Lecture Notes in Computer Science 16078

Founding Editors

Gerhard Goos
Juris Hartmanis

Editorial Board Members

Elisa Bertino, *Purdue University, West Lafayette, IN, USA*
Wen Gao, *Peking University, Beijing, China*
Bernhard Steffen ⓘ, *TU Dortmund University, Dortmund, Germany*
Moti Yung ⓘ, *Columbia University, New York, NY, USA*

The series Lecture Notes in Computer Science (LNCS), including its subseries Lecture Notes in Artificial Intelligence (LNAI) and Lecture Notes in Bioinformatics (LNBI), has established itself as a medium for the publication of new developments in computer science and information technology research, teaching, and education.

LNCS enjoys close cooperation with the computer science R & D community, the series counts many renowned academics among its volume editors and paper authors, and collaborates with prestigious societies. Its mission is to serve this international community by providing an invaluable service, mainly focused on the publication of conference and workshop proceedings and postproceedings. LNCS commenced publication in 1973.

Othon Michail · Giuseppe Prencipe
Editors

Algorithmics of Wireless Networks

21st International Symposium, ALGOWIN 2025
Warsaw, Poland, September 18–19, 2025
Proceedings

 Springer

Editors
Othon Michail
University of Liverpool
Liverpool, UK

Giuseppe Prencipe
University of Pisa
Pisa, Italy

ISSN 0302-9743　　　　　　ISSN 1611-3349　(electronic)
Lecture Notes in Computer Science
ISBN 978-3-032-09119-2　　　ISBN 978-3-032-09120-8　(eBook)
https://doi.org/10.1007/978-3-032-09120-8

© The Editor(s) (if applicable) and The Author(s), under exclusive license to Springer Nature Switzerland AG 2026

This work is subject to copyright. All rights are solely and exclusively licensed by the Publisher, whether the whole or part of the material is concerned, specifically the rights of translation, reprinting, reuse of illustrations, recitation, broadcasting, reproduction on microfilms or in any other physical way, and transmission or information storage and retrieval, electronic adaptation, computer software, or by similar or dissimilar methodology now known or hereafter developed.
The use of general descriptive names, registered names, trademarks, service marks, etc. in this publication does not imply, even in the absence of a specific statement, that such names are exempt from the relevant protective laws and regulations and therefore free for general use.
The publisher, the authors and the editors are safe to assume that the advice and information in this book are believed to be true and accurate at the date of publication. Neither the publisher nor the authors or the editors give a warranty, expressed or implied, with respect to the material contained herein or for any errors or omissions that may have been made. The publisher remains neutral with regard to jurisdictional claims in published maps and institutional affiliations.

This Springer imprint is published by the registered company Springer Nature Switzerland AG
The registered company address is: Gewerbestrasse 11, 6330 Cham, Switzerland

If disposing of this product, please recycle the paper.

Preface

This volume contains the papers presented at the *21st International Symposium on Algorithmics of Wireless Networks*, held at the University of Warsaw, Poland, on September 18–19, 2025, as part of ALGO 2025.

The International Symposium on Algorithmics of Wireless Networks (ALGOWIN), previously known as ALGOSENSORS, is an international forum dedicated to the algorithmic aspects of wireless networks. It covers algorithmic issues arising in wireless networks of all types of computational entities, static or mobile, including sensor networks, sensor-actuator networks, autonomous robots, and drones. The focus is on the design and analysis of algorithms, models of computation, graph and network algorithms, and experimental analysis.

The program committee of ALGOWIN 2025 consisted of Davide Bilò (University of L'Aquila), Paolo Boldi (University of Milan), Quentin Bramas (University of Strasbourg), Arnaud Casteigts (University of Geneva), Shantanu Das (Aix-Marseille University), Giuseppe Antonio Di Luna (University of Rome Sapienza), Shlomi Dolev (Ben-Gurion University of the Negev), Thomas Erlebach (Durham University), Chryssis Georgiou (University of Cyprus), Olga Goussevskaia (Federal University of Minas Gerais), Ralf Klasing (CNRS and University of Bordeaux), Evangelos Kranakis (Carleton University), George Mertzios (Durham University), Othon Michail (Co-chair, University of Liverpool), Nils Morawietz (Friedrich Schiller University Jena), Alfredo Navarra (University of Perugia), Lorenzo Palazzetti (University of Perugia), Giuseppe Prencipe (Co-chair, University of Pisa), Christoforos Raptopoulos (University of Patras), Christian Scheideler (Paderborn University), Christian Schindelhauer (University of Freiburg), George Skretas (Hasso Plattner Institute), Paul Spirakis (University of Liverpool), Tami Tamir (Reichman University), Sébastien Tixeuil (Sorbonne University), and Prudence Wong (University of Liverpool).

In response to the call for papers, 24 submissions were received. Each submission was reviewed by at least three program committee members and trusted external reviewers, and evaluated on its quality, originality, and relevance to the symposium. The committee decided to accept 13 papers for presentation at ALGOWIN 2025 and inclusion in its proceedings. The program also included an invited talk by Thomas Erlebach (Durham University), titled "Temporal Graphs: Exploration and Realization".

The program committee selected the paper "Round-wasynchronous amnesiac flooding" by Oluwatobi Alafin, George Mertzios, and Paul Spirakis for the Best Paper Award and decided to share the Best Student Paper Award between "Approximating temporal modularity on graphs of small underlying treewidth" by Vilhelm Agdur, Jessica Enright, Laura Larios-Jones, Kitty Meeks, Fiona Skerman, and Ella Yates, and "Capturing an Invisible Robber using Separators" by Igor Potapov, Tymofii Prokopenko, and John Sylvester. These awards were kindly sponsored by Springer.

Above all, we thank the authors who submitted papers to ALGOWIN. We also thank the invited speaker for his talk, as well as the program committee members and external reviewers for their invaluable contributions to the paper selection process, which resulted in a strong program. We are grateful to the ALGOWIN steering committee, and especially to its Chair, Sotiris Nikoletseas, for his full support throughout the process. Warm thanks go to the ALGO 2025 organizing committee, chaired by Marcin Pilipczuk and Paweł Rzążewski, for enabling us to hold ALGOWIN as part of the ALGO symposium and for handling all organizational matters. We also thank Springer for publishing the proceedings of ALGOWIN 2025 in the LNCS series and for their support and sponsorship. Finally, we acknowledge EasyChair for facilitating the submission of papers, the review process, and the collection of final versions.

September 2025

Othon Michail
Giuseppe Prencipe

Organization

Program Committee Chairs

Othon Michail   University of Liverpool, UK
Giuseppe Prencipe   University of Pisa, Italy

Program Committee

Davide Bilò	University of L'Aquila, Italy
Paolo Boldi	University of Milan, Italy
Quentin Bramas	University of Strasbourg, France
Arnaud Casteigts	University of Geneva, Switzerland
Shantanu Das	Aix-Marseille University, France
Giuseppe Antonio Di Luna	University of Rome Sapienza, Italy
Shlomi Dolev	Ben-Gurion University of the Negev, Israel
Thomas Erlebach	Durham University, UK
Chryssis Georgiou	University of Cyprus, Cyprus
Olga Goussevskaia	Federal University of Minas Gerais (UFMG), Brazil
Ralf Klasing	CNRS and University of Bordeaux, France
Evangelos Kranakis	Carleton University, Canada
George Mertzios	Durham University, UK
Othon Michail (Co-chair)	University of Liverpool, UK
Nils Morawietz	Friedrich Schiller University Jena, Germany
Alfredo Navarra	University of Perugia, Italy
Lorenzo Palazzetti	University of Perugia, Italy
Giuseppe Prencipe (Co-chair)	University of Pisa, Italy
Christoforos Raptopoulos	University of Patras, Greece
Christian Scheideler	Paderborn University, Germany
Christian Schindelhauer	University of Freiburg, Germany
George Skretas	Hasso Plattner Institute, Germany
Paul Spirakis	University of Liverpool, UK
Tami Tamir	Reichman University, Israel
Sébastien Tixeuil	Sorbonne University, France
Prudence Wong	University of Liverpool, UK

Steering Committee

Sotiris Nikoletseas (Chair)	University of Patras and CTI, Greece
Jie Gao	Rutgers University, USA
Magnús M. Halldórsson	Reykjavik University, Iceland
Bhaskar Krishnamachari	University of Southern California, USA
P. R. Kumar	Texas A&M University, USA
José Rolim	University of Geneva, Switzerland
Christian Scheideler	Paderborn University, Germany
Paul Spirakis	University of Liverpool, UK

Organization Chairs

Marcin Pilipczuk	University of Warsaw, Poland
Paweł Rzążewski	Warsaw University of Technology & University of Warsaw, Poland

Additional Reviewers

Duncan Adamson
Nicolas Bonichon
Giorgos Demosthenous
Alessia Di Fonso
Michelle Döring
Efthyvoulos Drousiotis
Caterina Feletti

Ling-Ju Hung
Dominik Pajak
Francesco Piselli
Gokarna Sharma
Akira Suzuki
Georg Tennigkeit

Contents

Distributed Weak Independent Sets in Hypergraphs: Upper and Lower
Bounds 1
   Duncan Adamson, Will Rosenbaum, and Paul G. Spirakis

Approximating Temporal Modularity on Graphs of Small Underlying
Treewidth 17
   *Vilhelm Agdur, Jessica Enright, Laura Larios-Jones, Kitty Meeks,
Fiona Skerman, and Ella Yates*

Round-Asynchronous Amnesiac Flooding 32
   Oluwatobi Alafin, George B. Mertzios, and Paul G. Spirakis

Optimizing the Number of Drones for Aerial Power-Line Maintenance 46
   *Francesco Betti Sorbelli, Sajjad Ghobadi, Lorenzo Palazzetti,
and Cristina M. Pinotti*

Almost Tight Oracles for Fastest-Path Queries on Temporal Trees 61
   *Davide Bilò, Luciano Gualà, Stefano Leucci, Guido Proietti,
and Alessandro Straziota*

Temporal Orienteering with Changing Fuel Costs 76
   Timothée Corsini, Jessica Enright, Laura Larios-Jones, and Kitty Meeks

Parameterised Algorithms for Temporally Satisfying Reconfiguration
Problems 89
   Tom Davot, Jessica Enright, and Laura Larios-Jones

Temporal Cycle Detection and Acyclic Temporalizations 104
   *Davi de Andrade, Júlio Araújo, Allen Ibiapina, Andrea Marino,
Jason Schoeters, and Ana Silva*

Graph Traversal via Connected Mobile Agents 119
   Saswata Jana, Giuseppe F. Italiano, and Partha Sarathi Mandal

Time-Optimal Asynchronous Minimal Vertex Covering by Myopic Robots
on Graph 135
   *Saswata Jana, Subhajit Pramanick, Adri Bhattacharya,
and Partha Sarathi Mandal*

Linear Search for Capturing an Oblivious Mobile Target
in the Sender/Receiver Model 151
   Khaled Jawhar and Evangelos Kranakis

A Logarithmic Approximation Algorithm for the Activation
Edge-Multicover Problem 166
   Zeev Nutov, Avner Huri, and Guy Kortsarz

Capturing an Invisible Robber Using Separators 181
   Igor Potapov, Tymofii Prokopenko, and John Sylvester

Author Index 197

Distributed Weak Independent Sets in Hypergraphs: Upper and Lower Bounds

Duncan Adamson[1] (✉) , Will Rosenbaum[2] , and Paul G. Spirakis[2]

[1] University of St Andrews, St Andrews, UK
duncan.adamson@st-andrews.ac.uk
[2] University of Liverpool, Liverpool, UK

Abstract. In this paper, we consider the problem of finding weak independent sets in a distributed network represented by a hypergraph. In this setting, each edge contains a set of r vertices rather than simply a pair, as in a standard graph. A k-weak independent set in a hypergraph is a set where no edge contains more than k vertices in the independent set. We focus on two variations of this problem. First, we study the problem of finding k-weak maximal independent sets, k-weak independent sets where each vertex belongs to at least one edge with k vertices in the independent set. Second we introduce a weaker variant that we call (α, β)-independent sets where the independent set is β-weak, and each vertex belongs to at least one edge with at least α vertices in the independent set.

Given a hypergraph H of rank r and maximum degree Δ, we provide a LLL formulation for finding an (α, β)-independent set when $(\beta - \alpha)^2/(\beta + \alpha) \geq 6\log(16r\Delta)$, an $O(\Delta r/(\beta - \alpha + 1) + \log^* n)$ round deterministic algorithm finding an (α, β)-independent set, and a $O(\Delta^2(r - k)\log r + \Delta \log r \log^* r + \log^* n)$ round algorithm for finding a k-weak maximal independent set. Additionally, we provide zero round randomized algorithms for finding (α, β) independent sets, when $(\beta - \alpha)^2/(\beta + \alpha) \geq 6c\log n + 6$ for some constant c, and finding an m-weak independent set for some $m \geq r/2k$ where k is a given parameter. Finally, we provide lower bounds of $\Omega(\Delta + \log^* n)$ and $\Omega(r + \log^* n)$ on the problems of finding k-weak maximal independent sets for some values of k.

1 Introduction

Independent sets are a key tool in distributed networks, allowing nodes within a graph to assert themselves as leaders over their immediate neighbors so as to help with the allocation of resources. This is of particular importance in the distributed setting, where nodes likely do not have full information of the complete graph. The best known version of the independent set problem is the *maximal independent set* (MIS) problem. Informally, in non-hypergraphs, an independent set is a subset of vertices such that no pair of vertices belongs to an edge in the graph. Such a set is maximal if every vertex either belongs to the set, or has some neighbor in the set. As this property is *locally checkable* [17], each vertex in the graph can determine whether it satisfies this condition by considering only the local neighborhood. In other words, once an algorithm to find an MIS has terminated, each vertex can determine if the algorithm was locally successful by checking if it belongs to the independent set, and if any of its neighbors do.

Finding independent sets in distributed graphs is one of the most heavily studied problems in distributed computing. Starting with the classic algorithm due to Linial [16,17], there has been a successive series of improvements in terms of both deterministic [1,6,7,21] and randomized [11,13–15] algorithms. At the same time, there has been a significant body of work determining the lower bound on the number of rounds required for distributed algorithms in general [8,9], and finding a MIS in particular [2,4,5]. As it stands, the current state-of-the-art for solving MIS deterministically, in terms of the maximum degree of the graph, matches the lower bound, giving an $O(\Delta + \log^* n)$ round algorithm for finding an MIS in an n node graph, with a maximum degree of Δ.

We extend the problem of finding an MIS to hypergraphs with the motivation of coordinating communication within wireless networks. In this setting, a hyperedge represents a given network, with the vertices representing devices that may connect one of these networks. The primary problem with such a network is in balancing the number of devices that interact between different networks. In this setting, we need some number of devices to act as coordinators within, and between, networks. On one hand, each network can only support a certain number of highly active vertices. On the other, some level of redundancy is necessary, ensuring that if one device loses connection, there are still some coordinators available. With this in mid, we consider two generalisations of MIS to the hypergraph setting. First, we consider the *weak-MIS problem*, which is perhaps the best studied generalisation. A set of nodes S is a *weak-MIS* if no hyperedge in the graph is a subset of S. This is the primary version studied in the distributed setting, with both positive, algorithmic results [15] and lower bounds [3]. In this paper, we consider two further generalizations of the independent set problem to hypergraphs, k-weak independent sets, and (α, β)-independent sets. A k-weak independent set is a set S such that the intersection between any edge in the graph and S has size at most k. Such a set is maximal if every vertex in the hypergraph either belongs to S, or belongs to some edge containing k other vertices in S. An (α, β)-independent set is a β-weak independent set S, where each vertex is either in S, or belongs to at least one edge containing α vertices in S. Note that a (k, k)-independent set is thus a k-weak MIS. We note that both definitions are locally checkable.

Of particular interest to our paper are the works of Kutten et al. [15], Kuhn and Zheng [14], and Balliu et al. [3], all of which analyze the MIS problem on hypergraphs. In [15], Kutten et al. provide a $O(\log^2 n)$ round randomized algorithm for solving maximal independent sets within hypergraphs containing n nodes. This is done by way of a network decomposition, partitioning the hypergraph into a collection of low diameter components, i.e. components for which the distance between any pair of nodes is minimized, in this case $O(\log n)$. Once partitioned, each component may "centralize" the topology of the local neighborhood into a single node, that can then solve the problem, broadcasting the solution to the other nodes in its component. Building upon this, Kuhn and Zheng [14] provide an $O(\log n)$ round algorithm for finding an MIS in a *linear* hypergraph, a hypergraph where no pair of edges share more than a single common vertex. They further introduce and provide an $O(\log^2 n)$ round algorithm for the *generalized MIS problem*, a problem roughly equivalent to our k-weak MIS problem, but with a variable for each edge determining the maximum number of vertices in the edge that may belong to the set. Finally, in [3], Balliu et al. provide a pair of deterministic algorithms for finding an MIS in a hypergraph. Given a hypergraph of rank r, maximum degree Δ, and n nodes, the authors show that an MIS can be found in both $O(\Delta^2 \log r + \Delta \log r \log^* r + \log^* n)$ rounds, and in $O(\Delta^{O(\Delta)} \log^* r + \log^* n)$ rounds.

We note two tools that can be applied directly to get naive solutions for finding either a k-weak MIS, or an (α, β)-IS. First is the graph decomposition algorithm of Ghaffari and Grunau [12], allowing a deterministic graph decomposition in $\tilde{O}(\log^2 n)$ rounds into components of diameter $O(\log n)$ using $O(\log n)$ colors, and thus either problem can be solved in $O(\log^2 n)$ rounds. Second, there is the $O(\Delta)$-coloring algorithm of Maus and Tonoyan [18], finding such a coloring in $O(\sqrt{(\Delta)}(\log \Delta) + \log^* n)$ rounds. By finding such a coloring on the underlying graph (with maximum degree Δr), we can iterate over each color class, allowing vertices to add themselves to the set without risk of conflict in $O(\Delta r)$ rounds.

Our Contributions. While k-weak MIS was (implicitly) introduced in [14], we believe our definition of (α, β)-independent set is novel. Our primary formal contributions consist of upper and lower-bounds for finding independent sets in hypergraphs in the LOCAL model. For deterministic lower bounds, in Sect. 3 we show the following:

- Any algorithm for finding a 1-weak MIS requires $\Omega(\Delta + r + \log^* n)$ rounds (Theorems 1 and 3).
- For any odd value k, finding a k-MIS in a hypergraph of rank $2k$ requires $\Omega(\Delta + \log^* n)$ rounds (Theorem 4).

For upper bounds, we provide a collection of deterministic and randomized algorithms solving several cases of (α, β)-IS and k-weak MIS. In all of these results, we assume that H is a hypergraph on n vertices with rank r and maximum degree Δ, and that α and β satisfy $1 \leq \alpha \leq \beta < r$.

- In Sect. 4 we provide an LLL formulation for finding an (α, β)-IS when $(\beta - \alpha)^2/(\beta + \alpha) \geq 6\log(16r\Delta)$, allowing an $O(\log^2 n)$ round deterministic algorithm (Corollary 1). Using this formulation, we show that when $(\beta - \alpha)^2/(\beta + \alpha) \geq 6\log n + 6$, an (α, β)-IS can be found in zero communication rounds with high probability (Corollary 2).

- In Sect. 5, we describe a deterministic algorithm for finding an (α, β)-IS in $O(\Delta r/(\beta - \alpha + 1) + \log^* n)$ rounds (Theorem 5). This result generalizes the "trivial" $O(r\Delta + \log^* n)$-round algorithm for finding a k-weak MIS, which corresponds to this result when $k = \alpha = \beta$.
- In Sect. 5 we provide a $O(\Delta^2(r-k)\log r + \Delta \log r \log^* r + \log^* n)$ round algorithm for finding a k-weak MIS (Theorem 6). This result generalizes a result of Balliu et al. [3], who give an algorithm with similar running time in the case that $k = r - 1$ and each edge is of uniform rank r.

2 Preliminaries

Let $H = (V, E)$ be a hypergraph consisting of the set of vertices, V, and edges E. Each edge in E contains some (non-empty) subset of vertices from V. The *rank* of an edge e is the number of vertices in the edge. The *rank* of the graph is equal to the maximum rank of any edge in E. The *degree* of a vertex v is the number of edges in E containing v. The maximum degree of H is the maximum degree of any vertex in v. By convention, we denote the rank of a hypergraph by r, and the degree by Δ. Given a pair of vertices v, u in V, the *distance* between v and u, denoted $dist(v, u)$ is the minimum number of edges needed to form a contiguous path between v and u. For example, $dist(v, v) = 0$, $dist(v, u) = 1$ if and only if $\exists e \in E$ such that $\{v, u\} \subseteq e$.

The *underlying graph* of the hypergraph $H = (V, E)$ is the graph $G = (V, E')$ formed by replacing each edge $e \in E$ with a clique containing every vertex in e, i.e. $E' = \{(v, u) \mid \exists e \in E \text{ such that } \{u, v\} \subseteq e\}$. Given a subset of vertices $S \subseteq V$, the graph *induced* by S is the graph $H' = \{S, E'\}$ where $E' = \{e \cap S \mid e \in E\}$, i.e. the graph formed by removing every vertex in $V \setminus S$.

An *independent set* S in a hypergraph (V, E) is a subset of vertices where, for any pair $u, v \in S$, where $u \neq v$, $\nexists e \in E$ such that $(u, v) \in e$. A ψ-*coloring* $\boldsymbol{\Psi}$ of a hypergraph (V, E) is a mapping of the set of vertices to some set of ψ-colors, assumed to be the set of integers $1, 2, \ldots, \psi$. A ψ-coloring is *valid* if $\forall v, u \in V$ where $v \neq u$, either $\nexists e \in E$ such that $(v, u) \in e$ or $\boldsymbol{\Psi}(v) \neq \boldsymbol{\Psi}(u)$.

Definition 1 (k-weak IS). *Given a hypergraph $G = (V, E)$ of rank r, a k-weak independent set, denoted k-weak IS, is a subset $V' \subseteq V$ such that, for every $e \in E$, $|e \cap V'| \leq k$, i.e. no edge contains more than k vertices in V'. A k-weak independent set V' is maximal (a k-weak MIS) if no super set of V' is a k-weak independent set, i.e. each vertex not in V' is adjacent to at least one edge containing k members of V'.*

Problem 1. In a given communication model, what is the minimum number of rounds needed to find a *maximal k-weak independent set* in the graph G (with high probability)?

In the case that some edge $e \in E$ has rank less than or equal to k, it is possible that every vertex in e belongs to the independent set. Further, a 1-weak independent set on a hypergraph H corresponds to the traditional definition of an independent set on the underlying graph. For convenience, in non-hypergraphs, we denote 1-weak maximal independent sets as simply MIS. We now define a generalized version of independent sets, (α, β)-weak independent sets.

Definition 2 ((α, β)-IS). *Given a hypergraph $H = (V, E)$ of rank r, an (α, β)-weak independent set, denoted (α, β)-IS, is a subset $V' \subseteq V$ such that, for every $e \in E$, $|e \cap V'| \leq \beta$, and every vertex v belongs to at least one edge e such that $|e \cap V'| \geq \alpha$.*

Problem 2. Given a hypergraph $H = (V, E)$ of rank r, and pair $\beta, \alpha \in \mathbb{N}$ such that $\beta \geq \alpha$, what is the minimum number of rounds needed to find an (α, β)-IS (with high probability)?

Model of Computation. In this paper, we primarily consider the LOCAL model of distributed computing. In this model, each vertex in the graph is assigned a unique ID, and is aware of the local neighborhood, i.e. the edges it belongs to and the IDs of the vertices in each edge. Each round consists of a period of computation, followed by each vertex sending some message to each neighbor. We do not place any bound on the size of the messages in this model. We note that some cited work uses the CONGEST model, a restriction of the LOCAL model where each vertex may only send messages of size $O(\log n)$.

3 Lower Bounds for Weak MIS

Before providing our solutions to Problem 1, we first provide a pair of lower bounds of $\Omega(r + \log^* n)$ and $\Omega(\Delta + \log^* n)$ for deterministic algorithms solving 1-weak MIS, and a $\Omega(\Delta + \log^* n)$ lower bound for finding a k-MIS in a hypergraph of rank $2k$, for an odd value of k.

Theorem 1. *Consider the family of r-uniform hypergraphs with maximum degree Δ such that $r\Delta \log(r\Delta) = O(\log n)$. Then in this family, computing a 1-weak MIS requires $\Omega(r)$ rounds in the local model.*

The idea of the proof of Theorem 1 is to give a reduction from hypergraph maximal matching. To this end, we employ the lower bound of [3]:

Theorem 2 (Balliu et al. [3]). *For the family of r-uniform hypergraphs with maximum degree Δ and $r\Delta \log(r\Delta) = O(\log n)$, computing a maximal matching requires $\Omega(r\Delta)$ rounds in the LOCAL model.*

Proof (Proof of Theorem 1). Suppose we have an algorithm A that computes a 1-weak MIS in $T = T(\Delta, r, n)$ rounds. Given a hypergraph $G = G_0$, define a sequence of hypergraphs $G = G_0, G_1, \ldots, G_\Delta$ and sets of hyperedges $M_1, M_2, \ldots, M_\Delta$ as follows. Given G_{i-1} compute M_i and G_i by:

1. Apply A to compute a 1-weak MIS S_i in G_{i-1}.
2. For each vertex $v \in S_i$, choose an edge e_v incident to v arbitrarily and add e_v to M_i. Note that this can be done in a single round of LOCAL given the output of A.
3. Form G_i by removing from G_{i-1} all vertices u incident to edges in M_i and all edges incident to those vertices.

We claim that $M = \bigcup_{i=1}^{\Delta} M_i$ is a maximal matching in G.

First observe that each M_i is a matching in G_{i-1}. Next, note that if $e \notin M_i$ is an edge removed in Step 3 above, then e intersects some edge $e' \in M_i$, hence e cannot be in any matching that contains the edges from M_i.

Next consider an edge e in G_i—i.e., an edge that is neither in M_i nor was it removed in Step 3. Since S_i is a 1-weak MIS in G_{i-1}, it must be the case that every vertex $v \in e$ is also contained in another edge e' that intersects S_i on some vertex v'. Since e was not removed in Step 3, $e' \notin M_i$. However, since $v' \in e'$, e' is removed in Step 3. Thus, every vertex v in G_i has at least one incident edge removed from G_{i-1}. Combining these observations, we find:

- every edge $e \in G_i$ is disjoint from every edge in $M_1 \cup M_2 \cup \cdots \cup M_i$, and
- the maximum degree of G_i is $\Delta - i$.

By the second point above, G_Δ is an independent set of vertices. Also, by the first point and the observation that each M_i is a matching, we find that $M = \bigcup_{i=1}^{\Delta} M_i$ is a matching as well. Finally, M is maximal because every removed edge intersects some edge in M. The procedure invokes A to find a 1-weak MIS Δ times, and after each invocation, only $O(1)$ rounds of communication are performed. Therefore, the total running time of the procedure is $O(\Delta T)$. By Theorem 2, the running time must be $\Omega(r\Delta)$, hence $T = \Omega(r)$.

The lower bound of $\Omega(r)$ is perhaps surprising given the upper bounds for $r - 1$-weak MIS in [3] and our Theorem 6 whose r-dependence is sublinear.

We complement our $\Omega(r + \log^* n)$ lower bound with a pair of $\Omega(\Delta + \log^* n)$ lower bounds on finding an MIS in Hypergraphs, complementing the above bounds. First, we show an $\Omega(\Delta + \log^* n)$ lower bound for finding a 1-weak independent set on the family of hypergraphs of even rank. Secondly, we present an $\Omega(\Delta + \log^* n)$ lower bound for finding a k-weak independent set for odd values of k on the family of hypergraphs of rank $2k$. Both are due to a reduction from the $\Omega(\Delta + \log^* n)$ lower bound on finding an MIS on regular graphs due to Balliu et al. [2].

Theorem 3. *Consider the family of r-uniform hypergraphs with maximum degree Δ such that r is even. Then in this family, computing a 1-weak MIS requires $\Omega(\Delta + \log^* n)$ rounds in the local model.*

Proof. Consider a (non-hyper) graph $G = (V, E)$ of maximum degree Δ. We construct a hypergraph $G' = (V', E')$ as follows. For each vertex $v \in V$, we create a set of $r/2$ vertices $v_1, v_2, \ldots, v_{r/2}$ in V'. For each edge $(v, u) \in E$, we add the edge $(v_1, v_2, \ldots, v_{r/2}, u_1, u_2, \ldots, u_{r/2})$ to E'. Observe that a 1-weak MIS in G' can be converted into an MIS for G as follows. Consider some $v_i \in V'$ such that v_i is in the MIS, then, for any $u_j \in V'$ such that there exists some edge $e \in E'$ for which $v_i, u_j \in e$, u_j is not in the MIS. We add to the MIS for G any vertex v such that some vertex v_i is in the MIS of G', getting a maximal independent set of G. As there is known to be a lower bound of $\Omega(\Delta + \log^* n)$ for finding such an MIS for graphs, we get the stated lower bound.

We can use the same technique to obtain a $\Omega(\Delta)$ lower bound for k-weak MIS for an odd value of k, and hypergraph of rank $(2k)$. The high-level idea is the same as above, with the difference that instead, we construct the hypergraph with k copies of each vertex, and use the odd parity of k to only add vertices in the original graph G to the independent set of G if at least $k/2$ of the corresponding vertices in the hypergraph belong to the corresponding k-weak independent set. This allows a more general bound, relating the rank and weakness of the set in a closer manner than before. We now formalize our construction.

Construction. Given a graph $G = (V, E)$, and $k \in \mathbb{N}$ where k is odd, we construct the hypergraph $H = (V', E')$ as follows. For each vertex $v_i \in V$, we add k vertices into V', labelled $v_{i,1}, v_{i,2}, \ldots, v_{i,k}$. For each edge $(v_i, v_j) \in E$, we add the hyperedge $(v_{i,1}, v_{i,2}, \ldots, v_{i,k}, v_{j,1}, v_{j,2}, \ldots, v_{j,k})$ to E'.

Theorem 4. *Consider the family of $2k$-uniform hypergraphs with maximum degree Δ such that k is odd. Then in this family, computing a k-weak MIS requires $\Omega(\Delta + \log^* n)$ rounds in the local model.*

Proof. Let H be constructed as above for the graph G, and let S be a k-weak maximal independent set in H. Observe that each vertex $v_{i,\ell}$ must belong to at least one edge with k vertices in the independent set. Further, as $\{v_{i,\ell} \mid \ell \in [1,k]\} \subset e$ or $\{v_{i,\ell} \mid \ell \in [1,k]\} \cap e = \emptyset$, for every $e \in E'$, we have that all vertices in $\{v_{i,\ell} \mid \ell \in [1,k]\}$ share the same set of edges containing k vertices in S. Now, let e be some edge such that $|e \cap S| = k$, and let $e = (v_{i,1}, v_{i,2}, \ldots, v_{i,k}, v_{j,1}, v_{j,2}, \ldots, v_{j,k})$. Observe that, as k is odd, either $|\{v_{i,1}, v_{i,2}, \ldots, v_{i,k}\} \cap S| > k/2$ or $|\{v_{j,1}, v_{j,2}, \ldots, v_{j,k}\} \cap S| > k/2$.

Consider the set $S' \subseteq V$ in the original graph G, where $v_i \in S'$ if and only if $|\{v_{i,1}, v_{i,2}, \ldots, v_{i,k}\} \cap S| > k/2$. Observe that, given any pair v_i, v_j where $(v_i, v_j) \in E$, and $v_i \in S'$, we have that $|\{v_{j,1}, v_{j,2}, \ldots, v_{j,k}\} \cap S| < k/2$, by definition of a k-weak independent set in H. Therefore, by construction, $v_j \notin S'$. In the other direction, if $v_j \notin S'$, then observe that there must be some edge $e \in E'$ where $|e \cap S| = k$ and $\{v_{j,1}, v_{j,2}, \ldots, v_{j,k}\} \subset e$. Now, let $e = (v_{j,1}, v_{j,2}, \ldots, v_{j,k}, v_{\ell,1}, v_{\ell,2}, \ldots, v_{\ell,k})$ be such an edge, and observe that $|\{v_{\ell,1}, v_{\ell,2}, \ldots, v_{\ell,k}\} \cap S| > k/2$. Therefore, $(v_j, v_\ell) \in E$ and $v_\ell \in S'$. Thus, for any v_j not in S', there exists at least one vertex adjacent to v_j in G that is in S' and, conversely, for any $v_i \in S'$, no vertex adjacent to v_i belongs to S'. Hence S' is a maximal independent set, and thus, by the previous bound of $\Omega(\Delta + \log^* n)$ rounds on finding an MIS in G holds for finding a k-weak independent set on H.

4 LLL Formulation

With our lower bounds in mind, we now begin to provide positive results to the problem. We first present a formulation of this problem using the Lovasz Local Lemma as a means to find an (α, β)-independent set for some range of parameters.

Recall that the Lovasz Local Lemma (LLL) [10] gives sufficient conditions for a probability space to have an outcome that avoids a set of "bad" events. More formally, suppose $B_1, B_2, \ldots, B_m$ are events in a probability space Ω such that each B_i is independent of all but d other events. The LLL asserts that if for all $\Pr(E_i) \leq p$ and $ep(d+1) \leq 1$, then there exists an outcome $\omega \in \Omega$ that is not contained in any of the E_i. While the original formulation is non-constructive, an efficient constructive, and distributed solution was found by Moser and Tardös in [20]. In the distributed setting, each event B_i is represented by a vertex in the network and B_i and B_j share an edge if and only if the events B_i and B_j are not independent. An *LLL formulation* of a distributed problem P is a reduction from P to the LLL.

The idea of our LLL formulation is that we associate with each vertex $v \in V$ with a $\{0,1\}$-random variable with the interpretation that $v = 1$ if and only if v is contained in the independent set. Thus, an outcome (i.e., an assignment of $\{0,1\}$-values to each v) corresponds to an (α, β)-MIS if and only if (1) for each edge $e \in E$, $\sum_{v \in e} v \leq \beta$, and (2) for each vertex $v \in V$, either $v = 1$ or v is contained in an edge e with $\sum_{u \in e} u \geq \alpha$. In the LLL formulation, events B correspond to violations of (1) and (2). We make the following observations assuming that $H = (V, E)$ has rank r with maximum degree at most Δ:

1. Type 1 events B_e and B_f are independent unless their corresponding edges e and f intersect. Therefore B_e is independent of all but Δr type 1 events.
2. Type 2 events B_v and B_u are independent unless their corresponding vertices v and u are neighbors. Thus, again, B_v is independent of all but at most Δr other such type 2 events.
3. A type 1 event B_e and type 2 event B_v are independent unless $v \in e$. Thus, B_e is independent of all but r type 2 events, and B_v is independent of all but Δ type 1 events.
4. Every event is a function of the 1-hop neighborhood of some vertex $v \in V$. Therefore, communication in the LLL network can be simulated in the underlying graph with one additional communication round in the LOCAL model.

Combining the observations 1–3 above, we obtain the following.

Lemma 1. *Consider the LLL formulation described above where H is a hypergraph with rank r and maximum degree Δ. Then each event B is independent of all but $d \leq \Delta r + \Delta + r \leq 2\Delta r - 1$ other events.*

In order to complete the LLL formulation of finding an (α, β)-MIS, we must define a probability measure on the outcomes such that probabilities p of the events satisfy $ep(d+1) \leq 1$. To this end, we prove the following lemma.

Lemma 2. *Suppose H is a hypergraph with rank r and maximum degree Δ. Suppose α, β with $0 < \alpha \leq \beta \leq r - 1$ satisfy*

$$\frac{(\beta - \alpha)^2}{\beta + \alpha} \geq 6 \log(16 r \Delta). \tag{1}$$

Then there is an LLL formulation of finding (α, β)-independent sets in H.

Proof. Let $\mu = \frac{\beta + \alpha}{2}$ denote the midpoint between α and β. Consider the probability measure determined by choosing each $v = 1$ with probability $q = \mu/r$ (and $v = 0$ with probability $1 - q$) independently. For each edge e, let $X_e = \sum_{v \in e} v$, so that $\mathbb{E}(X_e) = \mu$. We make the following observations:

- if $X_e \leq \beta$, then the event B_e does not occur
- if $X_e \geq \alpha$ the for every $v \in e$, the event B_v does not occur

Observe that both conditions above are satisfied if $|X_e - \mu| \leq \frac{\beta - \alpha}{2}$. To bound the probability that the latter condition does not hold, we apply the following Chernoff bound [19]: if X is a sum of independent 0-1 random variables with expected value μ, then for δ satisfying $0 < \delta < 1$, we have

$$\Pr(|X - \mu| > \delta \mu) \leq 2 \exp(-\mu \delta^2 / 3). \tag{2}$$

Applying (2) with $\delta = \frac{\beta - \alpha}{\beta + \alpha}$, we obtain

$$\Pr\left(|X - \mu| > \frac{\beta - \alpha}{2}\right) \leq 2 \exp\left(-\frac{(\beta - \alpha)^2}{6(\beta + \alpha)}\right). \tag{3}$$

This expression is an upper bound on the probability, p of any bad event B. Hence, by appling (1) to the second inequality, we get

$$ep(d+1) < 4 \cdot 2 \exp\left(-\frac{(\beta - \alpha)^2}{6(\beta + \alpha)}\right) \cdot (2\Delta r) \leq 16 \Delta r \exp(-\ln(16 \Delta r)) = 1.$$

Corollary 1. *There exists a deterministic distributed algorithm to find an (α, β)-MIS in an e-rank hypergraph $H = (V, E)$ with maximum degree Δ in $O(\log^2 |V|)$ rounds of the LOCAL model for any α, β satisfying $\frac{(\beta - \alpha)^2}{\beta + \alpha} \geq 6 \log(16 r \Delta)$.*

A Zero Round Protocol. We note that for larger values of $\beta - \alpha$, the concentration inequality in (1) is strong enough to guarantee that the set S formed by selecting each vertex independently to be in S with probability $q = \mu/r$ is an (α, β)-MIS with high probability. In particular, we get the following:

Corollary 2. *Suppose α and β satisfy $\frac{(\beta - \alpha)^2}{\beta + \alpha} \geq 6c \log n + 6$. Then there exists a zero-round randomized distributed algorithm that finds an (α, β)-MIS with probability at least $1 - \frac{1}{n^c}$.*

5 Deterministic Algorithms

We now provide a set of deterministic algorithms to find a (α, β)-IS, or a k-MIS. Both approaches are based on the idea of finding *defective colorings* of the graph. A k-defective coloring is a coloring such that no more than k vertices in a given edge share the same color.

Finding an (α, β)-IS in $O(\Delta r/(\beta - \alpha + 1))$ Rounds. We now provide a deterministic algorithm for finding an (α, β)-IS in $O(\Delta r/(\beta - \alpha + 1))$ rounds. For the remainder of this section we assume that we have an r-rank hypergraph $H = (V, E)$ in the LOCAL model. Further, we assume that every vertex v knows the values of β and α used, and the edges incident to v. We define the parameter $\delta = \beta - \alpha + 1$.

Outline. Our algorithm operates in a two-stage manner. First, we find a δ-*edge defective coloring*, a coloring where no edge contains more than δ colors of a given class. Then, we iterate through each class, activating any vertices of the given color, which can then choose to add themselves to the independent set or not.

To determine the δ-defective edge coloring, we have each edge partition itself into δ sets of size r/δ. We construct a new graph by replacing each hyperedge with the new sets, thus getting a hypergraph of rank r/δ, and finding an $\psi = O(\Delta r/\delta)$ coloring on the underlying graph of this new hypergraph. Once this coloring is found, we iterate through each color class from 1 to ψ, activating at round i all vertices with the ith color. Any active vertex v that belongs only to edges with fewer than α vertices in the independent set will add itself to the set. Otherwise, v excludes itself.

The key observation is that after the edge coloring, for any edge containing the vertex v, there are at most δ vertices sharing the same color as v. Therefore, if every edge incident to v contains less than α vertices in the independent set, v can add itself to the set, without any risk of the number of any edge incident to v containing more than β vertices in the independent set.

Finding a δ-Defective Coloring. For each edge $e \in E$, we construct δ sets of size r/δ, $e_1, e_2, \ldots, e_\delta$. For simplicity, if $E = \{v_1, v_2, \ldots, v_r\}$ where $ID(v_1) < ID(v_2) < \cdots < ID(v_\delta)$, we have $e_i = \{v_{(i-1)r/\delta+1}, v_{(i-1)r/\delta+2}, \ldots, v_{ir/\delta}\}$. Let $H' = \{V, E'\}$ be the hypergraph formed by replacing each edge in $e \in E$ with the sets $e_1, e_2, \ldots, e_\delta$, formally $E' = \bigcup_{e \in E}\{e_1, e_2, \ldots, e_\delta\}$. Correspondingly, let G' be the underlying graph of H'. Now, let $\Psi : V \mapsto 1, 2, \ldots, \Delta r/\delta + 1$ be a coloring of the underlying graph G', corresponding to a maximum degree $+ 1$ coloring of G'. Note that as G' is a regular graph, Ψ can be found in $O(\sqrt{(\Delta r/\delta)}(\log \Delta r/\delta) + \log^* n)$ rounds by the algorithm due to Maus and Tonoyan [18]. Now, observe that as each edge in H' is properly colored, and the edge $e \in E$ in the original hypergraph contains α such sets, for any color $\chi \in [\Delta r/\delta + 1]$, $|e \cap \{v \in V \mid \Psi(v)\}| \leq \delta$. Thus Ψ is a δ-defective coloring of H. See Algorithm 1 for pseudo code.

Algorithm 1. δ-defective coloring algorithm on the graph $H = (V, E)$ of rank r for vertex $v \in V$. We assume E only contains the edges incident to v.

1: **procedure** δ-DEFECTIVECOLOR
2:     Split each edge e into c subsets $e_1, e_2, \ldots, e_\delta$, with v in e_i.
3:     $H' \leftarrow (V, \bigcup_{e \in E} \{e_1, e_2, \ldots, e_\delta\})$
4:     $G' \leftarrow$ Underlying Graph of H'
5:     $\Psi \leftarrow (\Delta r/\delta)$-COLOR$(G', v)$
6:     **Return** Ψ.
7: **end procedure**

Lemma 3. *Given a hypergraph H of rank r, and value $\delta \leq r$, there exists an that finds a δ-defective coloring of H using $\Delta r/\delta + 1$ colors can be found in $O(\sqrt{(\Delta r/\delta)}(\log \Delta r/\delta) + \log^* n)$ rounds.*

Forming an Independent Set. Using the δ-defective coloring Ψ, we now find the independent set. We iterate through the set of colors, activating at each round the set of vertices in the given color class. When active, each vertex is given the chance to add itself to the independent set, or to mark itself as inactive. Formally, at round i, any vertex v where $\Psi(v) = i$ will add itself to the independent set S if and only if $\forall e \in E$ either $v \notin e$ or $v \in e$ and $|e \cap S| < \alpha$. Therefore, after v has been activated, either v is in the independent set S, or v is incident to at least one edge containing α vertices in the independent set, locally satisfying the properties of an (α, β)-IS.

Theorem 5. *There exists an algorithm constructing an (α, β)-IS in $O(\Delta r/\delta + \log^* n)$ rounds in any hypergraph $H = (V, E)$ of rank r.*

Proof. We prove this by an inductive argument. First, note that any vertex v where $\Psi(v) = 1$ will, by construction, add itself to the independent set S. As there can be at most α vertices in any edge colored 1, no edge after this step contains more than β vertices in the independent set.

Now consider some vertex v where $\Psi(v) = i$, and assume that after the first $i - 1$ color classes have been activated, no edge contains more than β vertices in the independent set. If v is incident to at least one edge with more than α vertices in the independent set, then v may not add itself to the independent set. Note that v is locally satisfied as it belongs to at least one edge containing at least α-vertices in the independent set. Otherwise, if no such edge is incident to v, v adds itself to the independent set. As no edge contains more than $\delta = \beta - \alpha + 1$ vertices in the color class i, and a vertex will only add itself to the independent set if there are fewer than α vertices in the independent set in every edge it is incident to, no edge can, after color class i has been activated, contain more than β vertices in the independent set. Thus after being activated, v is either in the independent set, or incident to one edge with at least α vertices in the independent set. In either case, the locally checkable properties of the set are satisfied. By inductive argument, we have the claim of correctness.

To determine the round complexity, observe that the α-defective coloring can be found in $O(\sqrt{(\Delta r/\alpha)}(\log \Delta r/\alpha) + \log^* n)$ rounds. As this coloring uses at most $\Delta r/\alpha + 1$ colors, the second step of the algorithm requires $O(\Delta r/\alpha)$ rounds, giving the total complexity of $O(\Delta r/\alpha + \log^* n)$.

Algorithm 2. $O(\Delta r/\delta)$ round coloring algorithm for some vertex v in the hypergraph $H = (V, E)$.

1: **procedure** EDGEPARTITIONIS(Hypergraph H, $(\alpha, \beta) \in \mathbb{N}^2$)
2:     $\Psi \leftarrow \delta$-DEFECTIVECOLOR()
3:     $\psi \leftarrow |\Psi|$
4:     $A \leftarrow \emptyset$ % Set of vertices adjacent to v in the independent set.
5:     **for** $i \in [\psi]$ **do**
6:       **if** $\Psi(v) = i$ **then**
7:         **if** $\forall e \in \{v \in e \mid e \in E\}, |e \cap A| \leq \alpha$ **then**
8:           Mark as in the independent set
9:           Broadcast that v is adding itself to the independent set.
10:        **else**
11:           Mark as not in the independent set
12:           Broadcast that v is not adding itself to the independent set.
13:        **end if**
14:     **else**
15:        Add to A any adjacent vertex that adds itself to the independent set.
16:     **end if**
17:     **end for**
18: **end procedure**

Finding k-MIS for Large k. Here, we describe an algorithm that finds a k-weak MIS in $O(\Delta^2(r - k)\log r + \Delta \log r \log^* r + \log^* n)$ rounds. Note that in the regime where r is much larger than Δ and k is close to r, this gives an asymptotic improvement over the "trivial" $O(r\Delta + \log^* n)$ algorithm of finding a $r\Delta + 1$ coloring in the underlying graph, then iterating over each color class. This result generalizes of a result of Balliu et al. [3], which gives an $O(\Delta^2 \log r + \log r \log^* r + \log^* n)$ time algorithm for finding an $(r - 1)$-weak MIS, which is comparable our result for $k = r - 1$.

The idea of our algorithm is to iterate the procedure described of Sect. 5 to find an (α, β)-MIS $\Delta \log r$ times with $\beta = k$. On the first iteration, we obtain at $(k/2, k)$-MIS. In subsequent iterations, we consider only "active" vertices that have not yet joined the IS. In each iteration of the procedure, each edge e with a_e active vertices (and $i_e = r - a_e$ elements in the IS) partitions its active vertices, and the active vertices color themselves to give an edge-defective coloring as in Sect. 5. This is done such that each color class contains at most $(k - i_e)/2$ colors, hence adding all vertices of any one color class will not violate the k-independence of the IS. Given this coloring, we then iterate over color classes, and each vertex adds itself to the IS greedily as in the previous section.

After each iteration of the procedure above, we observe that the following holds: for each vertex v, either v is added to the IS, or v is incident to some edge e whose "saturation" (i.e., $|e \cap S|$ increased from $k - \delta$ to $k - \delta/2$. Note that each edge can only increase its saturation in this way at most $\log r$ times before it contains k elements in the IS. Thus, after at most $\Delta \log r$ phases, each vertex v has either been added to the IS or is incident to a saturated edge. In what follows below, we describe a slight modification of this procedure that computes a k-MIS. We now introduce some notation. Suppose S is an independent set in $H = (V, E)$ and k is an integer with $1 \leq k \leq r - 1$.

- The *saturation* of an edge e is $\text{sat}(e) = |e \cap S|$. We say e is *saturated* if $\text{sat}(e) = k$.
- We say that v is *active* if (1) $v \notin S$, and (2) v is not contained in a saturated edge.
- We denote the set of active vertices in e by A_e and say that e is *inactive* if $A_e = \varnothing$.
- We say that e is in *phase* φ if $(1 - 2^{-\varphi-1})k < \text{sat}(e) \leq (1 - 2^{-\varphi})k$. We denote the phase of e by $\varphi(e)$.

Lemma 4. *If a edge e is in phase $\varphi = \log r + 1$, then e is saturated. In particular, each edge's phase can increase at most $\log r$ times before the edge is either saturated or inactive.*

Algorithm 3. k-weak MIS

1: **procedure** KWEAKMIS(H)
2:    $S \leftarrow \varnothing$ ▷ The IS
3:    **for each** edge e, $A_e \leftarrow e$ ▷ Active vertices in e
4:    **for each** iteration $i = 1, 2, \ldots, 1 + \Delta \log r$ **do**
5:       **if** $|A_e| \geq 4(r - k)$ **then**
6:          partition A_e into $\lfloor |A_e|/4 \rfloor$ parts of size at most 5
7:       **else**
8:          keep A_e as a single part
9:       **end if**
10:      $H' \leftarrow$ the hypergraph induced by this edge partition
11:      properly color H' with $4\Delta(r - k) + 1$ colors
12:      **for** each color class c **do**
13:         $V_c \leftarrow$ vertices of color c
14:         **if** $v \in V_c$ and each $e \ni v$ satisfies $|V_c \cap e| \leq k - \text{sat}(e)$ **then**
15:            v adds itself to S and removes itself from A_e
16:         **end if**
17:      **end for**
18:      **if** v is is incident to a saturated edge **then**
19:         remove v from all incident A_e
20:      **end if**
21:    **end for**
22: **end procedure**

The main procedure assumes that the vertices in the input are properly colored (in the underlying graph) with $O(\Delta^2 r^2)$ colors. Such a coloring can be found in $O(\log^* n)$ rounds using the algorithm of Linial [17].

Theorem 6. *Let $H = (V, E)$ be an r-uniform hypergraph with maximum degree at most Δ. Then on input H, Algorithm 3 produces a k-weak MIS in $O(\Delta^2(r-k)\log r + \Delta \log r \log^* r + \log^* n)$ rounds in the LOCAL model.*

Proof. We first establish the correctness of the procedure. To this end, let v be an arbitrary vertex and $e_1, e_2, \ldots, e_d$ its incident edges. Suppose $v \notin S$ at the beginning of an iteration i of the loop in lines 4–21. For $j = 1, 2, \ldots, d$, let $f_j \subseteq e_j$ denote the part of e_j containing v in the partition formed in Lines 5–9. By the choice of the size of the partitions, for each color c in the coloring we have

$$|V_c \cap e| \leq \frac{1}{2}(k - \text{sat}(e)) \tag{4}$$

This expression is clearly true when $|V_c| = 1$ (i.e., A_e is maintained as a single part). On the other hand, if $|A_e| \geq 4(r-k)$ (hence A_e is partitioned into multiple parts), then we have $|V_c \cap e| \leq \frac{1}{4}|A_e| < \frac{1}{2} \cdot \frac{3}{4}|A_e| \leq \frac{1}{2}(|A_e| - (r-k)) \leq \frac{1}{2}(k - \text{sat}(e))$, where the final inequality holds because $|A_e| + \text{sat}(e) \leq r$.

By (4), if v does not add itself to S in Line 15, it must be that some incident edge e' increased its phase ϕ during this iteration of the the loop. To see this, suppose v does not added to S in iteration i in which v is colored c. Then v has some incident edge e such that $|V_c \cap e| > k - \text{sat}(e)$. However, at the beginning of iteration (4) was satisfied, hence $k - \text{sat}(e)$ must have halved during iteration i, implying that its phase, $\phi(e)$ increased. As v is incident to at most Δ edges, and each incident edge can increase its phase at most $\log r$ times before becoming saturated or inactive (Lemma 4), after $\Delta \log r$ iterations, either v added itself to S, or it is incident to some saturated edge (hence inactive). Thus, S is a k-weak MIS.

For the running time analysis, we can initially color all of the vertices with $\Delta^2 r^2$ colors in $O(\log^* n)$ rounds using Linial's algorithm [17]. To color the hypergraph H' in Line 11, observe that each part of the partition has size at most $\max 5, 4(r-k)$. Therefore, the underlying graph of H' has maximum degree at most $O(\Delta(r-k))$. Given the initial coloring, the coloring algorithm of [18] has running time $O(\sqrt{\Delta(r-k)} + \log^*(r^2\Delta^2)) = O(\Delta(r-k) + \log^* r)$. Iterating over the colors takes $O(\Delta(r-k))$ rounds, so the overall running time is $O(\Delta^2(r-k)\log r + \Delta \log r \log^* r + \log^* n)$.

Conclusion. In this paper, we have provided an overview of the k-MIS and (α, β)-IS problems, showing lower bounds in terms of both r and Δ on finding a 1-MIS, and in terms of Δ on finding a k-MIS for certain values of k. In the other direction, we have provided a set of algorithmic results for finding both k-weak independent sets, and (α, β) independent sets. Our lower bound results suggest that finding k-weak MIS may be computationally costly, but the weaker (α, β)-IS admits efficient algorithms for some range of parameters. Thus, in applications where some form of maximal independent set is desirable, an (α, β)-IS may offer sufficient "maximality" while allowing for significantly faster algorithms. The primary open question is closing the gaps between upper and lower bounds. In particular, as our current bounds apply only for k-weak MIS, a bound as a function of α and β for (α, β)-IS would be an interesting extension. We conjecture that, in general, there is an $\Omega(\Delta(r-\beta)/(1+\beta-\alpha)+\log^* n)$ general lower bound, with the intuition that the problem becomes easier as the gap between α and β grows, while also becoming easier as more vertices can be allowed into the set.

References

1. Awerbuch, B., Goldberg, A.V., Luby, M., Plotkin, S.A.: Network decomposition and locality in distributed computation. In: FOCS, vol. 30, pp. 364–369. Citeseer (1989)
2. Balliu, A., Brandt, S., Hirvonen, J., Olivetti, D., Rabie, M., Suomela, J.: Lower bounds for maximal matchings and maximal independent sets. J. ACM (JACM) **68**(5), 1–30 (2021)
3. Balliu, A., Brandt, S., Kuhn, F., Olivetti, D.: Distributed maximal matching and maximal independent set on hypergraphs, pp. 2632–2676 (2023)
4. Balliu, A., Brandt, S., Kuhn, F., Olivetti, D.: Improved distributed lower bounds for mis and bounded (out-) degree dominating sets in trees. In: Proceedings of the 2021 ACM Symposium on Principles of Distributed Computing, pp. 283–293 (2021)
5. Balliu, A., Brandt, S., Olivetti, D.: Distributed lower bounds for ruling sets. SIAM J. Comput. **51**(1), 70–115 (2022)
6. Barenboim, L., Elkin, M.: Distributed $(\delta+1)$-coloring in linear (in δ) time. In: Proceedings of the Forty-First Annual ACM Symposium on Theory of Computing, pp. 111–120 (2009)
7. Barenboim, L., Elkin, M., Pettie, S., Schneider, J.: The locality of distributed symmetry breaking. J. ACM (JACM) **63**(3), 1–45 (2016)
8. Brandt, S.: An automatic speedup theorem for distributed problems. In: Proceedings of the 2019 ACM Symposium on Principles of Distributed Computing, pp. 379–388 (2019)
9. Brandt, S., et al.: A lower bound for the distributed lovász local lemma. In: Proceedings of the Forty-Eighth Annual ACM Symposium on Theory of Computing, pp. 479–488 (2016)
10. Erdos, P., Lovász, L.: Problems and results on 3-chromatic hypergraphs and some related questions. Infinite Finite Sets **10**(2), 609–627 (1975)
11. Ghaffari, M.: An improved distributed algorithm for maximal independent set. In: Proceedings of the Twenty-Seventh Annual ACM-SIAM Symposium on Discrete Algorithms, pp. 270–277. SIAM (2016)
12. Ghaffari, M., Grunau, C.: Near-optimal deterministic network decomposition and ruling set, and improved mis. In: 2024 IEEE 65th Annual Symposium on Foundations of Computer Science (FOCS), pp. 2148–2179. IEEE (2024)
13. Ghaffari, M., Grunau, S., Rozhoň, V.: Improved deterministic network decomposition. In: Proceedings of the 2021 ACM-SIAM Symposium on Discrete Algorithms (SODA), pp. 2904–2923. SIAM (2021)
14. Kuhn, F., Zheng, C.: Efficient distributed computation of mis and generalized mis in linear hypergraphs. arXiv preprint arXiv:1805.03357 (2018)

15. Kutten, S., Nanongkai, D., Pandurangan, G., Robinson, P.: Distributed symmetry breaking in hypergraphs. In: Kuhn, F. (ed.) DISC 2014. LNCS, vol. 8784, pp. 469–483. Springer, Heidelberg (2014). https://doi.org/10.1007/978-3-662-45174-8_32
16. Linial, N.: Distributive graph algorithms global solutions from local data. In: 28th Annual Symposium on Foundations of Computer Science (sfcs 1987), pp. 331–335. IEEE (1987)
17. Linial, N.: Locality in distributed graph algorithms. SIAM J. Comput. **21**(1), 193–201 (1992)
18. Maus, Y., Tonoyan, T.: Local conflict coloring revisited: linial for lists. In: 34th International Symposium on Distributed Computing (DISC 2020), pp. 16–1. Schloss Dagstuhl–Leibniz-Zentrum für Informatik (2020)
19. Mitzenmacher, M., Upfal, E.: Chernoff Bounds, pp. 61–89. Cambridge University Press (2005)
20. Moser, R.A., Tardos, G.: A constructive proof of the general lovász local lemma. J. ACM **57**(2), 1–15 (2010)
21. Panconesi, A., Rizzi, R.: Some simple distributed algorithms for sparse networks. Distrib. Comput. **14**(2), 97–100 (2001)

Approximating Temporal Modularity on Graphs of Small Underlying Treewidth

Vilhelm Agdur[1], Jessica Enright[2], Laura Larios-Jones[2](✉), Kitty Meeks[2], Fiona Skerman[1], and Ella Yates[2]

[1] Department of Mathematics, Uppsala University, Uppsala, Sweden
{vilhelm.agdur,fiona.skerman}@math.uu.se
[2] School of Computing Science, University of Glasgow, Glasgow, UK
{jessica.enright,laura.larios-jones,kitty.meeks}@glasgow.ac.uk,
3032195Y@student.gla.ac.uk

Abstract. Modularity is a very widely used measure of the level of clustering or community structure in networks. Here we consider a recent generalisation of the definition of modularity to temporal graphs, whose edge-sets change over discrete timesteps; such graphs offer a more realistic model of many real-world networks in which connections between entities (for example, between individuals in a social network) evolve over time. Computing modularity is notoriously difficult: it is NP-hard even to approximate in general, and only admits efficient exact algorithms in very restricted special cases. Our main result is that a multiplicative approximation to temporal modularity can be computed efficiently when the underlying graph has small treewidth. This generalises a similar approximation algorithm for the static case, but requires some substantially new ideas to overcome technical challenges associated with the temporal nature of the problem.

Keywords: Modularity · Community structure · Temporal graphs · Parameterised algorithms · Treewidth

1 Introduction

One of the most common methods for community detection on static graphs is *modularity optimisation*, where we define an objective function on partitions of the vertices, and attempt to solve the resulting optimisation problem by various means. The computational problem is notoriously intractable: exact optimisation is known to be NP-Hard [6], even restricted to d-regular graphs (for any $d \geq 9$) and two-part partitions [9]; moreover, it is NP-hard even to compute a multiplicative approximation [10]. In the parameterised setting, the problem is W[1]-hard parameterised simultaneously by the pathwidth and feedback vertex number of the input graph [22]; the problem is however in FPT parameterised by either the vertex cover number [22] or max leaf number [15] of the input graph. More generally, there is an fpt-algorithm parameterised by the treewidth of the input graph which computes a multiplicative approximation to the maximum modularity [22].

In this paper we are concerned with computing a modularity-like quantity on networks which evolve over time. In the real world, it is often the case that static graphs are not an appropriate model – online social contacts change over time [13], different bird species are present in the winter and in the summer [29], and brain structure is affected by hormonal cycles [25]. Temporal graphs [19] are one of the most widely used models for such networks: a temporal graph is a pair (G, λ) where G is the underlying static graph and $\lambda : E(G) \to 2^\mathbb{N}$ assigns to each edge a (non-empty) set of timesteps at which it is active. This model describes networks where the vertex-set remains unchanged but the edge-set changes over discrete timesteps.

The problem of community detection in temporal graphs has received increasing attention over the last twenty years, going from approaches that try to leverage community detection methods in the static case [16,17,27,30,32] to online methods [3,14,20,31,33] and methods that construct an auxiliary static graph from the temporal graph and modify methods from the static case to apply to the auxiliary graph [4,12,18,24,28,34].

Here, we study temporal modularity as defined by Mucha et al. [24] which generalises classic modularity to a temporal graph setting, and has become a standard method [5,21,25,26]. This adaptation considers a partitioning of the vertices of the temporal graph which allows vertices to be in different parts at different times. The measure rewards partitions which have higher modularity within the static graph present at any particular time step and penalises moving vertices between parts. This measure exhibits a number of convenient properties: for example, if the temporal graph is the same at all times then the optimum partitions are exactly the same as for static modularity. Because the optimisation of this measure is a generalisation of the NP-hard static version, it is straightforwardly hard to optimise, thus motivating our interest in a parameterised approach.

Our main result is that one of the most general positive results from the static setting can be adapted to this notion of temporal modularity. Specifically, we show that there exists an fpt-algorithm, parameterised by treewidth of the underlying static graph (whose edge-set is the union of the edge-set at all timesteps), which computes a multiplicative approximation to the temporal modularity. Similarly to the analogous result in the static case, this algorithm relies on a dynamic program over a tree decomposition of the underlying graph (albeit with slightly more involved accounting than is needed in the static case). In the static case this was combined with an existing result that the maximum modularity can be approximated by considering only partitions with a constant number of parts; we prove an analogous result for the temporal case which we use here, but there is a further complication we must overcome for the temporal version. In order to avoid the number of states that must be considered in the dynamic program over the tree decomposition becoming prohibitively large, we must restrict the number of timesteps being considered. We show that we can in fact approximate the temporal modularity by considering separately the restriction of the temporal graph to short time-windows, provided these windows are chosen carefully.

The remainder of the paper is organised as follows. In Sect. 2 we introduce notation and key definitions. In Sect. 3 we list the crucial lemmas that allow us to approximate temporal modularity by solving a collection of simpler problems in which both the number of permitted parts and the number of timesteps is bounded. In Sect. 4 we describe how to solve this simpler problem on graphs of small treewidth via a dynamic programming approach, and then apply the results of Sect. 3 to obtain our overall approximation algorithm. In Sect. 5 we conclude with some final observations and directions for future work. For reasons of space, proofs of results marked with a star ($\star$) are omitted; for full details see [1].

2 Notation and Definitions

Here we introduce key definitions and notation. Throughout this work we use the Word-RAM model of computation, thus computing arithmetic operations on $\log n$-bit numbers in constant time. A problem is said to be *fixed-parameter tractable*, or fpt, with respect to a parameter k if there is an algorithm solving it in time $f(k) \cdot \text{poly}(n)$, where n is the size of the instance, and f is a computable function. The FPT complexity class contains all problems admitting an fpt algorithm.

A graph is a pair $G = (V, E)$ with vertex set V and edge set E; we denote the size of the vertex set as $n = |V|$, and the size of the edge set as $m = |E|$. Graphs here are simple, loopless, and undirected. The *degree* of a vertex v, denoted d_v, is the number of other vertices it is adjacent to. For a subset $A \subseteq V$ of the vertices of G, we write $E(A)$ for the set of edges between vertices in A, $e(A)$ for $|E(A)|$, and $\text{vol}(A) = \sum_{v \in A} d_v$.

Given a graph $G = (V, E)$ with $m = |E| \geq 1$ edges and a partition $\mathcal{A} = \{A_1, A_2, \ldots, A_k\}$ of its vertices, the *modularity* of this partition is given by

$$q(G, \mathcal{A}) = \sum_{A \in \mathcal{A}} \frac{e(A)}{m} - \frac{\text{vol}(A)^2}{(2\,m)^2},$$

and the modularity of G is the maximum over all partitions, that is,

$$q^*(G) = \max_{\mathcal{A}} q(G, \mathcal{A}).$$

For graphs G' with no edges let $q(G', \mathcal{A}) = 0$ for any partition and $q^*(G') = 0$. The modularity of any partition ranges between 0 and 1, where partitions that capture more clustering in the graphs score higher. The positive term rewards high numbers of edges within parts while the negative term penalises having large parts of high degree.

2.1 Temporal Graphs and Temporal Modularity

A *temporal graph* $\mathcal{G} = (G, \lambda)$ with lifetime T consists of a graph $G = (V, E)$ and a function $\lambda : E \to 2^{[T]}$, assigning each edge a set of times at which it is active. For each $t \in [T]$, the *snapshot* of $\mathcal{G}$ at time t is the graph $G_t = (V, E_t)$, where $E_t = \{e \in E \mid t \in \lambda(e)\}$. The degree of a vertex v in snapshot G_t is denoted by $d_{v,t}$. We denote the number of vertices in a temporal graph as $n = |V|$, and the number of edges in a snapshot G_t as $m_t = |E_t|$.

A partition $\mathcal{A}$ of a temporal graph into k parts is a function $\pi_{\mathcal{A}} : V \times [T] \to [k]$, assigning each vertex a labelled part at each time step. For each time t we get a partition $\mathcal{A}_t$ of G_t by taking

$$\mathcal{A}_t = \left\{ \pi_{\mathcal{A},t}^{-1}(1), \pi_{\mathcal{A},t}^{-1}(2), \ldots, \pi_{\mathcal{A},t}^{-1}(k) \right\},$$

where $\pi_{\mathcal{A},t}(v) = \pi_{\mathcal{A}}(v,t)$. An example of such a partition is illustrated in Fig. 1.

For a temporal graph $\mathcal{G}$ and a partition $\mathcal{A}$ of $\mathcal{G}$, we say that a vertex v is *loyal* at time t if $\pi_{\mathcal{A}}(v,t) = \pi_{\mathcal{A}}(v,t+1)$. We denote by $\mathcal{L}(\mathcal{A})$ the total number of loyal vertices, over all times - we call this the *loyalty contribution*. That is, if we define the *indicator function* that (v,t) and (v',t') are in the same part by:

$$\delta_{\mathcal{A}}((v,t),(v',t')) = \begin{cases} 1 & \text{if } \pi_{\mathcal{A}}(v,t) = \pi_{\mathcal{A}}(v',t') \\ 0 & \text{otherwise,} \end{cases}$$

then we have

$$\mathcal{L}(\mathcal{A}) = \sum_{v \in V} \sum_{t=1}^{T-1} \delta_{\mathcal{A}}((v,t),(v,t+1)).$$

Adapting [24], specifically for temporal graphs, we can now define temporal modularity.

Definition 1. *Given a temporal graph $\mathcal{G} = (G = (V,E), \lambda)$, a partition $\mathcal{A}$ of $\mathcal{G}$, and a tuning parameter $\omega \geq 0$, the* temporal modularity *of $\mathcal{A}$ is given by*

$$q_\omega(\mathcal{G}, \mathcal{A}) = \frac{1}{2\mu_\omega(\mathcal{G})} \left(\sum_{t=1}^{T} \sum_{A \in \mathcal{A}_t} \left(2e_{G_t}(A) - \frac{\text{vol}_{G_t}(A)^2}{2m_t} \right) + \omega \mathcal{L}(\mathcal{A}) \right), \quad (1)$$

where

$$\mu_\omega(\mathcal{G}) = \frac{1}{2}\omega n(T-1) + \sum_{t=1}^{T} m_t$$

is a normalisation factor. The temporal modularity *of $\mathcal{G}$ is given by $q_\omega^*(\mathcal{G}) = \max_{\mathcal{A}} q(\mathcal{G}, \mathcal{A})$.*

We will often omit the dependence on ω, and in most sections treat it as a given constant.

We sometimes consider the temporal modularity restricted to k parts, or *temporal k-modularity*, of $\mathcal{G}$, which is given by $q_{k,\omega}^*(\mathcal{G}) = \max_{\mathcal{A}, |\mathcal{A}| \leq k} q_\omega(\mathcal{G}, \mathcal{A})$.

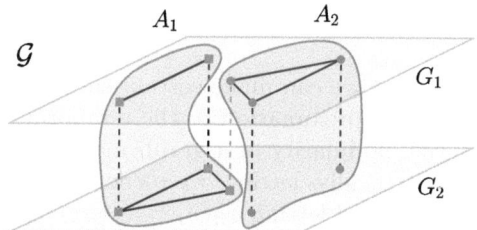

Fig. 1. A temporal graph $\mathcal{G}$ together with a two part vertex partition $\mathcal{A} = \{A_1, A_2\}$. Here four of the five vertices are loyal at time 1, as indicated with black dashed lines between the snapshots, while one vertex moves between parts. Note also that, unlike in the case of static modularity, it is beneficial for a part to be disconnected at time 2 as this increases the loyalty contribution.

In our algorithms, it will often be more convenient to compute the non-normalised temporal modularity of a temporal graph (or temporal subgraph); for completeness, we now define this notion.

Definition 2. *Given a temporal graph* $\mathcal{G} = (G, \lambda) = ((V, E), \lambda)$, *a partition* $\mathcal{A}$ *of this graph, and a tuning parameter* $\omega \geq 0$, *the* non-normalised temporal modularity *of* $\mathcal{A}$ *is given by*

$$\widetilde{q}_\omega(\mathcal{G}, \mathcal{A}) = \sum_{t=1}^{T} \sum_{A \in \mathcal{A}_t} \left(2e_{G_t}(A) - \frac{\mathrm{vol}_{G_t}(A)^2}{2m_t} \right) + \omega \mathcal{L}(\mathcal{A}). \quad (2)$$

The *non-normalised temporal modularity* of $\mathcal{G}$ is given by $\widetilde{q}_\omega^*(\mathcal{G}) = \max_{\mathcal{A}} \widetilde{q}(\mathcal{G}, \mathcal{A})$ and $\widetilde{q}_{k,\omega}^*(\mathcal{G}) = \max_{\mathcal{A}, |\mathcal{A}| \leq k} \widetilde{q}_\omega(\mathcal{G}, \mathcal{A})$ gives the *non-normalised temporal k-modularity* of $\mathcal{G}$.

Our main result in this paper is an approximate fpt-algorithm parameterised by treewidth. We use standard treewidth definitions and results as in [8].

Definition 3 [8]. *A* tree decomposition *of a graph G is a pair $(H, \mathcal{D})$ where H is a tree and $\mathcal{D} = \{\mathcal{D}(b) : b \in V(H)\}$ is a collection of subsets of $V(G)$, called* bags, *such that:*

1. *For every vertex $v \in V(G)$ there is at least one $b \in V(H)$ such that $v \in \mathcal{D}(b)$.*
2. *For every edge $uv \in E(G)$ there exists a node $b \in V(H)$ such that $u, v \in \mathcal{D}(b)$.*
3. *For every vertex $v \in V(G)$ the subgraph induced by the set of nodes $\{b : v \in \mathcal{D}(b)\}$ is connected.*

The width w *of the tree decomposition is the size of the largest bag minus 1.*

The *treewidth* is the minimum width over all possible tree decompositions of a graph. We use *nice* tree decompositions, which have restrictions on the relationships between adjacent bags. Any tree decomposition can, in polynomial time, be transformed into a nice tree decomposition without increasing the width, and without loss of generality we can assume any nice tree decomposition of width w has $\mathcal{O}(wn)$ nodes [8].

3 Approximations to Temporal Modularity

In this section, we prove that we can make certain simplifying assumptions and still retain a multiplicative approximation to the temporal modularity.

First we note that the modularity of a graph may also be defined as a sum over pairs of vertices. Specifically, letting $\pi_{\mathcal{A}}(v)$ denote the part that vertex v belongs to in a partition $\mathcal{A}$, and letting $\delta_{\mathcal{A}}(u,v) = \mathbf{1}_{\pi_{\mathcal{A}}(u)=\pi_{\mathcal{A}}(v)}$, we have that

$$q(G, \mathcal{A}) = \frac{1}{2m} \sum_{u,v \in G} \delta_{\mathcal{A}}(u,v) \left(\mathbf{1}_{uv \in E(G)} - \frac{d_u d_v}{2m} \right).$$

Using this, and our definition of loyalty, we get the following alternative form of the definition of temporal modularity:

Remark 1. We may equivalently define the temporal modularity score as

$$q_\omega(\mathcal{G}, \mathcal{A}) = \sum_{(u,t),(u',t') \in V(G) \times [T]} \delta_{\mathcal{A}}((u,t),(u',t')) \kappa_\omega(u, u', t, t') \tag{3}$$

where

$$\kappa_\omega(u, u', t, t') = \frac{1}{2\mu(\mathcal{G})} \left(\omega \mathbf{1}_{t=t'-1} \mathbf{1}_{u=u'} + \mathbf{1}_{t=t'} \left(\mathbf{1}_{uu' \in E_t} - \frac{d_{u,t} d_{u',t}}{2m_t} \right) \right)$$

is a constant that depends on $\mathcal{G}$ and ω but not on the partition $\mathcal{A}$.

Our next result is an analogue of the result of Dinh and Thai for the static setting [11, Lemma 3], which says that we can approximate the maximum modularity by considering only partitions with a fixed number of parts. We note that the Dinh-Thai result was previously exploited by Meeks and Skerman [22] to obtain an efficient approximation algorithm to compute static modularity on graphs of small treewidth.

Lemma 1 (⋆). Let $\mathcal{G}$ be a temporal graph with n vertices and lifetime T such that each snapshot has at least one edge. Fix an integer $k \geq 2$. Then

$$q^*_{k,\omega}(\mathcal{G}) \geq \left(1 - \frac{1}{k}\right) q^*_\omega(\mathcal{G}) + \frac{n\omega(T-1)}{k}.$$

We now prove two results that together show we can approximate the (non-normalised) temporal modularity by summing the temporal modularity of the graph restricted to suitably chosen short time windows. We first introduce some notation for the restriction of a temporal graph to a specified time interval. Given a temporal graph $\mathcal{G} = (G, \lambda)$ with lifetime T, and integers a, b with $1 \leq a \leq b \leq T$, we will write $\mathcal{G}_{[a,b]}$ for restriction of $\mathcal{G}$ to the time interval $[a, b]$; that is, $\mathcal{G}_{[a,b]} = (G, \lambda')$ where, for all $e \in E(G)$, $\lambda'(e) = \lambda(e) \cap \{a, a+1, \ldots, b\}$.

Lemma 2 ($\star$). *Let $\mathcal{G}$ be a temporal graph with lifetime T, and fix integers $0 = t_0 < t_1 < \cdots < t_\ell = T$. Then*

$$\sum_{i=0}^{\ell-1} \widetilde{q}^*(\mathcal{G}_{[t_i+1, t_{i+1}]}) \leq \widetilde{q}^*(\mathcal{G}).$$

We now show that it is possible to choose values of $t_1, \ldots, t_{\ell-1}$ so that each difference $t_i - t_{i-1}$ is small but we do not lose a large proportion of loyalty edges between timesteps t_i and t_{i+1}. Recall we define the loyalty contribution as $\mathcal{L}(\mathcal{A}) = \sum_{v \in V} \sum_{t=1}^{T-1} \delta_\mathcal{A}((v, t), (v, t+1))$. In the following lemma, we want to consider the contribution to this total from a single pair of consecutive timesteps; to this end, we define

$$\mathcal{L}(\mathcal{A}, t) = \sum_{v \in V} \delta_\mathcal{A}((v, t), (v, t+1)).$$

Lemma 3 ($\star$). *Let $\mathcal{G}$ be a temporal graph with lifetime T, and let d be a positive integer. Then there exist integers $0 = t_0 < t_1 < \cdots < t_\ell = T$ such that $t_j - t_{j-1} \leq 2d$ for each $1 \leq j \leq \ell$ and*

$$\sum_{i=0}^{\ell-1} \widetilde{q}(\mathcal{G}_{[t_i+1, t_{i+1}]}) \geq \left(1 - \frac{1}{d}\right) \widetilde{q}^*(\mathcal{G}).$$

4 Tree-Decomposition Based Algorithm

In this section, we describe our main algorithm, and prove that it efficiently computes an approximation to temporal modularity when the underlying graph has small treewidth.

Theorem 1. *Let $\mathcal{G}$ be a temporal graph with n vertices and lifetime T, and suppose that the underlying graph of $\mathcal{G}$ has treewidth at most w. Let c and d be positive integers. Then we can compute a $\left(1 - \left(\frac{1}{c} + \frac{2}{d}\right)\right)$-approximation to $q_\omega^*(\mathcal{G})$ in time $T^2 n^{\mathcal{O}(cd)} c^{\mathcal{O}(\mathrm{wd})} d^{\mathcal{O}(c)}$.*

As a subroutine, our approximation algorithm will use an algorithm which computes exactly the maximum temporal modularity achievable with a partition into c parts when both the underlying treewidth and lifetime are small.

Theorem 2. *Let $\mathcal{G}$ be a temporal graph with n vertices, lifetime T and underlying treewidth at most w. The non-normalised temporal c-modularity of $\mathcal{G}$, $\widetilde{q}_{c,\omega}^*(\mathcal{G})$, can be calculated in time $n^{\mathcal{O}(cT)} c^{\mathcal{O}(\mathrm{w}T)} T^{\mathcal{O}(c)}$.*

Theorem 2 is proved using fairly standard dynamic programming techniques over a *nice tree decomposition*, which is defined as follows.

Definition 4 [8]. *We call a tree decomposition $(H, \mathcal{D})$ nice if all leaves and the root of the tree contain empty bags and all non-leaf nodes are one of three types:*

- *Introduce node:* a node b with exactly one child b' such that $\mathcal{D}(b) = \mathcal{D}(b') \cup \{v\}$, for some vertex $v \notin \mathcal{D}(b')$.
- *Forget node:* a node b with exactly one child b' such that $\mathcal{D}(b) = \mathcal{D}(b') \setminus \{v\}$ for some vertex $v \in \mathcal{D}(b')$.
- *Join node:* a node b with exactly two children b_1 and b_2 such that $\mathcal{D}(b) = \mathcal{D}(b_1) = \mathcal{D}(b_2)$.

We define V_b to be the set of all vertices in $\mathcal{D}(b)$ and all bags below the node b. We call the set $V_b \setminus \mathcal{D}(b)$ the set of vertices that have been *forgotten* at b. By the third property from Definition 3 (i.e. that the subtree of the tree decomposition induced by the nodes containing any given vertex is connected) we know that these vertices occur strictly below $\mathcal{D}(b)$ in the tree.

We now describe the information we will store at each node of the nice tree decomposition in our algorithm. For any node $b \in V(H)$ a *state* of b consists of the following:

1. A partition function $\pi : \mathcal{D}(b) \times [T] \to [c]$.
2. A function $\alpha : [c] \to [mT]$, a count of all time-edges within each part that have at least one vertex forgotten.
3. A function $\beta : [c] \times [T] \to [2m]$, a count of the degree of all forgotten vertices within each time and part.
4. A number γ, a count of the total loyalty edges from forgotten vertices.

Lemma 4 ($\star$). *Let $\mathcal{G}$ be a temporal graph with n vertices, m edges, lifetime T and underlying treewidth at most w. Then there are $\mathcal{O}(2^{cT} c^{(\mathrm{w}+1)T} m^{c(T+1)} T^{c+1} n)$ states describing partitions into at most c parts at any node in a tree decomposition of $\mathcal{G}$.*

For a node $b \in V(H)$ a state $(\pi, \alpha, \beta, \gamma)$ of b is *valid* if there exists a partition function $\pi^* : V_b \times T \to [c]$ such that:

1. $\pi^*|_{\mathcal{D}(b) \times T} = \pi$,
2. for each $p \in [c]$, $\alpha(p)$ is the number of all time-edges in part p in π^* that have at least one vertex in $V_b \setminus \mathcal{D}(b)$ or equivalently $\alpha(p) = |\{(uv, t) : t \in [T], uv \in E_t, \pi^*(v, t) = \pi^*(u, t) = p \text{ and } \{u, v\} \cap V_b \setminus \mathcal{D}(b) \neq \emptyset\}|$,
3. for each time t and $p \in [c]$, $\beta(p, t)$ is the sum of degrees of all vertices in $V_b \setminus \mathcal{D}(b)$ in part p at time t in π^* or equivalently $\beta(p, t) = \sum_{\substack{u \in V_b \setminus \mathcal{D}(b) \\ \pi^*(u,t)=p}} d_{u,t}$,

    and
4. γ is the loyalty contribution from all vertices in $V_b \setminus \mathcal{D}(b)$ in π^*, equivalently $\gamma = \sum_{v \in V_b \setminus \mathcal{D}(b)} \sum_{t=1}^{T-1} \delta_{\pi^*}((v, t), (v, t+1))$.

If these conditions hold we say that the partition function π^* *supports* the valid state $(\pi, \alpha, \beta, \gamma)$.

We now describe how to determine the set of valid states for each type of node, given the sets of valid states for all of the node's children.

Lemma 5 ($\star$). *A state $(\pi, \alpha, \beta, \gamma)$ at a leaf node is valid if and only if:*

- π is the empty partition function,
- $\alpha(p) = 0$ for all $p \in [c]$,
- $\beta(p,t) = 0$ for all $p \in [c], t \in [T]$, and
- $\gamma = 0$.

Lemma 6 ($\star$). *Let b be an introduce node with child b' such that $\mathcal{D}(b) \setminus \mathcal{D}(b') = \{v\}$. Then $(\pi, \alpha, \beta, \gamma)$ is a valid state for b if and only if there exists a valid state $(\pi', \alpha', \beta', \gamma')$ for b' such that:*

1. $\pi|_{\mathcal{D}(b') \times [T]} = \pi'$,
2. $\alpha(p) = \alpha'(p)$ for all $p \in [c]$,
3. $\beta(p,t) = \beta'(p,t)$ for all $p \in [c], t \in [T]$, and
4. $\gamma = \gamma'$.

Lemma 7 ($\star$). *Let b be a forget node with child b' such that $\mathcal{D}(b) = \mathcal{D}(b') \setminus \{v\}$ for some $v \in \mathcal{D}(b')$. Then $(\pi, \alpha, \beta, \gamma)$ is a valid state of b if and only if there exists a valid state $(\pi', \alpha', \beta', \gamma')$ of b' such that:*

1. $\pi = \pi'|_{\mathcal{D}(b) \times [T]}$
2. $\alpha(p) = \alpha'(p) + |\{(u,t) : uv \in E_t, u \in \mathcal{D}(b), t \in [T] \text{ and } (u,t), (v,t) \in p\}|$ for all $p \in [c]$,
3. for all $p \in [c]$, $t \in [T]$,

$$\beta(p,t) = \begin{cases} \beta'(p,t) + d_{v,t} & \text{if } \pi'(v,t) = p \\ \beta'(p,t) & \text{otherwise,} \end{cases}$$

and

4. $\gamma = \gamma' + |\{t \in [T-1] : \pi'(v,t) = \pi'(v,t+1)\}|$.

Lemma 8 ($\star$). *Let b be a join node with children b_1 and b_2 such that $\mathcal{D}(b) = \mathcal{D}(b_1) = \mathcal{D}(b_2)$. Then $(\pi, \alpha, \beta, \gamma)$ is a valid state of b if and only if there exist valid states $(\pi_1, \alpha_1, \beta_1, \gamma_1)$ of b_1 and $(\pi_2, \alpha_2, \beta_2, \gamma_2)$ of b_2 such that:*

1. $\pi(v,t) = \pi_1(v,t) = \pi_2(v,t)$ for all $v \in \mathcal{D}(b)$ and $t \in [T]$,
2. $\alpha(p) = \alpha_1(p) + \alpha_2(p)$ for all $p \in [c]$,
3. $\beta(p,t) = \beta_1(p,t) + \beta_2(p,t)$ for all $p \in [c], t \in [T]$, and
4. $\gamma = \gamma_1 + \gamma_2$.

We also bound the time required to compute the maximum non-normalised temporal c-modularity of the graph given all valid states at the root.

Lemma 9 ($\star$). *Let $\mathcal{G}$ be a temporal graph with n vertices, m edges and lifetime T. Given the set of all valid states at the root of a nice tree decomposition of $\mathcal{G}$, the maximum non-normalised temporal c-modularity of $\mathcal{G}$, $\widetilde{q}_c^*(\mathcal{G})$, can be found in time $\mathcal{O}(2^{cT} m^{c(T+1)} T^{c+2} cn)$.*

We now have everything we need to prove Theorem 2.

Proof (Proof of Theorem 2). By Lemma 4, the maximum number of states at any node is $\mathcal{O}(2^{cT} c^{(w+1)T} m^{c(T+1)} T^{c+1} n)$.

We assume that all our leaf nodes are empty and from Lemma 5 the states at the leaf nodes are valid only when the partition is empty and the other functions are zero which can checked in constant time. To compute the valid states at the root we move up the nice tree decomposition of the graph starting at the leaf nodes until we reach the root where we will use Lemma 9 to calculate the non-normalised temporal c-modularity. To do this we consider our three types of parent child relationship and the time needed to find all valid states for the parent in each case.

First we consider an introduce node. Considering a state $(\pi, \alpha, \beta, \gamma)$ of the parent and a valid state $(\pi', \alpha', \beta', \gamma')$ of the child, by Lemma 6 we can check the validity of the parent by checking the equality of each of our functions. For the partition function we have to check that, for each time $t \leq T$ and vertex $u \neq v$ in the bag, $\pi(u,t) = \pi'(u,t)$, which takes at most $(w+1)T$ checks with each check taking constant time. For α we have to check that, for each part $p \in [c]$, we have $\alpha(p) = \alpha'(p)$, which takes c constant time checks. For β we have to check that, for each part $p \in [c]$ and time $t \leq T$, we have $\beta(p,t) = \beta'(p,t)$, which takes cT constant time checks. Finally, we have a single constant time check to see that $\gamma = \gamma'$. Therefore, checking the validity of a parent state can be done in time $\mathcal{O}(T(w+c))$. We want to check each possible pair of a parent and a child state, that is $n^{\mathcal{O}(cT)} c^{\mathcal{O}(wT)} T^{\mathcal{O}(c)}$.

Next we look at the time taken to check a forget node. Considering a state $(\pi, \alpha, \beta, \gamma)$ for the parent and a valid state $(\pi', \alpha', \beta', \gamma')$ for the child, by Lemma 7 we can check the validity by checking the relationship of each of our functions. For the partition function, we have to check for each time $t \in [T]$ and each vertex $u \neq v$ in the bag that we have $\pi(u,t) = \pi'(u,t)$, which takes wT constant time checks. For α, for each of the parts $p \in [c]$ we count the number of edges from v in the part in the child and then check this against the difference in our α values, which can be done in time $\mathcal{O}(cw^2 T)$. For β, for each part $p \in [c]$ and time $t \in [T]$ we count the degree of v in part p at time t in the child then check if this is equal to $\beta(p,t) - \beta'(p,t)$, which can be done in time $\mathcal{O}(cTw)$. Finally, for γ we count the loyalty of the vertex v and compare the difference in our loyalty scores to this value, which can be done in time $\mathcal{O}(T)$. Therefore, checking the validity of a parent state can be done in time $\mathcal{O}(cw^2 T)$. We need to check all possible combinations of parent and child states, and there are $\mathcal{O}((2^{cT} c^{(w+1)T} m^{c(T+1)} T^{c+1} n)^2)$ such combinations. This gives us total time $n^{\mathcal{O}(cT)} c^{\mathcal{O}(wT)} T^{\mathcal{O}(c)}$.

Finally, we consider the time needed to check that a join node is valid. Consider a parent state $(\pi, \alpha, \beta, \gamma)$ and valid states $(\pi_1, \alpha_1, \beta_1, \gamma_1)$ and $(\pi_2, \alpha_2, \beta_2, \gamma_2)$ for the two children. From Lemma 8 we know the relationship needed between each of the four functions for the parent state to be valid, we check these relationships. First, to check the partition function compatibility, for each vertex v in the bag and time t we check that $\pi(v,t) = \pi_1(v,t) = \pi_2(v,t)$ which takes time $\mathcal{O}(w+1)T$ checks. Then, for each part $p \in [c]$ we check that $\alpha(p) = \alpha_1(p) + \alpha_2(p)$

which takes time $\mathcal{O}(c)$. Similarly, for each part $p \in [c]$ and time $t \in [T]$ we check the value of $\beta(p,t)$ by comparing it to the sum of $\beta_1(p,t)$ and $\beta_2(p,t)$ which takes time $\mathcal{O}(cT)$. Finally, we check the loyalty γ by comparing it to the sum of γ_1 and γ_2, which is a single constant time check. Therefore, checking the validity of the parent takes time $\mathcal{O}(T(w+c))$. We need to check all possible combinations of two children and one parent state, and there are $\mathcal{O}\big((2^{cT}c^{(w+1)T}m^{c(T+1)}T^{c+1}n)^3\big)$ such combinations. This gives us total time $n^{\mathcal{O}(cT)}c^{\mathcal{O}(wT)}T^{\mathcal{O}(c)}$.

Given the valid states of its children, we can compute the valid states at any node in time $n^{\mathcal{O}(cT)}c^{\mathcal{O}(wT)}T^{\mathcal{O}(c)}$ regardless of what type of node it is. We can assume any nice tree decomposition has at most $\mathcal{O}(wn)$ nodes [8] so using our worst case complexity for each of these nodes, we can calculate all valid states at the root in $n^{\mathcal{O}(cT)}c^{\mathcal{O}(wT)}T^{\mathcal{O}(c)}$. From Lemma 9 the non-normalised temporal c-modularity at the root can be calculated in time $\mathcal{O}(2^{cT}m^{c(T+1)}T^{c+2}cn) \in n^{\mathcal{O}(cT)}T^{\mathcal{O}(c)}c$. Hence, the non-normalised temporal c-modularity for a graph of bounded tree width can be calculated in time $n^{\mathcal{O}(cT)}c^{\mathcal{O}(wT)}T^{\mathcal{O}(c)}$. □

We are now ready to prove Theorem 1. The strategy is to apply the algorithm of Theorem 2 to the restriction of our input graph to constant-length time intervals. We use a second simple dynamic program to determine the best set of short intervals to use for this, recalling from Lemma 3 that there exists at least choice that will result in a good approximation.

Proof (Proof of Theorem 1). Given any temporal graph $\mathcal{G}$ with lifetime T, let us define $\widetilde{q}_c^*(\mathcal{G}, d)$ to be

$$\max_{\substack{0=t_0<t_1<\cdots<t_\ell=T \\ t_i-t_{i-1}\leq d \text{ for all } 1\leq i\leq \ell}} \sum_{i=1}^{\ell} \widetilde{q}_c^*(\mathcal{G}_{[t_{i-1}+1,t_i]}).$$

Thus, $\widetilde{q}_c^*(\mathcal{G}, d)$ is the maximum possible sum of temporal c-modularities we can get from splitting the temporal graph into intervals of length at most d and maximising temporal modularity independently on each interval. By Lemmas 1, 2 and 3, we see that $\widetilde{q}_c^*(\mathcal{G}, d)$ is a $(1-(\frac{1}{c}+\frac{2}{d}))$-approximation to $\widetilde{q}^*(\mathcal{G})$. Given this approximation, we can easily compute a $(1-(\frac{1}{c}+\frac{2}{d}))$-approximation to $q^*(\mathcal{G})$ in time $\mathcal{O}(mT)$, simply multiplying by the normalisation factor. It therefore suffices to show that we can compute $\widetilde{q}_c^*(\mathcal{G}, d)$ in time $T^2 n^{\mathcal{O}(cd)} c^{\mathcal{O}(wd)} d^{\mathcal{O}(c)}$.

We achieve this by dynamic programming. Our goal is to compute a value $DP[s_1, s_2]$ for $1 \leq s_1 \leq s_2 \leq T$, such that

$$\left(1-(\frac{1}{c}+\frac{2}{d})\right) \widetilde{q}_c^*(\mathcal{G}_{[s_1,s_2]}, d) \leq DP[s_1,s_2] \leq \widetilde{q}_c^*(\mathcal{G}_{[s_1,s_2]}, d). \qquad (4)$$

We can then return the value of $DP[1,T]$ as our approximation to $\widetilde{q}_c^*(\mathcal{G}, d)$. We compute the table values as follows. We begin by initialising all table entries $DP[\mathcal{G}, s_1, s_2]$ such that $s_2 - s_1 < d$ by running the algorithm of Theorem 2 with input $\mathcal{G}_{[s_1,s_2]}$ and recording the result. This follows from the fact that the intervals are smaller than d, so $\widetilde{q}_c^*(\mathcal{G}_{[s_1,s_2]}, d) = \widetilde{q}_c^*(\mathcal{G}_{[s_1,s_2]})$. The remaining entries in the table, where $s_2 - s_1 \geq d$, are computed using the recurrence

$$DP[s_1, s_2] = \max_{1 \leq i \leq d-1} \{DP[s_1, s_1 + i] + DP[s_1 + i + 1, s_2]\}.$$

Correctness: We argue, by induction on $s_2 - s_1$, that Equation (4) holds for all table entries. For the base case, note that for entries with $s_2 - s_2 < d$ this follows immediately from the fact that the algorithm of Theorem 2 gives an $\left(1 - \left(\frac{1}{c} + \frac{2}{d}\right)\right)$-approximation to the non-normalised maximum temporal modularity. Suppose now that $s_2 - s_1 \geq d$. It follows immediately from the inductive hypothesis that $DP[s_1, s_2] \leq \widetilde{q}^*(\mathcal{G}_{[s_1,s_2]}, d)$, so it remains only to show the lower bound on $DP[s_1, s_2]$. For this, fix a sequence $s_1 - 1 = t_0 < t_1 < \cdots < t_\ell = s_2$ such that $\widetilde{q}^*(\mathcal{G}_{[s_1,s_2]}, d) = \sum_{j=1}^{\ell} \widetilde{q}^*(\mathcal{G}_{[t_{j-1}+1,t_j]})$ and $t_j - t_{j-1} \leq d$ for all $1 \leq j \leq \ell$. Fix $i = t_1 - s_1 - 1$. Then we can write

$$\widetilde{q}^*(\mathcal{G}_{[s_1,s_2]}, d) = \widetilde{q}^*(\mathcal{G}_{[s_1,s_1+i]}, d) + \sum_{j=1}^{\ell} \widetilde{q}^*(\mathcal{G}_{[t_{j-1}+1,t_j]})$$

$$\leq \widetilde{q}^*(\mathcal{G}_{[s_1,s_1+i]}, d) + \widetilde{q}^*(\mathcal{G}_{[s_1+i+1,s_2]}, d)$$

$$\leq \left(1 - (\frac{1}{c} + \frac{2}{d})\right)^{-1} DP[s_1, s_1 + i] + \left(1 - (\frac{1}{c} + \frac{2}{d})\right)^{-1} DP[s_1 + i + 1, s_2],$$

by the inductive hypothesis. Rearranging gives the required lower bound.

Running Time: We first consider the time required to compute the entries $DP[s_1, s_2]$ with $s_2 - s_1 < d$. There are $\mathcal{O}(dT)$ such entries. For each entry we invoke the algorithm of Theorem 2, which will run in time bounded by $n^{\mathcal{O}(cd)} c^{\mathcal{O}(\mathsf{w}d)} d^{\mathcal{O}(c)}$. Thus the time required for this initialisation phase is $\mathcal{O}(dT) \cdot n^{\mathcal{O}(cd)} c^{\mathcal{O}(\mathsf{w}d)} d^{\mathcal{O}(c)}$ which is bounded above by $T n^{\mathcal{O}(cd)} c^{\mathcal{O}(\mathsf{w}d)} d^{\mathcal{O}(c)}$. For each of the remaining entries, we take the minimum over $\mathcal{O}(d)$ sums of pairs of entries that have already been computed; computing each such entry takes time $\mathcal{O}(d)$. Since there are in total $\mathcal{O}(T^2)$ entries in the table, this second phase requires time $\mathcal{O}(dT^2)$. The total running time of the algorithm is at most $T^2 n^{\mathcal{O}(cd)} c^{\mathcal{O}(\mathsf{w}d)} d^{\mathcal{O}(c)}$, as required. □

5 Conclusions and Open Problems

To our best knowledge, the algorithm described here is the first with performance guarantees for computing temporal modularity. Given that temporal versions of problems that are tractable in the static case often become intractable even when the underlying graph is very severely restricted (e.g. even for paths [23] or stars [2]), it is somewhat surprising that here we are able to generalise one approach from the static case, at the expense of a worse approximation factor.

A key open question is whether any of the exact parameterised algorithms for computing static modularity can be generalised to the temporal setting. The vertex cover number of the underlying graph is a natural first candidate; note that this is strictly more restrictive than our treewidth-based approach, as vertex cover number bounds treewidth.

The approach using vertex cover number in the static setting [22] is unlikely to be fruitful here without new ideas: it relies on partitioning vertices outside of a vertex cover into a small number of sets with *identical* neighbourhoods; here, without also restricting the lifetime of the temporal graph, it is not possible to bound the number of different distinct neighbourhoods in terms of the vertex cover number. A more fruitful approach might be to consider parameterisation by a temporal analogue of this parameter, the *timed* vertex cover number [7].

Acknowledgments. We thank Matteo Magnani and Obaida Hanteer for useful discussions.

Jessica Enright is supported by EPSRC grant EP/T004878/1. and Kitty Meeks is supported by EPSRC grants EP/T004878/1 and EP/V032305/1. Fiona Skerman is supported by the Wallenberg AI, Autonomous Systems and Software Program (WASP) funded by the Knut and Alice Wallenberg Foundation. This project was partially supported by AI4Research at Uppsala University.

For the purpose of open access, the author(s) has applied a Creative Commons Attribution (CC BY) licence to any Author Accepted Manuscript version arising from this submission.

Disclosure of Interests. The authors have no competing interests to declare.

References

1. Agdur, V., Enright, J., Larios-Jones, L., Meeks, K., Skerman, F., Yates, E.: Approximating temporal modularity on graphs of small underlying treewidth. arXiv preprint arXiv:2507.17541 (2025)
2. Akrida, E.C., Mertzios, G.B., Spirakis, P.G., Raptopoulos, C.: The temporal explorer who returns to the base. J. Comput. Syst. Sci. **120**, 179–193 (2021)
3. Aynaud, T., Guillaume, J.L.: Static community detection algorithms for evolving networks. In: 8th International Symposium on Modeling and Optimization in Mobile, Ad Hoc, and Wireless Networks, pp. 513–519. IEEE (2010)
4. Bassett, D.S., Porter, M.A., Wymbs, N.F., Grafton, S.T., Carlson, J.M., Mucha, P.J.: Robust detection of dynamic community structure in networks. Chaos Interdisc. J. Nonlinear Sci. **23**(1) (2013)
5. Bianconi, G.: Multilayer Networks: Structure and Function. Oxford university press, Cambridge (2018)
6. Brandes, U., Delling, D., Gaertler, M., Gorke, R., Hoefer, M., Nikoloski, Z., Wagner, D.: On modularity clustering. IEEE Trans. Knowl. Data Eng. **20**(2), 172–188 (2007)
7. Casteigts, A., Himmel, A.S., Molter, H., Zschoche, P.: Finding temporal paths under waiting time constraints. Algorithmica **83**(9), 2754–2802 (2021)
8. Cygan, M., et al.: Parameterized Algorithms, vol. 5. Springer, Heidelberg (2015)
9. DasGupta, B., Desai, D.: On the complexity of newman's community finding approach for biological and social networks. J. Comput. Syst. Sci. **79**(1), 50–67 (2013)
10. Dinh, T.N., Li, X., Thai, M.T.: Network clustering via maximizing modularity: approximation algorithms and theoretical limits. In: 2015 IEEE International Conference on Data Mining, pp. 101–110. IEEE (2015)

11. Dinh, T.N., Thai, M.T.: Community detection in scale-free networks: approximation algorithms for maximizing modularity. IEEE J. Sel. Areas Commun. **31**(6), 997–1006 (2013)
12. DiTursi, D.J., Ghosh, G., Bogdanov, P.: Local community detection in dynamic networks. In: 2017 IEEE International Conference on Data Mining (ICDM), pp. 847–852. IEEE (2017)
13. Evkoski, B., Pelicon, A., Mozetič, I., Ljubešić, N., Kralj Novak, P.: Retweet communities reveal the main sources of hate speech. PLoS ONE **17**(3), e0265602 (2022)
14. Folino, F., Pizzuti, C.: An evolutionary multiobjective approach for community discovery in dynamic networks. IEEE Trans. Knowl. Data Eng. **26**(8), 1838–1852 (2013)
15. Garvardt, J., Komusiewicz, C.: Modularity clustering parameterized by max leaf number. In: 19th International Symposium on Parameterized and Exact Computation (IPEC 2024), pp. 16-1. Schloss Dagstuhl–Leibniz-Zentrum für Informatik (2024)
16. Greene, D., Doyle, D., Cunningham, P.: Tracking the evolution of communities in dynamic social networks. In: 2010 International Conference on Advances in Social Networks Analysis and Mining, pp. 176–183. IEEE (2010)
17. Hopcroft, J., Khan, O., Kulis, B., Selman, B.: Tracking evolving communities in large linked networks. Proc. Natl. Acad. Sci. **101**, 5249–5253 (2004)
18. Jian, J., Zhu, M., Sang, P.: Restricted Tweedie stochastic block models. arXiv preprint arXiv:2310.10952 (2023)
19. Kempe, D., Kleinberg, J., Kumar, A.: Connectivity and inference problems for temporal networks. J. Comput. Syst. Sci. **64**(4), 820–842 (2002)
20. Lin, Y.R., Chi, Y., Zhu, S., Sundaram, H., Tseng, B.L.: Facetnet: a framework for analyzing communities and their evolutions in dynamic networks. In: Proceedings of the 17th International Conference on World Wide Web, pp. 685–694 (2008)
21. Magnani, M., Rossi, L., Vega, D.: Analysis of multiplex social networks with R. J. Stat. Softw. **98**, 1–30 (2021)
22. Meeks, K., Skerman, F.: The parameterised complexity of computing the maximum modularity of a graph. Algorithmica **82**(8), 2174–2199 (2020)
23. Mertzios, G.B., Molter, H., Niedermeier, R., Zamaraev, V., Zschoche, P.: Computing maximum matchings in temporal graphs. J. Comput. Syst. Sci. **137**, 1–19 (2023)
24. Mucha, P.J., Richardson, T., Macon, K., Porter, M.A., Onnela, J.P.: Community structure in time-dependent, multiscale, and multiplex networks. Science **328**(5980), 876–878 (2010)
25. Mueller, J.M., et al.: Dynamic community detection reveals transient reorganization of functional brain networks across a female menstrual cycle. Netw. Neurosci. **5**(1), 125–144 (2021)
26. Nicosia, V., Tang, J., Mascolo, C., Musolesi, M., Russo, G., Latora, V.: Graph metrics for temporal networks. In: Temporal Networks, pp. 15–40 (2013)
27. Palla, G., Barabási, A.L., Vicsek, T.: Quantifying social group evolution. Nature **446**(7136), 664–667 (2007)
28. Paoletti, G., Gioacchini, L., Mellia, M., Vassio, L., Almeida, J.M.: Benchmarking evolutionary community detection algorithms in dynamic networks. arXiv preprint arXiv:2312.13784 (2023)
29. Pilosof, S., Porter, M.A., Pascual, M., Kéfi, S.: The multilayer nature of ecological networks. Nat. Ecol. Evol. **1**(4), 0101 (2017)
30. Rosvall, M., Bergstrom, C.T.: Mapping change in large networks. PLoS ONE **5**(1), e8694 (2010)

31. Seifikar, M., Farzi, S., Barati, M.: C-blondel: an efficient Louvain-based dynamic community detection algorithm. IEEE Trans. Comput. Soc. Syst. **7**(2), 308–318 (2020)
32. Sun, J., Faloutsos, C., Papadimitriou, S., Yu, P.S.: Graphscope: parameter-free mining of large time-evolving graphs. In: Proceedings of the 13th ACM SIGKDD International Conference on Knowledge Discovery and Data Mining, pp. 687–696 (2007)
33. Yuan, L., Zhang, X., Ke, Y., Lu, Z., Li, X., Liu, C.: Temporal community detection and analysis with network embeddings. Mathematics **13**(5), 698 (2025)
34. Zhang, M., Zhang, J., Dai, W.: Fast community detection in dynamic and heterogeneous networks. J. Comput. Graph. Stat. **33**(2), 487–500 (2024)

Round-Asynchronous Amnesiac Flooding

Oluwatobi Alafin[1], George B. Mertzios[2](✉)[ID], and Paul G. Spirakis[1][ID]

[1] Department of Computer Science, University of Liverpool, Liverpool, UK
{o.f.alafin,p.spirakis}@liverpool.ac.uk
[2] Department of Computer Science, Durham University, Durham, UK
george.mertzios@durham.ac.uk

Abstract. We present a comprehensive analysis of Round-Asynchronous Amnesiac Flooding (RAAF), a variant of Amnesiac Flooding that introduces round-based asynchrony through adversarial delays. We establish fundamental properties of RAAF, including termination characteristics for different graph types and decidability results under various adversarial models. Our key contributions include: (1) a formal model of RAAF incorporating round-based asynchrony, (2) a proof that flooding always terminates on acyclic graphs despite adversarial delays, (3) a construction showing non-termination is possible on any cyclic graph, (4) a demonstration that termination is undecidable with arbitrary computable adversaries, and (5) the introduction of Eventually Periodic Adversaries (EPA) under which termination becomes decidable. These results enhance our understanding of flooding processes in asynchronous settings and provide insights for designing robust distributed protocols.

Keywords: flooding protocol · amnesiac flooding · asynchronous protocol

1 Introduction

Flooding algorithms [2] serve as fundamental primitives in distributed computing for information dissemination, with applications ranging from network discovery to emergency broadcast systems. While traditional flooding maintains message histories to prevent redundant transmissions [3], such approaches become impractical in resource-constrained environments like sensor networks, IoT devices, or networks with high churn rates where maintaining consistent state is challenging.

Amnesiac Flooding (AF) addresses these limitations by eliminating message history, requiring nodes to make forwarding decisions based solely on current information [6]. However, existing AF analyses assume perfect synchrony—an unrealistic assumption in practical networks where delays, failures, and asynchrony are the norm rather than the exception.

G. B. Mertzios—Supported by the EPSRC grant EP/P020372/1.
P. G. Spirakis—Supported by the EPSRC grant EP/P02002X/1.

This paper introduces *Round-Asynchronous Amnesiac Flooding (RAAF)*, which bridges the gap between theoretical AF models and practical network conditions. RAAF maintains the memory-efficiency of amnesiac approaches while incorporating realistic asynchronous behaviour through adversarial delays; thus, our model can be also termed *Round-Delayed Amnesiac Flooding (RDAF)*. Our key insight is that even with minimal state and adverse conditions, we can characterise precise conditions under which flooding terminates, providing both positive results (guaranteed termination in acyclic networks) and fundamental limitations (undecidability with arbitrary adversaries).

The significance of our results extends beyond flooding protocols. By establishing when termination analysis becomes undecidable and identifying restricted adversary models (Eventually Periodic Adversaries) where it remains decidable, we contribute to the broader understanding of computability limits in asynchronous distributed systems.

While our model makes specific assumptions (such as nodes detecting blocked edges), these capture realistic scenarios and enable rigorous analysis of fundamental limits. The dichotomy between acyclic and cyclic graphs, and between arbitrary and periodic adversaries, reveals deep structural properties that inform the design of practical flooding protocols.

1.1 Model Context and Novelty

RAAF occupies a unique position in the spectrum of distributed system models. Unlike classical asynchronous models that allow arbitrary message delays and reorderings [3], or partially synchronous models that impose eventual bounds on communication delays [5], RAAF maintains a synchronous round structure while allowing adversarial edge-level asynchrony within rounds.

Adversarial Model Justification. A key aspect of our model is that nodes are aware of which outgoing edges are currently delayed by the adversary. While this may initially seem like a strong assumption, it captures several practical scenarios:

- **Failed transmission detection**: In many network protocols, nodes receive acknowledgments or can detect transmission failures through timeout mechanisms or carrier sensing.
- **Scheduled maintenance**: In managed networks, nodes may be informed of temporary link unavailability due to scheduled maintenance or known congestion patterns.
- **Visible network conditions**: In wireless networks, nodes can often detect poor channel conditions or interference that prevents successful transmission.

This modeling choice allows us to study the fundamental limits of flooding under adversarial conditions while maintaining some feedback about the network state. Alternative models where nodes lack this information would require additional mechanisms (such as acknowledgments or timeouts) that would fundamentally change the nature of the flooding protocol.

Memory Model and Amnesiac Nature. The term "amnesiac" in our context requires careful interpretation. Traditional amnesiac flooding assumes that nodes retain *no state* between rounds. Our variant relaxes this to what we call *structured amnesia*: nodes forget all message history but maintain a bounded amount of state (destination sets) that is recomputed based on current round information. Specifically:

- Nodes do not remember which nodes they have received messages from in previous rounds.
- Nodes only maintain destination sets that are *functionally determined* by the current round's receipts and delays.

This structured amnesia is motivated by resource-constrained environments where maintaining full message history is infeasible, but nodes can afford $O(|N(v)|)$ memory for immediate forwarding decisions, where $N(v)$ denotes the set of neighbours of node v. This represents a middle ground between full amnesia and traditional flooding.

1.2 Our Contributions

This paper makes several significant contributions:

1. **Formal Model**: A comprehensive mathematical framework for RAAF, including precise definitions for system state, adversarial delay functions, and termination conditions.
2. **Termination Analysis**: Proof that RAAF always terminates on acyclic graphs with provable bounds, and demonstration that any cyclic graph admits non-termination.
3. **Decidability Results**: Proof of undecidability for arbitrary computable adversaries via reduction from the halting problem, and introduction of the Eventually Periodic Adversary (EPA) model under which termination becomes decidable.

1.3 Organisation

Section 2 discusses related work. Section 3 presents our formal model and defines key properties. Section 4 demonstrates non-termination in cyclic graphs. Section 5 develops the theory of periodic infinite schedules, providing a framework for analysing recurrent behaviour. Section 6 proves undecidability for arbitrary computable adversaries. Section 7 introduces Eventually Periodic Adversaries (EPA), establishes decidability and provides complexity bounds. In the full version of the paper we show that all non-terminating schedules in the EPA model are periodic infinite schedules.

2 Related Work

Amnesiac Flooding originated with Hussak and Trehan's work [7], establishing fundamental properties in synchronous settings. Their analysis proved termination bounds—exactly e rounds for bipartite and between e and $e+d+1$ rounds for non-bipartite graphs (where e is source eccentricity, d is graph diameter)—demonstrating AF's asymptotic time optimality against the $\Omega(d)$ broadcast lower bound.

Turau [11] revealed deeper complexity aspects through the (k, c)-flooding problem: finding k nodes to guarantee termination within c rounds under concurrent flooding. Its NP-completeness highlighted inherent optimisation challenges. Sharp bounds showed significant disparities between bipartite and non-bipartite graphs, introducing a behaviour-preserving construction mapping between them.

Hussak and Trehan extended their analysis [8] to multi-source scenarios, proving $e(I)$-round termination for I-bipartite graphs with source set I. Their fixed-delay analysis showed termination by round $2d+\tau-1$ for single-edge delays of duration τ in bipartite graphs and established termination for multiple-edge fixed delays in cycles.

Bayramzadeh et al. [4] proved termination for multiple-message AF in the unranked full-send case, previously conjectured non-terminating, showing $D \cdot (2k-1)$ rounds for bipartite and $(2D+1) \cdot (2k-1)$ rounds for non-bipartite graphs (k messages). Their introduction of graph diameter knowledge as a parameter suggested new model variants.

Comparison with Asynchronous Flooding Models. Hussak and Trehan [7] briefly discuss an asynchronous variation of amnesiac flooding, and they demonstrate with a small example that this variation does not guarantee termination, in contrast to their synchronous model. In this model of [7], the adversary can decide a delay of message delivery on any link. Once a node sends a message, this message will definitely be delivered at some future round. In contrast, in our model, if a message from node u to node v is delayed by the adversary, the initiator node u keeps a note of this and tries to re-send the message to v again and again, until either (i) the message is delivered to v, or (ii) u receives the message from v, in which case u stops trying to send the message to v.

The possibility of a message not being delivered, due to the last case, makes non-termination in our model much less trivial, compared to [7]. We comprehensively investigate this model and we provide a periodic-schedule normal form for it: every infinite execution can be compressed into an ultimately periodic delay pattern, which in turn enables decidability and undecidability results. Summarizing, our model is complementary to the model of [7], and our work provides a rigorous framework that delineates the exact boundary between terminating and non-terminating behaviour.

Comparison with Stateless Flooding Approaches. The stateless flooding algorithm by Adamek et al. [1] achieves statelessness through a different mechanism than our structured amnesia. Their algorithm uses send queues where messages are discarded upon encountering "mates"—pairs of messages with swapped sender/receiver addresses. Crucially, their model assumes fair scheduling where every queued message is eventually transmitted or removed, without adversarial interference. This synchronous assumption fundamentally differs from our round-asynchronous model where an adversary controls edge availability.

While Adamek et al. prove termination under fair scheduling, we establish when termination remains decidable despite adversarial delays (EPA model) or becomes undecidable (arbitrary computable adversaries). Our structured amnesia—recomputing destination sets based on current round information—provides a framework for analysing flooding under hostile scheduling conditions that previous stateless approaches did not consider.

3 Model, Preliminaries and Notation

We first present the computational model for round-based asynchronous systems, then describe the RAAF protocol that operates within this model.

3.1 Computational Model

Network Structure. We consider a simple, finite, connected graph $G = (V, E)$ with a distinguished source node $g_0 \in V$ possessing initial message m_0. For every node v we denote by $N(v)$ the set of neighbours of v.

Round-Based Asynchrony. The system proceeds in synchronous rounds, but an adversary can selectively make edges unavailable for message transmission. Formally:

Definition 1 (Adversarial Delay Function). *A delay function* $d : \mathbb{N} \times V \times E \to \{0, 1\}$ *specifies for each round j, node v, and incident edge $e = \{v, u\}$ whether transmission from v along e is blocked ($d(j, v, e) = 1$) or allowed ($d(j, v, e) = 0$).*

Definition 2 (Finite Delay Property). *A delay function d satisfies the finite delay property if for every node-edge pair (v, e), any sequence of consecutive rounds where $d(j, v, e) = 1$ is finite. Formally, for all $v \in V$ and incident edges e, if $d(j, v, e) = 1$ for $j \in [t_1, t_2]$, then $t_2 - t_1$ is finite.*

Key Model Assumption. Nodes are aware of which of their incident edges are currently blocked. This models scenarios where transmission failures are detectable (e.g., through carrier sensing, acknowledgments, or network management protocols).

3.2 The RAAF Protocol

Within the above model, we define the Round-Asynchronous Amnesiac Flooding protocol.

Node State. Each node v maintains:

- $M(j,v) \in \{0,1\}$: whether v possesses the message in round j
- $s(j,v) \subseteq V$: source set - neighbours that successfully delivered the message to v in round j
- $\text{dest}(j,v) \subseteq V$: destination set - neighbours to which v intends to forward the message

Structured Amnesia. The protocol is called "amnesiac" because:

- Nodes do not maintain history: i.e. nodes don't remember which nodes they received messages from (or sent messages to) in previous rounds
- The destination set is functionally determined by recent receptions and current delays
- When destination sets empty and no delayed transmissions remain, nodes return to their initial state

The key insight is that while nodes maintain destination sets across rounds (not strictly amnesiac), this state is *recomputed* based on current information rather than accumulated history. When a node receives the message from new sources, it completely recomputes its forwarding strategy.

Protocol Operation. Each round j proceeds as follows:

1. **Delay Phase**: The adversary specifies $d(j,v,e)$ for all node-edge pairs
2. **Transmission Phase**: Each node v with $M(j-1,v) = 1$ attempts to transmit to all $u \in \text{dest}(j-1,v)$ where $d(j,v,\{v,u\}) = 0$
3. **Reception Phase**: Nodes receive messages from successful transmissions
4. **State Update Phase**: Nodes update their state according to the following rules:

State Update Rules. For node u transitioning from round j to $j+1$:
Message Possession:

$$M(j+1,u) = \begin{cases} 1 & \text{if } u \text{ has pending delayed transmissions from round } j \\ 1 & \text{if } u \text{ receives the message in round } j+1 \\ 0 & \text{otherwise} \end{cases}$$

Source Set:

$$s(j+1,u) = \{v \in V : \{v,u\} \in E, u \in \text{dest}(j,v), d(j+1,v,\{v,u\}) = 0\}$$

Destination Set: The update rule for destination sets captures the "structured amnesia":

$$\text{dest}(j+1,u) = \begin{cases} \{v \in \text{dest}(j,u) : d(j+1,u,\{u,v\}) = 1\} & \text{if continuing delayed transmission} \\ N(u) \setminus s(j+1,u) & \text{if newly receiving message} \\ \emptyset & \text{if no message possessed} \end{cases}$$

Observation 1 (Persistence of Destination Sets (PDS)). *Let $\{u,v\} \in E$. If u receives in round j from $w \neq v$ and does not receive from v in the same round, then v belongs to $\text{dest}(u)$ until u delivers to v or receives from v.*

A key property of the protocol is that when u receives the message from new sources, it *recomputes* its destination set as all neighbours except those that just delivered the message, effectively "forgetting" its previous forwarding intentions.

3.3 System Evolution and Termination

State Function. The system state is captured by $S : \mathbb{N} \times V \to \text{StateRecord}$ where $S(j, u) = (M(j, u), s(j, u), \text{dest}(j, u))$.

Round Function. The transmission function $r(j)$ records actual message transmissions in round j:

$$r(j) = \{(v, \{v, w\}) : v \in V, w \in \text{dest}(j-1, v), d(j, v, \{v, w\}) = 0\}$$

State Update Function. The state update function defines how node states evolve. For node v in round j, computing the next state requires:

- Current graph state $S(j, \cdot) : V \to \text{StateRecord}$
- Current delay decisions $d(j, \cdot, \cdot) : V \times E \to \{0, 1\}$
- Node's local state $S(j, v)$ and incident delays $d(j, v, \cdot)$

While updates depend on graph-wide state and delays, these parameters remain fixed when computing individual node updates in a given round. Thus, we can express the state update as:

$$S(j+1, v) := u(v, S(j, v), d(j, v, \cdot))$$

where u implicitly references the global state $S(j, \cdot)$ and delays $d(j, \cdot, \cdot)$ fixed for round j.

Initial Configuration. At round zero:

- Source: $S(0, g_0) = (1, \emptyset, N(g_0))$
- Others: $S(0, u) = (0, \emptyset, \emptyset)$ for $u \neq g_0$

Termination. We say that flooding has terminated "by" (at or before) round $t \in \mathbb{N}$ if $M(t, v) = 0$ for every $v \in V$, i.e. no node v has the message at round t. Clearly, this is equivalent with saying that $M(j, v) = 0$ for every $j \geq t$ and for every $v \in V$, i.e. if flooding has terminated by round t then no node has the message in any round after round t.

Definition 3. *The termination round t_{min} is defined as:*

$$t_{min} = \min\{t \in \mathbb{N} : M(k, u) = 0, \text{ for every } u \in V\}$$

Observation 2 (Persistence of Empty Destination Sets (PEDS)). *If a node's destination set is empty at round t, it remains empty in all subsequent rounds until the node receives the message.*

Lemma 1 (Empty Destination Sets and Termination). *All destination sets are empty at round t if and only if flooding has terminated by round t.*

4 Termination Dichotomy

It is not hard to establish that RAAF always terminates on acyclic graphs, regardless of the adversarial strategy. In the remainder of this section we focus on graphs that contain at least one cycle, where we prove that every such graph admits a non-terminating strategy under RAAF by constructing a periodic infinite schedule (Definition 7)[1] that maintains message circulation within the cycle.

Let $G = (V, E)$ be an arbitrary graph containing a cycle $C = (V_C, E_C)$ where $V_C = \{v_1, \ldots, v_n\}$ and $E_C = \{\{v_i, v_{i+1 \bmod n}\} : 1 \leq i \leq n\}$. Let c be the earliest round where a node in V_C receives the message. Among nodes receiving the message in round c, designate one as v_1 and number remaining cycle nodes sequentially[2]. We define the following delay function d:

$$d(j, u, e) = \begin{cases} 0 & \text{if } j - c \equiv i \pmod{n} \text{ and } e = \{v_i, v_{i+1 \bmod n}\} \\ 1 & \text{otherwise} \end{cases}$$

Property 1 (Cyclic Propagation Pattern). If, for every $i \in \mathbb{N}^+$, we have that node $v_{i \bmod n}$ of the cycle C transmits to node $v_{(i+1) \bmod n}$ of the cycle C at round round $c + i$, then we say that the *cyclic propagation pattern* is satisfied for cycle C.

Lemma 2. *The delay function d ensures cyclic propagation.*

Lemma 3 (Characterisation of Cyclic Pattern Disruption). *The cyclic propagation pattern (Property 1) is disrupted if and only if for some k, node $v_{k+1 \bmod n}$ transmits to $v_{k \bmod n}$ while $v_{k \bmod n}$ has the message but before $v_{k \bmod n}$ transmits to $v_{k+1 \bmod n}$.*

Lemma 4 (Non-disruption of Cyclic Pattern). *The cyclic propagation pattern cannot be disrupted by message flow in the reverse direction.*

Lemma 5 (External Message Preservation). *Receiving messages from nodes outside the cycle does not disrupt cyclic propagation.*

Theorem 1 (Cyclic Non-termination). *For any graph $G = (V, E)$ containing a cycle, there exists a valid delay function d such that flooding does not terminate.*

---

[1] When restricting schedule information only to the cycle.
[2] We require that $v_2 \neq g_0$. This is because we assume that $v_2 \notin s(c, v_1)$, and this condition would not be satisfied if $v_2 = g_0$.

5 Periodic Infinite Schedules

We introduce *Periodic Infinite Schedules (PIS)* as a framework for analysing certain non-terminating behaviours in RAAF systems, serving as a bridge between finite state descriptions and infinite executions.

Definition 4 (Configuration). *A configuration $\sigma(j)$ for round j is an ordered pair $(S(j, \cdot), r(j))$ where S and r are the state and round functions, capturing complete system state and message transmissions.*

Definition 5 (Schedule). *A schedule σ maps each round $j \in \mathbb{N}$ to its configuration. Given a valid delay function d, the schedule σ_d induced by d is as follows:*

1. $\sigma_d(0) = (S(0, \cdot), r(0))$
2. For $j > 0$, $\sigma_d(j) = (S(j, \cdot), r(j))$ where:
   - $S(j, v) = u(v, (S(j-1, v), d(j-1, v, \cdot)))$
   - $r(j) = \{(v, \{v, w\}) \in V \times E : M(j-1, v) = 1 \land w \in dest(j-1, v) \land d(j, v, \{v, w\}) = 0\}$

In the above definition, the schedule is "induced" as states and transmissions arise deterministically from applying the delay function according to our state evolution rules.

Definition 6 (Eventually Periodic Delay Function). *A delay function d is eventually periodic with period p if, for some $c \in \mathbb{N}$, we have that $d(i, v, \{v, u\}) = d(i+p, v, \{v, u\})$, for every round $i \geq c$ and for every node $v \in V$ and every edge $\{v, u\}$.*

Definition 7 (Periodic Infinite Schedule). *A schedule σ is periodic infinite if there exist natural numbers c (stabilisation round) and l (cycle length) where:*

1. $\sigma(j) = \sigma(j + l)$ for every $j \geq c$,
2. $r(c + k) \neq \emptyset$ for at least one $k \in \{0, 1, \ldots, l-1\}$.

In the above definition, the first condition establishes repeating behaviour after the stabilisation round c, while the second guarantees genuine non-termination through guaranteed transmissions. Now we establish three fundamental results characterising PIS behaviour:

Theorem 2 (IPIS: Identification of PIS). *Given a graph G and delay function d, the induced schedule σ_d is periodic infinite if:*

1. *d is eventually periodic (Definition 6) with period p,*
2. *$\exists c, l \in \mathbb{N}_{>0} : \forall u \in V : S(c, u) = S(c + l, u)$,*
3. *$l \bmod p = 0$,*
4. *$\exists j \in \{0, \ldots, l-1\} : r(c + j) \neq \emptyset$.*

Theorem 3 (NTPIS: Non-Termination of PIS). *Any periodic infinite schedule is non-terminating.*

Theorem 4 (EPIS: Existence of PIS). *If a graph admits a non-terminating schedule, it admits a periodic infinite schedule.*

Proof. Suppose that d induces a non-terminating schedule σ_d on G. The configuration space is finite, as it has at most $(2 \cdot 2^{|V|} \cdot 2^{|V|})^{|V|} \cdot 2^{2|E|}$ configurations. Therefore, as σ_d is a non-terminating schedule, there exists at least one configuration C which repeats infinitely often.

As the adversary respects the finite delay property, it follows that for every pair $(v, \{v, u\})$ there exists an infinite sequence of rounds, in which $(v, \{v, u\})$ is not delayed. Let j_1 be the first round in σ_d where configuration C appears. Due to the finite delay property, there exists some round $j_2 > j_1$ such that (i) the configuration C appears also at round j_2 and (ii) every pair $(v, \{v, u\})$ was allowed to transmit (i.e. it was not delayed by the adversary) at least once between rounds j_1 and j_2.

We now define a new delay function d', which is periodic with period $j_2 - j_1$ after round j_2, as follows:

- if $j \leq j_2$ then $d'(j, u, e) = d(j, u, e)$, for every (u, e),
- if $j > j_2$ then $d'(j, u, e) = d'(j - j_2 + j_1), u, e)$, for every (u, e).

Then the schedule $\sigma_{d'}$ induced by this new delay function d' is periodic after round j_2, with period $j_2 - j_1$.

These results establish that PIS capture the fundamental structure of non-termination in RAAF systems. While not all non-terminating schedules are periodic, any graph admitting non-termination must also admit a periodic infinite schedule. This insight reduces termination analysis to the study of periodic behaviours, bridging finite state descriptions and infinite executions.

6 Undecidability with Arbitrary Computable Adversaries

We prove that determining flooding termination in RAAF is undecidable when the adversary is an arbitrary computable function via reduction from the Halting problem [9]. The decision problem for the termination of RAAF is defined as follows:

RAAF-TERMINATION

- **Input:** A graph $G = (V, E)$, source node $g_0 \in V$, and computable delay function d.
- **Question:** Does flooding terminate on G with source g_0 under adversary d?

We first establish a basic non-terminating strategy on the triangle graph $G = (V, E)$ where:

- $V = \{\text{Source}, A, B\}$
- $E = \{\{\text{Source}, A\}, \{A, B\}, \{B, \text{Source}\}\}$

We now define the basic delay function d_0:

$$d_0(j, u, e) = \begin{cases} 1 & \text{if } j \bmod 3 = 0 \text{ and } e \neq \{\text{Source}, B\} \\ 1 & \text{if } j \bmod 3 = 1 \text{ and } e \neq \{\text{Source}, A\} \\ 1 & \text{if } j \bmod 3 = 2 \text{ and } e \neq \{A, B\} \\ 0 & \text{otherwise} \end{cases}$$

Lemma 6 (Basic Strategy Nonterminating). *The basic delay strategy d_0 creates a periodic infinite schedule.*

Proof. We demonstrate the basic strategy induces a periodic infinite schedule by verifying the conditions of Theorem 2:

1. The delay function d is eventually periodic with period $p = 3$. For all $i \geq 1$, $u \in V$, $e \in E$: $d(i, u, e) = d(i + 3, u, e)$. This follows from the three-round delay pattern in the strategy definition.
2. Taking $c = 3$ and $l = 6$, we observe from the state evolution in Table 1 that $S(3, u) = S(9, u)$ for all $u \in V$. The complete state evolution demonstrating this equality is shown below:
3. $l \bmod p = 0$ as $6 \bmod 3 = 0$.
4. In each cycle $[3, 9)$, transmission occurs. For instance, at round 4, we have $r(4) \neq \emptyset$.

Therefore, by Theorem 2, the schedule is periodic infinite with $c = 3$ and $l = 6$. By Theorem 3, we conclude it is non-terminating.

Table 1. State Evolution under Basic Strategy

Round 0	Round 1	Round 2	Round 3	Round 4
$S: (1, \emptyset, \{A, B\})$	$S: (1, \emptyset, \{B\})$	$S: (1, \emptyset, \{B\})$	$S: (1, \{B\}, \{A\})$	$S: (0, \emptyset, \emptyset)$
$A: (0, \emptyset, \emptyset)$	$A: (1, \{S\}, \{B\})$	$A: (0, \emptyset, \emptyset)$	$A: (0, \emptyset, \emptyset)$	$A: (1, \{S\}, \{B\})$
$B: (0, \emptyset, \emptyset)$	$B: (0, \emptyset, \emptyset)$	$B: (1, \{A\}, \{S\})$	$B: (1, \{S\}, \{A\})$	$B: (1, \emptyset, \{A\})$
Round 5	Round 6	Round 7	Round 8	textbfRound 9
$S: (0, \emptyset, \emptyset)$	$S: (1, \{B\}, \{A\})$	$S: (1, \{A\}, \{B\})$	$S: (1, \emptyset, \{B\})$	$S: (1, \{B\}, \{A\})$
$A: (1, \{B\}, \{S\})$	$A: (1, \emptyset, \{S\})$	$A: (1, \{S\}, \{B\})$	$A: (0, \emptyset, \emptyset)$	$A: (0, \emptyset, \emptyset)$
$B: (1, \{A\}, \{S\})$	$B: (0, \emptyset, \emptyset)$	$B: (0, \emptyset, \emptyset)$	$B: (1, \{A\}, \{S\})$	$B: (1, \{S\}, \{A\})$

Theorem 5 (Undecidability). *RAAF-TERMINATION is undecidable.*

Proof. Let M be an arbitrary Turing Machine M, and let x be an arbitrary input to M. Then we construct the following delay function on the triangle graph $G = (V, E)$:

$$d(j, u, e) = \begin{cases} 0 & \text{if } M \text{ halts on } x \text{ within } j \text{ steps} \\ d_0(j, u, e) & \text{otherwise} \end{cases}$$

where d_0 is the basic delay function defined above. We will prove that M halts on x if and only if flooding terminates under the delay function d.

($\Rightarrow$) Suppose that M halts on x after exactly t steps. Then $d(j, u, e) = 0$ for every $j \geq t$ and every u and e. Then flooding terminates by round $t + 2$.

($\Leftarrow$) Suppose that flooding terminates at round t, and assume for the sake of contradiction that M does not halt after any finite number of steps. Then $d(j, u, e) = d_0(j, u, e)$ for every j and every u and e, and thus d creates a periodic infinite schedule by Lemma 6. Therefore flooding does not terminate after any finite number of rounds, which is a contradiction.

This undecidability persists even under severe computational constraints:

Theorem 6 (Resilient Undecidability). *For any unbounded computable $f : \mathbb{N} \to \mathbb{N}$ with $\lim_{n \to \infty} f(n) = \infty$, an adversary with $O(f(n))$ time and space in round n can simulate $\lfloor f(n) \rfloor$ Turing machine steps, preserving undecidability.*

Proof. Let the adversary in round n simulate $\lfloor f(n) \rfloor$ Turing machine steps, applying no delays if halted, else d_0. Then the Turing machine halts after k steps if and only if flooding terminates after $f^{-1}(k)$ rounds. The theorem holds even for extremely slow-growing f like inverse Ackermann $\alpha(n) = \min\{m : A(m, m) > n\}$ where A is the Ackermann function [10].

This fundamental limitation motivates restricting adversary behaviour rather than computational power, leading to the EPA model.

7 Eventually Periodic Adversaries

To bridge the gap between undecidability and practical analysis, we introduce Eventually Periodic Adversaries (EPA), which restrict adversaries to eventually periodic behaviour while maintaining significant expressive power.

Definition 8 (Eventually Periodic Adversary). *An Eventually Periodic Adversary is a triple (d, c, l) where the delay function d is a computable function, $c \in \mathbb{N}$ is the stabilisation round, $l \in \mathbb{N}^+$ is the cycle length, and $d(i, u, e) = d(i + l, u, e)$ for every $i \geq c$, $u \in V$, and $e \in E$.*

Theorem 7 (EPA Decidability). *The termination problem for EPA-RAAF systems is decidable with time complexity $O(2^{2|V|^2 + 2|E|}(c + l))$.*

Theorem 8 (Lower Bound). *Any decision procedure for EPA-RAAF termination has time complexity $\Omega((c+l) \cdot |E|)$.*

The EPA model demonstrates that restricting adversary behaviour to eventual periodicity yields decidable termination while preserving significant expressive power, bridging the gap between undecidability for arbitrary computable adversaries and practical analysis needs. A non-trivial lower bound remains open.

8 Conclusions and Open Problems

We have established fundamental properties of Round-Asynchronous Amnesiac Flooding through rigorous mathematical characterisation. Our analysis yields a complete structural dichotomy: acyclic graphs guarantee termination with $O((B+1) \cdot e(g_0))$ bound for B-bounded delays, while cyclic graphs admit non-terminating adversarial strategies. This extends to a sharp complexity separation - termination is undecidable for arbitrary computable adversaries, but it becomes decidable for eventually periodic adversaries with time complexity at least $\Omega((c+l)|E|)$ and at most $O(2^{2^{|V|^2+2|E|}}(c+l))$.

Several theoretical challenges remain open. The complexity landscape invites tighter bounds for EPA-RAAF, while specific graph classes may admit improved parameterisation by structural properties. Natural model extensions include multiple messages and dynamic topologies with bounded modification rates.

Our dichotomy results establish fundamental limits on automated verification of asynchronous flooding protocols: while acyclic networks allow termination analysis, verification becomes undecidable in the presence of cycles unless the adversary exhibits eventual periodicity. This framework precisely characterises when efficient algorithmic analysis of asynchronous flooding behaviour is possible.

References

1. Adamek, J., Nesterenko, M., Robinson, J.S., Tixeuil, S.: Stateless reliable geocasting. In: Proceedings of SRDS 2017. IEEE Computer Society, Hong Kong, China (2017). https://hal.sorbonne-universite.fr/hal-01549915
2. Aspnes, J.: Flooding (2019). http://www.cs.yale.edu/homes/aspnes/pinewiki/Flooding.html
3. Attiya, H., Welch, J.: Distributed Computing: Fundamentals, Simulations and Advanced Topics. Wiley (2004)
4. Bayramzadeh, Z., Kshemkalyani, A.D., Molla, A.R., Sharma, G.: Weak amnesiac flooding of multiple messages. In: Echihabi, K., Meyer, R. (eds.) NETYS 2021. LNCS, vol. 12754, pp. 88–94. Springer, Cham (2021). https://doi.org/10.1007/978-3-030-91014-3_6
5. Dwork, C., Lynch, N.A.: Consensus in the presence of partial synchrony. J. ACM **35**(2), 288–323 (1988)
6. Hussak, W., Trehan, A.: On the termination of a flooding process. arXiv preprint arXiv:1907.07078 (2019). https://arxiv.org/abs/1907.07078

7. Hussak, W., Trehan, A.: Terminating cases of flooding. arXiv preprint arXiv:2009.05776 [cs.DC] (2020). https://arxiv.org/abs/2009.05776
8. Hussak, W., Trehan, A.: Termination of amnesiac flooding. Distrib. Comput. **36**(2), 193–207 (2023). https://doi.org/10.1007/s00446-023-00448-y
9. Lucas, S.: The origins of the halting problem. J. Logical Algebraic Methods Program. **121**, 100687 (2021)
10. Matos, A.B.: Total recursive functions that are not primitive recursive. Unpublished manuscript (2016). https://www.dcc.fc.up.pt/~acm/definitions.pdf. Accessed 18 Sept 2024
11. Turau, V.: Analysis of amnesiac flooding. CoRR abs/2002.10752 (2020). https://arxiv.org/abs/2002.10752

Optimizing the Number of Drones for Aerial Power-Line Maintenance

Francesco Betti Sorbelli, Sajjad Ghobadi(✉), Lorenzo Palazzetti, and Cristina M. Pinotti

Department of Computer Science and Mathematics, University of Perugia, Perugia, Italy
{francesco.bettisorbelli,sajjad.ghobadibabi,lorenzo.palazzetti, cristina.pinotti}@unipg.it

Abstract. Unmanned Aerial Vehicles (UAVs) are increasingly used in critical infrastructure maintenance due to their ability to improve safety, efficiency, and access in challenging environments. This paper focuses on optimizing drone-assisted equipment delivery for high-voltage power line maintenance, with the goal of minimizing the number of drones required to serve all pylons that lie on a line. Unlike prior work that maximizes delivery profit given a fixed fleet size, we aim to minimize the fleet size itself, addressing deployment constraints, such as load and energy, and coordination complexity. We introduce a new optimization problem, the *Minimum Drone Delivery Problem* (MDDP), and study three key variants: **unitary loads** (MDDP-U), **arbitrary loads** (MDDP-A), and **non-overlapping missions** (N-MDDP). We formulate MDDP as an Integer Linear Program and prove its *NP*-hardness. To solve it, we propose polynomial-time approximation algorithms and a heuristic. Extensive evaluations on synthetic datasets demonstrate the effectiveness and scalability of our approaches.

Keywords: Unmanned aerial vehicles · Approximation algorithms · Integer linear programming

1 Introduction

Over the last decade, the proliferation of Unmanned Aerial Vehicles (UAVs), such as *drones*, has significantly transformed various operational practices, from industrial inspections to last-mile logistics. These remotely operated systems have transitioned beyond recreational and niche applications, becoming crucial elements in sectors such as emergency response, precision agriculture, and urban package delivery. Drones offer substantial improvements in operational safety, efficiency, and access to challenging environments, surpassing traditional ground-based methods.

A particularly impactful application of drone technology is evident in the maintenance of high-voltage power lines [3,18,19]. Regular inspections and timely interventions are critical for preventing operational disruptions, enhancing safety, and reducing downtime. Traditionally, such operations have heavily relied on ground trucks equipped with elevated platforms, placing operators at considerable risk [2,9,11]. Drone-assisted maintenance provides a compelling alternative, substantially mitigating these occupational hazards. Recent literature has introduced innovative solutions involving coordinated drone and truck operations, where drones facilitate maintenance tasks and deliver tools and materials to pylons along power lines [22].

This paper focuses on optimizing drone-assisted power line maintenance, with the goal of minimizing the number of drones needed to inspect the pylons along the section of line that a maintenance truck can cover in a single workday. Unlike previous research that often focuses on selecting the pylons that maximize the profit, our approach emphasizes the minimization of the drone fleet size itself while serving all the pylons. Technological advancements now allow compact and medium-sized drones, such as the DJI FlyCart 30 (payload capacity of 30-40 kg), to deliver multiple items in a single flight efficiently. Thus, our model accommodates multi-package flights, significantly reducing the frequency of drone-truck interactions and improving overall operational efficiency.

We consider a scenario where a drone fleet, supported by a truck moving along a one-way road close to the power line, delivers equipment to subsequebt pylons requiring maintenance. The number of pylons served in one mission is constrained by the drones' payload and energy limits, adding complexity to the optimization. Additionally, the truck is limited to one-way movement along a high-traffic route, such as a highway, which further restricts mission planning flexibility.

The key contributions of our work are summarized as follows:
- We introduce a new optimization problem, the *Minimum Drone Delivery Problem* (MDDP), which aims to minimize the number of drones required for complete power line maintenance. We study two variants based on package load characteristics: **unitary** loads (MDDP-U, Sect. 4) and **arbitrary** loads (MDDP-A, Sect. 5), and also consider a variant with **non-overlapping** drone flights (N-MDDP, Sect. 6).
- We formulate MDDP as an Integer Linear Program (ILP) and prove its *NP*-hardness (Sect. 3), and propose polynomial-time approximation algorithms.
- We evaluate the proposed algorithms using synthetic datasets to assess their efficiency (Sect. 7).

Related work is discussed in Sect. 2, and the paper concludes in Sect. 8.

2 Related Works

The demand for automated maintenance of critical infrastructures such as power lines, wind turbines, and solar farms has increased significantly, particularly in the renewable energy sector. Offshore wind farms, often located far from the coast, pose logistical and safety challenges. This limits inspection frequency and effectiveness. Recent advances in drone technology offer safer and more efficient maintenance solutions [14].

Various autonomous systems have been proposed for such tasks. In [11], a multirobot system was introduced for deploying and retrieving a blade-inspection robot using drones. This was extended in [13] with adaptive monitoring strategies for heterogeneous fleets. Chung et al. [5] addressed routing and fleet sizing under wind constraints, while Baik et al. [1] studied coordinated routing of drones and a support truck using ILP formulations. Huang et al. [10] proposed energy-aware inspection with a mobile charging station and clustering heuristics. Autonomous delivery in wind farm was explored in [17], integrating behavior trees with connectivity management under EU regulations. Similarly, [8] tested an autonomous helicopter equipped with a winch for BVLoS part delivery, validating technical feasibility and regulatory compliance.

Efforts in power lines and solar plants have led to technological progress as well. For example, [15] developed a drone for cleaning power line insulators using vision-based tracking, while [16] proposed a TSP-based route planner for solar farm inspection.

These works primarily focus on time- and energy-efficient routing, often neglecting topological features such as the linear or grid layouts commonly found in power lines, solar panel rows, and wind farms. In addition, in this paper, we explicitly account for drone constraints—such as energy limits and payload capacity—which are frequently overlooked.

3 Problem Definition

We consider a power line maintenance scenario where a fleet of drones is deployed by a truck to perform inspection and maintenance tasks along a high-voltage power line. The drones are responsible for delivering maintenance tools and equipment to designed pylons along the power line in correspondence of each pylon. The considered fleet of drones is homogeneous, in other words every drone has the same capabilities. Our aim is to determine the minimum number of drones required to serve all the pylons while respecting operational constraints on payload and energy consumption.

3.1 System Model

Let A be a flat area. Within A, C refers to a *maintenance corridor* for a high-voltage *power line*, which is supported by a sequence of pylons. In parallel to C, there is a transportation road H and a truck is responsible for carrying a fleet of drones and the tools to be delivered at the pylons. Since A is a flat area, the road's height is fixed at 0. Maintenance operations require servicing a predefined set of *pylons* $P = \{p_1, p_2, \ldots, p_n\}$ inside C, where each $p_i \in P$ represents a specific pylon that needs a specific service.

The truck is located at a *depot* ϕ with coordinates $(x_\phi, y_\phi, 0)$ assumed to be positioned on the road. So, for simplicity, we set the origin of the truck's trajectory at the ϕ, i.e., $x_\phi = y_\phi = 0$. The pylon $p_i \in P$ has coordinates (x_{p_i}, y, z), where y is the lateral offset of C with respect to H and z is the height of the pylon's top where the load will be discharged. For easiness, since y and z are the same for all the pylons, we will use p_i to denote also x_{p_i}, the x-coordinate of point p_i. We assume that the pylons in P are given in increasing order of their x-coordinates, i.e., $p_i \leq p_{i+1}$, for $1 \leq i \leq n-1$. Additionally, each pylon $p_i \in P$ is associated with a *payload requirement* to be deployed at the top of the pylon itself. The weight of the payload of p_i is denoted by $\ell_i > 0$.

The truck moves along the one-way left-to-right route H, starting from the ϕ, and encountering the pylons in the order $p_1, \ldots, p_n$. We assume that the truck is not allowed to turn back. This constraint is central to the mission planning logic. No synchronization is assumed between the truck and the drones: the drones are dropped off sequentially as soon the truck encounters the leftmost pylon of their respective missions. At the end of the workday (i.e., when the last dropped off drone returns to H), the truck travels back to ϕ along the same road, picking up the drones in the reverse order in which they were dropped off. All drone missions begin and end on the road, ensuring compatibility with the truck's movement. To deliver tools to the pylons, each drone takes off from the truck carrying the tools to deliver. It serves a subset of pylons, and then lands waiting for the truck on its way back. Specifically, let $m_j = \{p_{j_1}, \ldots, p_{j_c}\}$ denote the set of pylons assigned to drone j. Since each mission serves at least one pylon, the total number of used drones is at most n. The pylons in m_j are sorted in increasing order of their x-coordinates in P, though they are not necessarily consecutive. The drone that serves m_j is dropped off in the point of H that corresponds to the x-coordinate of the first pylon in m_j, i.e., $(x_{p_{j_1}}, 0, 0)$. It ascends and flies diagonally to the top of p_{j_1}, following the slant line that connects $(x_{p_{j_1}}, 0, 0)$ and $(x_{p_{j_1}}, y, z)$, serves all the pylons in mission m_j, and finally lands at $(x_{p_{j_c}}, 0, 0)$, i.e., the point of H aligned with the last pylon in the mission, by traversing the slant line from $(x_{p_{j_c}}, y, z)$ to $(x_{p_{j_c}}, 0, 0)$. Each mission thus follows a left-to-right delivery pattern aligned with the truck's direction, while ensuring the drone returns to a known position along the truck's path for future pickup. Observe that each pylon is served exactly once.

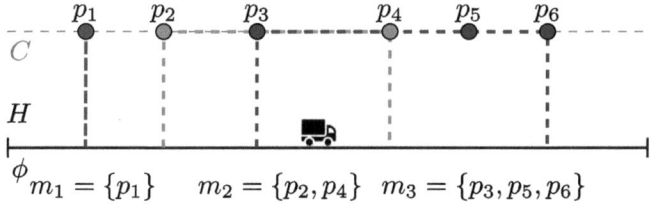

Fig. 1. Example of our problem: a truck carries three drones, the first one serves p_1, the second serves p_2 and p_4, and the third one serves p_3, p_5, and p_6.

Figure 1 illustrates an example, projecting the scene on 2D. A truck carries three drones, each assigned to serve a subset of pylons along a power line. The first drone serves p_1 only, the second serves p_2 and p_4 (skipping p_3), and the third covers p_3, p_5, and p_6 (skipping p_4). The truck travels from left to right, dropping off drones at the starting positions of their respective missions, i.e., p_1, p_2, and p_3. Each drone takes off from the truck, delivers tools to its assigned pylons in order, and returns to the road at the last pylon's position, awaiting pickup. After the last mission has been completed, the truck drives along the same path in the opposite direction (right to left) to collect the drones.

The total weight of the tools carried by drone j in its associated mission m_j is $\mathcal{L}(m_j) = \sum_{p_i \in m_j} \ell_i$. So, in the previous example in Fig. 1, the second drone may have skipped p_3 due to a payload constraint violation. Moreover, the energy cost of performing deliveries in m_j is computed based on the path that the drone travels to deliver individual tools in m_j, which is given by $\mathcal{E}(m_j) = \alpha(2\sqrt{y^2 + z^2} + (x_{p_{j_c}} - x_{p_{j_1}}))$, where α is the energy cost of the drone per unit distance. A mission m_j can be formed by a single pylon whose cost is simply $\mathcal{E}(m_j) = 2\alpha\sqrt{y^2 + z^2}$.

Assuming that a fleet of identical drones is available for performing the set of missions $\mathcal{M} = \{m_1, \ldots, m_{k \leq n}\}$. Each drone j, for $1 \leq j \leq k$, is subject to two primary constraints:

- **payload constraint**, a drone has a maximum payload capacity $L > 0$, so the total weight of the tools carried during a mission cannot exceed L, i.e., $\mathcal{L}(m_j) \leq L$;
- **energy constraint**, a drone has an energy budget $E > 0$, which limits the maximum distance it can travel along the power line, i.e., $\mathcal{E}(m_j) \leq E$.

Given two parameters E and L that denote the energy battery budget and payload capacity of the drones, respectively, and a set of n pylons P, we define the *Minimum Drone Delivery Problem* (MDDP) whose objective is to determine the minimum fleet size of drones (or, equivalently, set of missions $\mathcal{M}$) required to ensure that all pylons are served for maintenance, while satisfying both payload and energy constraints for each drone.

3.2 ILP Formulation

Let $\mathcal{D}$, with $|\mathcal{D}| = n$, be the set of drones that can be used to perform all the deliveries. For any $j \in \mathcal{D}$, let $y_j \in \{0, 1\}$ be a decision variable that is 1 if the drone j is used to perform deliveries; otherwise, it is 0. Moreover, let w_{ij} be a decision variable that is 1 if the pylon $p_i \in P$ is served by the drone $j \in \mathcal{D}$; otherwise, it is 0. For $j \in \mathcal{D}$ and $p_i, p_k \in P$, we also define a decision variable r_{ik}^j to be 1 if p_i and p_k are served by drone j; otherwise, $r_{ik}^j = 0$.

Therefore, the ILP formulation of MDDP is as follows.

$$\min \sum_{j=1}^{n} y_j \qquad (1)$$

s.t.

$$\sum_{j=1}^{n} w_{ij} = 1, \quad \forall p_i \in P \qquad (2)$$

$$\sum_{i=1}^{n} w_{ij} \leq n y_j, \quad \forall j \in \mathcal{D} \qquad (3)$$

$$\sum_{i=1}^{n} \ell_i w_{ij} \leq L y_j, \quad \forall j \in \mathcal{D} \qquad (4)$$

$$r_{ik}^j \leq w_{ij}, \quad \forall p_i \in P, p_k \in P, j \in \mathcal{D} \qquad (5)$$

$$r_{ik}^j \leq w_{kj}, \quad \forall p_i \in P, p_k \in P, j \in \mathcal{D} \tag{6}$$

$$w_{ij} + w_{kj} - 1 \leq r_{ik}^j, \quad \forall p_i \in P, p_k \in P, j \in \mathcal{D} \tag{7}$$

$$\alpha r_{ik}^j(|x_{p_i} - x_{p_k}|) \leq (E - (2\alpha\sqrt{y^2 + z^2}))y_j, \quad \forall p_i \in P, p_k \in P, j \in \mathcal{D} \tag{8}$$

Equations (5)–(8) are equivalent to the next quadratic constraint, much easier to understand.

$$\alpha w_{ij} w_{kj}(|x_{p_i} - x_{p_k}|) \leq (E - (2\alpha\sqrt{y^2 + z^2}))y_j, \quad \forall p_i \in P, p_k \in P, j \in \mathcal{D} \tag{9}$$

The objective function is represented by Eq. (1), which aims to minimize the number of drones employed. Concerning the constraints, Eq. (2) ensures that each pylon in P is assigned to exactly one drone, while Eq. (3) guarantees that a drone is used only if at least a pylon maintenance task is assigned to it. Similarly, Eq. (4) ensures that the total load of a drone does not exceed its maximum payload L. Equations (5)–(8) guarantee that each mission is energy feasible using linear constraints. Specifically, they ensure that, for each drone, the total energy consumed to serve any pair of pylons within its corresponding mission does not exceed the energy budget E.

In the following, we investigate MDDP under three variants: **Unitary loads** (MDDP-U), **Arbitrary loads** (MDDP-A), and **Non-overlapping missions** (N-MDDP). In MDDP-U, the load ℓ_i of each $p_i \in P$ is fixed to 1, while in MDDP-A, each pylon has a load $0 < \ell_i \leq L$. The third variant, N-MDDP, imposes an additional constraint that no two drone missions may overlap.

4 MDDP with Unitary Package Loads

In the unitary load variant of the MDDP (MDDP-U), each pylon has a load of 1. Consequently, the load constraint becomes a *cardinality* constraint, meaning that any mission may include at most L pylons. The energy constraint remains unchanged, requiring that the spatial spread of a mission, measured as the difference between the maximum and minimum positions (plus the commutes to/from the road), does not exceed E. Algorithm 1 presents a pseudocode for an optimal solution for MDDP-U. Such optimal solution returns a partition of the pylons into contiguous segments, non overlapping, each satisfying both the maximum cardinality L and the maximum spatial span E.

In NEAR-FIT (Algorithm 1), the set P is assumed to be sorted in increasing order of x-coordinates. The procedure sequentially removes pylons from P (Line 3), attempting to add each p_i to the current mission m as long as both the load and the energy constraints are satisfied (Line 5). When the addition of a new pylon p_i violates one of the two constraints, the current mission is finalized and added to overall solution $\mathcal{M}$ (Line 7), and a new mission is initialized (Line 8).

Therefore, we have the following theorem.

Theorem 1. *NEAR-FIT optimally solves MDDP-U.*

Algorithm 1: NEAR-FIT Algorithm

Data: Set of pylons P, energy budget E, load capacity L
Result: Minimum-size set of missions $\mathcal{M}$

1   $\mathcal{M} \leftarrow \varnothing, m \leftarrow \varnothing$;
2   **while** $P \not\subseteq \varnothing$ **do**
3      $p_i \leftarrow$ pop an element from P;
4   **if** $(\sum_{p_j \in m} \ell_j) + \ell_i \leq L$ **and** $\mathcal{E}(m \cup \{p_i\}) \leq E$ **then**
5         $m \leftarrow m \cup \{p_i\}$;
6   **else**
7         $\mathcal{M} \leftarrow \mathcal{M} \cup m$;
8         $m \leftarrow \{p_i\}$;
9   **return** $\mathcal{M}$;

Regarding the complexity of Algorithm 1, the `while` loop in Line 2 meets its ending conditions once the set P is empty. Since we pop one pylon at a time (Line 3), the time complexity of such a loop can be bounded by $\Theta(n)$ extractions. Moreover, checking the `if` condition in Line 4 takes constant time. Thus, the overall time complexity of the algorithm is $\Theta(n)$.

5 MDDP with Arbitrary package loads

In the arbitrary load variant of the MDDP (MDDP-A), each pylon $p_i \in P$ has a load ℓ_i such that $0 < \ell_i \leq L$. In this setting, we first show that the problem is NP-hard. Then, we propose two approximation algorithms, ENERGY-NEXT-LOAD and LOAD-NEXT-ENERGY, as well as a heuristic, BIN-COVER, to obtain suboptimal solutions for MDDP-A.

Theorem 2. *MDDP-A is NP-hard.*

5.1 Approximation Algorithms for MDDP-A

The first approximation algorithm is ENERGY-NEXT-LOAD and its pseudocode is given in Algorithm 2. It starts by relaxing the load constraints, and partitioning the pylons only based on the energy constraint. Specifically, it sets the load budget L' to the sum of all the loads, i.e., $L' = \sum_{p_i \in P} \ell_i$, and then invokes Algorithm 1 to generate a set of missions $\mathcal{M}'$ (Line 1). Each mission in $\mathcal{M}'$ satisfies the energy budget E but may exceed the original load budget L as $L \leq L'$. Next, for each mission in $\mathcal{M}'$, it applies the approximation algorithm proposed for the Bin Packing Problem (BPP) [6] to obtain a minimum-size set of missions that satisfies the load budget L (Line 4). Finally, it returns the union of all computed missions.

Theorem 3. *The* ENERGY-NEXT-LOAD *Algorithm is a 2β-approximation algorithm for MDDP-A, where β is the approximation ratio of any algorithm for BPP.*

Algorithm 2: ENERGY-NEXT-LOAD Algorithm

Data: Set of pylons P, energy budget E, load capacity L
Result: Minimum-size set of missions $\mathcal{M}$

1   $\mathcal{M}' \leftarrow$ Run Algorithm 1 with the load capacity $\sum_{p_i \in P} \ell_i$ and the energy budget E;
2   $\mathcal{M} \leftarrow \varnothing$;
3   **foreach** $m_j \in \mathcal{M}'$ **do**
4 | $\mathcal{M}'_j \leftarrow$ Run an approximation algorithm for BPP with the instance m_j and L [6] ;
5 | $\mathcal{M} \leftarrow \mathcal{M} \cup \mathcal{M}'_j$;
6   **return** $\mathcal{M}$;

Notice that the approximation ratio of Algorithm 2 depends on the specific approximation algorithm used for solving the BPP. For instance, the First-FIT algorithm guarantees $\beta = 1.7$ in $\mathcal{O}(n \log n)$ time [7], while the First-FIT-Decreasing algorithm yields $\beta = 11/9$ plus an additive error of $6/9$ in $\mathcal{O}(n \log n)$ time [6]. We now analyze the time complexity of the algorithm. Line 1 takes $\mathcal{O}(n)$. The **for** loop in Line 3 can be done in $\mathcal{O}(n \log n)$ because for any $m_j, m_k \in \mathcal{M}'$ we have $m_j \cap m_k = \varnothing$ and $\bigcup_{m_i \in \mathcal{M}'} m_i = P$. Thus, the overall time complexity of the algorithm is $\mathcal{O}(n \log n)$.

The second approximation algorithm is LOAD-NEXT-ENERGY and its pseudocode is given in Algorithm 3. LOAD-NEXT-ENERGY starts by relaxing the energy constraint. Infact, it applies an approximation algorithm for the BPP on the instance defined only by all the pylons P and the payload budget L (Line 1). Let $\mathcal{M}'$ be the obtained set. Note that every mission in $\mathcal{M}'$ satisfies the load budget L, while the energy budget E can be exceeded. Then, for each $m_j \in \mathcal{M}'$, the algorithm calls Algorithm 1 with the load budget $\sum_{p_i \in m_j} \ell_i \leq L$ and the energy budget E to compute a minimum-size set of missions (Line 4). Finally, the set of all obtained missions is reported.

Algorithm 3: LOAD-NEXT-ENERGY Algorithm

Data: Set of pylons P, energy budget E, load capacity L
Result: Minimum-size set of missions $\mathcal{M}$

1   $\mathcal{M}' \leftarrow$ Run an approximation algorithm proposed for BPP with the instance P and L [6];
2   $\mathcal{M} \leftarrow \varnothing$;
3   **foreach** $m_j \in \mathcal{M}'$ **do**
4 | $\mathcal{M}'_j \leftarrow$ Run Algorithm 1 with the instance m_j, the load capacity $\sum_{p_i \in m_j} \ell_i$, and the energy budget E;
5 | $\mathcal{M} \leftarrow \mathcal{M} \cup \mathcal{M}'_j$;
6   **return** $\mathcal{M}$;

	p_1	...	p_γ	$p_{\gamma+1}$	...	$p_{2\gamma}$	...	$p_{\gamma(\gamma-1)+1}$	...	p_{γ^2}
$\ell_i:$	1	...	γ	1	...	γ	...	1	...	γ
$x_{p_i}:$	1	...	γ	$2\gamma+1$	...	3γ	...	$2\gamma(\gamma-1)+1$	...	$2\gamma(\gamma-1)+\gamma$

Fig. 2. An instance of MDDP-A illustrating a tight bound for Theorem 4.

Therefore, we state the following theorem:

Theorem 4. *The approximation ratio of* LOAD-NEXT-ENERGY *Algorithm is* γ, *where* γ *is the size of* $\mathcal{M}'$ *generated in Line 1.*

We now present an instance that matches the bound γ shown in Theorem 4.

Example. Let $\gamma > 0$ be a positive integer. We construct an instance of MDDP-A such that the minimum number of drones returned by Algorithm 3 to serve all pylons is exactly γ times the optimal solution (see Fig. 2). Let P be the set of γ^2 pylons, i.e., $P = \{p_{1+\gamma j}, \ldots, p_{\gamma+\gamma j} : \forall 0 \leq j \leq \gamma - 1\}$. For each fixed j in $\{0, \ldots, \gamma - 1\}$, define the load of pylon $p_{k+\gamma j}$, for $k \in \{1, \ldots, \gamma\}$, as $\ell_{k+\gamma j} = k$, and its x-coordinate as $x_{p_{k+\gamma j}} = x_{p_{k+\gamma(j-1)}} + 2\gamma$. Note that when $j = 0$, we set $\ell_k = k$ and $x_{p_k} = k$ for every $k \in \{1, \ldots, \gamma\}$. We set the energy budget E to $\gamma + 1$ and the load budget L to $\sum_{\ell=1}^{\gamma} \ell$. Moreover, we assume that each drone consumes 1 unit of energy to take off from or land on the truck and the energy required to traverse one unit of distance is 1.

We now invoke Algorithm 3 on this instance. In Line 1, applying an optimal algorithm to the BPP returns a set $\mathcal{M}'$ consisting of γ missions. Note that $\mathcal{M}'$ is not unique and here we consider the solution that leads to the ratio of γ for Algorithm 3. Every $m_i \in \mathcal{M}'$, for $1 \leq i \leq \gamma$, contains exactly γ pylons, one from every subset of pylons $p_{1+\gamma j}, \ldots, p_{\gamma+\gamma j}$, for $0 \leq j \leq \gamma - 1$, with all selected pylons having distinct loads. Observe that for every $m_i \in \mathcal{M}'$, we have $\mathcal{L}(m_i) = L$. Now consider Line 4 in the algorithm. For every $m_i \in \mathcal{M}'$, invoking Algorithm 1 on m_i returns $|m_i| = \gamma$ missions, one for every pylon in m_i, because the energy consumption for a drone to fly between any pair of points in m_i, including the energy for take off and landing, is at least $\gamma + 2$. Therefore, the total number of missions returned by the algorithm is γ^2. However, the optimal algorithm will return the mission set $\mathcal{M}^*$ of size γ, where each mission contains the pylons $p_{1+\gamma j}, \ldots, p_{\gamma+\gamma j}$, for $0 \leq j \leq \gamma - 1$, i.e., $\mathcal{M}^* = \{\{p_{1+\gamma j}, \ldots, p_{\gamma+\gamma j}\} : \forall 0 \leq j \leq \gamma - 1\}$. Thus, there is an instance that matches the bound γ in Theorem 4.

Regarding the time complexity, Line 1 takes $\mathcal{O}(n \log n)$ and the `for` loop starting from Line 3 takes $\mathcal{O}(n)$. Thus, the overall time complexity of the algorithm is $\mathcal{O}(n \log n)$.

5.2 A Heuristic for MDDP-A

We present a heuristic, BIN-COVER, designed to retrieve a suboptimal solution to MDDP-A, and its pseudocode is reported in Algorithm 4. Unlike the proposed approximation algorithms, BIN-COVER generates a collection of missions, allowing pylons to appear in multiple missions, and then selects a minimum subset from them. Specifically, BIN-COVER uses the ordered list of pylons and computes a set of energy-feasible missions $\mathcal{M}'$. Then, for each $m_i \in \mathcal{M}'$, it applies a BPP procedure to match the load constraint, producing one or more missions that together cover all pylons in m_i. Finally, it collects all generated load and energy feasible missions and solves an instance of the minimum Set Cover Problem (SCP), where each mission corresponds to a set and the universe is the set of all pylons. In SCP, given a universe set $U = \{u_1, \ldots, u_n\}$ and a collection of subsets $\mathcal{D} = \{D_1, \ldots, D_m\}$ over U, the objective is to identify a minimum-size collection $\mathcal{D}' \subseteq \mathcal{D}$ whose union is U.

Algorithm 4: BIN-COVER Algorithm

Data: Set of pylons P, energy budget E, load capacity L
Result: Minimum-size set of missions $\mathcal{M}$

1 $\mathcal{B} \leftarrow \varnothing$;
2 $\mathcal{M}' \leftarrow$ For every pair of pylons in P, generate all energy-feasible missions;
3 **foreach** $m_i \in \mathcal{M}'$ **do**
4 $\quad$ $b_1, \ldots, b_k \leftarrow$ Run an algorithm for BPP on mission m_i with the budget L;
5 $\quad$ $\mathcal{B} \leftarrow \mathcal{B} \cup \{b_1\} \cup \ldots \cup \{b_k\}$;
6 $\mathcal{M} \leftarrow$ Run an algorithm for SCP with candidate sets $\mathcal{B}$ and universe P;
7 **return** $\mathcal{M}$;

The time complexity of the BIN-COVER can be inferred by examining its core components. The algorithm begins by computing energy-feasible missions starting from each pylon based on E (Line 2). Thanks to the fact that all pylons lie along a line, this step can be carried out efficiently. For each pylon p_i, the algorithm computes all energy-reachable pylons to its right, including p_i. Let us call this set $P_i \subseteq P$. Then, BIN-COVER considers all pylons between p_i and any $p_j \in P_i$ as a mission. Let $\mathcal{M}'$ be the resulted set with $|\mathcal{M}'| \leq n^2$. Consequently, for each $m_i \in \mathcal{M}'$, an algorithm for BPP [6] is called to enforce the payload constraint (Lines 3–4). These steps take $\mathcal{O}(n^3 \log n)$ time. Many of these missions may be redundant, as different iterations can generate overlapping coverage of pylons. To reduce the set to its minimal form, the algorithm applies a greedy approximation to the SCP [20], where the universe is the set of all pylons and the candidate sets are the generated bins (missions) (Line 6). By implementing the greedy strategy with a max-heap to select the most covering set at each step, this final phase takes in $\mathcal{O}(n \log n)$ time. Putting all components together, the total running time of BIN-COVER is $\mathcal{O}(n^3 \log n)$. As we will show empirically in Sect. 7, BC is the second best among all algorithms.

6 MDDP with Non-overlapping flights

In the non-overlapping mission variant of the MDDP (N-MDDP), drone flight paths must not intersect. Since only one drone is active at any given time, scheduling flight routes becomes significantly easier.

We first show that Algorithm 1, which begins at the leftmost pylon in P and sequentially assigns pylons to a drone while respecting load and energy constraints, returns an optimal solution for N-MDDP even considering arbitrary loads.

Lemma 1. *Algorithm 1 optimally solves the N-MDDP.*

Next, we show that any optimal solution to N-MDDP returns an approximate solution for MDDP-A. Note that employing the NEXT-FIT algorithm for BPP [12] in Algorithms 2 and 3 yields a set of non-overlapping missions, each containing consecutive pylons. Thus, both algorithms return feasible solutions to N-MDDP. Let $\mathcal{M}_1$ and $\mathcal{M}_2$ denote the sets of missions returned by Algorithms 2 and 3, respectively, and let opt_N be the number of missions in an optimal solution to N-MDDP. Then it follows that $\text{opt}_N \leq |\mathcal{M}_1|$ and $\text{opt}_N \leq |\mathcal{M}_2|$. According to Theorem 3, we have $\text{opt}_N \leq |\mathcal{M}_1| \leq 4\,\text{opt}$ when using NEXT-FIT with $\beta = 2$, and Theorem 4 implies $\text{opt}_N \leq |\mathcal{M}_2| \leq \gamma\,\text{opt}$, where opt is the number of drones used in an optimal solution to MDDP-A.

7 Performance Evaluation

In this section, we evaluate the performance of the proposed algorithms for solving MDDP-A using randomly generated instances.

We consider $n = \{20, 40, \ldots, 200\}$ pylons, which are "almost" regularly spaced along a road. The distance of the power line from the road is $y = 1\,\text{km}$, and the drones operate at an altitude of $z = 50\,\text{m}$. Each pylon p_i has an x-coordinate of $0.5 + \epsilon$, where ϵ is randomly selected from the interval $[-0.05, 0.05]\,\text{km}$. The choice of $0.5\,\text{km}$ is motivated by [21]. Thus, the distance between any pair of consecutive pylons p_i and p_{i+1} is approximately $0.5\,\text{km}$. Moreover, every delivery is assigned an integer load ℓ, randomly chosen between 1 and 5. We set the load capacity of the drones to $L = \{5, 10\}\,\text{kg}$ and their battery energy capacity to $E = \{2500, 5000\}\,\text{kJ}$. The energy consumption rate is fixed at $\alpha = 200\,\text{kJ/km}$ [4].

In the plots in Fig. 3, OPT refers to the optimal solution to MDDP-A which is computed using the ILP, OPT_N represents the optimal solution for N-MDDP, EL denotes the solution returned by the ENERGY-NEXT-LOAD approximated algorithm, LE corresponds to the solution computed by the LOAD-NEXT-ENERGY approximated algorithm, and BC denotes the solution generated by the BIN-COVER heuristic. We use the First-Fit-Decreasing algorithm for the BPP, which begins by sorting the items in decreasing order of their sizes. Then, for each item, the algorithm places it into the first bin that has enough remaining capacity. If no such bin exists, a new bin is opened and the item is

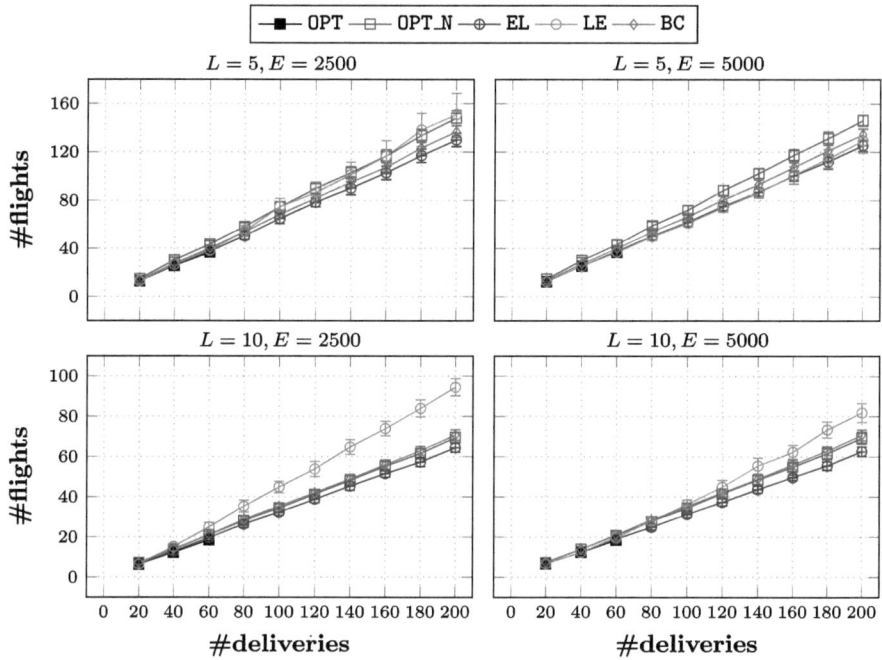

Fig. 3. Experimental results.

placed in it. For the SCP, we employ the greedy algorithm, which at each step selects the set that covers the maximum number of uncovered elements. We run each algorithm on 33 randomly generated instances using fixed parameter settings, and report the average result in terms of the number of drones used along with the standard deviation.

Firstly, note that the ILP was not able to return solutions for instances with more than $n = 60$ pylons. For small values of $n \leq 60$, the results produced by all algorithms closely match those of OPT. However, for large values of $n \geq 80$, the performance of LE degrades compared to the other algorithms and becomes the worst among them. Specifically, consider the plot with $L = 5$ and $E = 2500$. Since LE begins by applying the First-Fit-Decreasing algorithm to the BPP, it may result in missions (bins) fully loaded that include pylons very far, requiring the drone to spend more energy than E to serve them. Thus, dividing such missions according to energy constraints will lead to multiple missions that do not carry a full load but adhere to the energy limitations. This is exacerbated when the load budget is large and the energy budget is small, as seen in the plot for $L = 10$ and $E = 2500$. However, increasing the energy budget allows LE to group more pylons within a single mission, leading to improved performance.

Regarding OPT_N, its behavior is the same for a fixed L and varying values of E. This is because OPT_N jointly considers both load and energy constraints when partitioning pylons, and fixing the load constraint while increasing the energy budget, makes the load constraint to become the dominant. Consequently, further increases in E do not affect the results of OPT_N.

For BC, we observe that it is the second best among all algorithms, almost tied with EL. However, BC has a higher time complexity than EL. In fact, it first considers all energy feasible missions and then invokes the algorithm for BPP. Let $\mathcal{B}$ denote the all load and energy feasible missions computed by BC. Notably, the solutions computed by EL and LE are subsets of $\mathcal{B}$. However, since BC uses a suboptimal greedy algorithm for solving the SCP over $\mathcal{B}$, it may yield solutions that differ from those produced by EL and LE.

Finally, EL consistently outperforms all other algorithms. This is because of its initial step of partitioning pylons based on energy constraint, which avoids forming missions with widely spaced pylons. As a result, EL produces more spatially compact and energy-efficient missions compared to other algorithms.

8 Conclusion

We introduced the MDDP, a new optimization problem focused on minimizing the number of drones required for delivering maintenance equipment along power lines. Our model incorporates practical constraints, including payload limits, energy capacity, and the one-way movement of a support truck. We studied three meaningful variants: MDDP-U, MDDP-A, and N-MDDP, and proposed exact, approximate, and heuristic algorithms, supported by formal guarantees and experimental validation.

Future work will explore more realistic operational settings. These include allowing partial mission overlap to improve scheduling flexibility, enabling drone reuse through recharging mechanisms supported by the truck, and incorporating additional energy costs related to payload delivery. Addressing these aspects will enhance the applicability of our approach to real-world deployments.

Acknowledgments. This work was supported by the PRIN 2022 PNRR M4.C2.1.3 "BREADCRUMBS" project, funded by the European Union – Next Generation EU, grant number P2022K7ERB, CUP J53D23014990001, and partially supported by the "GNCS – INdAM". All authors are member of the GNCS-INdAM.

References

1. Baik, H., Valenzuela, J.: An optimization drone routing model for inspecting wind farms. Soft Comput. **25**(3), 2483–2498 (2020). http://dx.doi.org/10.1007/s00500-020-05316-6
2. Bernardini, S., et al.: A multi-robot platform for the autonomous operation and maintenance of offshore wind farms. In: Adaptive Agents and Multi-Agent Systems (2020). https://api.semanticscholar.org/CorpusID:216332969
3. Betti Sorbelli, F., Ghobadi, S., Palazzetti, L., Pinotti, C.M.: Power line maintenance using multi-package collaborative drone-truck system. In: 2025 21st International Conference on Distributed Computing in Smart Systems and the Internet of Things (DCOSS-IoT), pp. 328–335 (2025). https://doi.org/10.1109/DCOSS-IoT65416.2025.00061

4. Betti Sorbelli, F., Ghobadi, S., Pinotti, C.M.: Single-and multi-depot optimization for uav-based iot data collection in neighborhoods. ACM Trans. Sensor Networks **21**(1), 1–30 (2025). https://doi.org/10.1145/3704810
5. Chung, H.M., Maharjan, S., Zhang, Y., Eliassen, F., Strunz, K.: Placement and routing optimization for automated inspection with unmanned aerial vehicles: a study in offshore wind farm. IEEE Trans. Indust. Inform. **17**(5), 3032–3043 (2021). https://doi.org/10.1109/TII.2020.3004816
6. Dósa, G.: The tight bound of first fit decreasing bin-packing algorithm is FFD(I) ≤ 11/9 OPT(I) + 6/9. In: International Symposium on Combinatorics, Algorithms, Probabilistic and Experimental Methodologies, pp. 1–11. Springer (2007). https://doi.org/10.1007/978-3-540-74450-4_1
7. Dósa, G., Sgall, J.: First fit bin packing: a tight analysis. In: 30th International symposium on theoretical aspects of computer science (STACS 2013), pp. 538–549. Schloss Dagstuhl–Leibniz-Zentrum fuer Informatik (2013). https://doi.org/10.4230/LIPIcs.STACS.2013.538
8. Eck, C., Zgraggen, C., Birrer, M., Cour-Harbo, A.l.: Payload delivery to offshore wind turbines using unmanned helicopters. In: XPONENTIAL 2024, pp. 117–125. XPO24. Association for Unmanned Vehicle Systems International (2024). http://dx.doi.org/10.52202/075106-0010
9. Guo, J., Song, R., He, S.: Vehicle and onboard uav collaborative delivery route planning: considering energy function with wind and payload. J. Syst. Eng. Electron. **36**(1), 194–208 (2025). http://dx.doi.org/10.23919/JSEE.2025.000020
10. Huang, X., Wang, G.: Saving energy and highefficient inspection to offshore wind farm by the comprehensiveassisted drone. Int. J. Energy Res. **2024**(1), January 2024. http://dx.doi.org/10.1155/2024/6209170
11. Jiang, Z., Jovan, F., Moradi, P., Richardson, T., Bernardini, S., Watson, S., Weightman, A., Hine, D.: A multirobot system for autonomous deployment and recovery of a blade crawler for operations and maintenance of offshore wind turbine blades. J. Field Robot. **40**(1), 73–93 (2022). http://dx.doi.org/10.1002/rob.22117
12. Johnson, D.S.: Near-optimal bin packing algorithms. Ph.D. thesis, Massachusetts Institute of Technology (1973). http://hdl.handle.net/1721.1/57819
13. Jovan, F., Bernardini, S.: Adaptive temporal planning for multi-robot systems in operations and maintenance of offshore wind farms. In: Proceedings of the AAAI Conference on Artificial Intelligence 37(13), 15782–15788, June 2023. http://dx.doi.org/10.1609/aaai.v37i13.26874
14. Kocer, B.B., Orr, L., Stephens, B., Kaya, Y.F., Buzykina, T., Khan, A., Kovac, M.: An intelligent aerial manipulator for wind turbine inspection and repair. In: 2022 UKACC 13th International Conference on Control (CONTROL), pp. 226–227 (2022). https://doi.org/10.1109/Control55989.2022.9781451
15. Lopez Lopez, R., Batista Sanchez, M.J., Perez Jimenez, M., Arrue, B.C., Ollero, A.: Autonomous uav system for cleaning insulators in power line inspection and maintenance. Sensors **21**(24), 8488 (2021). http://dx.doi.org/10.3390/s21248488
16. Salahat, E., Asselineau, C.A., Coventry, J., Mahony, R.: Waypoint planning for autonomous aerial inspection of large-scale solar farms. In: IECON 2019 - 45th Annual Conference of the IEEE Industrial Electronics Society, pp. 763–769. IEEE, October 2019. http://dx.doi.org/10.1109/IECON.2019.8927123
17. Schopferer, S., et al.: Offshore wind farm delivery with autonomous drones: a holistic view of system architecture and onboard capabilities. Drones **9**(4), 295 (2025). http://dx.doi.org/10.3390/drones9040295

18. Stuhne, D., et al.: Design of a wireless drone recharging station and a special robot end effector for installation on a power line. IEEE Access **10**, 88719–88737 (2022). https://doi.org/10.1109/ACCESS.2022.3201351
19. Suarez, A., Salmoral, R., Garofano-Soldado, A., Heredia, G., Ollero, A.: Aerial device delivery for power line inspection and maintenance. In: 2022 International Conference on Unmanned Aircraft Systems (ICUAS), pp. 30–38 (2022). https://doi.org/10.1109/ICUAS54217.2022.9836039
20. Vazirani, V.V.: Approximation algorithms, vol. 1. Springer (2001). https://doi.org/10.1007/978-3-662-04565-7
21. Western Renewables Link: Transmission towers and conductors. https://www.westernrenewableslink.com.au/assets/resources/Transmission-towers-and-conductors.pdf. Accessed 14 May 2025
22. Yang, C., et al.: Bladeview: toward automatic wind Turbine inspection with unmanned aerial vehicle. IEEE Trans. Automation Sci. Eng. **22**, 7530–7545 (2025). https://doi.org/10.1109/TASE.2024.3464640

Almost Tight Oracles for Fastest-Path Queries on Temporal Trees

Davide Bilò[1], Luciano Gualà[2], Stefano Leucci[1], Guido Proietti[1,3], and Alessandro Straziota[2](✉)

[1] Department of Information Engineering, Computer Science and Mathematics, University of L'Aquila, L'Aquila, Italy
{davide.bilo,stefano.leucci,guido.proietti}@univaq.it
[2] Department of Enterprise Engineering, University of Rome "Tor Vergata", Rome, Italy
guala@mat.uniroma2.it, alessandro.straziota@uniroma2.it
[3] Istituto di Analisi dei Sistemi ed Informatica "A. Ruberti", CNR, Rome, Italy

Abstract. We investigate the trade-offs between size and query time that are attainable by *fastest-path oracles* for *temporal trees*, i.e., data structures capable of reporting the duration of a fastest point-to-point temporal path, possibly constrained to be within a given time window. For any parameter $t \geq 1$ of choice, we provide an oracle of size $O(M + \frac{M^2}{t^2})$ answering queries in time $O(t \log(1+L))$, where L is the maximum number of time-labels of a single edge, and M is the overall number of (not necessarily distinct) time-labels. We also prove a conditional lower bound that relies on the difficulty of the *Set Disjointness* problem, showing that the trade-offs obtained by our oracles are tight, up to polylogarithmic factors.

We also investigate the case of general temporal graphs and we provide some evidences that the problem becomes much more challenging even for the special case of temporal reachability queries with no time constraints.

Keywords: temporal graphs · fastest-path oracles · temporal reachability

1 Introduction

Temporal graphs, also known as time-evolving or dynamic graphs, are graphs in which each edge exists only in specific moments in time. They provide a natural model for systems where relationships between entities change over time, such as social networks or transportation systems. One of the most widely adopted formalizations of temporal graphs is the model of Kempe, Kleinberg, and Kumar [19], in which each edge e of a graph G is associated with a finite set $\lambda(e)$ of integer *time-labels*, representing the times at which the edge can be traversed. A *temporal path* in G is a path in G together with a choice of a time-label for each traversed edge, such that the encountered time labels are non-decreasing.

In this paper we tackle the problem on designing data structures capable of answering *point-to-point* queries on temporal graphs. These data structures are known as *oracles* and their quality is usually measured by the size/query-time trade-off they achieve. The design of oracles for *non-temporal* graphs has been the subject of extensive attention, which focused mainly on *reachability* and (exact or approximate) *distance* queries (see [4,13,14,17,22], just to mention a few).

On temporal graphs, the landscape of point-to-point queries becomes richer. Indeed, in addition to *temporal reachability* queries, which ask to report whether there exists at least one temporal path from a given staring vertex to a given destination vertex, one can consider *temporal distance* queries for many different and reasonable *temporal distance* measures. Two widely studied measures are the *earliest arrival time* and its symmetric counterpart, called *latest departure time*, where the former (resp. latter) is the smallest (resp. largest) time-label of the last (resp. first) edge among all temporal paths from the starting vertex to the destination vertex. Conveniently, these measures enjoy the following *optimal substructure* property: there always exists an earliest arrival (resp. latest departure) temporal path π between a pair of vertices, such that any prefix (resp. suffix) of π is also an earliest arrival (resp. latest departure) temporal path. This optimal substructure property has been exploited in [7] to provide oracles for earliest arrival and latest departure queries in *dynamic temporal forests* even in the *time-constrained* case, i.e., when the considered earliest arrival (resp. latest departure) temporal paths need to depart no earlier than (resp. arrive no later than) a specified time instant.

When designing oracles, one hopes to obtain a size that is almost linear, and query times that are constant or almost-constant, say polylogarithmic. Although these parameters might not always be simultaneously attainable, the case of earliest arrival and latest departure queries allows for this best-case scenario. Indeed, the oracles of [7] have linear size, and support queries and updates in polylogarithmic time w.r.t. the temporal forest's size.

Another distance measure that is relevant on temporal graphs is the *minimum duration*, defined as the minimum among the differences between the arrival time and the departure time of the temporal paths from the departure to the destination vertex. This measure captures, e.g., the duration of a fastest possible route to a destination in a road network. It would then be desirable to have *fastest-path oracles*, i.e., oracles capable of answering minimum duration queries, especially in the time-constrained case, i.e., when *both* a lower limit on the departure time and an upper limit on the arrival time of the considered path are imposed at query time. Unfortunately, no such non-trivial data structure is currently known, even for the special case of *static* (i.e., non-dynamic) temporal trees. This might be due, in part, to the fact that minimum duration paths appear to have a more complicated combinatorial structures, as they do not enjoy the same suboptimality property of earliest arrival and latest departure paths.

The above discussion begs the following questions:

- Can we design almost-linear size oracles capable of answering (possibly time-constrained) minimum duration queries in polylogarithmic time for the special case of temporal trees?
- More generally, what are the best attainable trade-offs between size and query time for temporal trees?
- What can be said about fastest-path oracles for general temporal graphs?

Our Results. We show that the answer to the first question is likely negative. Indeed, assuming that the Strong Set Disjointness conjecture holds [16], all fastest-path oracles for temporal trees having polylogarithmic query time, must have almost-quadratic size. More precisely, we prove the following conditional lower bound on the achievable size/query time trade off: any fastest-path oracle with query time t must have size $\widetilde{\Omega}(\frac{M^2}{t^2})$, where M is the overall number of (not necessarily distinct) time-labels in the temporal tree, even if only *unconstrained* minimum duration queries are allowed.[1] This provides a (conditional) separation between what is achievable for earliest arrival and latest departure queries (even in the time-constrained case) and (unconstrained) minimum duration queries, providing a formal backing to the intuition that minimum duration queries are harder to answer.

On the positive side, we answer the second question by showing that the above trade-off can actually be achieved, up to polylogarithmic factors. For any temporal tree T and any choice of $t \geq 1$, we show how to construct, in polynomial time, a fastest-path oracle for T having query time $O(t \log L)$ and size $O(M + \frac{M^2}{t^2})$, where L is the maximum number of time-labels on a single edge.[2] Such an oracle can answer time-constrained queries, and is *path-reporting* as it can return the edges (and the corresponding time-labels) of a temporal path achieving the minimum duration in constant additional time per edge.

Finally, we investigate whether similar trade-offs can be achieved for general temporal graphs, and we argue that this is a challenging, if not impossible, task. In detail, we show the above conditional lower bound of $\widetilde{\Omega}(\frac{M^2}{t^2})$ extends to the size of any oracle that has query time at most t, even for the simpler case of *unconstrained connectivity queries*. Moreover, we show that, while an oracle with polylogarithmic query time and size $O(M^2)$ is easy to obtain, designing non-trivial oracles for (unconstrained) temporal connectivity with a truly subquadratic size is a difficult problem, as it would imply novel oracles for non-temporal connectivity in *sparse directed acyclic graphs*, which is a major open problem in the area [18].

---

[1] An information-theoretic argument can be used to show that any oracle for time-constrained fastest-path queries must have size $\widetilde{\Omega}(M)$, regardless of the query time.
[2] To lighten the notation we will write $\log L$ in place of $\log(1 + L)$ in our asymptotic bounds throughout the paper.

Other Related Work. The closest related work is the aforementioned oracle of [7], which has linear size and maintains temporal forests that can be updated in $O(\log M)$ time per operation via the addition and removal of time-labels, and restricted types of edge additions and deletions. Such a data structure can answer time-constrained temporal reachability queries in time $O(\log M)$, and earliest arrival and latest departure queries in time $O(\log M \cdot \log L)$.

Concerning general temporal graphs, [8] provides a data structure capable of answering time-constrained *temporal reachability* queries when incremental updates are allowed (i.e., insertions of new edges and of new time-labels to existing edges). This data structure has size $O(n^2\tau)$, an amortized update time of $O(n^2 \log \tau)$ per operation, where n is the number of vertices of the temporal graph and τ is the number of distinct time-labels in the temporal graph, answers queries in $O(\log \tau)$ worst-case time, and can report a corresponding path in $O(\log \tau)$ worst-case time per edge. Later works considered the problem designing temporal reachability oracles that are optimized for external memory or have compact representations in practice [9,15].

Finally, we mention that the related line of research of designing spanners of temporal graphs, i.e., sparse subgraphs preserving temporal reachability, has also received considerable attention [1,5,6,10–12,19].

2 Preliminaries

A temporal graph is a graph $G = (V, E)$ where each edge $e \in E$ is associated with a finite set $\lambda(e)$ of integers, called *time-labels*. We denote the total number of (not necessarily distinct) time-labels as $M = \sum_{e \in E} |\lambda(e)|$, the maximum number of time-labels assigned to any single edge by $L = \max_{e \in E} |\lambda(e)|$, and the *lifetime* of the temporal graph, i.e., the number of distinct time labels, as $\tau = |\cup_{e \in E} \lambda(e)|$.

A temporal path π from a vertex u to a vertex $v \neq u$ is a sequence $\langle (e_1, t_1), \ldots, (e_k, t_k) \rangle$, where $(e_1, \ldots, e_k)$ is a simple path from u to v in G, $t_i \in \lambda(e_i)$ for $i = 1, \ldots, k$, and the sequence $\langle t_1, t_2, \ldots, t_k \rangle$ is monotonically non-decreasing. The departure (resp. arrival) time of π is t_1 (resp. t_k) and its duration is $t_k - t_1$. We denote by $\text{EA}(u, v, t_d)$ the earliest (i.e., smallest) arrival time among all temporal paths from u to v having departure time at least t_d. If no such temporal path exists, we let $\text{EA}(u, v, t_d) = +\infty$. Symmetrically, we denote by $\text{LD}(u, v, t_a)$ the latest (i.e., largest) departure time among all temporal paths from u to v having arrival time at most t_a or, if no such temporal path exists, $-\infty$. Finally, we use $\text{MD}(u, v, t_d, t_a)$ to denote the *(time-constrained)* minimum duration among all temporal paths from u to v departing at time at least t_d and arriving at time at most t_a, or $+\infty$ if no such temporal path exists. Correspondingly, we refer to the associated path as to a *fastest-path* between u and v. The special case in which $t_d = -\infty$ and $t_a = +\infty$ will be referred to as *unconstrained*, and in such a case t_d and t_a will be omitted in the query argument.

Finally, we observe that a fastest temporal path from u to v having departure time t is also an earliest arrival path which is constrained to depart at time at least t. This is formally stated in the following lemma, whose proof is provided in the full version of the paper.

Lemma 1. *Let $u, v \in V$ be two distinct vertices of a temporal tree T, let e be the edge incident to u in the unique path from u to v in T, and let $\mathcal{T} = \{\ell \in \lambda(e) \mid \ell \geq t_d \land EA(u, v, \ell) \leq t_a\}$. We have:*

$$MD(u, v, t_d, t_a) = \min_{\ell \in \mathcal{T}} (EA(u, v, \ell) - \ell).$$

The following corollary is a consequence of Lemma 1 and of the fact that $EA(u, v, \ell) \leq t_a$ if and only if $LD(u, v, t_a) \geq \ell$.

Corollary 1. $MD(u, v, t_d, t_a) = \min\limits_{\substack{\ell \in \lambda(e) \\ t_d \leq \ell \leq LD(u,v,t_a)}} (EA(u, v, \ell) - \ell)$.

3 Lower Bounds for Fastest-Path Queries on Trees

We now present a conditional lower bound on the size/query time trade-off of fastest-path oracles for temporal trees which relies on the Strong Set Disjointness Conjecture [16].

In the Set Disjointness Problem we are given a collection of m non-empty subsets $S_1, \ldots, S_m$ from a common universe U, and we want to pre-process all the sets $S_1, \ldots, S_m$ in order to build an oracle capable of answering the queries of the form: given two indices i, j report whether S_i and S_j are disjoint.

No oracle for the Set Disjointness problem having query time t and size polynomially smaller than $\frac{N^2}{t^2}$ is currently known, where $N = \sum_{i=1}^{m} |S_i|$. In fact, oracles with such parameters are conjectured not to exist.

Conjecture 1 (Strong Set Disjointness Conjecture in [16]). Any data structure for the Set Disjointness problem that answers queries in time t must use space $\widetilde{\Omega}(\frac{N^2}{t^2})$, where $N = \sum_{i=1}^{m} |S_i|$.

We label each element $x \in U$ with a distinct integer ℓ_x in $1, \ldots, |U|$, and we consider a star T with center vertex r and m leaves $u_1, \ldots, u_m$, where the set of time-labels of the generic edge (u_i, r) is $\{\ell_x \mid x \in S_i\}$. It is easy to see that $MD(u_i, u_j) = 0$ if and only if (u_i, r) and (u_j, r) share a common time-label, i.e., S_i and S_j intersect (see Fig. 1). Then, since $M = N$, we have that if the Strong Set Disjointness Conjecture holds, then any fastest-path oracle with query time t must have size $\widetilde{\Omega}(\frac{M^2}{t^2})$.

Observe that a modification of the above construction yields the same lower bound, up to polylogarithmic factors, on space/query-time trade-off of fastest-path oracles even when each vertex in T has degree at most 3. Indeed, we can choose T as a rooted binary tree that is complete up to the penultimate level, and has exactly m leaves $u_1, \ldots, u_m$. For a non-root vertex v, let $p(v)$ denote its parent in T. For each leaf u_i we choose $\lambda((u_i, p(u_i))) = \{\ell_x \mid x \in S_i\}$, while for

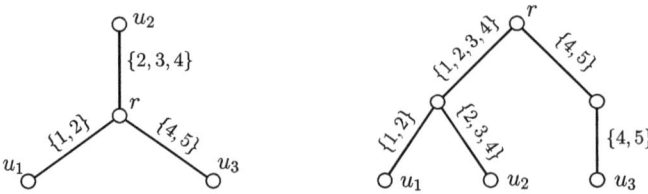

Fig. 1. On the left, the tree T built from Set Disjointness Problem with $U = \{1,2,3,4,5\}$, $S_1 = \{1,2\}$, $S_2 = \{2,3,4\}$, and $S_3 = \{4,5\}$. On the right, the equivalent reduction to a tree with maximum degree 3.

any generic internal non-root vertex v having v' and v'' as its two children we set $\lambda((v, p(v))) = \lambda((v', v)) \cup \lambda((v'', v))$.

Now, if S_i and S_j are disjoint, then $(u_i, p(u_i))$ and $(u_j, p(u_j))$ do not share any time-label and $\mathrm{MD}(u_i, u_j) > 0$. Conversely, if there exists some $x \in S_i \cap S_j$, then ℓ_x appears as a time-label of all edges in the unique path from u to v in T, hence $\mathrm{MD}(u_i, u_j) = 0$.

Since the height of T is $O(\log m)$, we have $M = O(N \log m) = O(N \log N)$ and we can state the following.

Theorem 1. *Assuming Conjecture 1, any fastest-path oracle for temporal trees answering queries in time t has size $\widetilde{\Omega}(\frac{M^2}{t^2})$, even if the input tree has maximum degree 3 and the oracle only supports unconstrained minimum duration queries.*

4 An Almost Tight Oracle for Temporal Trees

In this section we present our fastest-path oracle for temporal trees with query time $O(t \log L)$ and size $O(M + \frac{M^2}{t^2})$, which is essentially tight assuming Conjecture 1. For the sake of readability and in order to better highlight the used ingredients, we organize our discussion as follows: we start by presenting a simple temporal-oracle that does not allow tuning the size/query time trade-off; then we introduce a *bucketing* technique which allows saving space at the cost of slower queries, but still does not provide tight trade-offs; finally, by employing an additional *sparsification* phase, we further reduce the required space and achieve (conditionally) tight bounds, up to polylogarithmic factors.

Before discussing the details of our constructions, we start by describing some common ingredients that are shared by all our oracles.

4.1 Common Ingredients

Given any two distinct vertices u, v of a temporal tree T, we denote with $f_{u,v}$ the first edge along the unique path from u to v in T.

All of our oracles store some common information, which uses overall $O(M)$ space, and can be computed in polynomial time. In particular, we root the tree T is some arbitrary vertex r, and we maintain the following information:

- The rooted temporal tree T, where each vertex v stores a pointer to its parent $p(v)$ (if any), and each edge e also stores the list of time-labels in $\lambda(e)$ in sorted order;
- The depth d_v of each vertex v in (the rooted version of) T;
- A *level ancestor* oracle of T. This oracle can be queried with a vertex v and a non-negative integer i to obtain the i-th level ancestor of v in (the rooted version of) T, i.e., the ancestor of v at hop-distance exactly i from v. Notice that if such an ancestor exists, then it is unique. Level ancestor oracles that can be constructed in linear time, use linear space, and answer queries in constant query time are known [3].
- An oracle Φ that can answer EA and LD queries for T. Such an oracle with polynomial building time and linear size can be easily built by relying on ideas from [7]. More precisely, [7] shows how to answer EA and LD queries in time $O(\log M \cdot \log L)$ in the case of *dynamic* temporal forests. In our case, we can exploit the fact our temporal tree T is fixed to reduce the query time to $O(\log L)$. We also note that Φ can be made path-reporting, i.e., it can output the temporal paths corresponding to EA and LD queries (including an associated time-label for each traversed edge), in time $O(\log L)$ plus constant additional time per reported edge. The details of the construction of Φ can be found in the full version of the paper.

Observe that, using the above information, we can find $f_{u,v}$ in constant time for any $u \neq v$. Indeed, it suffices to check whether v is a descendant of u by testing if $d_v > d_u$ and if the $(d_v - d_u)$-th level ancestor of v is u. If the answer is affirmative, $f_{u,v}$ is the edge (u, w), where w is the $(d_v - d_u - 1)$-th level ancestor of v. If the answer is negative, $f_{u,v}$ is the edge $(u, p(u))$.

Whenever we need to answer a $\text{MD}(u, v, t_d, t_a)$ query, we first perform some preliminary steps. In details, we (i) compute $f_{u,v}$; (ii) find the successor t'_d of t_d and its 0-indexed rank[3] r'_d among the time-labels in $\lambda(f_{u,v})$, and (iii) find $t'_a = \text{LD}(u, v, t_a)$ and the 0-indexed rank r'_a of t'_a among the time-labels in $\lambda(f_{u,v})$. This requires time $O(\log L)$.

Then, if $t'_d > t'_a$, we can immediately answer the query with $+\infty$. Otherwise, we delegate the responsibility of answering the query to the specific oracle constructions described in the rest of this section, where the specific query-answering algorithms have access to u, v, t_a, t_d and to the precomputed values $f_{u,v}, t'_d, t'_a$, r'_d, and r'_a. Finally, since all of our delegated queries can also report the departure time t^*_d of a fastest (time-constrained) temporal path from u to v, we have that an earliest arrival path from u to v departing at time t^*_d is actually a (time-constrained) fastest-path (see Lemma 1 and the preceding discussion). Hence, we can report such a path using additional constant time per edge by performing a path-reporting $\text{EA}(u, v, t^*_d)$ query to Φ.

---

[3] The 0-indexed rank of an element x in a set of integers S is the number of elements smaller than x in S.

4.2 Plain Range Minimum Queries

We now describe a simple construction of an oracle with size $O(nM)$ and logarithmic query time.

Construction. The main idea of the construction is that of storing a collection of inner data structures $\mathcal{R}_{u,v}$, one for each ordered pair of distinct vertices u, v in T. All (delegated) queries of the form $\mathrm{MD}(u, v, \cdot, \cdot)$ will be answered by consulting $\mathcal{R}_{u,v}$. More precisely, each $\mathcal{R}_{u,v}$ is a data structure that stores a static array of η integers $x_1, x_2, \ldots, x_\eta$ and that can answer *range minimum queries*, i.e., given two indices i, j with $1 \le i \le j \le \eta$, it can report an index in $\arg\min_{i \le h \le j} x_h$ and the corresponding value of the minimum. Such a data structure can be built in time $O(\eta)$, requires $O(\eta)$ space to be stored, and is able to answer each query in constant time (see, e.g., [2].).

For a fixed ordered pair of distinct vertices u, v, we store $|\lambda(f_{u,v})|$ integers $x_1, x_2, \ldots$ in $\mathcal{R}_{u,v}$. In particular, if $\ell_1, \ell_2, \ldots$ are the time-labels in $\lambda(f_{u,v})$, in increasing order, then we choose $x_i = \mathrm{EA}(u, v, \ell_i) - \ell_i$. Intuitively, x_i encodes the fact that the fastest among all temporal paths from u to v in T that depart from u at time exactly ℓ_i has duration x_i.

Size Analysis. To analyze the size of our oracle, observe that, for any fixed destination vertex v, we have $\sum_{u \in V \setminus \{v\}} |\lambda(f_{u,v})| = \sum_{e \in E} |\lambda(e)|$ since each edge in T appears exactly once in each of the two sums. Then, the overall space, up to multiplicative constants, is upper bounded by $\sum_{u \in V} \sum_{v \in V \setminus \{u\}} (1 + |\lambda(f_{u,v})|) = n(n-1) + \sum_{v \in V} \sum_{u \in V \setminus \{v\}} |\lambda(f_{u,v})| \le nM + n \sum_{e \in E} |\lambda(e)| = 2nM$, where we used $M \ge n - 1$.

Answering a Query. To answer a (delegated) $\mathrm{MD}(u, v, t_d, t_a)$ query, we use the precomputed values r'_d and r'_a, and we employ $\mathcal{R}_{u,v}$ to retrieve the minimum value x_h among all x_i with $r'_d \le i \le r'_a$ in constant time. The answer is exactly x_h and a suitable departure time t^*_d of a corresponding fastest-path can be chosen as ℓ_h. Correctness follows from Corollary 1. Overall, the query requires time $O(\log L) + O(1) = O(\log L)$.

Lemma 2. *There exists a fastest-path oracle for temporal trees having polynomial building time, size $O(nM)$, and query time $O(\log L)$. The oracle can report a fastest-path in additional $O(1)$ time per edge.*

4.3 Range Minimum Queries and Bucketing

Although the oracle of Lemma 2 is conditionally tight for polylogarithmic query times (up to polylogarithmic factors in the size) due to Theorem 1, it does not allow tuning the trade-off between space and query time. In this section we describe an oracle that allows for such trade-off via a positive integer parameter b of choice. In particular, we will achieve query time $\widetilde{O}(b)$ using $O(M + \frac{nM}{b})$ space.

Construction. For a fixed ordered pair u, v of distinct vertices, let $\ell_1, \ell_2, \ldots$ be the time-labels in $\lambda(f_{u,v})$, in increasing order, and logically partition them into $k + 1 = \left\lceil \frac{|\lambda(f_{u,v})|}{b} \right\rceil$ buckets $B_0, B_1, \ldots, B_k$, each containing b time-labels, except possibly B_k which might be under-full. More precisely, we let $B_i = \{\ell_{ib+1}, \ell_{ib+2}, \ldots, \ell_{(i+1)b}\}$ for $i = 0, \ldots, k - 1$, and $B_k = \{\ell_{kb+1}, \ldots, \ell_{|\lambda(f_{u,v})|}\}$. Then, for each bucket B_i with $i < k$, we compute $x_i = \min_{\ell \in B_i}(\mathrm{EA}(u, v, \ell) - \ell)$, and we store all integers $x_0, \ldots, x_{k-1}$ (if any) in a data structure $\mathcal{R}_{u,v}$ supporting range minimum queries (such a data structure is described in Sect. 4.2).

Our oracle also stores a static dictionary $\mathcal{D}$ whose keys are all pairs u, v for which the time-labels of $f_{u,v}$ are partitioned into more than one bucket (i.e., those for which $|\lambda(f_{u,v})| > b$). The value associated to the generic key u, v is a pointer to $\mathcal{R}_{u,v}$. Such a dictionary can be built in polynomial time, has linear size in the number of stored keys, and has constant lookup time [20].

Size Analysis. In addition to the $O(M)$ space needed to store the common information, the additional size of our data structure, up to multiplicative factors, is upper bounded by $\sum_{u \in V} \sum_{v \in V \setminus \{u\}} \frac{|\lambda(f_{u,v})|}{b} = \frac{nM}{b}$.

Answering a Query. To answer a (delegated) query $\mathrm{MD}(u, v, t_d, t_a)$, we use the precomputed values r'_d and r'_a to find the indices $i = \left\lceil \frac{r'_d}{b} \right\rceil$ and $j = \left\lceil \frac{r'_a}{b} \right\rceil$ of the buckets B_i, B_j such that $t'_d \in B_i$ and $t'_a \in B_j$.

If $i = j$ we return $\min_{t'_d \leq \ell \leq t'_a}(\mathrm{EA}(u, v, \ell) - \ell)$ by querying Φ $O(b)$ times, where each query requires time $O(\log L)$.

Otherwise, when $i < j$, we return the minimum among the following three quantities: (i) $\min_{\substack{\ell \in B_i \\ \ell \geq t'_d}}(\mathrm{EA}(u, v, \ell) - \ell)$, (ii) $\min_{\substack{\ell \in B_j \\ \ell \leq t'_a}}(\mathrm{EA}(u, v, \ell) - \ell)$, and (iii) $\min_{i < h < j} x_h$. Observe that (i) and (ii) can be found by performing at most $O(b)$ queries to Φ, each of which requires $O(\log L)$ time, while (ii) can be found in constant time by first looking up (the pointer to) $\mathcal{R}_{u,v}$ in $\mathcal{D}$ and then querying $\mathcal{R}_{u,v}$. The overall query time is hence $O(b \log L)$.

Observe that the same asymptotic time suffices to also find the departure time t^*_d of a corresponding fastest-path. This is trivial when $i = j$ and when $i < j$ and the minimum duration is attained by (i) or (ii). When $i < j$ the minimum duration is attained by (iii), then we know the bucket B_h containing the first time-label of fastest-path. Then, we can choose $t^*_d = \min_{\ell \in B_h}(\mathrm{EA}(u, v, \ell) - \ell)$.

Lemma 3. *For any positive integer parameter b, there exists a fastest-path oracle for temporal trees having polynomial building time, size $O(M + \frac{nM}{b})$, and query time $O(b \log L)$. The oracle can report a fastest-path in additional $O(1)$ time per edge.*

4.4 Range Minimum Queries, Bucketing, and Sparsification

The oracle of Lemma 3 still does not achieve the (conditionally) optimal trade-off curve of Theorem 1. Instead of applying the bucketing technique on all pairs of vertices, we can instead restrict the creation of buckets to only the subset of vertex pairs. This allows us to reduce the memory requirements of our oracle without increasing the query time, which yields asymptotically tight trade-offs (up to polylogarithmic factors, and conditioned on Conjecture 1).

Construction. Our construction is parameterized by two positive integers b and h. We say that an edge e is *heavy* if $|\lambda(e)| \geq h$, otherwise e is *light*.

For each ordered pair u, v of distinct vertices such that $f_{u,v}$ and $f_{v,u}$ are both heavy, we apply the bucketing technique from the previous construction. Namely, we partition $\lambda(f_{u,v})$ into $k + 1 = \left\lceil \frac{|\lambda(f_{u,v})|}{b} \right\rceil$ buckets $B_0, B_1, \ldots, B_k$ containing b time-labels each, except possibly for the last bucket. Then, we compute $x_i = \min_{\ell \in B_i}(\text{EA}(u, v, \ell) - \ell)$ for all $i = 0, \ldots, k-1$, and we store $x_0, \ldots, x_{k-1}$ in a data structure $\mathcal{R}_{u,v}$ supporting range minimum queries.

All the above pairs u, v for which $k \geq 1$ are then stored as keys in a static dictionary $\mathcal{D}$, with a pointer to the corresponding $\mathcal{R}_{u,v}$ data structure as their associated value.

Size Analysis. In addition to the $O(M)$ space required to store the common information, we only need to account for the overall number N of integers stored in the data structures $\mathcal{R}_{u,v}$ (such a quantity is also an asymptotic upper bound to the $\mathcal{D}$).

Let H be the set of all heavy edges and observe that, since each heavy edge has at least h time-labels, we must have $M \geq \sum_{f \in H} |\lambda(f)| \geq |H| \cdot h$, which implies $|H| \leq \frac{M}{h}$. Observe further that we can map each ordered pair of distinct non-adjacent vertices u, v to the ordered pair of distinct edges $f_{u,v}, f_{v,u}$, and that such mapping μ is bijective. Then, if $f, f' = \mu(u, v)$, we can charge the pair f, f' a *cost* $c(f, f')$ equal to the number of integers stored due to the ordered pair of vertices u, v. Since $c(f, f') = 0$ whenever at least one of f and f' is light, and $c(f, f') \leq \frac{|\lambda(f)|}{b}$, we have that the overall contribution of all non-adjacent ordered pairs of vertices is upper bounded by:

$$\sum_{f \in H} \sum_{f' \in H \setminus \{f\}} c(f, f') \leq \frac{1}{b} \sum_{f' \in H} \sum_{f \in H} |\lambda(f)| \leq \frac{1}{b} \sum_{f' \in H} M = \frac{|H| \cdot M}{b} \leq \frac{M^2}{bh}.$$

For an ordered pair of adjacent vertices u, v, we have that the number of integers stored due to u, v is at most $\frac{|\lambda((u,v))|}{b}$. Then, the overall contribution of all such pairs is at most $\frac{2}{b} \sum_{e \in E} |\lambda(e)| = \frac{2M}{b}$.

We can conclude that the overall size of our oracle is $O(M + \frac{M^2}{bh})$.

Answering a Query. We start by stating the following property of fastest-paths, whose proof is given in the full version of the paper, that will be instrumental to our query-answering procedure.

Lemma 4. $\min\limits_{\substack{\ell \in \lambda(f_{u,v}) \\ t_d \leq \ell \leq LD(u,v,t_a)}} (EA(u,v,\ell) - \ell) = \min\limits_{\substack{t \in \lambda(f_{v,u}) \\ EA(u,v,t_d) \leq \ell \leq t_a}} (\ell - LD(u,v,\ell)).$

To answer a (delegated) query $\mathrm{MD}(u,v,t_d,t_a)$, we identify the edges $f_{u,v}$ and $f_{v,u}$ (where $f_{u,v}$ has been precomputed, and $f_{v,u}$ can be found in constant time), and we check whether they are heavy. We let $i = \left\lceil \frac{r'_d}{b} \right\rceil$, $j = \left\lceil \frac{r'_a}{b} \right\rceil$, and we continue the query according to the following cases:

- If both $f_{u,v}$ and $f_{v,u}$ are heavy, and $i = j$, then we answer by returning $\min_{t'_d \leq \ell \leq t'_a}(\mathrm{EA}(u,v,\ell) - \ell)$, which can be found by querying Φ $O(b)$ times.
- If both $f_{u,v}$ and $f_{v,u}$ are heavy and $i < j$, then we answer by returning the minimum among the following three quantities: (i) $\min_{\substack{\ell \in B_i \\ \ell \geq t'_d}}(\mathrm{EA}(u,v,\ell) - \ell)$, (ii) $\min_{\substack{\ell \in B_j \\ \ell \leq t'_a}}(\mathrm{EA}(u,v,\ell) - \ell)$, and (iii) $\min_{i < h < j} x_k$. Here (i) and (ii) can be found with $O(b)$ queries to Φ, while (iii) can be found by first looking up $\mathcal{R}_{u,v}$ using $\mathcal{D}$, and then performing a single query to $\mathcal{R}_{u,v}$;
- If $f_{u,v}$ is light, then we return $\min_{\substack{\ell \in \lambda(f_{u,v}) \\ t'_d \leq \ell \leq t'_a}}(\mathrm{EA}(u,v,\ell) - \ell)$ by performing at most h queries to Φ;
- Otherwise, $f_{v,u}$ must be light. We first compute $t' = \mathrm{EA}(u,v,t_d)$, and then we return $\min_{\substack{\ell \in \lambda(f_{v,u}) \\ t' \leq \ell \leq t_a}}(\ell - \mathrm{LD}(u,v,\ell))$ (see Lemma 4) by performing at most h queries to Φ.

Hence, the overall query time is $O(\max\{b + h\} \log L)$. In order to compute the departure time t_d^* of a corresponding (time-constrained) fastest-path, observe that the first three cases can be handled as already described in Sect. 4.3. Regarding the last case, since the time-label ℓ for which the minimum duration d is achieved is exactly the arrival time of a fastest temporal path, we can choose t_d^* as the difference between ℓ and d. Choosing $b = h$, we obtain the following:

Theorem 2. *For any positive integer parameter t, there exists a fastest-path oracle for temporal trees having polynomial building time, size $O(M + \frac{M^2}{t^2})$, and query time $O(t \log L)$. The oracle can report a fastest-path in additional $O(1)$ time per edge.*

5 On the Hardness of Handling General Temporal Graphs

In this section we argue that designing oracles for general temporal graphs is challenging, even when the oracle only needs to answer temporal connectivity queries. We first give a conditional lower bound for this simpler type of query, showing impossibility results similar to the ones proved for fastest queries on trees if Conjecture 1 holds. Then, we argue that it is easy to construct oracles achieving trivial trade-offs: one construction has quadratic size and answers fastest-path queries in logarithmic time, while the other has linear space and answers connectivity queries in linear time. Finally, we argue than constructing non-trivial truly subquadratic oracles for temporal connectivity would result in new oracles for connectivity in *non-temporal* directed acyclic graphs, which is a major open problem in the area.

The proof of the following theorem can be found in the full version of the paper.

Theorem 3. *Assuming Conjecture 1, any oracle for temporal graphs that can answer temporal connectivity queries in time t has size $\widetilde{\Omega}(\frac{M^2}{t^2})$. The same holds even when $\tau = 3$, the maximum degree is 3, and all edges have a single time-label.*

Hence, if one interested in temporal connectivity oracles proving *fast* query times, say polylogarithmic, then the above lower bound (conditionally) rules out any construction with truly subquadratic size. Interestingly, it is easy to construct an oracle with quadratic size even for the more general case of time-constrained fastest-path queries. Consider all tuples $\mu = \langle u, t_u, v, t_v \rangle$ with $u, v \in V(G)$, $t_u \in \Lambda(u)$, and $t_v \in \Lambda(v)$, where $\Lambda(w)$ denotes the set of all time-labels that appear in at least one edge incident to vertex w. For each such tuple μ we can precompute $d_\mu = \text{MD}(u, v, t_u, t_v)$, and we can store all pairs μ, d_μ as key/value pairs of a static dictionary $\mathcal{D}$ having size $O\left((\sum_e |\lambda(e)|)^2\right) = O(M^2)$ and constant query time [20]. The oracle consists of $\mathcal{D}$ and of all sets $\Lambda(w)$ for $w \in V$, where the time-labels in $\Lambda(w)$ have been sorted. A query $\text{MD}(u, v, t_d, t_a)$ can be answered in $O(\log M)$ time by looking up the successor of t'_d of t_d in $\Lambda(u)$, looking up the predecessor of t'_a of t_a in $\Lambda(v)$, and by returning the value stored in $\mathcal{D}$ for the key $\langle u, t'_d, v, t'_a \rangle$.

Another trivial connectivity oracle stores the entire temporal graph and answers (possibly time-constrained) connectivity queries in linear time by exploring the graph at query time [21].

One might wonder whether other non-trivial trade-offs are attainable (up to polylogarithmic factors) for temporal connectivity oracles. We show that this would imply the existence of novel oracles for connectivity in *non-temporal* sparse directed acyclic graphs (DAGs), solving a major open problem in the area. Indeed, consider a DAG H with η vertices $v_1, \ldots, v_\eta$, in topological order, and construct a temporal graph (G, λ) from H by splitting each directed edge (v_i, v_j) into two undirected temporal edges $(v_i, x_{i,j})$ and $(x_{i,j}, v_j)$, where $x_{i,j}$ is a new vertex. Edge $(v_i, x_{i,j})$ has a single time-label i, and edge $(x_{i,j}, v_j)$ has a single time-label j (see Fig. 2). Given two vertices $u, v \in V(H)$, u is connected to v in H if and only if u is temporally connected to v in G. This implies that any oracle construction achieving a certain size-time trade-off for temporal connectivity can be used to obtain the same trade-off for non-temporal connectivity on *sparse* DAGs (i.e., DAGS with $O(\eta)$ of edges). However, no non-trivial oracles for connectivity in DAGs are currently known, even for the sparse case [18].

6 Conclusions and Open Problems

Besides the model of temporal graphs of Kempe et al., more general notions of temporal graphs accounting for *latencies* have also been considered [21]. In this

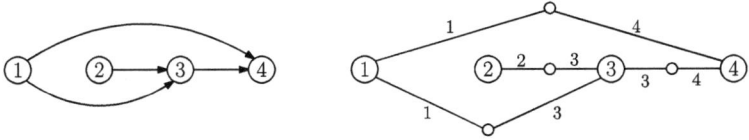

Fig. 2. Reduction from an instance of connectivity on DAG (on the left), to an instance of temporal connectivity on temporal graph (on the right).

model, time-labels are pairs (ℓ, d) of positive integers encoding the fact that the corresponding edge can be traversed from any endvertex starting at time ℓ in order to reach the other endvertex at time $\ell + d$. This model also captures the notion of *strict* temporal path as a special case, namely when all edge traversal durations d are identically 1.

All our (conditional) lower bounds apply to the case of strict temporal paths with minor modifications,[4] and hence also to the more general case of arbitrary latencies. Interestingly, our upper bounds (including that of the oracle Φ supporting EA and LD queries) also extend to the case of latencies in a straightforward way, with no asymptotic difference in their size or query time.

Among the problems left open, one that we deem particularly interesting is that of understanding whether static temporal paths are easier than static temporal trees, i.e., whether they admit fastest-path oracles with better space/query-time trade-offs. The problem of designing fastest-path oracles supporting updates is also worth studying, both for general temporal graphs and in the special case of temporal forests.

References

1. Angrick, S., et al.: How to reduce temporal cliques to find sparse spanners. In: Chan, T.M., Fischer, J., Iacono, J., Herman, G. (eds.) 32nd Annual European Symposium on Algorithms, ESA 2024, 2–4 September 2024, Royal Holloway, London, United Kingdom. LIPIcs, vol. 308, pp. 11:1–11:15. Schloss Dagstuhl - Leibniz-Zentrum für Informatik (2024). https://doi.org/10.4230/LIPICS.ESA.2024.11
2. Bender, M.A., Farach-Colton, M.: The LCA problem revisited. In: Gonnet, G.H., Viola, A. (eds.) LATIN 2000. LNCS, vol. 1776, pp. 88–94. Springer, Heidelberg (2000). https://doi.org/10.1007/10719839_9
3. Bender, M.A., Farach-Colton, M.: The level ancestor problem simplified. Theor. Comput. Sci. **321**(1), 5–12 (2004). https://doi.org/10.1016/J.TCS.2003.05.002

---

[4] Namely, in the first construction of Sect. 3 (in which T is a star), we can assign the generic i-th element of U to the *two* time-labels $3i-2$ and $3i-1$, so that two distinct sets S_i, S_j intersect iff $MD(u_i, u_j) = 1$. In the modified construction in which T is binary tree of height $h = O(\log m)$, we can assign each element in U to h consecutive time-labels, while ensuring that any two time-labels associated to distinct elements differ by at least $2h$. Then, two distinct sets S_i, S_j intersect iff $MD(u_i, u_j) < 2h$. Observe that M only increases by a multiplicative $O(\log m)$ factor.

4. Bilò, D., Chechik, S., Choudhary, K., Cohen, S., Friedrich, T., Schirneck, M.: Improved distance (sensitivity) oracles with subquadratic space. In: 65th IEEE Annual Symposium on Foundations of Computer Science. FOCS 2024, Chicago, IL, USA, 27–30 October 2024, pp. 1550–1558. IEEE (2024). https://doi.org/10.1109/FOCS61266.2024.00097
5. Bilò, D., D'Angelo, G., Gualà, L., Leucci, S., Rossi, M.: Sparse temporal spanners with low stretch. In: Chechik, S., Navarro, G., Rotenberg, E., Herman, G. (eds.) 30th Annual European Symposium on Algorithms. ESA 2022, 5–9 September 2022, Berlin/Potsdam, Germany. LIPIcs, vol. 244, pp. 19:1–19:16. Schloss Dagstuhl - Leibniz-Zentrum für Informatik (2022). https://doi.org/10.4230/LIPICS.ESA.2022.19
6. Bilò, D., D'Angelo, G., Gualà, L., Leucci, S., Rossi, M.: Blackout-tolerant temporal spanners. J. Comput. Syst. Sci. **141**, 103495 (2024). https://doi.org/10.1016/J.JCSS.2023.103495
7. Bilò, D., Gualà, L., Leucci, S., Proietti, G., Straziota, A.: Temporal queries for dynamic temporal forests. In: Mestre, J., Wirth, A. (eds.) 35th International Symposium on Algorithms and Computation. ISAAC 2024, 8–11 December 2024, Sydney, Australia. LIPIcs, vol. 322, pp. 11:1–11:16. Schloss Dagstuhl - Leibniz-Zentrum für Informatik (2024). https://doi.org/10.4230/LIPICS.ISAAC.2024.11
8. Brito, L.F.A., Albertini, M.K., Casteigts, A., Travençolo, B.A.N.: A dynamic data structure for temporal reachability with unsorted contact insertions. Soc. Netw. Anal. Min. **12** (2021). https://api.semanticscholar.org/CorpusID:231847148
9. Brito, L.F.A., Albertini, M.K., Travençolo, B.A.N.: A dynamic data structure for representing timed transitive closures on disk. CoRR abs/2306.13937 (2023). https://doi.org/10.48550/ARXIV.2306.13937
10. Carnevale, D., Casteigts, A., Corsini, T.: Dismountability in temporal cliques revisited. In: Meeks, K., Scheideler, C. (eds.) 4th Symposium on Algorithmic Foundations of Dynamic Networks. SAND 2025, 9–11 June 2025, Liverpool, UK. LIPIcs, vol. 330, pp. 6:1–6:18. Schloss Dagstuhl - Leibniz-Zentrum für Informatik (2025). https://doi.org/10.4230/LIPICS.SAND.2025.6
11. Casteigts, A., Peters, J.G., Schoeters, J.: Temporal cliques admit sparse spanners. J. Comput. Syst. Sci. **121**, 1–17 (2021). https://doi.org/10.1016/J.JCSS.2021.04.004
12. Casteigts, A., Raskin, M., Renken, M., Zamaraev, V.: Sharp thresholds in random simple temporal graphs. SIAM J. Comput. **53**(2), 346–388 (2024). https://doi.org/10.1137/22M1511916
13. Chechik, S.: Approximate distance oracles with improved bounds. In: Servedio, R.A., Rubinfeld, R. (eds.) Proceedings of the Forty-Seventh Annual ACM on Symposium on Theory of Computing. STOC 2015, Portland, OR, USA, 14–17 June 2015, pp. 1–10. ACM (2015). https://doi.org/10.1145/2746539.2746562
14. Dey, D., Gupta, M.: Nearly optimal fault tolerant distance oracle. In: Mohar, B., Shinkar, I., O'Donnell, R. (eds.) Proceedings of the 56th Annual ACM Symposium on Theory of Computing. STOC 2024, Vancouver, BC, Canada, 24–28 June 2024, pp. 944–955. ACM (2024). https://doi.org/10.1145/3618260.3649697
15. Fernando Afra Brito, L., Keese Albertini, M., Augusto Nassif Travençolo, B., Navarro, G.: Dynamic compact data structure for temporal reachability with unsorted contact insertions. Comput. J. **67**(10), 2984–2994 (2024). https://doi.org/10.1093/comjnl/bxae063
16. Goldstein, I., Lewenstein, M., Porat, E.: On the hardness of set disjointness and set intersection with bounded universe. In: Lu, P., Zhang, G. (eds.) 30th International

Symposium on Algorithms and Computation. ISAAC 2019, 8–11 December 2019, Shanghai University of Finance and Economics, Shanghai, China. LIPIcs, vol. 149, pp. 7:1–7:22. Schloss Dagstuhl - Leibniz-Zentrum für Informatik (2019). https://doi.org/10.4230/LIPICS.ISAAC.2019.7

17. Holm, J., de Lichtenberg, K., Thorup, M.: Poly-logarithmic deterministic fully-dynamic algorithms for connectivity, minimum spanning tree, 2-edge, and biconnectivity. J. ACM **48**(4), 723–760 (2001). https://doi.org/10.1145/502090.502095

18. Kaplan, H., Mulzer, W., Roditty, L., Seiferth, P.: Reachability oracles for directed transmission graphs. Algorithmica **82**(5), 1259–1276 (2020). https://doi.org/10.1007/S00453-019-00641-1

19. Kempe, D., Kleinberg, J.M., Kumar, A.: Connectivity and inference problems for temporal networks. J. Comput. Syst. Sci. **64**(4), 820–842 (2002). https://doi.org/10.1006/JCSS.2002.1829

20. Ružić, M.: Constructing efficient dictionaries in close to sorting time. In: Aceto, L., Damgård, I., Goldberg, L.A., Halldórsson, M.M., Ingólfsdóttir, A., Walukiewicz, I. (eds.) ICALP 2008. LNCS, vol. 5125, pp. 84–95. Springer, Heidelberg (2008). https://doi.org/10.1007/978-3-540-70575-8_8

21. Wu, H., Cheng, J., Huang, S., Ke, Y., Lu, Y., Xu, Y.: Path problems in temporal graphs. Proc. VLDB Endow. **7**(9), 721–732 (2014). https://doi.org/10.14778/2732939.2732945

22. Wulff-Nilsen, C.: Faster deterministic fully-dynamic graph connectivity. In: Khanna, S. (ed.) Proceedings of the Twenty-Fourth Annual ACM-SIAM Symposium on Discrete Algorithms. SODA 2013, New Orleans, Louisiana, USA, 6–8 January 2013, pp. 1757–1769. SIAM (2013). https://doi.org/10.1137/1.9781611973105.126

Temporal Orienteering with Changing Fuel Costs

Timothée Corsini[1], Jessica Enright[2], Laura Larios-Jones[2](✉), and Kitty Meeks[2]

[1] LaBRI, CNRS, University of Bordeaux, Bordeaux INP, Talence, France
`timothee.corsini@labri.fr`
[2] School of Computing Science, University of Glasgow, Glasgow, UK
`{jessica.enright,laura.larios-jones,kitty.meeks}@glasgow.ac.uk`

Abstract. The Orienteering problem asks whether there exists a walk which visits a number of sites without exceeding some fuel budget. In the variant of the problem we consider, the cost of each edge in the walk is dependent on the time we depart one endpoint and the time we arrive at the other endpoint. This mirrors applications such as travel between orbiting objects where fuel costs are dependent on both the departure time and the length of time spent travelling. In defining this problem, we introduce a natural generalisation of the standard notion of temporal graphs: the pair consisting of the graph of the sites and a cost function, in which costs as well as shortest travel times between pairs of objects change over time. We believe this model is likely to be of independent interest. The problem of deciding whether a stated goal is feasible is easily seen to be NP-complete; we investigate three different ways to restrict the input which lead to efficient algorithms. These include the number of times an edge can be used, an analogue of vertex-interval-membership width, and the number of sites to be visited.

Keywords: Orienteering · TSP · Temporal graphs · Parameterized complexity · Color coding

1 Introduction

The ORIENTEERING problem, also known as SELECTIVE TRAVELLING SALESMAN [16] or the BANK ROBBER [3] problem, asks for a path in a graph which visits some number of vertices such that the sum of the costs on the edges of the path is at most a given budget. Note that, when the number of vertices to be visited is the same as the number of vertices in the graph, ORIENTEERING becomes the classical TRAVELLING SALESMAN PROBLEM (TSP) [13]. As with TSP, many versions of ORIENTEERING have been studied (see [19] for a survey).

Our variation of the ORIENTEERING problem is CHANGING COST TEMPORAL ORIENTEERING. In this variant, we look for a walk which visits the designated number of vertices with fuel costs at most the given budget. The cost of a walk is given by the sum of the costs of the edges at the time they are traversed, where the cost of an edge is given by a function dependent on the edge, departure time at one endpoint, and arrival time at the other endpoint. Note that looking for a walk rather than a path allows us to revisit vertices. Our variant of the problem is inspired by scheduling travel to objects in near-earth orbit [17]. Since these objects are in orbit and the distances between them change over time, so too do the associated fuel costs. In addition, one may choose to expend more fuel to arrive at the destination faster, or take a cheaper and slower journey. Our model allows both waiting at a vertex until the journey to the next vertex is cheaper, and for making longer, but more fuel-efficient, journeys.

In order to describe this problem formally, we introduce a new notion of *temporal cost graphs*, a generalisation of the well-studied notion of temporal graphs which allows for the cost of travelling between two vertices to change over time; we believe that this mathematical object will prove useful for the study of other problems. We observe that our problem – CHANGING COST TEMPORAL ORIENTEERING – generalises star exploration, known to be NP-complete even under strong restrictions [1,7]. We therefore focus our attention on restricted cases in which we can hope to recover tractability. Informally, we design efficient algorithms by restricting any one of the following:

- the number of times at which it is possible to either enter or leave a vertex with finite travel cost (Sect. 2);
- the maximum, taken over all timesteps, of the number of vertices possible for the orienteer's current location, assuming they have only used finite fuel and are not permanently stranded on the current object (Sect. 3);
- the target number of objects we must visit (Sect. 4).

We note that our second restriction (found in Sect. 3) is a generalisation of vertex-interval-membership width. In the interest of space, most proofs are deferred to the arXiv version.

1.1 Related Work

The ORIENTEERING problem [14] is described by Vansteenwegan [19] as a combination of the KNAPSACK Problem [15] and TSP. When the vertices are weighted, the problem has also been referred to as PRIZE COLLECTING TSP [4] or TSP WITH PROFITS [11]. Note that we allow the walk to revisit vertices, however some variants of the problem do not allow this and instead require a tour of the visited vertices. Blum et al. [5] give a constant factor approximation algorithm for the ORIENTEERING problem that demands a tour given a specified starting vertex. Similar methods are used by Chekuri et al. [9] for the variant where vertices can be revisited to obtain a $(2 + \varepsilon)$-approximation.

Fomin and Lingas [12] introduce the TIME-DEPENDENT ORIENTEERING problem which, given a clique and a travel time function which depends on the current absolute time, asks for a tour that visits k vertices before a deadline. In a survey of different notions of time-varying graphs, Casteigts et al. [8] gives a model which has a latency function over the edge-time pairs which describes how long it takes to cross an edge at a given time. This latency function operates in the same way as the travel time function used by Fomin and Lingas. They show that their generalisation of the ORIENTEERING problem is $(2+\epsilon)$-approximable if the ratio between the maximum and minimum travel times is bounded by a constant. Our problem is related in also computing on a graph and with a travel time function, but differs in allowing the fuel cost to be vary arbitrarily with the travel time, in explicitly using a different underlying graph, and allowing vertices to be revisited. As a result, their results cannot be easily adapted to our setting.

Other time-dependent variations of ORIENTEERING are considered by Buchin et al. [6]. In their work, they search for a walk on a graph whose vertices are labelled with intervals at which each vertex can be visited. They show that the problem is weakly NP-hard when the underlying graph is a path and with unit costs on the edges. Buchin et al. also consider a variant of the problem where edges, rather than vertices, are labelled with intervals in which they can be used. This is an analogue of ORIENTEERING for temporal graphs. For this problem, they show tractability when the underlying graph is a path, and hardness when it is a tree. They extend some of their structural results to the original ORIENTEERING problem.

Capturing our space-related motivation, López-Ibáñez et al. [17] present the ASTEROID ROUTING problem which asks for the optimal sequence for visiting a set of asteroids, starting from Earth's orbit, in order to minimise both the cost and the time taken. They give four algorithms and compare their efficacy in an experimental study.

1.2 Problem Definition and Basic Observations

A *temporal graph* is usually defined as a pair $(G = (V, E), \lambda)$, where G is a static graph and the function $\lambda : E \to 2^T$ attributes to each edge a set of time labels at which the edge is said to be *active*. To define our problem, we begin by introducing a generalisation of this notion in which each edge of the static graph has an associated traversal cost, which depends on both the departure and arrival times as well as the direction of travel (we include the arrival time as well as departure time as an input to the cost function as one can imagine a scenario in which the orienteer has a choice between a fast but costly route or a slower but more fuel-efficient trajectory departing at the same time). This also generalises the time-varying graph model given in the survey by Casteigts et al. [8]. This leads us to the following definition.

Definition 1 (Temporal cost graph). *A temporal cost graph is a static graph G paired with a cost function $F : V \times V \times [T] \times [T] \to \mathbb{N}_0 \cup \{\infty\}$ which takes an ordered tuple consisting of a starting vertex v_1, a destination vertex v_2, a departure time t_1 and an arrival time t_2 and assigns a fuel cost. We require that $F(v_1, v_2, t_1, t_2) = \infty$ whenever $t_1 \geq t_2$, $F(v, v, t_1, t_2) = 0$ for all v and any $t_1 < t_2$, and that $F(v_1, v_2, t_1, t_2) > 0$ whenever $v_1 \neq v_2$.*

We assume throughout that temporal cost graphs are encoded in such a way (e.g. using a hash table) that, given any tuple (u, v, t_1, t_2), we can look up the value of $F(u, v, t_1, t_2)$ in constant time.

Notice that our definition of temporal cost graphs generalises the standard definition of temporal graphs. Given a temporal graph (G, λ), we can obtain an equivalent temporal cost graph by taking the same underlying graph G and setting $F(u, v, t_1, t_2) = 1$ if and only if the edge uv is active at time t_1, and $t_2 = t_1 + 1$. If this is not the case, the quadruple is assigned infinite cost by F.

We now define the key concept of a valid walk in a temporal cost graph. In a temporal cost graph generated from a standard temporal graph, this is equivalent to the notion of a strict temporal walk.

Definition 2 (Valid walk). *A valid walk on a temporal cost graph (G, F) is a sequence of quadruples $(u_1, v_1, t_1, t'_1), (u_2, v_2, t_2, t'_2), \ldots, (u_\ell, v_\ell, t_\ell, t'_\ell)$ such that:*

- *for each $1 \leq i < \ell$, $v_i = u_{i+1}$,*
- *for each $1 \leq i \leq \ell$, $t_i < t'_i$ and $F(u_i, v_i, t_i, t'_i) < \infty$, and*
- *for each $1 \leq i < \ell$, $t'_i \leq t_{i+1}$.*

We define the cost of a valid walk W to be $\sum_{(u_i, v_i, t_i, t'_i) \in W} F(u_i, v_i, t_i, t'_i)$.

Note that, since each quadruple (u_i, v_i, t_i, t'_i) in a valid walk is required to have finite cost, it must be the case that $t_i < t'_i$. Also note that we use the convention that staying at a vertex incurs no cost.

We can now give the formal definition of our problem.

CHANGING COST TEMPORAL ORIENTEERING (CCTO)
Input: A temporal cost graph (G, F), source vertex v_s, sink vertex v_t, a target $k \in \mathbb{N}$ and a budget $f \in \mathbb{N}$.
Question: Is there a valid walk W from v_s to v_t that visits at least k distinct vertices and has cost at most f?

For avoidance of doubt: we count the source and sink vertices in the number of vertices visited by a valid walk. We also assume without loss of generality that the underlying graph of the input temporal cost graph is connected.

We now define two important properties of temporal cost graphs which we shall refer to when designing our algorithms. These are the analogues of the notions of lifetime and temporality, respectively, for temporal graphs.

Definition 3 (Lifetime). *The lifetime T of a temporal cost graph (G, F) is the latest arrival time t' of an edge such that there exist vertices v, u and a departure time t with $F(v, u, t, t') < \infty$.*

Definition 4 (Maximum traversal number). *Let $e = uv$ be an edge in G. The maximum traversal number of e in the temporal cost graph (G, F) is the largest integer j such that there exists a sequence $(t_1, t'_1), (t_2, t'_2), \ldots, (t_j, t'_j)$ of pairs of times such that:*

- *for each $1 \leq i \leq j$, we have $\min\{F(u, v, t_i, t'_i), F(v, u, t_i, t'_i)\} < \infty$, and*
- *for each $1 \leq i \leq j - 1$, we have $t'_i \leq t_{i+1}$.*

Crucially, the maximum traversal number of an edge e in (G, F) provides an upper bound on the number of times that e can be used in any valid walk.

We conclude this section by observing that CCTO is NP-complete. Recall that our definition of temporal cost graphs generalises the standard definition of temporal graphs so, if a problem is hard on temporal graphs, the analogous problem is hard on temporal cost graphs. It is therefore easy to deduce NP-hardness of CCTO from the NP-hardness of the following problem on temporal graphs, which is known to be NP-hard even when every edge is active at no more than four timesteps [1,7]; here S_n is a star with n leaves, and our goal is to visit every leaf before returning to the centre.

STAREXP
Input: A temporal star (S_n, λ) with centre x.
Question: Is there an ordering $v_1, \ldots, v_n$ of the leaves of S_n and a sequence $t_1, t_2, \ldots, t_{2n}$ of times with $t_i < t_{i+1}$ for each $1 \leq i \leq 2n-1$ such that, for each $1 \leq j \leq n$, we have $t_{2j-1}, t_{2j} \in \lambda(xv_j)$?

Given the input (S_n, λ) to an instance of STAREXP, we can easily construct an equivalent instance of CCTO. Suppose that the latest time at which any edge in (S_n, λ) is active is τ. We define a cost function $F : V(S_n) \times V(S_n) \times [\tau+1] \times [\tau+1]$ by setting $F(u, v, t_1, t_2) = 1$ if $t_1 \in \lambda(uv)$ and $t_2 = t_1 + 1$, and $F(u, v, t_1, t_2) = \infty$ otherwise. It is then immediate that $(S_n, x, x, F, n+1, 2n)$ is a yes-instance for CCTO if and only if (S_n, λ) is a yes-instance for STAREXP – recall that S_n has $n+1$ vertices. We further note that CCTO is clearly in NP (with the sequence of edges traversed together with the departure and arrival times acting as a certificate) so we conclude that CCTO is NP-complete.

It is natural to ask – especially as we will show in Sect. 4 that CCTO is in FPT parameterised by the number k of vertices to be visited – whether NP-hardness relies on the fact that our target number of objects to visit is equal to the number of vertices. In fact, we can easily adapt the reduction described above to give NP-hardness when $k = \mathcal{O}(n^c)$ for any $c \in (0, 1]$. Let $(S_{n'}, x, x, F, n'+1, 2n')$ be an instance of CCTO constructed via the reduction above. We then add $\Theta((n')^{1/c})$ additional leaves so that the total number of vertices is n and we have $n' = \mathcal{O}(n^c)$. We extend F to these additional vertices by making it possible to traverse the edges to the new leaves with cost 1 only at times $\tau+1$ and $\tau+2$. The key observation is that we can visit at most one of these new vertices in any walk of finite cost, so if we increase our budget by 2 and the target number of vertices to visit by one, this instance is again equivalent to the original instance of STAREXP.

2 Trees and Bounded Maximum Traversal Number

We begin by designing algorithms to solve CCTO on temporal cost graphs with restricted underlying graphs and cost functions. This uses a generalisation of the notion of the time expanded graph of a temporal graph, and the fact that this is a directed acyclic graph. We consider several different restrictions on the input, each of which allows us to ensure that we have a path consisting of h edges if and only if we visit at least $g(h)$ distinct vertices in the corresponding walk on the original graph for some computable function g.

We begin by defining the time expanded cost graph; a generalisation of the *time expanded graph* of a temporal graph. Here, for a temporal graph (G, λ), the time expanded graph is a directed graph with vertices u_t for each $u \in V(G)$ and $t \in [\tau]$. For all $u \in V(G)$, there is an arc from u_t to $u_{t'}$ if $t' > t$ and for all $v \in V(G)$, there is an arc from u_t to v_{t+x} if $t \in \lambda(u, v)$ and x is the travel time of such edge at time t. Assuming that the travel times are strictly greater than 0, the time expanded graph is a directed acyclic graph (DAG).

Definition 5 (Time expanded cost graph). *The* time expanded cost graph *of a temporal cost graph (G, F) with lifetime T is a directed graph consisting of a vertex u_t for each $u \in V(G)$ and $t \in [T]$. For all $u, v \in V(G)$, there is an arc from u_{t_1} to v_{t_2} if $F(u, v, t_1, t_2) < \infty$. We call such a graph where the arcs $v_{t_1} u_{t_2}$ are labelled with $F(v, u, t_1, t_2)$ weighted.*

Note that, since the cost of staying at a vertex is 0, there is an arc u_t to $u_{t'}$ in the time expanded cost graph if $t' > t$. As with a time expanded graph, a time expanded cost graph is a DAG. We construct the time-expanded cost graph of a temporal cost graph by adding the necessary vertices and adding arcs where needed for every pair of vertices and pair of increasing times.

Lemma 1. *Given a temporal cost graph (G, F) with n vertices and lifetime T, we can construct its time expanded cost graph in $O(n^2 T^2)$ time.*

Our first result is in the setting where the underlying graph G is a tree, the source and sink are the same vertex s, and the maximum traversal number of any edge in the temporal cost graph (G, F) is at most 3. The intuition of the following result is that, if the underlying graph is a tree, the source and sink are the same vertex, and the maximum traversal number of any edge is 3, any edge can only be used at most twice on a valid walk. We use this fact paired with an auxiliary graph on which we look for a path from a source vertex to a sink vertex. The auxiliary graph is similar to the time expanded cost graph with additional features that we use to keep track of the number of vertices visited by the walk.

To construct the auxiliary graph H, for each $u \in V(G)$, $t \in [T]$ and $i \in [k]$ we add a vertex $u_{t,i}$. If a vertex u is closer to s than a vertex v in G, we add an arc labelled $F(u, v, t_1, t_2)$ from $u_{t_1, i}$ to $v_{t_2, i'}$ where $i' = \min\{i + 1, k\}$ and only if $F(u, v, t_1, t_2)$ is finite. If u is further from s than v is, we add an arc labelled $F(u, v, t_1, t_2)$ from $u_{t_1, i}$ to $v_{t_2, i}$ if and only if $F(u, v, t_1, t_2)$ is finite. That is, we only increment i if we are visiting a new vertex and we have not yet visited k vertices. A sketch of the auxiliary graph construction is given in Fig. 1.

Theorem 1. *CCTO is solvable in $O((nTk)^2)$ time for any instance $((G, F), s, s, k, f)$ where G is a tree with n vertices, the source and sink are the* same vertex s, the lifetime of (G,F) is T, and the maximum traversal number of any edge in (G,F) is at most 3.

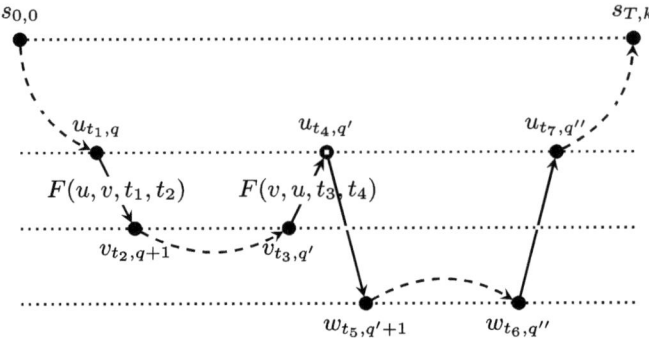

Fig. 1. A weighted path in the auxiliary graph H from $s_{0,0}$ to $s_{T,k}$ is equivalent to a walk from s to itself in the original graph traversing at least k distinct vertices in G. Horizontal dotted lines signify the distance of the corresponding vertices from s in the original graph, dashed arcs replace segments of the walk. For simplicity, the weights are only labelled on the first two arcs pictured.

We can also generalise Theorem 1 to the case where some of the edges can be allowed to have maximum traversal number greater than three.

Theorem 2. *Let (G,F) be a temporal cost graph where G is a tree with n vertices, the lifetime of (G,F) is T and let E' be a subset of edges in G such that the subgraph induced by E' is a forest containing at most ℓ leaves. If every edge in $E(G) \setminus E'$ has maximum traversal number 3, we can solve CCTO on any instance $((G,F), v_s, v_t, k, f)$ in $O(k^2 T^2 n^{2\ell+2})$ time.*

Using similar arguments, we can show that CCTO is solvable in polynomial time in more general graphs with a more restricted cost function. Here we do not explicitly restrict the underlying graph, but we require that there are at most 3 finite cost moves we can make from any starting point.

Theorem 3. *Let (G,F) be a temporal cost graph with n vertices and lifetime T such that, for each vertex $v \in V(G)$ there are only three distinct triples u, t_1, t_2 such that either $F(v, u, t_1, t_2)$ or $F(u, v, t_1, t_2)$ (or both) is finite. Then, CCTO is solvable on any instance $((G,F), v_s, v_t, k, f)$ in $O((nTk)^2)$ time.*

3 Vertex-Interval-Traversal Number

Bumpus and Meeks [7] introduce the parameter *vertex-interval-membership width*, $\omega(G, \lambda)$ of a temporal graph (G, λ), and give an algorithm which computes $\omega(G, \lambda)$ in time $O(\omega(G, \lambda)\tau)$ where τ is the latest time an edge in (G, λ)

is active. The vertex-interval-membership width is calculated by finding the *vertex-interval-membership sequence* of the temporal graph (G, λ). This is the sequence $(F_t)_{t \in [\tau]}$ of vertex-subsets of (G, λ) where $F_t := \{v \in V(G) : \exists i \leq t \leq j$ and $u, w \in V(G)$ such that $i \in \lambda(uv)$ and $j \in \lambda(wv)\}$. The vertex-interval-membership width is $\omega((G, \lambda)) := \max_{t \in \tau} |F_t|$. Roughly speaking, for many problems this parameter bounds the number of vertices of interest at any time (where, for example, a vertex may be considered interesting at time t if we could have reached it before t and subsequently depart at some time after t) [10].

We generalise the definition of vertex-interval-membership sequence to define an analogous parameter for temporal cost graphs.

Definition 6 (Vertex-interval-traversal width). *The* vertex-interval-traversal sequence *of a temporal cost graph (G, F) with lifetime T is the sequence $(H_t)_{t \in [T]}$ of vertex-subsets of G where $H_t := \{v \in V(G) : \exists i \leq t \leq j, t_1, t_2 \in [T]$ and $u, w \in V(G)$ such that $F(u, v, t_1, i) < \infty$ and $F(v, w, j, t_2) < \infty\}$. Note that u and w may be the same vertex. The* vertex-interval-traversal width *is $\varphi((G, F)) := \max_{t \in [T]} |H_t|$.*

We begin by observing that we can compute the vertex-interval-traversal sequence efficiently.

Lemma 2. *Let G be a graph with cost function F with lifetime T such that every edge of G has finite cost for at least one pair of times. Then we can find the vertex-interval-traversal sequence of (G, F) in time $O(n^2 T^2)$.*

Equipped with this notion, we give the following result. Our algorithm functions by dynamic programming over the vertex-interval-traversal sequence. At each time t, we find a set of states corresponding to valid walks which record the last vertex on the walk, the number of vertices traversed on the walk before t which are not in the bag H_t, the set of vertices in H_t traversed by the walk, and the fuel cost of the walk so far.

Theorem 4. *Given a temporal cost graph (G, F) with n vertices, lifetime T, and vertex-interval-traversal width φ, we can solve CCTO in $O(2^{2\varphi} T(\varphi k f)^2 + n^2 T^2)$ time, or $O(2^{2\varphi} T(\varphi k f)^2)$ time when the vertex-interval-traversal sequence is given.*

4 Target Number of Objects

In this section we use a colour-coding argument to show that CCTO is tractable with respect to the number of vertices we are required to visit:

Theorem 5. *Given a temporal cost graph (G, F) with n vertices and lifetime T, and a natural number k indicating the target number of vertices to visit, CCTO is solvable in time $k^{O(k)} T^4 n^4 \log n$.*

Intuitively, using a given arbitrary colouring of the input graph with k colours and an ordering of those colours, we give an algorithm which efficiently verifies whether there exists a valid walk of cost at most f in which at least one vertex of each colour is visited, and the order in which the first vertex of each colour is visited matches the specified order. In particular, this ensures that the walk traverses at least k distinct vertices (although for some colourings and orderings our algorithm may well find walks traversing more than k distinct vertices). Pairing this algorithm with a standard colour-coding technique solves CCTO. Our algorithm makes use of two auxiliary cost functions. The first gives us the minimum cost of a valid walk from one vertex to another given the departure and arrival times of the walk.

Lemma 3. *Let $(G = (V, E), F)$ be a temporal cost graph with n vertices and lifetime T. We can compute, in time $O(n^3 T^4)$, a function $\hat{F} : V \times V \times [T] \times [T] \to \mathbb{N}$ such that, for each pair of (not necessarily adjacent) vertices (u, v) and each pair of times (t_1, t_2), we have that $\hat{F}(u, v, t_1, t_2)$ is the minimum cost of any valid walk from u to v departing at time t_1 and arriving at time t_2 (or ∞ if no such walk exists).*

Using Lemma 3, we now show how to solve a variant of CCTO in which objects have colours, and there are restrictions on the order in which we must visit objects of different colours. The colourful version of our problem is defined as follows:

COLOURFUL CHANGING COST TEMPORAL ORIENTEERING (CCCTO)
Input: A temporal cost graph $(G = (V, E), F)$, a source vertex v_s, sink vertex v_t, a target value $k \in \mathbb{N}$, a colouring $c : V \setminus \{v_s, v_t\} \to [k-2]$, and budget $f \in \mathbb{N}$.
Question: Is there a valid walk in (G, F) from v_s to v_t that visits at least one vertex of each colour and has cost at most f?

The idea of colour coding is to repeatedly solve the colourful version of the problem on instances whose colourings are drawn from an (n, k)-perfect hash family.

Definition 7 (*(n, k)-perfect hash family*). *An (n, k)-perfect hash family $\mathcal{F}$ is a family of functions from $[n]$ to $[k]$ such that for every set S of size k there exists a function c in $\mathcal{F}$ that is injective on S.*

In general, the colour-coding method works as follows. If we know there is a solution to some problem that contains exactly k vertices, we can be sure there is at least one colouring in the family under which these k vertices all receive different colours, and so this colouring will give a yes-instance for the colourful problem. This is exactly the approach used to solve problems such as k-PATH [2].

Here there is subtle but technically important difference from this standard application of the method, because the colourful version of our problem looks for solutions using *at least* one vertex of each colour, not exactly one. This is necessary for two reasons. First, as we have a specified sink vertex, it may be that the least costly walk from source to sink that visits at least k vertices in fact visits more than k vertices (and we cannot simply truncate after the first k). More importantly, as we are looking for walks rather than paths, we may wish to return to previously visited vertices on the way to a new one; since we want to avoid keeping track of all vertices previously visited (this would require us to consider $n^{\Theta(k)}$ possibilities in the worst case) we cannot distinguish between revisiting a vertex we have already counted and visiting a new vertex with the same colour, so we must allow the inclusion of multiple vertices with the same colour.

We will in fact consider all possible orders in which colours might *first* appear on an optimal walk meeting our requirements. Given a permutation π of the set C of colours, we say that a valid walk W *respects* π if the order in which colours first appear on W matches the order given by π. Our second auxiliary cost function gives us the minimum cost of a walk from the source to a vertex which arrives by a specified time and respects a specified colouring. We then solve CCCTO by iterating over all permutations π and using the algorithm given in the following lemma.

Lemma 4. *Given a temporal cost graph $(G = (V, E), F)$ with n vertices and lifetime T, a vertex $v_s \in V$, a colouring $c : V \to [k] \cup \{0\}$ with $c^{-1}(0) = \{v_s\}$ and a permutation π' of $[k]$, we can find in time $O(kn^4T^4)$ the minimum cost of a valid walk that respects π, the permutation of $[k] \cup \{0\}$ obtained from π by adding 0 at the start.*

We now use Lemma 4 to solve the colourful version of our problem by trying each possible order in which the colours can first appear on the walk.

Theorem 6. *Given a temporal cost graph (G, F) with n vertices and lifetime T, we can solve CCCTO on (G, F) in $O(k!n^4T^4)$ time.*

We now show how to use our algorithm for CCCTO to solve the uncoloured version of the problem. We will make use of the following result about (n, k)-perfect families of hash functions, due to Naor et al. [18].

Theorem 7 ([18]). *For any n, $k \geq 1$, an (n, k)-perfect hash family of size $e^k k^{O(\log k)} \log n$ can be found in time $e^k k^{O(\log k)} n \log n$.*

We can now prove Theorem 5.

Proof (Proof of Theorem 5). Given input $((G = (V, E), F), v_s, v_t, k, f)$ to CCTO, our algorithm proceeds as follows.

1. Compute an $(n-2, k)$-perfect hash family $\mathcal{F}$, using the algorithm of Theorem 7.
2. For each function $g \in \mathcal{F}$, let c_g be the corresponding colouring of $V \setminus \{v_1, v_2\}$. Run the algorithm of Theorem 6 on the instance $((G, F), v_s, v_t, k, c_g, f)$ of CCCTO; if this algorithm returns YES, we return YES and halt.
3. Return NO.

It is immediate that, if the algorithm returns YES, we have a yes-instance: CCCTO simply introduces additional constraints compared with CCTO, so if we have a yes-instance to the former with any colouring this certainly corresponds to a yes-instance for the latter. Conversely, suppose that $((G = (V, E), F), v_s, v_t, k, f)$ is a yes-instance of CCTO, and let W be a walk witnessing this fact. Let $v_1, \ldots, v_{k-2}$ be the first $k-2$ vertices other than v_s and v_t on this walk (and note that $k-2$ such vertices must exist, since otherwise it would not visit the requisite number of vertices). By definition of an (n, k)-perfect hash family, there must be some $g \in \mathcal{F}$ such that c_g assigns a different colour to each of $v_1, \ldots, v_{k-2}$. It follows that $((G = (V, E), F), v_s, v_t, k, c_g, f)$ is a yes-instance for CCCTO, so our algorithm will return YES in the iteration corresponding to c_g.

We now consider the running time. Step 1 takes time $e^k k^{O(\log k)} n \log n$ by Theorem 7. We repeat Step 2 a total of $e^k k^{O(\log k)} \log n$ times, and each repetition takes time $O(k! n^4 T^4)$ by Theorem 6. Step 3 takes constant time. The overall running time is therefore $k^{O(k)} T^4 n^4 \log n$. □

Note that if we assume that all costs are integral and positive, the number of objects we visit cannot exceed the budget by more than one. This gives us the following corollary.

Corollary 1. *If all costs assigned by F are integral and positive, CCTO is in FPT with respect to f, the budget of fuel.*

5 Conclusion and Future Work

We have introduced a generalisation of temporal graphs, named temporal cost graphs and used this to define the problem CHANGING COST TEMPORAL ORIENTEERING. We have shown CCTO to be tractable when the underlying graph is a tree and the maximum traversal number of any edge under the function F is restricted. We also show tractability when vertex-interval-traversal width, or number of vertices to be visited k are restricted. These restrictions may not be reasonable in a real-world setting and so a natural step for future work could include an investigation of parameters which both give us tractability and are bounded in real-world applications of this model. In particular, these could arise from the complex but periodic nature of distances between orbiting objects.

Another possible avenue for future work is to investigate approximation algorithms for CCTO. To the best of the authors' knowledge, the closest problem to CCTO for which there exists an approximation algorithm is Time-Dependent Orienteering, for which there exists a $(2+\varepsilon)$-approximation algorithm [12]. Their algorithm cannot be simply adapted to solve CCTO because their problem does not allow vertices to be revisited in a solution. Another possibility would be to start from the algorithm given by Chekuri et al. [9] for the Orienteering problem where walks are allowed. However, this will likely require a significantly worse approximation factor or an exponential runtime caused by the addition of the fuel cost function to the problem.

Acknowledgments. Timothée Corsini is supported by ANR TEMPOGRAL ANR-22-CE48-0001. Jessica Enright and Kitty Meeks is supported by EPSRC grants EP/T004878/1 and EP/V032305/1. Jessica Enright is supported by EPSRC grant EP/T004878/1. For the purpose of open access, the author(s) has applied a Creative Commons Attribution (CC BY) licence to any Author Accepted Manuscript version arising from this submission.

Disclosure of Interests. The authors have no competing interests to declare.

References

1. Akrida, E.C., Mertzios, G.B., Spirakis, P.G., Raptopoulos, C.: The temporal explorer who returns to the base. J. Comput. Syst. Sci. **120**, 179–193 (2021)
2. Alon, N., Yuster, R., Zwick, U.: Color-coding. J. ACM **42**(4), 844–856 (1995). https://doi.org/10.1145/210332.210337
3. Awerbuch, B., Azar, Y., Blum, A., Vempala, S.: Improved approximation guarantees for minimum-weight k-trees and prize-collecting salesmen. In: Proceedings of the twenty-seventh annual ACM Symp. Theor. Comput. 277–283 (1995)
4. Balas, E.: The prize collecting traveling salesman problem. Networks **19**(6), 621–636 (1989)
5. Blum, A., Chawla, S., Karger, D.R., Lane, T., Meyerson, A., Minkoff, M.: Approximation algorithms for orienteering and discounted-reward tsp. SIAM J. Comput. **37**(2), 653–670 (2007)
6. Buchin, K., Hagedoorn, M., Li, G., Rehs, C.: Orienteering (with time windows) on restricted graph classes. In: International Conference on Current Trends in Theory and Practice of Computer Science, pp. 151–165. Springer (2025)
7. Bumpus, B.M., Meeks, K.: Edge exploration of temporal graphs. corr, abs/2103.05387. arXiv preprint arXiv:2103.05387 (2021)
8. Casteigts, A., Flocchini, P., Quattrociocchi, W., Santoro, N.: Time-varying graphs and dynamic networks. Int. J. Parallel Emergent Distrib. Syst. **27**(5), 387–408 (2012)
9. Chekuri, C., Korula, N., Pál, M.: Improved algorithms for orienteering and related problems. ACM Trans. Algorithms (TALG) **8**(3), 1–27 (2012)
10. Enright, J., Hand, S.D., Larios-Jones, L., Meeks, K.: Families of tractable problems with respect to vertex-interval-membership width and its generalisations. arXiv preprint arXiv:2505.15699 (2025)
11. Feillet, D., Dejax, P., Gendreau, M.: Traveling salesman problems with profits. Transp. Sci. **39**(2), 188–205 (2005). https://doi.org/10.1287/trsc.1030.0079, publisher: INFORMS
12. Fomin, F.V., Lingas, A.: Approximation algorithms for time-dependent orienteering. Inf. Process. Lett. (2002)
13. Gavish, B., Graves, S.C.: The travelling salesman problem and related problems. Working Paper, Massachusetts Institute of Technology, Operations Research Center, July 1978, https://dspace.mit.edu/handle/1721.1/5363, Accepted 28 May 2004 T19:35:47Z
14. Golden, B.L., Levy, L., Vohra, R.: The orienteering problem. Naval Res. Logist. (NRL) **34**(3), 307–318 (1987). https://doi.org/10.1002/1520-6750(198706)34:3⟨307::AID-NAV3220340302⟩3.0.CO;2-D

15. Kellerer, H., Pferschy, U., Pisinger, D.: Knapsack Problems. Springer, Berlin, Heidelberg (2004). https://doi.org/10.1007/978-3-540-24777-7
16. Laporte, G., Martello, S.: The selective travelling salesman problem. Discret. Appl. Math. **26**(2), 193–207 (1990). https://doi.org/10.1016/0166-218X(90)90100-Q
17. López-Ibáñez, M., Chicano, F., Gil-Merino, R.: The asteroid routing problem: a benchmark for expensive black-box permutation optimization. In: Jiménez Laredo, J.L., Hidalgo, J.I., Babaagba, K.O. (eds.) EvoApplications 2022. LNCS, vol. 13224, pp. 124–140. Springer, Cham (2022). https://doi.org/10.1007/978-3-031-02462-7_9
18. Naor, M., Schulman, L., Srinivasan, A.: Splitters and near-optimal derandomization. In: Proceedings of IEEE 36th Annual Foundations of Computer Science, pp. 182–191 (1995). https://doi.org/10.1109/SFCS.1995.492475
19. Vansteenwegen, P., Souffriau, W., Oudheusden, D.V.: The orienteering problem: a survey. Eur. J. Oper. Res. **209**(1), 1–10 (2011)

Parameterised Algorithms for Temporally Satisfying Reconfiguration Problems

Tom Davot[1,2], Jessica Enright[2], and Laura Larios-Jones[2(✉)]

[1] Univ Angers, LERIA, SFR MATHSTIC, 49000 Angers, France
tom.davot@univ-angers.fr
[2] School of Computing Science, University of Glasgow, Glasgow, UK
jessica.enright@glasgow.ac.uk, l.larios-jones.1@research.gla.ac.uk

Abstract. Given a static vertex-selection problem (e.g. independent set, dominating set) on a graph, we can define a corresponding temporally satisfying reconfiguration problem on a temporal graph which asks for a sequence of solutions to the vertex-selection problem at each time such that we can reconfigure from one solution to the next. We can think of each solution in the sequence as a set of vertices with tokens placed on them; our reconfiguration model allows us to slide tokens along active edges of a temporal graph at each time-step.

We show that it is possible to efficiently check whether one solution can be reconfigured to another, and show that approximation results on the static vertex-selection problem can be adapted with a lifetime factor to the reconfiguration version. Our main contributions are fixed-parameter tractable algorithms with respect to: enumeration time of the related static problem; the combination of temporal neighbourhood diversity and lifetime of the input temporal graph; and the combination of lifetime and treewidth of the footprint graph.

Keywords: parameterised algorithms · temporal graphs · reconfiguration

1 Introduction

In many classical graph problems in static settings, the aim is to select a subset of vertices respecting some specified property, while minimizing or maximizing the number of selected vertices (e.g. maximum independent set, minimum dominating set, maximum clique). Recently, reconfiguration versions of classical vertex-selection problems have been studied on static graphs, where the goal is typically to determine whether one valid solution can be transformed into another through a sequence of small modifications [8,26].

Formally, reconfiguration versions of vertex-selection problems in static graphs can be defined as follows. Let Π be a vertex-selection problem such as INDEPENDENT SET or DOMINATING SET. Reconfiguration problems on static graphs are often defined with a starting and end solution S and T respectively.

The aim is to determine if there is a sequence of vertex sets starting with S and ending with T such that each is a solution for Π and consecutive sets are adjacent in the space of solutions. The definition of solution adjacency varies according to model. In the *token sliding model*, a solution can be seen as a set of tokens placed on the vertices of G [20]. A solution S_1 is adjacent to another solution S_2 if we can transform S_1 into S_2 by sliding one token of S_1 along an edge uv of G such that $S_1 \setminus S_2 = \{u\}$ and $S_2 \setminus S_1 = \{v\}$. Both INDEPENDENT SET RECONFIGURATION and DOMINATING SET RECONFIGURATION have been studied in parameterised [1,3] and classical [7,27] settings.

Hearn and Demain [20] show that INDEPENDENT SET RECONFIGURATION under token sliding is PSPACE-complete even in planar graphs with bounded degree. It is also known to be PSPACE-complete when restricted to other classes of graphs such as split graphs [2], bipartite graphs [25], and graphs of bounded bandwidth [30]. On the positive side, there are polynomial time algorithms when restricted to trees [12], interval graphs [5], bipartite permutation graphs [16] and line graphs [21].

For DOMINATING SET RECONFIGURATION under token sliding, the problem is also known to be PSPACE-complete when restricted to split, bipartite and bounded tree-width graphs [19], or restricted to circle graphs [6]. The problem is polynomial-time solvable on dually chordal graphs, cographs [19] and on circular-arc graphs [6].

While these reconfiguration problems provide valuable insights into how dynamic solutions can evolve in static graphs, they cannot model scenarios where the underlying structure of the graph evolves. This motivates the study of reconfiguration in a temporal setting, where the set of edges changes in each time-step. Based on some vertex selection problem, we define a *temporally satisfying reconfiguration problem*, which differs slightly from the common reconfiguration setup: instead of being given a starting and end solution, we instead ask if there exists a sequence of solutions for each time-step such that each set can be reconfigured into the next via token sliding. Moreover, while the token sliding model in static settings only allows one token to move at a time, we generalise by allowing all tokens to move along available edges simultaneously at each time-step. Verheije studied a version of this problem for DOMINATING SET on temporal graphs [29], under the name MARCHING DOMINATING. He developed an exact exponential-time algorithm to determine whether a solution of DOMINATING SET with at most k tokens can be maintained in a temporal graph. TEMPORAL ARBORESCENCE RECONFIGURATION has also been studied and shown to be NP-hard when the temporal graph only consists of two time-steps [13]. Importantly, in our model, we require the vertices selected at any time to be a solution to the vertex-selection problem on the snapshot at that time. This is what gives these reconfiguration problems the name "temporally satisfying". We also note that all of our results hold on the restrictions of the problems where the start and end solution are given – as is typically the case in static reconfiguration problems.

The paper is organised as follows: in Sect. 2, we introduce basic graph and temporal graph notation. In Sect. 3, we formally introduce temporally satisfying reconfiguration problems and define a transformation of any vertex-selection problem on a static graph into a temporally satisfying reconfiguration problem. In Sect. 4, we describe two preliminary results on temporal graphs, showing we can check if a specified sequence is temporally reconfigurable, and giving an approximation result. In Sects. 5, 6, and 7 we give parameterised algorithmic results: in Sect. 5, we study the parameterisation of temporally satisfying reconfiguration problems by the enumeration time of their static versions; in Sect. 6, we parameterise by temporal neighbourhood diversity and lifetime; finally, in Sect. 7, we parameterise by treewidth of the footprint graph. To save space the proofs are omitted. They can be found in the arXiv version of this work.

2 Notation

Where possible, we use standard graph theoretic notation, and direct the reader to [18] for detail. A static graph is a pair $G = (V, E)$ where $V(G) = V$ is the vertex set and $E(G) = E$ is the edge set. We also use standard definitions and notation of parameterised algorithmics as in [11]. A *matching* $M \subseteq E(G)$ of graph G is a set of edges that are pairwise disjoint. A matching M is *perfect* if each vertex $v \in V(G)$ is in exactly one edge in M. Finally, given two subsets of vertices X and Y, we say that there is a *perfect matching between* X and Y if there exists a perfect matching in the bipartite subgraph H with $V(H) = X \cup Y$ and $E(H) = \{xy \mid xy \in E(G), x \in X, y \in Y\}$.

2.1 Temporal Graphs

A *temporal graph* $\mathcal{G}$ is a pair (G, λ), where G is a static graph and $\lambda : E(G) \to 2^{\mathbb{N}}$ is a function called the *time-labelling function*; for each edge $e \in E(G)$, $\lambda(e)$ denotes the set of time-steps at which e is active. The *lifetime* of $\mathcal{G}$, denoted by $\tau_{\mathcal{G}}$, is the maximum time-step at which an edge is active, i.e., $\tau_{\mathcal{G}} = \max \bigcup_{e \in E(G)} \lambda(e)$. When $\mathcal{G}$ is clear from the context, we may drop the subscript and simply write τ. For a temporal graph $\mathcal{G} = (G, \lambda)$ and $t \in [\tau]$, the *snapshot* of $\mathcal{G}$ at time-step t is the static graph G_t that consists of all the edges of G that are active at time-step t, i.e., $V(G_t) = V(G)$ and $E(G_t) = \{e \in E(G) \mid t \in \lambda(e)\}$. For $v \in V(G_t)$, we use $N_t(v)$ (resp. $N_t[v]$) to denote the set of neighbours (resp. closed neighbours) of v in the graph G_t. The *footprint* of a temporal graph is the static graph formed by taking the union of the temporal graph at all time-steps.

3 Temporally Satisfying Reconfiguration Problems

We now define temporally satisfying reconfiguration problems and give some intuition. Here we define a temporally satisfying reconfiguration problem from a static graph vertex selection problem: any optimisation problem in which we choose a set of vertices that respect some property, with the aim of either maximising or minimising the number of vertices in the selected set. Intuitively, we can think of a set of selected vertices as a set of tokens placed on those vertices. Then, we require the vertices indicated by tokens to meet a required property at each time-step, and allow movement over an edge of each token at every time-step. Importantly, each vertex can only contain at most one token. At each time-step and for each token, we have two possibilities: either to keep the token on the same vertex or to move the token to an adjacent vertex. We then ask for the optimum number of tokens such that we respect the required property at each time and can also reconfigure the tokens from each time-step to the next.

Formally, let $T_1, T_2 \subseteq V(G)$ be two sets of selected vertices in a temporal graph $\mathcal{G}$. We say that T_1 is *reconfigurable* into T_2 at time-step t if it is possible to move the tokens from the vertices of T_1 to the vertices of T_2 in G_t. Observe that T_1 is reconfigurable into T_2 at time-step t if there is a bijection $b : T_1 \to T_2$, called a *reconfiguration bijection*, such that for each $(u,v) \in b$, either $u = v$ (i.e. the token remains on the same vertex) or $uv \in G_t$ (i.e. the token moves from u to v on the edge uv).

Notice that if T_1 is reconfigurable into T_2, then we have $|T_1| = |T_2|$. Let $T = (T_1, \ldots, T_\tau)$ be a sequence such that for all $i \in [\tau]$, $T_i \subseteq V(G)$. We say that T is a *reconfigurable sequence* of $\mathcal{G}$ if for each time-step $t \in [\tau - 1]$, T_t is reconfigurable into T_{t+1} at time-step t. We denote by $|T| = |T_1| = \cdots = |T_\tau|$ the *size* of the sets in the reconfigurable sequence T. In a temporally satisfying reconfiguration problem, we aim to find a reconfigurable sequence such that at each time-step t, the set of selected vertices T_t respects a specific property Π in G_t. This gives the formal basis for transforming a static vertex selection problem to a temporally satisfying reconfiguration problem. Consider the following generic vertex selection graph problem in a static setting:

Π STATIC GRAPH PROBLEM
Input: A static graph G.
Question: Find a minimum/maximum set of vertices X that respects property Π in G.

The corresponding temporally satisfying reconfiguration problem can be formulated as follow:

TEMPORAL Π RECONFIGURATION PROBLEM
Input: A temporal graph $\mathcal{G} = (G, \lambda)$ with lifetime τ.
Question: Find a reconfigurable sequence $T = (T_1, \ldots, T_\tau)$ of $\mathcal{G}$ of minimum/maximum size $|T|$ such that each T_t respects property Π in G_t.

For the sake of simplicity, we refer to "static problem" to exclusively refer to a vertex selection problem in a static graph while "temporally satisfying reconfiguration problem" will refer to a temporally satisfying reconfiguration version of a static problem. Notice that, since any static graph is a temporal graph of lifetime 1, if a static problem is NP-hard, then the corresponding temporally satisfying reconfiguration problem is also NP-hard. More generally, any lower bounds on complexity can be transferred from the static problem to the temporally satisfying reconfiguration problem. As an example, we will use two classical problems, DOMINATING SET and INDEPENDENT SET to illustrate the methods used throughout the paper.

Example 1 (Dominating Set). *A dominating set $D \subseteq V(G)$ is a set of vertices such that for each $v \in V(G)$, we have $N[v] \cap D \neq \emptyset$.*

A classical optimisation problem is to find a dominating set of minimum size in a static graph. This problem is known to be NP-complete [17].

Example 2 (Independent Set). *An independent set $I \subseteq V(G)$ is a set of pairwise non-adjacent vertices.*

Finding an independent set of maximum size is one of Karp's NP-complete problems [22]. In the following, we refer to the temporally satisfying reconfiguration versions of DOMINATING SET and INDEPENDENT SET as TEMPORAL DOMINATING SET RECONFIGURATION and TEMPORAL INDEPENDENT SET RECONFIGURATION, respectively.

4 Preliminary Results

In the remainder of this paper we present a number of algorithmic results; here we start with several initial results first showing that we can efficiently check if a given sequence is reconfigurable, and then presenting a condition for a reconfiguration problem to belong to the same approximation class as its static version.

4.1 Checking if a Sequence is Reconfigurable

We show that testing if a sequence $(T_1, \ldots, T_\tau)$ is a reconfigurable sequence of a temporal graph $\mathcal{G} = (G, \lambda)$ can be done in polynomial time. We begin with the smaller problem of checking whether one state can be reconfigured into another. This can be done by computing a perfect matching in a bipartite graph that captures what set changes are possible between time-steps. Details and proofs are deferred to the full version of the paper.

Lemma 1. *Let G be a static graph and let T_1 and T_2 be two subsets of vertices. We can determine in $\mathcal{O}((|V(G)|+|E(G)|) \cdot \sqrt{|V(G)|})$ time if T_1 is reconfigurable into T_2.*

We now extend the previous result to show that testing if a sequence is reconfigurable can also be done in polynomial time.

Corollary 1. *Let $\mathcal{G} = (G, \lambda)$ be a temporal graph. Let $T = (T_1, \ldots, T_\tau)$ be a sequence such that for all $i \in [\tau]$, $T_i \subseteq V(G)$. We can determine whether T is a reconfigurable sequence in $\mathcal{O}(\tau \cdot (|V(G)| + |E(G)| \cdot \sqrt{|V(G)|}))$ time.*

4.2 Approximation

We now turn our attention to the approximation of temporally satisfying reconfiguration problems. An optimisation problem belongs to the approximation class $f(n)$-APX if it is possible to approximate this problem in polynomial time with a $\mathcal{O}(f(n))$ approximation factor. Let Π_S be a minimisation static problem. A f-approximation algorithm for Π_S is a polynomial time algorithm that, given a graph G, returns an approximate solution X_{app} such that $|X_{app}| \leq f(G) \cdot |X_{opt}|$, where X_{opt} is an optimal solution for Π_S in G.

Theorem 1. *Let Π_S be a minimisation static graph problem such that for any solution S and any vertex v, $S \cup \{v\}$ is also a solution. Let Π_T be the corresponding temporally satisfying reconfiguration version of Π_S. If Π_S is f-approximable, then Π_T is $\tau \cdot f$-approximable.*

DOMINATING SET is known to be Log-APX-complete [15], *i.e.* there is a polynomial-time *log*-approximation algorithm and there is no polynomial-time approximation algorithm with a constant ratio. Thus, we obtain the following result.

Corollary 2. *There is a $(\tau \cdot \log)$-approximation algorithm for* TEMPORAL DOMINATING SET RECONFIGURATION.

5 Fixed-Parameter Tractability with Respect to the Enumeration Time of the Static Version

We show in this section that if the number of solutions for a static problem Π_S can be bounded by some function $f(G)$, then the temporally satisfying reconfiguration version is in FPT with respect to $f(G)$.

Lemma 2. *Let Π_S be a static problem and let Π_T be the temporally satisfying reconfiguration version of Π_S. Let $\mathcal{G} = (G, \lambda)$ be a temporal graph such that for all $t \in [\tau]$, all solutions in G_t for Π_S can be enumerated in $\mathcal{O}(f(G))$. We can solve Π_T in $\mathcal{O}(f(G)^2 \cdot \tau \cdot (|V(G)| + |E(G)|) \cdot \sqrt{|V(G)|})$ time.*

Let $|E|_{\max}$ denote $\max_{t \in [\tau]} |E_t|$, the maximum number of edges in any snapshot of the temporal graph $\mathcal{G}$. We use Lemma 2 to show inclusion of TEMPORAL DOMINATING SET RECONFIGURATION in FPT with respect to $|E|_{\max}$. First, we show that the number of dominating sets is bounded by a function of $|E|_{\max}$ in each snapshot.

Lemma 3. *Let $\mathcal{G} = (G, \lambda)$ be a temporal graph. For each $t \in [\tau]$, all dominating sets of G_t can be enumerated in $\mathcal{O}(2^{|E|_{max}} \cdot |E|_{max})$ time.*

Now, we can conclude that TEMPORAL DOMINATING SET RECONFIGURATION is in FPT with respect to $|E|_{\max}$.

Corollary 3. TEMPORAL DOMINATING SET RECONFIGURATION *can be solved in $\mathcal{O}(4^{|E|_{max}} \cdot \tau \cdot (|V(G)| + |E(G)| \cdot \sqrt{|V(G)|}))$ time.*

6 Fixed Parameter Tractability by Lifetime and Temporal Neighbourhood Diversity

In this section we present a fixed-parameter algorithm, parametrised by lifetime and the temporal neighbourhood diversity of the temporal graph, to solve a class of temporally satisfying reconfiguration problems that we call *temporal neighbourhood diversity locally decidable*.

We need a number of algorithmic tools to build toward this overall result. First, in Subsect. 6.1, we give definitions and notation necessary for this section, including defining temporal neighbourhood diversity, as well as the class of temporal neighbourhood diversity locally decidable problems. These build on analogous definitions in static graphs.

Then, in Subsect. 6.2 we describe an overall algorithm to solve our restricted class of problems that is in FPT with respect to temporal neighbourhood diversity and lifetime. This algorithm uses a critical subroutine that constitutes the majority of the technical detail, and is presented in Subsect. 6.3. The subroutine uses a reduction to the efficiently-solvable circulation problem to give the key result (in Lemma 6). The result allows us to efficiently generate an optimal reconfigurable sequence that is compatible with a candidate reconfiguration sequence of a type specific to temporal neighbourhood diversity locally decidable problems.

6.1 Definitions

Neighbourhood diversity is a static graph parameter introduced by Lampis [24]:

Definition 1 (Neighbourhood Diversity [24]). *The* neighbourhood diversity *of a static graph G is the minimum value k such that the vertices of G can be partitioned into k classes $V_1, \ldots, V_k$ such that for each pair of vertices u and v in a class V_i, we have $N(u) \setminus \{v\} = N(v) \setminus \{u\}$. We call $V_1, \ldots, V_k$ a* neighbourhood diversity partition *of G.*

Notice that each set V_i of P forms an independent set or a clique. Moreover, for any pair of sets V_i and V_j either no vertex of V_i is adjacent to any vertex of V_j or every vertex of V_i is adjacent to every vertex of V_j. We distinguish two types of classes: V_i is a *clique-class* if $G[V_i]$ is a clique and V_i is an *independent-class* otherwise.

Definition 2 (Neighbourhood diversity graph). *Let G be a static graph with neighbourhood diversity partition $V_1, \ldots, V_k$. The* neighbourhood diversity graph *of G, denoted ND_G is the graph obtained by merging each class V_i into a single vertex. Formally, we have $V(ND_G) = \{V_1, \ldots, V_k\}$ and $E(ND_G) = \{V_i V_j \mid \forall v_i \in V_i, \forall v_j \in V_j, v_i v_j \in E(G)\}$.*

For clarity, we use the term class when referring to a vertex of ND_G, in order to distinguish between the vertices of G and the vertices of ND_G.

Let X be a set of vertices and Y be a set of classes. We say that X and Y are *compatible* if each class V_i belongs to Y if and only if V_i intersects X, that is, $\forall V_i : (V_i \cap X \neq \emptyset \Leftrightarrow V_i \in Y)$. Notice that there is exactly one subset of classes that is compatible with a set of vertices X whereas several subsets of vertices of G can be compatible with a set of classes Y.

We now introduce the concept of a neighbourhood diversity locally decidable problem – we do this first in the static setting in order to build into the temporal setting. Intuitively, these are problems for which, given a set of classes Y, we can determine the minimum and maximum number of vertices to select in each class that are realised by at least one solution compatible with Y, if such a solution exists. The formal definition is as follows:

Definition 3 (Neighbourhood diversity locally decidable). *A static graph problem Π_S is $f(n)$-neighbourhood diversity locally decidable if for any static graph G with n vertices and every subset of classes Y of ND_G, the following two conditions hold:*

(a) there is a computable function $check_{\Pi_S}(Y)$ with time complexity $\mathcal{O}(f(n))$ that determines if there is a solution for Π_S in G that is compatible with Y,
(b) if there is such a solution, then there exist two computable functions $low_{\Pi_S} : \mathcal{P}(V(ND_G)) \times V(ND_G) \to \mathbb{N}$ and $up_{\Pi_S} : \mathcal{P}(V(ND_G)) \times V(ND_G) \to \mathbb{N}$ with time complexity $\mathcal{O}(f(n))$ such that, for all subsets $X \subseteq V(G)$, X is a solution for Π_S and is compatible with Y if and only if, for all $V_i \in V(ND_G)$, $low_{\Pi_S}(Y, V_i) \leq |V_i \cap X| \leq up_{\Pi_S}(Y, V_i)$.

In other words, low_{Π_S} and up_{Π_S} are necessary and sufficient lower and upper bounds for the number of selected vertices in each class in a solution to our problem in the graph of low neighbourhood diversity.

Notice that it is easy to compute a solution of minimum (respectively maximum) size that is compatible with a subset of classes Y (if such a solution exists), by arbitrarily selecting exactly $low_{\Pi_S}(V_i)$ (resp. $up_{\Pi_S}(V_i)$) vertices inside each class. Hence, Π_S is solvable in $\mathcal{O}(2^k \cdot f(n))$, where k is the neighbourhood diversity of the graph. Indeed, it suffices to enumerate every subset of classes and keep the best solution. It follows that if $check_{\Pi_S}$, low_{Π_S} and up_{Π_S} are polynomial time functions, Π_S is in FPT when parameterised by neighbourhood diversity.

The problems DOMINATING SET and INDEPENDENT SET are $f(n)$-neighbourhood diversity locally decidable.

Lemma 4. DOMINATING SET *is $f(n)$-neighbourhood diversity locally decidable where $f(n) \in O(n)$.*

Lemma 5. INDEPENDENT SET *is $f(n)$-neighbourhood diversity locally decidable where $f(n) \in O(n)$.*

In Temporal Graphs. We now extend the concept of neighbourhood diversity locally decidable problems to a temporal setting. We use temporal neighbourhood diversity introduced by Enright et al. [14].

Definition 4 (Temporal Neighbourhood Diversity [14]). *The temporal neighbourhood diversity of a temporal graph $\mathcal{G} = (G, \lambda)$ is the minimum value k such that the vertices of G can be partitioned into k classes $V_1, \ldots, V_k$ such that for each pair of vertices u and v in a class V_i, we have $N_t(u) \setminus \{v\} = N_t(v) \setminus \{u\}$ at each time-step $t \in [1, \tau]$. We call $V_1, \ldots, V_k$ a temporal neighbourhood diversity partition of $\mathcal{G}$.*

As for the static parameter, we can use a graph to represent the partition.

Definition 5 (Temporal neighbourhood diversity graph). *Let $\mathcal{G} = (G, \lambda)$ be a temporal graph with temporal neighbourhood partition $V_1, \ldots, V_k$. The temporal neighbourhood diversity graph of $\mathcal{G}$, denoted $TND_\mathcal{G}$ is the temporal graph obtained by merging every class V_i into a single vertex. Formally, we have $V(TND_\mathcal{G}) = \{V_1, \ldots, V_k\}$, $E(TND_\mathcal{G}) = \{V_i V_j \mid \forall v_i \in V_i, \forall v_j \in V_j, v_i v_j \in E(G)\}$ and $\lambda(V_i V_j) = \lambda(u_i u_j)$ for any vertices $u_i \in V_i$ and $u_j \in V_j$.*

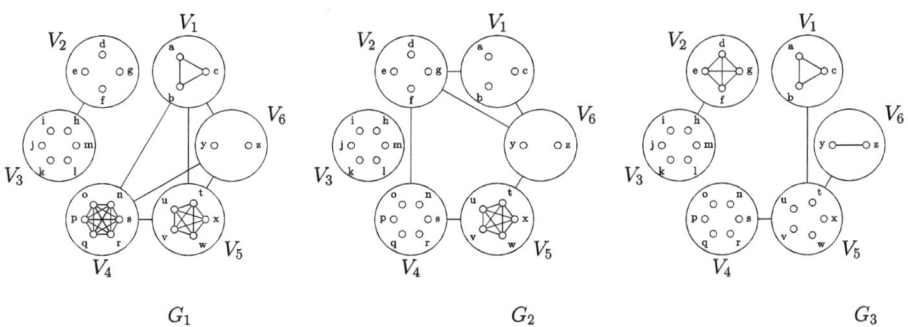

Fig. 1. Example of temporal neighbourhood diversity graph $TND_\mathcal{G}$ of a temporal graph $\mathcal{G} = (G, \lambda)$. An edge between two sets V_i and V_j indicates that each vertex of V_i is adjacent to all vertices of V_j.

An example of a temporal neighbourhood diversity graph is depicted in Fig. 1. Let Π_T be a temporally satisfying reconfiguration problem. We call Π_T $f(n)$-*temporal neighbourhood diversity locally decidable* if the static version Π_S of Π_T is $f(n)$-neighbourhood diversity locally decidable. In both of the problems we consider $f(n) = n$. For a temporal graph $\mathcal{G} = (G, \lambda)$, we denote by $low^t_{\Pi_T}$ and $up^t_{\Pi_T}$ the functions giving the lower and upper bounds on the number of selected vertices in a class V_i needed to obtain a solution for Π_S in G_t, as in Definition 3.

6.2 FPT Algorithm with Respect to Temporal Neighbourhood Diversity and Lifetime

We now formulate an FPT algorithm using temporal neighbourhood diversity and lifetime to solve a $f(n)$-temporal neighbourhood diversity locally decidable reconfiguration problem Π_T in a temporal graph $\mathcal{G} = (G, \lambda)$. A candidate *sequence* is a sequence $Y = (Y_1, \ldots, Y_\tau)$ such that for each $t \in [\tau]$, Y_t is a subset of classes of the temporal neighbourhood diversity partition. We say that Y is *valid* if $check_{\Pi_T}(Y_t) = \text{true}$ for all $t \in [\tau]$. Let $T = (T_1, \ldots, T_\tau)$ be a reconfigurable sequence for $\mathcal{G}$. For the sake of simplicity, we say that the two sequences Y and T are compatible if for each $t \in [\tau]$, T_t and Y_t are compatible.

The principle of the algorithm is to iterate through each candidate sequence Y and, if Y is valid, compute an optimal reconfigurable sequence T compatible with Y. Then, we return the optimal solution among all solutions associated to valid candidate sequences. Notice that there are at most $2^{tnd \cdot \tau}$ candidate sequences to consider, where tnd is the temporal neighbourhood diversity of the input graph. Hence, we can expect the algorithm to be efficient if the temporal graph has small temporal neighbourhood diversity and short lifetime. If Π_T is $f(n)$-temporal neighbourhood diversity locally decidable, we show in Subsect. 6.3 how to compute an optimal reconfigurable sequence compatible with a candidate sequence, if one exists, by solving an instance of the circulation problem. Combining the observation that there are at most $2^{tnd \cdot \tau}$ candidate sequences to consider and the result from Subsect. 6.3 gives us the following result, which we restate at the end of that subsection.

Lemma. *Let $\mathcal{G} = (G, \lambda)$ be a temporal graph and let Π_T be an $f(n)$-temporal neighbourhood diversity locally decidable reconfiguration problem. Π_T is solvable in $\mathcal{O}(2^{(tnd \cdot \tau)} \cdot (\tau \cdot tnd \cdot f(n) + \tau^{11/2} \cdot tnd^8))$ time where tnd is the temporal neighbourhood diversity of $\mathcal{G} = (G, \lambda)$.*

6.3 Computing an Optimal Reconfigurable Sequence Compatible with a Candidate Sequence

In this subsection, we present an efficient method for computing an optimal reconfigurable sequence T compatible with a particular valid sequence Y. Note that it is inefficient to compute T by exhaustively generating all possible sequences in $\mathcal{G}$ and selecting the best one compatible with Y, as this would have time complexity of $\mathcal{O}(2^{\tau \cdot |V(G)|})$ for each candidate sequence making it impractical.

Our algorithm uses an instance of the circulation problem as a subroutine, with details deferred to the arXiv version. The circulation problem is a variation of the network flow problem on digraphs for which there are upper and lower bounds on the capacities of the arcs.

Formally, a *circulation graph* $\overrightarrow{F} = (F, c, l, u)$ consists of a directed graph F, along with a cost function $c : A(F) \to \mathbb{N}$ on the arcs and two functions on the arcs $l : A(F) \to \mathbb{N}$ and $u : A(F) \to \mathbb{N}$, representing the lower and upper bounds of the flow capacities. The digraph F also has two designated vertices sou and tar representing the source and the target vertices of the flow, respectively.

In the circulation problem, we want to find a *circulation flow* between sou and tar, which is a function $g : A(F) \to \mathbb{N}$ that respects two constraints:

(a) *Flow preservation*: the flow entering in any vertex $v \in V(F) \setminus \{sou, tar\}$ is equal to the flow leaving it, that is, $\sum_{u \in N^+(v)} g(u,v) = \sum_{u \in N^-(v)} g(v,u)$.
(b) *Capacity*: for all arcs $(u,v) \in A(F)$, the amount of flow over (u,v) must respect the capacity of (u,v), that is, $l(u,v) \leq g(u,v) \leq u(u,v)$.

Formally, the circulation problem is defined as follows.

CIRCULATION PROBLEM
Input: A circulation digraph $\vec{F}$ with capacity $c(a)$ on each arc a, a source vertex sou and a target vertex tar.
Question: Find a circulation flow g that minimises $\sum_{a \in A(F)} g(a) \cdot c(a)$.

The circulation problem is known to be solvable in $\mathcal{O}(|A(F)|^{5/2} \cdot |V(F)|^3)$ [28]. Notice that the circulation problem can easily be transformed into a maximisation problem by modifying all positive costs into negative costs.

Intuitively, we encode a candidate sequence for a temporally satisfying reconfiguration problem as an instance of the circulation problem in which each timestep is encoded as two layers of the digraph in the circulation problem and the arcs and capacities model the reconfigurability constraints between timesteps as well as the requirement that a set of vertices meets the required property at each time.

This gives us the tools to produce the following Lemma:

Lemma 6. *Let Π be a $f(n)$-neighbourhood diversity locally decidable problem, let $\mathcal{G} = (G, \lambda)$ be a temporal graph with lifetime τ and temporal neighbourhood diversity tnd and let Y be a valid candidate sequence. It is possible to compute an optimal reconfigurable sequence T compatible with Y in $\mathcal{O}(\tau \cdot tnd \cdot f(n) + \tau^{11/2} \cdot tnd^8)$ time.*

We now have the necessary tools for the overall algorithmic result:

Lemma 7. *Let $\mathcal{G} = (G, \lambda)$ be a temporal graph and let Π be an $f(n)$-temporal neighbourhood diversity locally decidable reconfiguration problem. Π is solvable in $\mathcal{O}(2^{(tnd \cdot \tau)} \cdot (\tau \cdot tnd \cdot f(n) + \tau^{11/2} \cdot tnd^8))$ time where tnd is the temporal neighbourhood diversity of $\mathcal{G} = (G, \lambda)$.*

Corollary 4. *Let $\mathcal{G} = (G, \lambda)$ be a temporal graph with temporal neighbourhood diversity tnd and lifetime τ. TEMPORAL DOMINATING SET RECONFIGURATION and TEMPORAL INDEPENDENT SET RECONFIGURATION are solvable in $\mathcal{O}(2^{(tnd \cdot \tau)} \cdot (\tau^{11/2} \cdot tnd^8))$ time in $\mathcal{G}$.*

7 Fixed-Parameter Tractability with Respect to Lifetime and Treewidth of Footprint

Courcelle's celebrated theorem [9,10] tells us that any static graph problem that can be encoded in monadic second-order logic (MSO) is in FPT with respect to the treewidth of the graph and the length of the MSO expression. We make use of this standard tool to argue that if a static problem Π_S is definable in the monadic second-order logic, then its reconfiguration version Π_T is FPT when parameterized by the treewidth of the footprint and the lifetime of the temporal graph. The definition of treewidth is given in [4,23]. Roughly, it is a measure of how "tree-like" a static graph is.

Theorem 2 (Courcelle's theorem [9,10]). *Let G be a simple graph of treewidth tw and a fixed MSO sentence ϕ, there exists an algorithm that tests if $G \models \phi$ and runs in $\mathcal{O}(f(tw, |\phi|) \cdot |G|)$ time, where f is a computable function.*

Intuitively, we use a static auxiliary graph to encode the temporal graph $\mathcal{G}$ of size a linear factor of τ larger than $\mathcal{G}$. Then, using the MSO formula of the static problem, we encode the corresponding temporally satisfying reconfiguration problem by adapting the original formula to the auxiliary graph and adding the reconfiguration constraints at every timestep. This gives us a formula which is a factor of τ longer than the formula encoding the static problem.

Theorem 3. *Let Π_T be a reconfiguration problem such that its static version Π_S is expressable with an MSO formula $\phi(H)$. Let $\mathcal{G} = (G, \lambda)$ be a temporal graph such that the treewidth of G is tw. There is an algorithm to determine if there is a reconfigurable sequence of size k for Π_T in $\mathcal{G}$ in $\mathcal{O}(f(tw, \tau, |\phi|) \cdot \tau \cdot |G|)$ time.*

Corollary 5. TEMPORAL DOMINATING SET RECONFIGURATION *and* TEMPORAL INDEPENDENT SET RECONFIGURATION *are solvable in $\mathcal{O}(f(tw, \tau) \cdot \tau \cdot |G|)$ time.*

8 Conclusion and Future Work

Motivated by both the ability of temporal graphs to model real-world processes and a gap in the theoretical literature, we have defined a general framework for formulating vertex-selection optimisation problems as a temporally satisfying reconfiguration problems, and have described several associated algorithmic tools.

While hardness results on static vertex selection problems will straightforwardly imply hardness for their corresponding reconfiguration versions, we have described several algorithmic approaches, including an approximation algorithm and several fixed-parameter tractable algorithms.

Several areas of future work present themselves: first, further investigation of which problems can be solved using our results, or which other temporal parameters are useful here. Secondly, because temporal problems are so frequently harder than corresponding static ones, it may be interesting to establish negative results that are stronger than those in the static setting, such as $W[k]$-completeness results that consider the lifetime as a parameter. Finally, we could explore a more restrictive version of the model, where the number of tokens allowed to move at each time step is bounded, or there are other restrictions on the speed of change of the vertex set.

Acknowledgments. Tom Davot and Jessica Enright are supported by EPSRC grant EP/T004878/1. For the purpose of open access, the author(s) has applied a Creative Commons Attribution (CC BY) licence to any Author Accepted Manuscript version arising from this submission.

Disclosure of Interests. The authors have no competing interests.

References

1. Bartier, V., Bousquet, N., Dallard, C., Lomer, K., Mouawad, A.E.: On girth and the parameterized complexity of token sliding and token jumping. Algorithmica **83**(9), 2914–2951 (2021). https://doi.org/10.1007/S00453-021-00848-1
2. Belmonte, R., Kim, E.J., Lampis, M., Mitsou, V., Otachi, Y., Sikora, F.: Token sliding on split graphs. Theory Comput. Syst. **65**(4), 662–686 (2021). https://doi.org/10.1007/S00224-020-09967-8
3. Bodlaender, H.L., Groenland, C., Swennenhuis, C.M.F.: Parameterized complexities of dominating and independent set reconfiguration. In: Golovach, P.A., Zehavi, M. (eds.) 16th International Symposium on Parameterized and Exact Computation, IPEC 2021, Lisbon, Portugal, 8–10 September 2021. LIPIcs, vol. 214, pp. 9:1–9:16. Schloss Dagstuhl - Leibniz-Zentrum für Informatik (2021). https://doi.org/10.4230/LIPICS.IPEC.2021.9
4. Bodlaender, H.L., Kloks, T.: Efficient and constructive algorithms for the pathwidth and treewidth of graphs. J. Algorithms **21**(2), 358–402 (1996). https://doi.org/10.1006/JAGM.1996.0049
5. Bonamy, M., Bousquet, N.: Token sliding on chordal graphs. In: Bodlaender, H.L., Woeginger, G.J. (eds.) WG 2017. LNCS, vol. 10520, pp. 127–139. Springer, Cham (2017). https://doi.org/10.1007/978-3-319-68705-6_10
6. Bousquet, N., Joffard, A.: TS-reconfiguration of dominating sets in circle and circular-arc graphs. In: Bampis, E., Pagourtzis, A. (eds.) FCT 2021. LNCS, vol. 12867, pp. 114–134. Springer, Cham (2021). https://doi.org/10.1007/978-3-030-86593-1_8
7. Bousquet, N., Joffard, A., Ouvrard, P.: Linear transformations between dominating sets in the tar-model. In: Cao, Y., Cheng, S., Li, M. (eds.) 31st International Symposium on Algorithms and Computation, ISAAC 2020, 14–18 December 2020, Hong Kong, China (Virtual Conference). LIPIcs, vol. 181, pp. 37:1–37:14. Schloss Dagstuhl - Leibniz-Zentrum für Informatik (2020). https://doi.org/10.4230/LIPICS.ISAAC.2020.37
8. Bousquet, N., Mouawad, A.E., Nishimura, N., Siebertz, S.: A survey on the parameterized complexity of reconfiguration problems. Comput. Sci. Rev. **53**, 100663 (2024). https://doi.org/10.1016/J.COSREV.2024.100663
9. Courcelle, B.: On context-free sets of graphs and their monadic second-order theory. In: Ehrig, H., Nagl, M., Rozenberg, G., Rosenfeld, A. (eds.) Graph Grammars 1986. LNCS, vol. 291, pp. 133–146. Springer, Heidelberg (1987). https://doi.org/10.1007/3-540-18771-5_50
10. Courcelle, B.: Chapter 5 - graph rewriting: an algebraic and logic approach. In: Van Leeuwen, J. (ed.) Formal Models and Semantics, pp. 193–242. Handbook of Theoretical Computer Science. Elsevier, Amsterdam (1990). https://doi.org/10.1016/B978-0-444-88074-1.50010-X. https://www.sciencedirect.com/science/article/pii/B978044488074150010X

11. Cygan, M., Fomin, F.V., Kowalik, Ł, Lokshtanov, D., Marx, D., Pilipczuk, M., Pilipczuk, M., Saurabh, S.: Parameterized Algorithms. Springer, Cham (2015). https://doi.org/10.1007/978-3-319-21275-3
12. Demaine, E.D., et al.: Polynomial-time algorithm for sliding tokens on trees. In: Ahn, H.-K., Shin, C.-S. (eds.) ISAAC 2014. LNCS, vol. 8889, pp. 389–400. Springer, Cham (2014). https://doi.org/10.1007/978-3-319-13075-0_31
13. Dondi, R., Lafond, M.: On the complexity of temporal arborescence reconfiguration. In: 3rd Symposium on Algorithmic Foundations of Dynamic Networks (SAND 2024), pp. 10–1. Schloss Dagstuhl–Leibniz-Zentrum für Informatik (2024)
14. Enright, J.A., Hand, S.D., Larios-Jones, L., Meeks, K.: Structural parameters for dense temporal graphs. CoRR **abs/2404.19453** (2024). https://doi.org/10.48550/ARXIV.2404.19453
15. Escoffier, B., Paschos, V.T.: Completeness in approximation classes beyond APX. Theor. Comput. Sci. **359**(1–3), 369–377 (2006). https://doi.org/10.1016/J.TCS.2006.05.023
16. Fox-Epstein, E., Hoang, D.A., Otachi, Y., Uehara, R.: Sliding token on bipartite permutation graphs. In: Elbassioni, K., Makino, K. (eds.) ISAAC 2015. LNCS, vol. 9472, pp. 237–247. Springer, Heidelberg (2015). https://doi.org/10.1007/978-3-662-48971-0_21
17. Garey, M.R., Johnson, D.S.: Computers and Intractability; A Guide to the Theory of NP-Completeness. W. H. Freeman & Co., USA (1990)
18. Golumbic, M.: Algorithmic Graph Theory and Perfect Graphs. Annals of Discrete Mathematics. North Holland (2004). https://books.google.co.uk/books?id=8xo-VrWo5_QC
19. Haddadan, A., et al.: The complexity of dominating set reconfiguration. Theor. Comput. Sci. **651**, 37–49 (2016). https://doi.org/10.1016/J.TCS.2016.08.016
20. Hearn, R.A., Demaine, E.D.: PSPACE-completeness of sliding-block puzzles and other problems through the nondeterministic constraint logic model of computation. Theoret. Comput. Sci. **343**(1), 72–96 (2005). https://doi.org/https://doi.org/10.1016/j.tcs.2005.05.008. https://www.sciencedirect.com/science/article/pii/S0304397505003105, game Theory Meets Theoretical Computer Science
21. Ito, T., Demaine, E.D., Harvey, N.J.A., Papadimitriou, C.H., Sideri, M., Uehara, R., Uno, Y.: On the complexity of reconfiguration problems. Theor. Comput. Sci. **412**(12–14), 1054–1065 (2011). https://doi.org/10.1016/J.TCS.2010.12.005
22. Karp, R.M.: Reducibility among Combinatorial Problems, pp. 85–103. Springer, Boston (1972). https://doi.org/10.1007/978-1-4684-2001-2_9
23. Gupta, V., Rassias, M.T.: Computation and Approximation. SM, Springer, Cham (2021). https://doi.org/10.1007/978-3-030-85563-5
24. Lampis, M.: Algorithmic meta-theorems for restrictions of treewidth. Algorithmica **64**(1), 19–37 (2012). https://doi.org/10.1007/S00453-011-9554-X
25. Lokshtanov, D., Mouawad, A.E.: The complexity of independent set reconfiguration on bipartite graphs. ACM Trans. Algorithms **15**(1), 7:1–7:19 (2019). https://doi.org/10.1145/3280825
26. Mouawad, A.E., Nishimura, N., Raman, V., Simjour, N., Suzuki, A.: On the parameterized complexity of reconfiguration problems. Algorithmica **78**(1), 274–297 (2017). https://doi.org/10.1007/S00453-016-0159-2
27. Suzuki, A., Mouawad, A.E., Nishimura, N.: Reconfiguration of dominating sets. J. Comb. Optim. **32**(4), 1182–1195 (2016). https://doi.org/10.1007/S10878-015-9947-X

28. Tardos, É.: A strongly polynomial minimum cost circulation algorithm. Comb. **5**(3), 247–256 (1985). https://doi.org/10.1007/BF02579369
29. Verheije, M.: Algorithms for domination problems on temporal graphs. Master's thesis, Utrecht University (2021)
30. Wrochna, M.: Reconfiguration in bounded bandwidth and tree-depth. J. Comput. Syst. Sci. **93**, 1–10 (2018). https://doi.org/10.1016/J.JCSS.2017.11.003

Temporal Cycle Detection and Acyclic Temporalizations

Davi de Andrade[1(✉)], Júlio Araújo[2], Allen Ibiapina[3], Andrea Marino[4], Jason Schoeters[4], and Ana Silva[2]

[1] Gran Sasso Science Institute, L'Aquila, Italy
davi.deandradeiacono@gssi.it
[2] Universidade Federal do Ceará, Fortaleza, Brazil
[3] IRIF, CNRS & Université Paris Cité, Paris, France
[4] Università degli Studi di Firenze, Florence, Italy

Abstract. In directed graphs, a cycle can be seen as a structure that allows its vertices to loop back to themselves, or as a structure that allows pairs of vertices to reach each other through distinct paths. We extend these concepts to temporal graph theory, resulting in multiple interesting definitions of a "temporal cycle". For each of these, we consider the problems of CYCLE DETECTION and ACYCLIC TEMPORALIZATION. For the former, we are given an input temporal digraph, and we want to decide whether it contains a temporal cycle. Regarding the latter, for a given input (static) digraph, we want to time the arcs such that no temporal cycle exists in the resulting temporal digraph. We are also interested in ACYCLIC TEMPORALIZATION where we bound the lifetime of the resulting temporal digraph. For these two problems, multiple results are presented, including polynomial and fixed-parameter tractable search algorithms, polynomial-time reductions from 3-SAT and NOT-ALL-EQUAL 3-SAT, and temporalizations resulting from arbitrary vertex orderings which solve all but one specific case.

Keywords: Temporal graphs · Search algorithms · Connectivity · Cycles · Directed acyclic graphs · Detection · Temporalization · NP-completeness · Fixed-parameter tractability · Polynomial-time algorithms · Bounded lifetime

1 Introduction

A *temporal digraph with lifetime* τ is a pair $\mathcal{D} = (D, \lambda)$ where D is a directed graph (or digraph), called *underlying* digraph, and λ is a function from the arcs $A(D)$ to $2^{[\tau]} \setminus \emptyset$, called *time function*, or *temporalization*. Temporal graphs are powerful for analyzing dynamic relationships and patterns over time. They are

---

This paper was partially funded by Italian PNRR CN4 Centro Nazionale per la Mobilità Sostenibile, NextGeneration EU - CUP, B13C22001000001. MUR of Italy, under PRIN Project no. 2022ME9Z78 - NextGRAAL: Next-generation algorithms for constrained GRAph visuALization, PRIN PNRR Project no. P2022NZPJA - DLT-FRUIT: A user centered framework for facilitating DLTs FRUITion.

widely applied in social networks (e.g., trend detection, influencer analysis), epidemiology (disease spread modeling), and transportation (route optimization), and in general in contexts where evolving connections are key to understanding behavior, predicting events, and optimizing performance [12,16,19,20].

In temporal digraphs, a path[1] from a vertex x to a vertex y, called a *temporal x,y-path*, is meaningful only if the times on its arcs follow a strictly increasing or non-decreasing sequence. The former, known as *strict model*, is applied, for example, in the representation of a public transportation system where each arc in the path corresponds to a bus or train that must be taken at a time which is later than the previous transport. The latter, called *non-strict model*, allows transitions to occur instantaneously. This is useful for scenarios such as daily route availability, where multiple edges may be traversed in the same day if they are accessible.

Cycles in Static Digraphs. In static digraphs, a cycle is a simple path with at least one edge that starts and finishes at the same vertex. Cycles are fundamental structures within digraphs and they come up in a wide variety of applications, from computer science to engineering, biology, and social network analysis. For example, cycles are important in network routing to avoid routing loops and enhance efficiency. In operating systems and databases, deadlocks can be represented as cycles in a resource-allocation graph. In biochemical networks and protein interaction networks, cycles can represent feedback loops or recurring processes. The study of cycles, cycle detection, and cycle characterization is therefore central to graph theory and its applications in the real world. The following **fundamental properties** of cycles in static digraphs trivially hold and are equivalent in the static context: *(i)* there exists a vertex x in the cycle such that from x we can traverse the cycle and go back to x; *(ii)* there exists a pair of vertices x,y in the cycle, such that x is able to reach y and y is able to reach x using the arcs involved in the cycle; *(iii) for every* vertex x in the cycle, starting from x, we can traverse the cycle and go back to x; and *(iv) for every* pair of vertices x,y in the cycle, x is able to reach y and y is able to reach x using the arcs involved in the cycle. As said, for static digraphs, all of the four statements are equivalent and, note that *(iii)* is the *for every* version of *(i)* and *(iv)* is the *for every* version of *(ii)*.

Cycle Definitions in Temporal Graphs. Inspired by the properties *(i)-(iv)* above, we can define cycles in temporal digraphs, looking for cycles in the underlying digraph whose times satisfy such properties. Interestingly, while these properties are equivalent in static digraphs, in temporal digraphs they differ, and it makes sense to study both the *for every* and the *there exists* variations.

We define the following types of cycles, considering (now and in the remainder of the paper) only non-trivial temporal paths. In particular, given a temporal digraph $\mathcal{D} = (D, \lambda)$ (without self-loops) and a cycle C of D, we say that C is a temporal:

simple-cycle   if there exists a temporal x,x-path P such that $A(P) = A(C)$, for some $x \in V(C)$;

---

[1] All paths are considered to be directed paths.

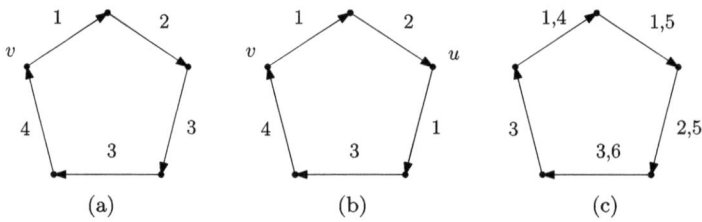

Fig. 1. Examples of a simple-cycle, weak-cycle, and strong-cycle respectively, using the non-strict model.

weak-cycle if there exist a temporal x,y-path P and a temporal y,x-path P' such that $A(P) \cup A(P') = A(C)$, for some pair $x,y \in V(C)$;

strong-cycle if there exists a temporal x,x-path P such that $A(P) = A(C)$, for every $x \in V(C)$.

See Fig. 1 for an example using the non-strict model. Figure 1a corresponds to a simple-cycle as there is a vertex, namely v, able to reach itself. Figure 1b corresponds to a weak-cycle, as there is a pair of vertices, namely v and u, such that v is able to go to u and u is able to go to v. Note that this is not a simple-cycle because the two paths do not compose to allow v (or any other vertex) to go back to itself. Finally, Fig. 1c corresponds to a strong-cycle as every vertex is able to go back to itself.

Note that the definitions of simple, weak, and strong cycles correspond to properties *(i)*, *(ii)*, and *(iii)*, respectively. We miss only property *(iv)*, which can be regarded as the *for every* version of a weak cycle. However, it is easy to prove that this in fact would be equivalent to a strong-cycle. Note additionally that every strong-cycle is also a simple-cycle, as the former is the *for every* version of the latter, and that every simple-cycle C is a weak-cycle (just consider $y = x$).

Problem Definition.

The first problem that arises naturally, is the detection of our temporal cycles, as described next where Type T can be simple-cycle, weak-cycle, or strong-cycle.

T Cycle Detection

Input: Temporal digraph $\mathcal{D}$

Question: Does $\mathcal{D}$ contain a temporal cycle of Type T?

We are interested in the time complexity of such problems. Note that we do not require the temporal cycle to be of at least some given size k, since this would be trivially NP-complete, by reducing from Hamiltonian Cycle.

Detecting a temporal cycle can also be seen as recognizing whether the given temporal graph is acyclic, which relates to the problem of recognizing DAGs[2] in the static context, which can be done easily through a search algorithm. Observe that constructing a DAG D from a given graph G, i.e., orienting the edges of G so that D does not contain any cycle, can be trivially done by picking an ordering of

---
[2] Used short for Directed Acyclic Graph.

$V(G)$ and orienting all edges from earlier to later vertices. When adapted to the temporal context, such orientation would clearly still work, but what happens when the digraph is already known and, instead, we want to find a time function that produces a temporal DAG? We then propose the DAG construction problem on the temporal context, presented below. We bring attention to the fact that DAGs are perhaps the most important class of digraphs, given that they not only model many practical applications (e.g. scheduling [21], version history [3], causal networks like Bayesian Networks [22], etc.), but also have interesting structural properties that lead to efficient algorithms (e.g. single source shortest paths and longest path [6], k disjoint paths for fixed k [9]), and inspires a series of width measures that try to mimic the successful treewidth concept on undirected graphs (see e.g. [10,13]). Hence, concerning constructing DAGs, the problem we deal with is the one of assigning a set of time labels to the arcs of a digraph, i.e. of designing a *temporalization*, in order to avoid temporal cycles to appear. In the following definition, we recall that Type T can be simple-cycle, weak-cycle, or strong-cycle.

T ACYCLIC TEMPORALIZATION
Input: (Static) digraph D
Question: Does there exist a temporalization $\lambda : A(D) \to 2^{\mathbb{N}} \setminus \{\emptyset\}$ such that $\mathcal{D} = (D, \lambda)$ admits no temporal cycles of Type T?

We do not allow the empty set to be assigned to arcs for the clear reason that doing so for all arcs would be a trivial solution. Note however that we can assume any solution to have exactly one time per arc, since adding more could only create more temporal cycles. This is why, whenever we talk about acyclic temporalization, we write simply the number i instead of $\{i\}$ when assigning such a set as the set of time labels of some arc.

Our Contributions.

Our results for the non-strict model are summarized in Table 1. Starting with CYCLE DETECTION in Sect. 3, we present polynomial-time algorithms to detect weak-cycles and simple-cycles, both using a temporal search algorithm as a subroutine. For STRONG CYCLE DETECTION, we prove the problem to be NP-complete through a reduction from 3-SAT. We also provide a complex search algorithm running in FPT time w.r.t. the lifetime parameter, in which search paths are encoded as time values corresponding to the search, which, together with a blocking technique when backtracking, allows us to efficiently solve the problem.

Concerning ACYCLIC TEMPORALIZATION, we can always trivially answer yes for strong-cycles by picking any ordering of the vertices, then assigning times to arcs going from earlier to later vertices with 1, and arcs going from later to earlier vertices with 2. This was first noted in [2] while dealing with DAG decomposition of static graphs. As for simple-cycles and weak-cycles, if we are allowed to use higher lifetime, we can also construct acyclic temporalizations by using an ordering of the vertices. This can always be done for simple-cycles, except when the girth[3] of D is 2, in which case the answer is trivially no. Sim-

---
[3] The girth of a (di)graph is defined as the size of the smallest cycle in the (di)graph.

Table 1. Main results for our problems on CYCLE DETECTION and ACYCLIC TEMPORALIZATION, concerning weak-cycles, simple-cycles, and strong-cycles.

CYCLE DEF	PROBLEMS		
	CYCLE DETECTION	ACYCLIC TEMPORALIZATION	
		Lifetime 2	Lifetime Unbounded
weak-cycle	Poly (Proposition 1)	NP-complete (Theorem 4)	no if girth ≤ 3 open if girth $= 4$ yes if girth ≥ 5 (Theorem 3)
simple-cycle	Poly (Proposition 2)	NP-complete (Theorem 3)	no if girth ≤ 2 yes if girth ≥ 3 (Theorem 2)
strong-cycle	NP-complete (Theorem 1) FPT w.r.t. lifetime (Theorem 2)	always yes (Proposition 4)	

ilarly, the answer is always **yes** for weak-cycles when the girth is at least 5, trivially always **no** when the girth is at most 3, and we leave open the case of girth 4. The latter temporalization makes a bijection from $A(D)$ to $[m]$, where $m = |A(D)|$. If instead the lifetime is bounded, we prove that SIMPLE ACYCLIC TEMPORALIZATION and WEAK ACYCLIC TEMPORALIZATION become NP-hard for lifetime 2. We do this through reductions from NOT-ALL-EQUAL 3-SAT. We note that these results apply to the non-strict model, as in the case of the strict one, if there are no digons, i.e. a cycle of length two, it is sufficient to give time 1 to all the arcs, that is, the answer is always **yes**. If there are digons, the answer for weak-cycles is trivially **no**, while for the other types it is still **yes** applying the same strategy.

Related Works.

We are not aware of a systematic study of cycles in temporal graphs. We can find in the literature studies about simple-cycles, for instance concerning Eulerian temporal cycles [5,17], and Hamiltonian cycles, also referred to as temporal vertex exploration returning to the base [1] (where the latter is a constrained version of the temporal vertex exploration problem where there is no need to go back to the starting vertex [7,8]). On the other hand, as far as we know, surprisingly, we are the first ones to introduce the notion of weak-cycle and strong-cycle.

Detecting a cycle in static graphs can be easily done by applying a BREADTH-FIRST SEARCH (BFS) or a DEPTH-FIRST SEARCH (DFS) from any vertex. Indeed, when the search explores an edge which leads to an already visited vertex, then a cycle has been detected, and when this does not occur, then no cycle exists. In digraphs, a similar idea works, although instead of an already visited vertex triggering detection, the vertex has to be in the current search path as well. In [24], (polynomial-time) search algorithms are presented for temporal graphs. Among these, one computes earliest arrival paths from the root vertex to the other vertices, or in other words, it computes earliest arrival times (earliest among all possible temporal paths) from the root to the other vertices. Informally, the search progresses by selecting earliest incident edges such that they obey the temporal order of the created temporal paths. In [23], this result is presented again, but complemented by a similar algorithm for computing latest departure times between vertices.

Concerning ACYCLIC TEMPORALIZATION, we highlight that this falls into the so-called network realization problem framework, where we are given a static graph and we have to assign time to the arcs in order to meet some property. Some of the properties considered in the literature are: ensure reachability [14]; and meet exact/upper bounds on the fastest path durations among its vertices on periodic temporal graphs [15,18]. Another close relation to this notion of acyclic temporalization is the one of *Good edge-labeling* [4]. A *labeling* of the edges of a given simple undirected graph G is an assignment of a real number to each edge of G. It is said to be *good* if, for any pair of vertices $u, v \in V(G)$, there do not exist two non-decreasing u, v-paths, with respect to the edge labels. In particular, labels can be assumed to be distinct, i.e. strict and non-strict cases are equivalent in this context. Note that this notion is similar, but not equivalent, to the case of WEAK ACYCLIC TEMPORALIZATION. In [4], the authors use the notion of good edge-labeling to prove that there exist particular optical networks and set of requests to be assigned wavelengths such that, if one wants to assign distinct wavelengths to requests sharing an arc, then the number of wavelengths can be arbitrarily large.

Finally, let us mention the problem of computing a temporal feedback edge set as discussed in [11], which also aims to achieve acyclic temporal graphs. However, unlike our approach of assigning suitable times to ensure acyclicity, their method considers a given temporal undirected graph and focuses on removing a subset of temporal edges (referred to as time-edges) or edges (referred to as connection sets) to eliminate all simple cycles.

Structure of the Paper.

In Sect. 2, we present our notation and definitions. In Sect. 3, we present our results about detecting cycles, and in Sect. 4 the results about acyclic temporalization. Results marked with a ($\star$) indicate that the proof (and/or corresponding lemmas etc.) are omitted or sketched for space constraints.

2 Preliminaries

Given a digraph D of lifetime τ, a *walk* in D is a sequence $W = (v_1, e_1, v_2, \ldots, v_q, e_q, v_{q+1})$ of alternating vertices and arcs of D where $e_i = v_i v_{i+1}$ for each $i \in [q]$. It is a *path* if $v_1, \ldots, v_{q+1}$ are all distinct and a *cycle* if $v_1, \ldots, v_q$ are all distinct and $v_1 = v_{q+1}$. We denote by $V(W)$ the set $\{v_1, \ldots, v_{q+1}\}$ and by $A(W)$ the set $\{e_1, \ldots, e_q\}$. It is said that W has *length* q and *order* $q+1$ if W is not a cycle, and *order* q otherwise. In this paper, we work on simple digraphs, so we can omit the arcs from the sequence, writing $W = (v_1, v_2, \ldots, v_q, v_{q+1})$

instead. Given a temporal directed graph $\mathcal{D} = (D, \lambda)$, the *set of vertices* of $\mathcal{D}$ is equal to $V(D)$, the *set of arcs* of $\mathcal{D}$ is equal to $A(D)$, the set of *temporal vertices* of $\mathcal{D}$ is equal to $V(D) \times [\tau]$, and the set of *temporal arcs* of $\mathcal{D}$ is equal to $\{(e, t) \mid e \in A(D) \text{ and } t \in \lambda(e)\}$. These are denoted, respectively, by $V(\mathcal{D})$, $A(\mathcal{D})$, $V^T(\mathcal{D})$, and $A^T(\mathcal{D})$. Given vertices $v_1, v_{q+1} \in V(D)$, a *temporal v_1, v_{q+1}-walk* in $\mathcal{D}$ is defined as a sequence of vertices and times $W = (v_1, t_1, v_2, \cdots, t_q, v_{q+1})$ such that, for each $i \in [q]$, there exists $e_i = v_i v_{i+1} \in A(D)$, $t_i \in \lambda(e_i)$, and $t_i \leq t_{i+1}$. An equivalent definition exists concerning temporal edges. It is said to be *strict* if $t_i < t_{i+1}$ for every $i \in [q]$, and *non-strict* otherwise. It is called a temporal v_1, v_{q+1}-*path* if all vertices are distinct. We also say that W *starts or departs at time* t_1 and *finishes or arrives at time* t_q. The set $\{v_1, \ldots, v_{q+1}\}$ is denoted by $V(W)$ and the set $\{e_1, \ldots, e_q\}$, by $A(W)$. Additionally, the set $\{(a_i, t_i) \mid i \in [q]\}$ is denoted by $A^T(W)$.

We write $\text{EAT}(u, v)$ to be the *earliest arrival time* from vertex u to vertex v, defined as the earliest arrival time among all temporal paths from u to v. Special cases include $\text{EAT}(u, u) = 0$, and $\text{EAT}(u, v) = +\infty$ if u cannot reach v. Similarly, $\text{LDT}(u, v)$ is the *latest departure time* from vertex u to vertex v, defined as the latest departure time among all temporal paths from u to v. Special cases include $\text{LDT}(u, u) = \tau$, and $\text{LDT}(u, v) = -\infty$ if u cannot reach v. As mentioned in the introduction, earliest arrival times and latest departure times can be computed in polynomial time [23,24]. We use these algorithms as a black box for CYCLE DETECTION.

3 Cycle Detection

In this section we describe our results for the CYCLE DETECTION problem. By computing earliest arrival times, we obtain the first two polynomial-time results for simple-cycles and weak-cycles. In the remainder, namely Sect. 3.1, we prove hardness for STRONG CYCLE DETECTION and give an FPT algorithm with regards to the lifetime τ.

Proposition 1. WEAK CYCLE DETECTION *is polynomial-time solvable.*

Proof. In order to detect a weak-cycle, it suffices to test for every pair $x, y \in V(\mathcal{D})$, whether x reaches y and y reaches x. This means determining whether the earliest arrival times between these vertices are finite. Indeed, suppose this is the case and let $P_{xy} = (v_1 = x, t_1, \ldots, t_p, v_{p+1} = y)$ (resp. $P_{yx} = (v'_1 = y, t'_1, \ldots, t'_q, v'_{q+1} = x)$) be a temporal path in $\mathcal{D}$ from x to y (resp. from y to x). If P_{xy} and P_{yx} intersect only in x and y, we are done. So suppose that they intersect in at least one other vertex and let i be minimum such that $v_i \in (V(P_{xy}) \cap V(P_{yx})) \setminus \{x, y\}$. Now, let Q be the temporal x, v_i-path contained in P_{xy} and Q' be the temporal v_i, y-path contained in P_{yx}. By the choice of v_i, observe that Q' cannot intersect Q on an internal vertex. It follows that the concatenation of Q and Q' forms a weak-cycle in $\mathcal{D}$. □

Proposition 2. SIMPLE CYCLE DETECTION *is polynomial-time solvable.*

Proof. To detect a simple-cycle that starts in a vertex v in a given temporal digraph $\mathcal{D} = (D, \lambda)$, we go over each arc $vr \in A(D)$, and check whether $\text{EAT}(r, v) \leq \max(\lambda(vr))$. If this holds, then a simple-cycle exists, formed by the temporal path from r to v concatenated with arc vr. If no vertex r can reach any of their incoming neighbors v in time before using the arc vr, then no simple-cycle exists. Thus, it suffices to repeat the above procedure for every $v \in V(\mathcal{D})$. □

3.1 Detecting Strong-Cycles

The algorithms detecting simple-cycles and weak-cycles can efficiently use the black box for EAT because, intuitively, the temporal paths corresponding to these EAT concatenate nicely into a cycle structure when there is only one or two vertices that need to reach themselves or each other. This nice concatenation cannot be ensured when multiple such vertices and thus multiple temporal paths exist, which is the case for strong-cycles.

This difficulty makes STRONG CYCLE DETECTION NP-complete, as shown next by reducing from 3-SAT. Interestingly, the lifetime of the digraph resulting from the reduction depends on the size of the formula. This is not by chance, as indeed, in the remainder, we prove that the problem is FPT with respect to the lifetime.

Hardness of Detecting a strong-cycle. In order to prove hardness of detecting a strong-cycle, we present first the *auxiliary cycle* structure that will be useful when assigning times to the arcs of the constructed digraph.

Definition 1. *The* auxiliary cycle *of order n is the temporal digraph whose vertex set is $\{v_0, v_1, v_2, \ldots, v_{n-1}\}$ and arc set is $\{e_0 = v_{n-1}v_0\} \cup \{e_i = v_{i-1}v_i \mid 1 \leq i \leq n-1\}$, with $\lambda(e_0) = \{0, n, 2n, 3n, \ldots, (n-1)n\}$ and $\lambda(e_i) = \{n-i, 2n-i, 3n-i, \ldots, (n-1)n-i\}$ for each $1 \leq i \leq n-1$. See Fig. 2a for an example.*

Proposition 3. *Given an auxiliary cycle $\mathcal{A}$ of order n, there exists exactly one temporal v, v-path for each $v \in V(\mathcal{A})$. Moreover, given v_i and v_k such that $i \neq k$ and $n-1 \notin \{i, k\}$, these paths do not share temporal arcs.*

Proof. Let $\mathcal{A}$ be an auxiliary cycle of order n. First, note that given $v_i \in V(\mathcal{A})$ such that $i \neq n-1$, $W_{v_i} = (v_i, t_i^1, v_{i+1}, t_i^2, \ldots, v_{n-1}, t_i^{n-i}, v_0, t_i^{n-i+1}, \ldots, t_i^n, v_i)$, where $t_i^j = j(n-1) - i$, is a temporal v_i, v_i-path.

We now prove that W_{v_i} is the only temporal v_i, v_i-path for each vertex v_i. Notice that, in W_{v_i}, each time t_i^j is the minimum possible that maintains the temporal path. Indeed, for any $j > 1$, the times smaller than t_i^j on the same arc are at most $t_i^j - n = (j-1)(n-1) - i - 1$, which is smaller than $t_i^{j-1} = (j-1)(n-1) - i$. Moreover, if we take a time greater than t_i^j on the same arc, the last time must be at least $t_i^n + n = n^2 - i$, by construction. Note that the last arc in the temporal v_i, v_i-path is e_i, whose greatest time is equal to $(n-1)n - i$, which is smaller than $n^2 - i$. Therefore, it is not possible to take a time greater than t_i^j for any j. W_{v_i} is thus the only temporal v_i, v_i-path. Additionally, we prove that W_{v_i} and W_{v_k} are disjoint, for $i \neq k$. Since $i \neq k$, it follows that $t_i^j \neq t_k^j$, and thus the times are all different. □

Let us refer to the times that each vertex $v_i \neq v_{n-1}$ requires to reach itself in the auxiliary cycle, as $L^{\circlearrowleft}(v_i) = \{(n-1)-i, 2(n-1)-i, 3(n-1)-i, ..., n(n-1)-i\}$. Note that vertex v_{n-1} admits exactly one temporal v_{n-1}, v_{n-1}-path as well, and that it uses times $\{0\} \cup L^{\circlearrowleft}(v_0) \setminus \max(L^{\circlearrowleft}(v_0))$. Together with Proposition 3, we thus have that every auxiliary cycle is a strong-cycle.

Theorem 1. $(\star)$ STRONG CYCLE DETECTION *is NP-complete.*

Proof. (Sketch) STRONG CYCLE DETECTION is in NP, because a solution subgraph $\mathcal{C}$ can be verified to be a cycle in the underlying graph, and deciding whether each vertex reaches itself can be done by checking whether $\text{EAT}(v, u)$ in $\mathcal{C}$ is at most $\max(\lambda(u,v))$, for each arc $uv \in A(\mathcal{C})$, similarly to Proposition 1.

To prove this problem is NP-hard, we reduce 3-SAT to it. Let the generic instance of 3-SAT be the CNF formula ϕ of n variables $x_0, x_1, ..., x_{n-1}$ and m clauses $C_0, C_1, ..., C_{m-1}$. Let the literals of clause C_i be denoted as $\ell_{i,1}, \ell_{i,2}$, and $\ell_{i,3}$. Let us build an instance of CYCLE DETECTION as the temporal digraph $\mathcal{D}(\phi)$ as follows. Initially, add three auxiliary cycles $\mathcal{A}^1$, $\mathcal{A}^2$, and $\mathcal{A}^3$, all of order $4m+1$. Let the corresponding vertices of $\mathcal{A}^1$, $\mathcal{A}^2$ and $\mathcal{A}^3$ be referred to as v_i^1, v_i^2, and v_i^3 respectively, for every $i \in \{0, ..., 4m\}$. Note that for any three vertices v_i^1, v_i^2, and v_i^3, $L^{\circlearrowleft}(v_i^1) = L^{\circlearrowleft}(v_i^2) = L^{\circlearrowleft}(v_i^3)$. Let us simply refer to these times as $L^{\circlearrowleft}(v_i)$ instead. Now, for each $i \in \mathbb{N}$, merge[4] the three vertices v_{4i}^1, v_{4i}^2, and v_{4i}^3, and refer to this merged vertex as v_{4i} (see Fig. 2). Note that this also merges vertices v_{4m}^1, v_{4m}^2, and v_{4m}^3 into vertex v_{4m}. For each clause C_i, add time 0 to arcs $v_{4i+2}^1 v_{4i+3}^1$, $v_{4i+3}^1 v_{4(i+1)}$, $v_{4i+1}^2 v_{4i+2}^2$, $v_{4i+3}^2 v_{4(i+1)}$, $v_{4i+1}^3 v_{4i+2}^3$, and $v_{4i+2}^3 v_{4i+3}^3$. Finally, for each literal $\ell_{i,j}$ corresponding to some variable x_k, and each literal $\ell_{g,h}$ which corresponds to $\neg x_k$, remove from arc $v_{4g} v_{4g+1}^h$ all times in $L^{\circlearrowleft}(v_{4i+j})$ (which results in removing one time from the arc). This concludes the transformation.

We omit the proof of correctness for space constraints. The key idea is that if path $(v_{4i+1}^j, v_{4i+2}^j, v_{4i+3}^j)$ is part of a strong-cycle, then the corresponding literal $\ell_{i,j}$ is set to true. □

Fixed-Parameter Tractability W.r.t. Lifetime. To detect strong-cycles, a modified depth-first search is employed on every outgoing arc $a_r = rv$ of every possible root vertex r. This search aims to iteratively construct a strong-cycle by exploring arcs from r, creating and extending a *search path* P, until reaching r again. During the search, time values corresponding to temporal paths along the search path are updated. Then, unsuccessful and dead-end search paths backtrack and employ a "blocking" mechanism of said time values on the backtracked arcs. This stops successive search paths from exploring along this arc if the corresponding time values of the search path are already blocked. Essentially, this restrains the running time to be superpolynomial in the lifetime parameter τ only, as arcs are explored at most as many times as there exist

---

[4] We define merging of vertices in temporal digraphs as in static digraphs, and times on arcs of pre-merged vertices remain on corresponding arcs of post-merged vertices.

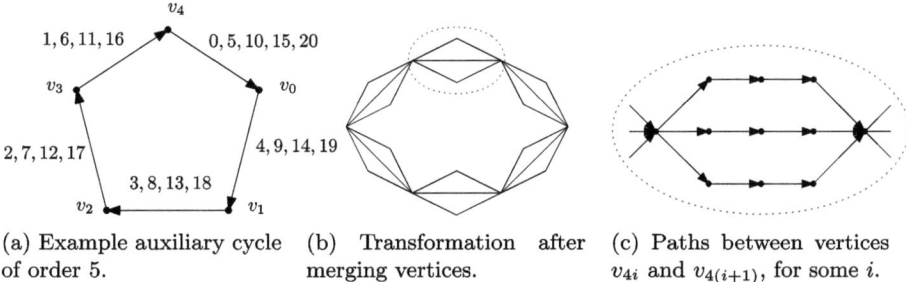

(a) Example auxiliary cycle of order 5. (b) Transformation after merging vertices. (c) Paths between vertices v_{4i} and $v_{4(i+1)}$, for some i.

Fig. 2. Example of the transformation for a 3-SAT formula. Starting with three auxiliary cycles such as the one shown in Fig. 2a, merge every fourth vertex such as shown in Fig. 2b. Each clause is represented as three paths between merged vertices in the created CYCLE DETECTION instance (see the blue dotted selection in Fig. 2b, and a more detailed view of these paths in Fig. 2c). Thus, in Fig. 2b, 6 clauses have been transformed. For clarity, times on the arcs have been omitted from Fig. 2b and Fig. 2c.

combinations of time values, while still allowing the detection of a strong cycle if one exists.

Due to the description of the algorithm, and the corresponding proofs, being long and technical, we omit them from this space-constrained version.

Theorem 2. (⋆) STRONG CYCLE DETECTION *is fixed-parameter tractable with the parameter being the lifetime.*

4 Acyclic Temporalization

Given a directed graph D, a *temporalization of D* is an assignment of a non-empty set of time labels λ to each arc of D. In this section, for each type of temporal cycle, we are interested in finding temporalizations that do not contain such cycles. In the following, we first give an easy solution for STRONG ACYCLIC TEMPORALIZATION, we then focus in Sect. 4.1 and in Sect. 4.2 respectively on simple-cycles and weak-cycles. Both these sections first analyze the unbounded lifetime case, i.e. we can use as many time values as we want to solve ACYCLIC TEMPORALIZATION, and then, we focus on the bounded lifetime case, which turns out to be NP-complete for both for $\tau = 2$ using similar reductions.

In this section, we often use the following temporalization, referred to as *lexicographic temporalization* (Fig. 3).

Definition 2 (lexicographic temporalization). *Assign an arbitrary order to $V(D)$. For all arcs uv such that $u > v$ (suppose there are m' such arcs) assign in an incremental manner one time per arc in lexicographic order, thus assigning times 1 to m' to these arcs. For the other arcs, being arcs uv such that $u < v$, assign in an incremental manner one time per arc in reverse lexicographic order, starting from time $m' + 1$ (and thus ending with time m).*

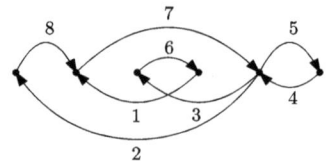

Fig. 3. Lexicographic temporalization with $m = 8$ and $m' = 4$.

Lemma 1. *Any digraph with the lexicographic temporalization results in a temporal graph which has temporal paths of length at most two.*

Proof. Consider two arcs uv and vw such that $u < v < w$ in the arbitrary ordering. The lexicographic temporalization ensures that $\lambda(vw) < \lambda(uv)$, meaning no temporal path exists using these successive arcs. The same holds for arcs wv and vu, and for arcs uw and wv, again with $u < v < w$. The remaining case is arcs wu and uv which the temporalization does allow to form a temporal path, but the temporal path is then stuck by the previous case analysis. □

The following easy proposition allows us to concentrate only on simple-cycles and weak-cycles in the remainder of the section, as for strong-cycles we can use the same strategy as in [2] to obtain a temporalization which will use only two values, i.e. providing a **yes** answer for STRONG ACYCLIC TEMPORALIZATION already for $\tau = 2$. In particular, it is enough to order the vertices of the input digraph and assign times to the arcs as follows: uv arcs such that $u < v$ are assigned time 1, and time 2 otherwise.

Proposition 4. *Let D be a directed graph. Then there always exists a temporalization $\lambda : A(D) \to 2^{[2]} \setminus \emptyset$ of D such that (D, λ) contains no strong-cycles.*

Proof. By construction, there is no cycle in timestep 1 nor in timestep 2. Now, if $C = (v_1, v_2, \ldots, v_q)$ is a cycle in D, suppose without loss of generality, that $\lambda(v_1 v_2) = 1$ and $\lambda(v_q v_1) = 2$. Then clearly C does not contain any non-trivial temporal v_q, v_q-path. □

4.1 Simple-Cycles

The following result characterizes the answer to SIMPLE ACYCLIC TEMPORALIZATION with respect to the girth of the input digraph.

Lemma 2. SIMPLE ACYCLIC TEMPORALIZATION *is always* **yes** *when the girth of the input digraph is at least 3, and* **no** *otherwise.*

Proof. By Lemma 1, the application of the lexicographic temporalization ensures that any cycle of size at least 3 cannot be a simple-cycle, since a temporal path of length at least 3 is required. Hence, graphs of girth at least 3 can always be made acyclic through the lexicographic temporalization. Concerning graphs of girth 2, we trivially note that no temporalization can avoid a simple-cycle. □

Lifetime at Most 2. In the following, we prove that SIMPLE ACYCLIC TEMPORALIZATION becomes NP-hard when the lifetime of the resulting temporal digraph is constrained to be at most 2. To this aim, we first observe the following property.

Proposition 5. *Let $\mathcal{D} = (D, \lambda)$ be a temporal digraph with lifetime 2. If $\mathcal{D}$ has no simple-cycles, then D has no cycles on less than 4 vertices. Additionally, if $C = (a, e_1, b, e_2, c, e_3, d, e_4, a)$ is a cycle in D, then $|\lambda(e_i)| = 1$ for every e_i, and $\lambda(e_1) = \lambda(e_3) \neq \lambda(e_2) = \lambda(e_4)$.*

Proof. First observe that if $\mathcal{D}$ has a cycle on 2 vertices, (a, e_1, b, e_2, a), then whatever assignment we give to e_1 and e_2 will give us either a non-trivial temporal a, a-path or a non-trivial temporal b, b-path. Now consider that $\mathcal{D}$ has a cycle on 3 vertices, $C = (a, e_1, b, e_2, c, e_3, a)$. We can suppose, without loss of generality that $1 \in \lambda(e_1)$. Indeed if this is not the case, then C is contained in timestep 2, a contradiction as $\mathcal{D}$ has no simple-cycles. Similarly, we can suppose that $2 \in \lambda(e_3)$. As $\lambda(e_2)$ is non-empty, we get a non-trivial temporal a, a-path, a contradiction.

For the second part, let $C = (a, e_1, b, e_2, c, e_3, d, e_4, a)$ be a cycle in D. First, we argue that $\lambda(e_1) \cap \lambda(e_2) = \emptyset$. Indeed, if it is not the case, then one can verify that in such case (a, e_1, b, e_2, c) behave as a single arc and we can apply an argument analogous to the previous paragraph to arrive to a contradiction. This gives us actually that no two consecutive arcs of C can be active in a single timestep of $\mathcal{D}$. As $\tau = 2$ and $\lambda(e_i) \neq \emptyset$ for every $i \in [4]$, the proposition follows. □

We are now ready to construct our reduction. We reduce from MONOTONE NAE 3-SAT. Let ϕ be a formula on variables $x_1, \ldots, x_n$ and clauses $c_1, \ldots, c_m$. For each variable x_i, add to D a $2 \times (2m-1)$ grid as in Fig. 4a. Formally, add vertices $\{a_1^i, \ldots, a_{2m-1}^i, b_1^i, \ldots, b_{2m-1}^i\}$. Denote by "even vertices" the vertices having an even number subscript, and by "odd vertices" the ones having an odd number subscript. Now, for each $i \in [n]$, add the arcs $a_{2j-1}^i a_{2j}^i$ and the arcs $a_{2j+1}^i a_{2j}^i$ for $j \in [m-1]$ (in words, make the set $A^i = \{a_1^i, \ldots, a_{2m-1}^i\}$ form a path from a_1^i to a_{2m-1}^i and direct arcs such that even vertices are sinks). Furthermore, for each $i \in [n]$, add the arcs $b_{2j}^i b_{2j-1}^i$ and the arcs $b_{2j}^i b_{2j+1}^i$ for $j \in [m-1]$ (in words, again add a path, and direct arcs such that now the odd vertices are sinks). Denote the arcs added thus far as "horizontal arcs", as portrayed in Fig. 4a. Finally, add the matching $\{b_{2j-1}^i a_{2j-1}^i, a_{2j}^i b_{2j}^i \mid j \in [m]\}$ (in words, the arcs between odd vertices point from b to a and arcs between even vertices from a to b). Refer to these arcs as "vertical arcs", again as portrayed in Fig. 4a. Denote by D_i the gadget related to variable x_i. Observe that for each $j \in [m]$, we have a cycle $C_j^i = (a_{2j-1}^i, a_{2j}^i, b_{2j}^i, b_{2j-1}^i, a_{2j-1}^i)$ on 4 vertices. By Proposition 5, we know that all vertical arcs within D_i are going to be given the same time, i.e. either 1 or 2. Similarly, all horizontal arcs will be assigned the other time. Hence, the idea is to use the vertical arcs to transfer the time

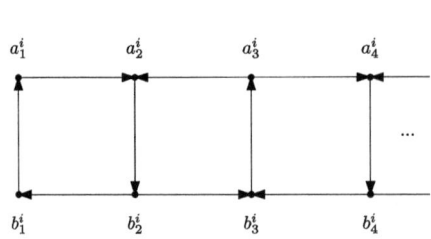
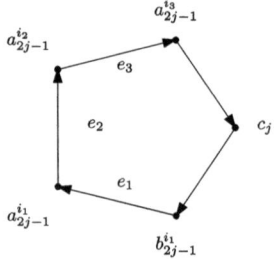

(a) Variable gadget, with $2m-1$ a_j^i vertices and $2m-1$ b_j^i vertices per variable gadget.

(b) Clause gadget, with vertices of edges e_j identified with vertices of variable gadgets.

Fig. 4. Gadgets for the reduction for SIMPLE ACYCLIC TEMPORALIZATION.

corresponding to the truth assignment of variable x_i. This is formalized in the next paragraph in the construction of the clause gadgets.

Now, consider clause $c_j = (x_{i_1} \vee x_{i_2} \vee x_{i_3})$. We will link the appropriate arcs within the gadgets of $x_{i_1}, x_{i_2}, x_{i_3}$ in a way that they cannot all be assigned the same time. See Fig. 4b to follow the construction. First create vertices c_j in D. Then, identify (or merge) vertices $a_{2j-1}^{i_1}$ and $b_{2j-1}^{i_2}$ in to one vertex (say $a_{2j-1}^{i_1}$), and vertices $a_{2j-1}^{i_2}$ and $b_{2j-1}^{i_3}$ in to one vertex (say $a_{2j-1}^{i_2}$). Denote by e_1, e_2 and e_3 the arcs $b_{2j-1}^{i_1} a_{2j-1}^{i_1}$, $a_{2j-1}^{i_1} a_{2j-1}^{i_2}$ and $a_{2j-1}^{i_2} a_{2j-1}^{i_3}$, respectively; after this operation, e_1, e_2, e_3 form a path, denoted by P_j. Finally, add arcs $a_{2j-1}^{i_3} c_j$ and $c_j b_{2j-1}^{i_1}$. For each $j \in [2m-1]$, we denote by C_j the set of vertices in "column j", i.e., $C_j = \{a_j^i, b_j^i \mid i \in [n]\}$. Observe that C_j induces a subgraph which is a matching with a path on three vertices P_j if j is odd; otherwise C_j induces a perfect matching from a's to b's. In either case, C_j induces an acyclic subgraph.

Theorem 3. ($\star$) SIMPLE ACYCLIC TEMPORALIZATION *with bounded lifetime* $\tau = 2$ *is* NP-*complete. In other words,* SIMPLE ACYCLIC TEMPORALIZATION *is para-*NP-*hard with regards to the lifetime parameter.*

4.2 Weak-Cycles

Similar results as in Sect. 4.1 can be proved for WEAK ACYCLIC TEMPORALIZATION. In particular, we show that whenever the girth is different from 4 we know an exact answer for our problem, while we leave open the case where the girth is 4. We also prove hardness for the problem when the lifetime is bounded to be at most 2. We omit here the corresponding proofs for space constraints.

Lemma 3. ($\star$) WEAK ACYCLIC TEMPORALIZATION *is always* **yes** *when the girth of the input digraph is at least 5, and* **no** *if girth is at most 3.*

Theorem 4. ($\star$) WEAK ACYCLIC TEMPORALIZATION *with bounded lifetime* $\tau = 2$ *is* NP-*complete. In other words,* WEAK ACYCLIC TEMPORALIZATION *is para-*NP-*hard with regards to the lifetime parameter.*

5 Conclusion

We present multiple manners of extending the concept of a cycle in temporal graphs. For each of these, interesting problems are studied in terms of algorithmics and tractability (see again Table 1). Almost all problems in this paper have been solved (in terms of tractability or feasability), except for WEAK ACYCLIC TEMPORALIZATION for girth 4 graphs. We leave this as an open problem.

References

1. Akrida, E.C., Mertzios, G.B., Spirakis, P.G., Raptopoulos, C.L.: The temporal explorer who returns to the base. J. Comput. Syst. Sci. **120**, 179–193 (2021)
2. Bang-Jensen, J., Bessy, S., Gonçalves, D., Picasarri-Arrieta, L.: Complexity of some arc-partition problems for digraphs. Theor. Comput. Sci. **928**, 167–182 (2022). https://doi.org/10.1016/J.TCS.2022.06.023
3. Bartlang, U.: Architecture and Methods for Flexible Content Management in Peer-to-Peer Systems. Springer (2010). https://doi.org/10.1007/978-3-8348-9645-2
4. Bermond, J.C., Cosnard, M., Pérennes, S.: Directed acyclic graphs with the unique dipath property. Theoret. Comput. Sci. **504**, 5–11 (2013)
5. Bumpus, B.M., Meeks, K.: Edge exploration of temporal graphs. Algorithmica **85**(3), 688–716 (2023)
6. Cormen, T.H., Leiserson, C.E., Rivest, R.L., Stein, C.: Introduction to Algorithms. MIT press (2022)
7. Erlebach, T., Hoffmann, M., Kammer, F.: On temporal graph exploration. J. Comput. Syst. Sci. **119**, 1–18 (2021)
8. Erlebach, T., Spooner, J.T.: Parameterised temporal exploration problems. J. Comput. Syst. Sci. **135**, 73–88 (2023)
9. Fortune, S., Hopcroft, J., Wyllie, J.: The directed subgraph homeomorphism problem. Theoret. Comput. Sci. **10**(2), 111–121 (1980)
10. Ganian, R., Hliněný, P., Kneis, J., Langer, A., Obdržálek, J., Rossmanith, P.: On digraph width measures in parameterized algorithmics. Discret. Appl. Math. **168**, 88–107 (2014)
11. Haag, R., Molter, H., Niedermeier, R., Renken, M.: Feedback edge sets in temporal graphs. Discret. Appl. Math. **307**, 65–78 (2022). https://doi.org/10.1016/J.DAM.2021.09.029
12. Holme, P.: Modern temporal network theory: a colloquium. Eur. Phys. J. B **88**(9), 1–30 (2015). https://doi.org/10.1140/epjb/e2015-60657-4
13. Johnson, T., Robertson, N., Seymour, P.D., Thomas, R.: Directed tree-width. J. Comb. Theory Ser. B **82**(1), 138–154 (2001)
14. Klobas, N., Mertzios, G.B., Molter, H., Spirakis, P.G.: The Complexity of Computing Optimum Labelings for Temporal Connectivity. In: Szeider, S., Ganian, R., Silva, A. (eds.) 47th International Symposium on Mathematical Foundations of Computer Science (MFCS 2022). Leibniz International Proceedings in Informatics (LIPIcs), vol. 241, pp. 62:1–62:15. Schloss Dagstuhl – Leibniz-Zentrum für Informatik, Dagstuhl, Germany (2022). https://doi.org/10.4230/LIPIcs.MFCS.2022.62

15. Klobas, N., Mertzios, G.B., Molter, H., Spirakis, P.G.: Temporal Graph Realization from Fastest Paths. In: Casteigts, A., Kuhn, F. (eds.) 3rd Symposium on Algorithmic Foundations of Dynamic Networks (SAND 2024). Leibniz International Proceedings in Informatics (LIPIcs), vol. 292, pp. 16:1–16:18. Schloss Dagstuhl – Leibniz-Zentrum für Informatik, Dagstuhl, Germany (2024). https://doi.org/10.4230/LIPIcs.SAND.2024.16
16. Latapy, M., Viard, T., Magnien, C.: Stream graphs and link streams for the modeling of interactions over time. Soc. Netw. Anal. Min. **8**(1), 1–29 (2018). https://doi.org/10.1007/s13278-018-0537-7
17. Marino, A., Silva, A.: Eulerian walks in temporal graphs. Algorithmica **85**(3), 805–830 (2023)
18. Mertzios, G.B., Molter, H., Spirakis, P.G.: Realizing temporal transportation trees (2024). https://arxiv.org/abs/2403.18513
19. Michail, O.: An introduction to temporal graphs: an algorithmic perspective. Internet Math. **12**(4), 239–280 (2016)
20. Nicosia, V., Tang, J., Mascolo, C., Musolesi, M., Russo, G., Latora, V.: Graph metrics for temporal networks. In: Temporal networks, pp. 15–40. Springer (2013). https://doi.org/10.1007/978-3-642-36461-7_2
21. Sapatnekar, S.: Timing. Springer (2004). https://doi.org/10.1007/b117318
22. Shmulevich, I., Dougherty, E.R.: Probabilistic Boolean networks: the modeling and control of gene regulatory networks. SIAM (2010)
23. Wu, H., Cheng, J., Huang, S., Ke, Y., Lu, Y., Xu, Y.: Path problems in temporal graphs. Proc. VLDB Endow. **7**(9), 721–732 (2014)
24. Xuan, B.B., Ferreira, A., Jarry, A.: Computing shortest, fastest, and foremost journeys in dynamic networks. Int. J. Found. Comput. Sci. **14**(02), 267–285 (2003)

Graph Traversal via Connected Mobile Agents

Saswata Jana[1], Giuseppe F. Italiano[2], and Partha Sarathi Mandal[1](✉)

[1] Indian Institute of Technology Guwahati, Guwahati, India
psm@iitg.ac.in
[2] Luiss University, Rome, Italy

Abstract. This paper considers the Hamiltonian walk problem in the multi-agent coordination framework, referred to as k-agents Hamiltonian walk problem (k-HWP). In this problem, a set of k connected agents collectively compute a spanning walk of a given undirected graph in the minimum steps. At each step, the agents are at k distinct vertices and the induced subgraph made by the occupied vertices remains connected. In the next consecutive steps, each agent may remain stationary or move to one of its neighbours. To the best of our knowledge, this problem has not been previously explored in the context of multi-agent systems with connectivity. As a generalization of the well-known Hamiltonian walk problem (when $k = 1$), k-HWP is NP-hard. We propose a $(3 - \frac{1}{21})$-approximation algorithm for 2-HWP on arbitrary graphs. For the tree, we define a restricted version of the problem and present an optimal algorithm for arbitrary values of k. Finally, we formalize the problem for k-uniform hypergraphs and present a $2(1 + \ln k)$-approximation algorithm. This result is also adapted to design an approximation algorithm for k-HWP on general graphs when $k = O(1)$.

Keywords: Approximation Algorithms · Graph Traversal · Mobile Agent · Hamiltonian Walk · Hypergraphs

1 Introduction

Graph traversal is a fundamental problem in computer science and robotics, where the goal is to visit every node of a graph at least once. A key objective of graph traversal is to minimize the number of steps needed to traverse the entire graph. Typically, such tasks can be accomplished by a single agent. However, relying on a single agent can be inefficient, prone to failure, and unsuitable for large or complex environments. These limitations motivate the need for multi-agent systems, where the agents coordinate among themselves to traverse the whole graph while reducing the traversal time and handling failures effectively.

S. Jana—Supported by Prime Minister's Research Fellowship (PMRF) scheme of the Govt. of India (PMRF-ID: 1902165).

One major challenge in coordinating multiple agents is ensuring safe and reliable communication during the traversal. In many practical systems, such as swarm robotics or drone networks, connectivity among agents is essential to maintain real-time coordination, prevent collisions, and quickly react to unexpected failures. In addition, the connectivity constraint also plays a key role in fault-tolerant settings. For instance, if one agent fails, the connected agents can detect the failure and either compensate for the loss or design a strategy to recover the lost functionality.

Preliminaries, Related Works and Problem Definition: Let $G = (V, E)$ be a simple undirected connected graph (without self-loops and multiple edges), where V is the set of vertices and E is the set of edges. An edge between two vertices v_i and v_j is denoted by (v_i, v_j). Let $n = |V|$ be the number of vertices and $m = |E|$ be the number of edges of G. $N(v)$ is the open neighbourhood of the vertex $v \in V$, consisting of all its neighbours, while $N[v]$ is the closed neighbourhood of v, defined as $N[v] = N(v) \cup \{v\}$. A sequence of distinct vertices $P = \{v_1, v_2, \cdots, v_p\}$ is called a *path* of the graph G if $(v_i, v_{i+1}) \in E \ \forall i \in \{1, 2, \cdots, p-1\}$. Whenever both endpoints of a path v_1 and v_p are explicitly mentioned, we denote the path as $P_{v_1 v_p}$. Additionally, if $v_1 = v_p$, the sequence is called a *cycle* of the graph G. If G admits a path of length $(n-1)$, then the path is called a *Hamiltonian path*. Similarly, if a graph has a cycle of length n, then the cycle is called a *Hamiltonian cycle*, and the graph is called *Hamiltonian graph*. In other words, a graph is called *Hamiltonian* if there exists a cycle that passes through each vertex of G exactly once. The problem of finding a Hamiltonian cycle in a graph, or checking whether a given graph is Hamiltonian, is known as the *Hamiltonian cycle problem*, which is one of Karp's 21 NP-complete problems [13]. Given that a class of graphs lacks a Hamiltonian path or cycle, there is growing interest in determining a minimum-length spanning walk of those graphs. A *walk* is a path with some possible repeated vertices. If both endpoints of the walk are the same (or different), the walk is termed a closed (or open) walk. A walk is a *spanning walk* of G if it passes through each vertex of G at least once. A closed spanning walk of minimum length is termed as *Hamiltonian walk*. The length of a Hamiltonian walk of the graph G is known as *Hamiltonian number* and denoted as $h^+(G)$. If $h^+(G) = n$, the graph G is Hamiltonian and vice versa. $n \leq h^+(G) \leq 2(n-1)$. It is well known that $h^+(G) = 2n - 2$ iff G is a tree [8]. An open spanning walk of G is a spanning walk with different endpoints, and we use the notation $h^-(G)$ to denote the length of the minimum open spanning walk of G. Finding the minimum-length open spanning walk of a graph is known as the *open Hamiltonian walk problem*. If the graph G is Hamiltonian, then $h^-(G) = (n-1)$. However, the converse is not true.

The challenge of finding an open spanning walk is closely related to the classic *traveling salesman problem* (TSP), in which the objective is to locate a minimum weight Hamiltonian cycle in a given complete weighted graph. Christofides-Serdyukov [5,16] proposed a $\frac{3}{2}$-approximation algorithm for TSP if the weight function satisfies the triangular inequality. After decades, Karlin et al. [12] give a randomized $\frac{3}{2} - \epsilon$ approximation algorithm for some $\epsilon > 10^{-36}$. A polynomial time approximation scheme (PTAS) exists for some special instances of the TSP, such as for Euclidean TSP [2,15], planar TSP [1,9,14], and bounded genus TSP [6]. The *multiple traveling salesman problem* [4] is a generalization of the TSP, where multiple salesmen independently (no restriction to the connectivity) visit the vertices of the graph. Hoogeveen [10] modified Christofide's heuristic to find a minimum weight Hamiltonian path of a given weighted complete graph when the weights satisfy the triangular inequality. The modified heuristic also gives a $\frac{3}{2}$ approximation factor, which is still the best-known factor for the problem. We can apply the modified Christofides heuristic to find an open spanning walk for an undirected, unweighted, and connected graph G by converting it into a complete weighted graph. To do this, we assign a weight equal to one to each existing edge and add all missing edges with a weight equal to the length of the shortest paths between corresponding vertices.

We address the open Hamiltonian walk problem from the perspective of a mobile agent that explores the entire graph G in a minimum number of steps, starting from an arbitrary vertex. At each step, the agent can move to one of its neighbouring vertices. Therefore, any minimum open-spanning walk constitutes a feasible solution. Additionally, we can apply the modified Christofide's heuristic [10] to obtain a $\frac{3}{2}$-approximation algorithm for the problem. In this paper, we formulate the generalized version of the Hamiltonian walk problem, which we named as *k-agent Hamiltonian Walk problem* (k-HWP), where a set of k (≥ 1) agents collectively explore the graph. The constraint is that at any instant of time $t(\geq 0)$, k agents must lie on k distinct vertices of G, so that the subgraph induced by the vertices occupied by the k agents must be connected. Initially, the agents can start from any arbitrary vertices that satisfy the above constraints. In the next step, all agents move synchronously to one of their neighbouring vertices or choose to remain stationary. Let $A = \{a_1, a_2, \cdots, a_k\}$ be the set of k agents. We use v_i^t to denote the vertex v_i occupied by a agent a_i at the t-th step. We denote the *configuration* at the t-th step by $\mathcal{C}_t$, and defined by the k-tuple $(v_1^t, v_2^t, \cdots, v_k^t)$, where $v_i^t \neq v_j^t, \forall i \neq j$ and the subgraph induced by the set of vertices $\{v_1^t, v_2^t, \cdots, v_k^t\} \subseteq V$ is connected. For convenience, we slightly abuse the notation $\mathcal{C}_t$ to denote the set $\{v_1^t, v_2^t, \cdots, v_k^t\}$ and, more generally, any arbitrary configuration. Two configurations, $\mathcal{C}_t$ and $\mathcal{C}_{t'}$, are said to be *adjacent* if $\forall i \in \{1, 2, \cdots, k\}$ either $v_i^t = v_i^{t'}$ or $(v_i^t, v_i^{t'}) \in E$. We imagine a graph whose vertices correspond to configurations, where two vertices are adjacent if the corresponding configurations are adjacent. We refer to the edge between two adjacent vertices, i.e., configurations, as a *transition edge*. The objective of k-HWP is to find a sequence of configurations $\{\mathcal{C}_0, \mathcal{C}_1, \cdots, \mathcal{C}_l\}$ with a *minimum length* (i.e., l is minimum) such that each vertex of G appears in at least one configuration in the sequence, and there is a transition edge between every two consecutive configurations. In other words, the objective is to find an open spanning walk of configurations $\{\mathcal{C}_t\}_{t=0}^l$ of minimum length, where each vertex in this walk is a k-tuple configuration and $\cup_{t=0}^l \cup_{i=1}^k v_i^t = V$. We denote the length of this open walk by $h_k^-(G)$. If there are $(l+1)$ many configurations in the walk, then $h_k^-(G) = l$. When $k = 1$, $h_1^-(G)$ coincides with $h^-(G)$. An open walk of configurations is called a *transition walk*. Since we focus solely on the open walk in this paper, we use $h_k(G)$, instead of $h_k^-(G)$, to denote the length of the minimum open spanning walk of configurations for the graph G with k agents. The NP-completeness of k-HWP follows from the fact that when $k = 1$, it is equivalent to the Hamiltonian walk problem, which is known to be NP-complete. We present the formal definition of k-HWP below.

Definition 1 (Problem: k-HWP). *Consider an undirected connected graph G and a collection of k agents. The goal is to find a sequence of configurations of minimum length such that each successive pair in the sequence is adjacent, and every vertex in G is included at least once in one of these configurations.*

When $k = 2$, any configuration represents an edge of G. Therefore, we can interpret the problem as traversing the graph through its edges.

Definition 2 (r-transition edge). *The transition edge between two configurations $\mathcal{C}_t$ and $\mathcal{C}_{t'}$ is said to be a r-transition edge if $\mathcal{C}_{t'}$ has exactly r vertices that are not in $\mathcal{C}_t$.*

For example of a r-transition edge, let $k = 4$, $\mathcal{C}_t = (v_1, v_2, v_3, v_4)$ and $\mathcal{C}_{t'} = (v_5, v_2, v_4, v_6)$. If $\mathcal{C}_t$ and $\mathcal{C}_{t'}$ are adjacent, then the edge between them is called a 2-transition edge. The transition edges of k-HWP can be categorized into k distinct classes based on the value of $r \in \{1, 2, \cdots, k\}$. We disregard 0-transition edges, which indicate that agents either remain stationary or rearrange their positions without visiting new vertices. Since our objective is to identify a transition walk of minimum length, we consistently strive to minimize the number of configurations encountered during any transition walk. Due to page limits, some proofs and pseudocode are deferred to the full version of the paper [11].

1.1 Our Contribution

In this paper, our contributions are the following:

- We define k-agents Hamiltonian walk problem (k-HWP).
- For the tree, we propose an optimal algorithm when $k \leq 3$. For any value of k, we present an optimal algorithm for the restricted version of the problem on tree, where we only allow 1-transition edges (Theorem 3).
- We give a $(3 - \frac{1}{21})$-approximation algorithm on arbitrary graphs for $k = 2$ (Theorem 4).
- We extend the problem definition to hypergraphs and propose a $2(1 + \ln k)$-approximation algorithm for k-uniform hypergraphs (Theorem 5). This algorithm is further developed into an approximation algorithm for k-HWP, when $k = O(1)$ (Theorem 6).

2 Algorithms for Tree

Since the k-HWP problem is NP-hard for general graphs, our goal is to explore specific graph classes where optimal solutions can be achieved. This section examines k-HWP problem on acyclic graphs and presents results for a constrained version of the problem. First, we describe an optimal strategy (1-HWP-FOR-TREE) to solve 1-HWP for tree. This serves as a foundation for understanding the generalized strategy (for arbitrary values of k), which we discuss later in the section. A vertex is called *leaf* (or *pendant*) if it has degree one. The diameter of the graph G, denoted $diam(G)$, is the length of the longest path.

Description of the Algorithm (1-HWP-FOR-TREE): Let $P^* = P_{v_1^* v_2^*}$ be a longest path of the tree G. Then, both v_1^* and v_2^* must be leaves of G. The agent starts the traversal from v_1^* and aims to eventually reach v_2^* while traversing all the vertices. If multiple unexplored vertices are available, it prioritizes those not located on P^*. Whenever all adjacent vertices are explored, it backtracks to its parent vertex. A parent vertex of v is the vertex from which the vertex v is explored for the first time. We omit the analysis and the pseudocode of the algorithm due to space constraints. Our analysis leads to the following theorem.

Theorem 1. *Algorithm* 1-HWP-FOR-TREE *provides an optimal solution for 1-HWP in polynomial time, when the input graph G is a tree.*

Using the above strategy, we now design an algorithm for a restricted version of k-HWP on trees, where the restriction is on the type of transition edges allowed between two configurations. We begin with the following structural property.

Theorem 2. *If G is a tree and the edge between two configurations $\mathcal{C}_t$ and $\mathcal{C}_{t'}$ in the k-HWP is an r-transition edge, then $r \leq \lfloor \frac{k}{2} \rfloor$, where $k \geq 2$.*

Proof. We first prove that there must exist a vertex v in $\mathcal{C}_t \cap \mathcal{C}_{t'}$. Suppose, on the contrary, that $\mathcal{C}_t \cap \mathcal{C}_{t'} = \emptyset$. In such a scenario, there exist two distinct paths between the vertices v_i^t and v_j^t, where v_i^t and v_j^t are the positions of the agents a_i and a_j, respectively, in the configuration $\mathcal{C}_t$. Since the induced graph $G[\mathcal{C}_t]$ made by the vertices of $\mathcal{C}_t$ is connected, there exists a path between v_i^t and v_j^t that entirely lies in $G[\mathcal{C}_t]$. An alternative path proceeds via the edge $(v_i^t, v_i^{t'})$, followed by a path within $G[\mathcal{C}_{t'}]$ from $v_i^{t'}$ to $v_j^{t'}$, and concludes with the edge $(v_j^{t'}, v_j^t)$. The existence of two such distinct paths contradicts the fact that there is always a unique path between two vertices in a tree.

Now consider a vertex $v_i^{t'} \in \mathcal{C}_{t'} \setminus \mathcal{C}_t$. We claim that $v_i^t \in \mathcal{C}_{t'}$. Otherwise, there would exist two paths between some $v \in \mathcal{C}_t \cap \mathcal{C}_{t'}$ and $v_i^{t'}$: one passing through v_i^t and the other does not, which is again a contradiction. Hence, for every $v_i^{t'} \in \mathcal{C}_{t'} \setminus \mathcal{C}_t$, the corresponding $v_i^t \in \mathcal{C}_t \cap \mathcal{C}_{t'}$. In other words, for each new vertex of the current configuration ($\mathcal{C}_{t'}$), we always have a unique vertex that is part of both the current and previous configuration ($\mathcal{C}_t$). Thus the proof. □

The above result implies that when $k \leq 3$, all transition edges are necessarily 1-transition edges. For larger values of k, between the movements of one configuration to the other, the agents might encounter $k/2$ new vertices. To simplify the transition structure and enable the design of an optimal algorithm, we consider a restricted version of k-HWP, where each transition edge must be a 1-transition edge, regardless of the number of agents (k). We refer to this problem as k-*agents restricted Hamiltonian walk problem* (k-RHWP). We present a polynomial-time algorithm, k-RHWP-FOR-TREE, that computes an optimal solution to the k-RHWP on trees. The optimal length of the k-RHWP on G is denoted by $h_k^r(G)$. Note that $h_2^r(G) = h_2(G)$ and $h_3^r(G) = h_3(G)$. We introduce subsequent definitions (Definition 3, 4), which are limited to the tree.

Definition 3 (Problem: k-RHWP). *Consider an undirected connected graph G along with a collection of k agents. The objective is to find a sequence of configurations of minimum length such that between every two consecutive configurations in the sequence there is a 1-transition edge, and every vertex of G is included at least once in one of these configurations.*

Definition 4 (Explored edge or vertex). *Let C_t and $C_{t'}$ be two adjacent configurations in a transition walk of k-RHWP; then there exists exactly one vertex $v_i^{t'} \in C_{t'} \setminus C_t$. We say that the edge $(v_i^t, v_i^{t'})$ is explored (or encountered) by the transition from C_t to $C_{t'}$ or the vertex $v_i^{t'}$ is explored (or encountered).*

Next, we describe the algorithm k-RHWP-FOR-TREE for solving k-RHWP on trees. We designate one of the agents as the head, who explores the graph. All other agents either follow the head or remain stationary to maintain connectivity.

Description of the Algorithm (k-RHWP-FOR-TREE): Let $P^* = P_{v_1^* v_2^*}$ be a longest path of G. All vertices are initially unexplored. Agents are initially deployed using the strategy 1-HWP-FOR-TREE. The agent a_i is placed at the vertex v_i^0, the i-th explored vertex by 1-HWP-FOR-TREE. So, the initial configuration C_0 equals $(v_1^0, v_2^0, \cdots, v_k^0)$, where $v_1^0 = v_1^*$. We refer to the vertices v_k^0 and v_1^0 as the *head* (v_H) and the *tail* (v_T) of the current configuration, respectively. Additionally, we apply the terms head and tail to agents at v_H and v_T, respectively. The head takes priority in exploring the graph. If the head encounters a situation where it finds all its neighbours as explored, it locates the nearest occupied vertex that has at least one unexplored neighbour. This vertex then becomes the new head, while the previous head is designated as the new tail. If the head has multiple unexplored neighbours, it selects the vertex v, which does not lie on P^*, as its next target of movement and sets $parent(v) = v_H$. If the neighbours of all the occupied vertices (including head) in the current configuration are explored, the agent a_i closest to P^* becomes the new head, while the previous head becomes the new tail. In this case, agent a_i decides its target as $parent(v')$, where v' is the current position of a_i. Once the head sets its target for the next movement, all the agents lying on the path between head and tail, including the tail, will move simultaneously in the direction of the head, while all other agents remain stationary. If the tail is not a leaf vertex of the induced graph G', which is formed by all occupied vertices, then moving the tail would disconnect G'. In such a case, we assign the tail to one of the leaf vertices of G', excluding both the head and the vertex nearest to P^*, if possible. Once all the agents between v_H and v_T have moved to their designated targets, we update the head and tail accordingly. Whenever the vertex v_2^* becomes the head, the algorithm terminates. We leave out the analysis and pseudocode of the algorithm due to page constraints. Our analysis leads to the following theorem.

Theorem 3. *Algorithm* K-RHWP-FOR-TREE *provides an optimal solution for k-RHWP in polynomial time, when the input graph G is a tree.*

3 Algorithms for Arbitrary Graph in Case of k = 2

Here, we present an approximation algorithm for the 2-HWP on an arbitrary graph G. We start by introducing a simple algorithm that achieves an asymptotic approximation factor of 3, using the relationship between $h_1(G)$ and $h_2(G)$.

Lemma 1. $h_1(G) \leq 2 \cdot h_2(G) + 1$.

The Approximation Algorithm for 2-HWP: Let $W_1 = \{v_1, v_2, \cdots, v_{l+1}\}$ be a spanning walk of configurations with one agent using some known β-approximation algorithm for the open Hamiltonian walk problem. Then $l \leq \beta \cdot h_1(G)$. The walk W_1 can be converted to a spanning walk of configurations W_2 with two agents, where $W_2 = \{(v_1, v_2), (v_2, v_3), \cdots, (v_l, v_{l+1})\}$. The length of the walk W_2 is $(l-1) \leq \beta \cdot h_1(G) - 1 \leq 2\beta \cdot h_2(G) + (\beta - 1)$, by Lemma 1. The best known approximation factor for the Hamiltonian walk problem is $3/2$ by Hoogeveen [10]. Hence, we have a solution of size at most $(3h_2(G) + 1)$.

Now, we want to find out if there is an approximation algorithm for 2-HWP that has an approximation factor less than 3. Theorem 4 conclusively confirms the possibility. The proposed algorithm uses two subroutines. One is modified Christofide's heuristic [10] to find the minimum-weight Hamiltonian path in a complete weighted graph. The other is an approximation algorithm for the *maximum weighted r-set packing problem* ($max_r SPP$) [18], where we are given a collection of weighted sets, each of which contains at most r elements from a fixed universe of finite elements. The goal is to find a sub-collection of pairwise disjoint sets with the maximum total weight.

Overview of the Improved Algorithm for 2-HWP: First, we create a weighted set-packing instance from the given unweighted graph G (Sect. 3.1). Then, we apply an approximation algorithm of the set-packing problem to get a solution, and from that solution, we construct a tree $Tr(G)$ that spans all the vertices of V (Sect. 3.2). Next, we find an open Hamiltonian walk in the tree $Tr(G)$, which gives us the required solution (Sect. 3.3). The proofs of all lemmas are excluded due to page limits.

3.1 Creating a Set-Packing Instance from G

From a given instance of 2-HWP, we first create an instance of $max_6 SPP$, denoted as $\mathcal{I}_{SP}(G)$. The motivation behind the construction is to select all possible cases from which we can get a 2-transition edge. These transitions may arise from a cycle of length four (C_4) or a grid of size 2×3 or any combination of the two. Finding such a disjoint collection of sets is preferable, as it reduces repeated visits to certain vertices. This can be achieved by applying the set-packing algorithm. However, it is possible that two C_4's intersect at a single vertex (as shown in Fig. 1). In such cases, all vertices of two C_4's can be traversed using 4 configurations. So, selecting only disjoint sets does not fully satisfy our objective. We define several types of packing sets to adapt such subgraphs in our solution.

We construct four types of weighted sets: two corresponding to each 4-length cycle $C = \{v_1, v_2, v_3, v_4\}$, and two corresponding to each 2×3 grid $D = \{v_1, v_2, v_3, v_4, v_5, v_6\}$ in G. Note that G may not contain any C_4. In that case, we have a simpler algorithm with a better approximation factor, which is discussed at the end of the section (Theorem 2). However, our main focus is the arbitrary case where the graph may be dense and contains many C_4's.

- (Type-I) A set $C_1^1 = C$ with weight four.
- (Type-II) Four sets, each of the form $C_2^i = C \setminus \{v_i\} \cup \{u_C^i\}$ with weight three for $1 \leq i \leq 4$, where u_C^i is a dummy variable corresponding to v_i, not belonging to V and not previously used in the construction process.
- (Type-III) A set $D = \{v_1, v_2, v_3, v_4, v_5, v_6\}$ with weight six.
- (Type-IV) For each set D of Type-III, we create another six sets, each of the form $D \setminus \{v_i\} \cup \{w_D^i\}$ with weight five for $1 \leq i \leq 6$, where w_D^i is a dummy variable corresponding to v_i, not belonging to V and not previously used.

We call all these sets the *packing set*. The weights are assigned according to how many vertices a packing set contains from the vertex set V. Note that $\{v_1, v_2, v_3, v_4\}$ being a cycle of length four, between the configurations (v_1, v_2) and (v_4, v_3), there is a transition edge. Similarly, if $\{v_1, v_2, v_3, v_4, v_5, v_6\}$ is a grid

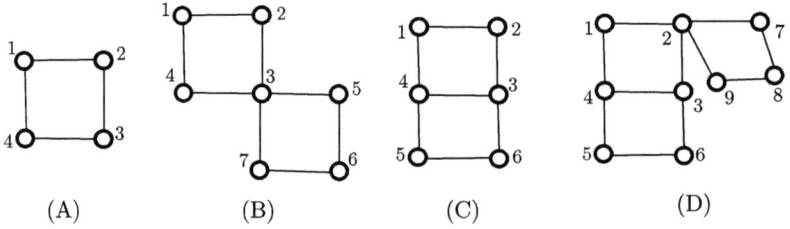

Fig. 1. (A) A Type-I set $\{1, 2, 3, 4\}$, (B) A Type-I set $\{1, 2, 3, 4\}$ and a Type-II set $\{u, 5, 6, 7\}$, where u is a dummy variable of the vertex 3, (C) A Type-III set $\{1, 2, 3, 4, 5, 6\}$, (D) A Type-I set $\{2, 7, 8, 9\}$ and a Type-IV set $\{1, v, 3, 4, 5, 6\}$, where v is the dummy variable of the vertex 2. These packing sets are used to accommodate the above-mentioned subgraphs in our solution.

of size 2 × 3, there must be two transition edges between (v_1, v_2) and (v_4, v_3), and between the configurations (v_4, v_3) and (v_5, v_6).
G can have at most $\binom{n}{4}$ cycles of length four. For each such cycle, we create one Type-I packing set and four Type-II packing sets. Furthermore, G has at most $\binom{n}{6}$ grids of size 2 × 3. For each such grid, we make one Type-III packing set and six Type-IV packing sets. Thus, for a given graph G, we create at most $5 \cdot \binom{n}{4} + 7 \cdot \binom{n}{6} = O(n^6)$ sets, where each set is of size at most six and the universal set of the procedure is $V \cup (\cup_{C \in G} \cup_{i=1}^{4} u_C^i) \cup (\cup_{D \in G} \cup_{j=1}^{6} w_D^j)$, where C is a 4 length cycle and D is a 2 × 3 grid in G. All u_C^i and w_D^j ($\forall i, j$) are distinct.

$max_k SPP$ is NP-hard and since the introduction of the set packing problem, a significant research has been conducted in the past few decades for the weighted, unweighted, and online cases [1,3,7,17,18]. The best known polynomial-time approximation algorithm of the weighted k-set packing problem is given by Thiery and Ward [18], achieving a factor slightly less than $\frac{2}{k+1}$, which asymptotically approaches $\frac{4}{2k+1}$ as k grows. We define $max_6(\mathcal{I})$ to represent the problem $max_6 SPP$ for the instance $\mathcal{I}$. We denote the optimal value of $max_6(\mathcal{I}_{SP}(G))$ by $w(OPT_{SP}(G))$. Then the following lemma holds:

Lemma 2. $h_2(G) \geq (n - \frac{w(OPT_{SP}(G))}{2} - 1)$.

Our first step in designing an approximation algorithm is to create a tree $Tr(G)$ based on the approximate solution of $max_6(\mathcal{I}_{SP}(G))$. There are two types of vertices in the tree $Tr(G)$: some are the vertices of G, and the remaining ones are the edges of G, which we refer to as *contracted vertices*. We discuss the construction process in the following section.

3.2 Construction of the Tree Tr(G) that Spans V

Let Sol be one of the approximation solutions of $max_6(\mathcal{I}_{SP}(G))$. Let $w(Sol_{SP}(G))$ be the value (weight) of the solution returned by Sol. Now we do the following:

- For each Type-I packing set $\{v_1, v_2, v_3, v_4\} \in Sol$ of weight four, we add two contracted vertices (v_1, v_2), (v_4, v_3) to $Tr(G)$ and connect them by an edge. Adding this edge spans 4 distinct vertices of G and creates a new component.
- For each Type-II packing set $(C = \{v_1, v_2, v_3, v_4\}) \setminus \{v_i\} \cup \{u_C^i\} \in Sol$ of weight three for some $1 \leq i \leq 4$, we add two contracted vertices (v_1, v_2) and (v_4, v_3) to $Tr(G)$, and connect them with an edge, which span three distinct vertices of G, since the vertex v_i is already in another packing set $S \in Sol$. Let $v_j \in C$ and $v_l \in S$ be the associated vertices contracted with v_i. We then add an edge between (v_i, v_j) and (v_i, v_l), ensuring that all the vertices of C and S are part of the same connected component of $Tr(G)$.
- For each Type-III packing set $\{v_1, v_2, v_3, v_4, v_5, v_6\} \in Sol$ of weight six, we build three contracted vertices (v_1, v_2), (v_4, v_3), (v_5, v_6) and add to $Tr(G)$. We join the edges between the first and last two, which span six distinct vertices of V and create one new component.

- For each Type-IV packing set $D = (\{v_1, v_2, v_3, v_4, v_5, v_6\}) \setminus \{v_i\} \cup \{w_D^i\} \in Sol$ of weight five for some $1 \leq i \leq 6$, we select three contracted vertices (v_1, v_2), $(v_4, v_3), (v_5, v_6)$ and add them to $Tr(G)$ with the edges between the first and last two, which span five distinct vertices (except v_i) of V, where v_i is present in another packing set $S \in Sol$. Let $v_j \in C$ and $v_l \in S$ be the associated vertices contracted with v_i. We also placed an edge between (v_i, v_j) and (v_i, v_l) that makes all the vertices of C and S in one component of $Tr(G)$.

The number of vertices in V included by the above procedure is $w(Sol_{SP}(G))$. Let, $Sol = Sol(I) \cup Sol(II) \cup Sol(III) \cup Sol(IV)$, where $Sol(i)$ consists of all the packing sets of Type-i, $i \in \{I, II, III, IV\}$. So, the total number of edges added after the procedure is $\frac{w(Sol(I)_{SP}(G))}{4} + \frac{2 \cdot w(Sol(II)_{SP}(G))}{3} + \frac{w(Sol(III)_{SP}(G))}{3} + \frac{3 \cdot w(Sol(IV)_{SP}(G))}{5}$. The number of trees in the forest $Tr(G)$ (disjoint union of trees) after the procedure is $\frac{w(Sol(I)_{SP}(G))}{4} + \frac{w(Sol(III)_{SP}(G))}{6}$. The number of vertices in V yet to be spanned is $(n - w(Sol_{SP}(G)))$. Since the graph G is connected, we can always find a contracted vertex (v, v') in $Tr(G)$ such that $v \in V$ is not spanned by the above procedure. We add the vertex v' to the forest $Tr(G)$ and join the edge between the vertex v and the contracted vertex (v, v'). After this, we again select a vertex from V that is not present in the forest $Tr(G)$ and connect it to one of the vertices of $Tr(G)$. We continue the procedure until it spans all the vertices of V. The procedure includes $(n - w(Sol_{SP}(G)))$ additional edges to span all remaining $(n - w(Sol_{SP}(G)))$ vertices of V. Thereafter, we make the forest $Tr(G)$ connected or a single tree. To do so, we find two trees Tr_1 and Tr_2 of the forest $Tr(G)$ such that there is an edge $e = (v_1, v_2) \in E$ such that v_1 is present in the tree Tr_1 and v_2 is present in the tree Tr_2. We include a contracted vertex (v_1, v_2) in the forest $Tr(G)$. Then we connect an edge between (v_1, v_2) and the vertex of Tr_1 which contains v_1, and another edge between (v_1, v_2) and the vertex of Tr_2 which contains v_2. Since there is a $n_c = \frac{w(Sol(I)_{SP}(G))}{4} + \frac{w(Sol(III)_{SP}(G))}{6}$ number of trees after the first phase of the procedure, the last phase of the procedure needs exactly $(2n_c - 2)$ many edges. Hence, the total number of edges added after all the procedures is,

$$len(Tr(G)) = \frac{w(Sol(I)_{SP}(G))}{4} + \frac{2 \cdot w(Sol(II)_{SP}(G))}{3} + \frac{w(Sol(III)_{SP}(G))}{3}$$
$$+ \frac{3 \cdot w(Sol(IV)_{SP}(G))}{5} + (n - w(Sol_{SP}(G)))$$
$$+ 2 \cdot (\frac{w(Sol(I)_{SP}(G))}{4} + \frac{w(Sol(III)_{SP}(G))}{6}) - 1 \quad (1)$$

3.3 Finding an Open Hamiltonian Walk on the Tree $Tr(G)$

The above procedure implies that an open Hamiltonian walk of $Tr(G)$ with one agent corresponds to an open walk of configurations with two agents that spans all the vertices in V. Theorem 1 guarantees that for a tree with diameter d and $(n-1)$ edges, the length of the optimal open Hamiltonian walk is

$2(n-1)-d$. To find a better approximation result, here we give an alternative way to find the open Hamiltonian walk of $Tr(G)$ by using modified Christofide's heuristic proposed by Hoogeveen [10]. The heuristic applies to the complete weighted graph with weight function satisfying the triangular inequality. Therefore, we first convert our constructed tree $Tr(G)$ into a complete weighted graph $Tr^*(G)$ as follows: each existing edge of $Tr(G)$ is assigned a weight of one, while each missing edge between two vertices tr_1 and tr_2 is given a weight equal to the length of the shortest path between them in the line graph of G or in G, depending on whether the vertex is contracted or not. If tr_1 or tr_2 is a non-contracted vertex (i.e., in V), we compute the length between them in G. However, if both tr_1 and tr_2 are contracted vertices, we calculate the shortest length in the line graph of G. By assigning weights this way, the triangular inequality is preserved. Next, similar to the modified Christofide's heuristic, we first find the minimum spanning tree (MST_{Tr^*}) of the newly created graph $Tr^*(G)$, which gives the tree $Tr(G)$. Then we find the minimum matching (MM_{Tr^*}) between all the odd-degree vertices, except for two. The detail and analysis of this heuristic can be found in [10]. Let $cost(MST_{Tr^*})$ and $cost(MM_{Tr^*})$ be the cost of the MST_{Tr^*} and MM_{Tr^*}, respectively. We keep two odd-degree vertices unmatched as we look for the path, not the cycle. By adding the matching edges, all the vertices in $Tr(G)$ become even-degree vertices except two, which is sufficient to get an Eulerian path (a path traversing each edge exactly once). The length of this Eulerian path is $cost(MST_{Tr^*}) + cost(MM_{Tr^*}) = len(Tr(G)) + cost(MM_{Tr^*})$.

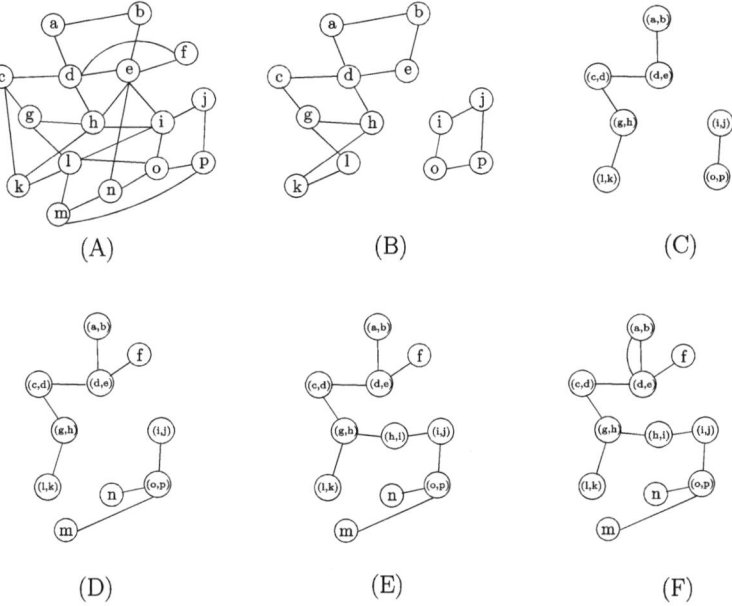

Fig. 2. Illustrating a step-by-step execution of the algorithm

This path can be easily modified to obtain an open walk of a configuration of G with two agents, without changing its length. Hence, if the complete procedure as discussed above is referred to as ALG_2, then the length of the transition walk returned by ALG_2 is $t_{ALG_2} = len(Tr(G)) + cost(MM_{Tr^*})$.

A step-by-step execution of the algorithm is shown in Fig. 2. Figure 2(A) represents base graph G. Figure 2(B) depicts all the packing sets $\{i, j, p, o\}$, $\{a, b, e, u\}$, $\{c, d, h, g, l, k\}$ selected by Sol, where u is the dummy vertex for d. Figure 2(C) shows the creation of the forest $Tr(G)$. $\{i, j, p, o\}$ being a Type-I packing set, we incorporate two vertices (i, j), (o, p) within $Tr(G)$ and insert an edge between them. $\{c, d, h, g, k, l\}$ being a Type-III packing set, we add three vertices (c, d), (g, h), (l, k), and subsequently insert edges to connect them. $\{a, b, e, u\}$ being a Type-II packing set and u being the dummy variable of d, we draw an edge between (a, b) and (d, e) and between (c, d) and (d, e). Figure 2(D) describes the process of connecting all the leftover vertices $\{f, m, n\}$ of G to $Tr(G)$. Figure 2(E) portrays of converting the forest $Tr(G)$ into tree, where we select an edge (h, i) that links them. Then, we insert the vertex (h, i) and connect it to both (g, h) and (i, j). In Fig. 2(F) we convert two odd-degree contracted vertices vertices (a, b) and (d, e), obtained from the same Type-II packing set, into even-degree by adding an edge between them. A bound on $cost(MM_{Tr^*})$ is provided in the lemma below for the final analysis of the procedure ALG_2.

Lemma 3. $cost(MM_{Tr^*}) \leq \frac{1}{2}(h_1(G) + n\_odd_c)$, where n_odd_c is the number of odd-degree contracted vertices in the tree $Tr(G)$.

By using the above lemma, we have $t_{ALG_2} \leq len(Tr(G)) + \frac{1}{2}(h_1(G) + n_{odd_c})$. To prove the following lemma, we modify the tree $Tr(G)$ as follows. Let tr_1 and tr_2 be two contracted vertices corresponding to some Type-I or Type-II packing set. If both tr_1 and tr_2 are odd-degree vertices in the tree $Tr(G)$, then we add another edge between them. This modification increases the number of edges of $Tr(G)$ by one, while decreasing the number of odd-degree contracted vertices by two. Let t'_{LAG_2} be the length of the transition walk returned by our algorithm ALG_2 after this modification. Then $t'_{ALG_2} \leq len(Tr(G)) - 1 + \frac{1}{2}(h_1(G) + n_{odd_c} - 2) = len(Tr(G)) + \frac{1}{2}(h_1(G) + n_{odd_c})$. Thus, the upper bound on the length of the walk remains unaltered. Therefore, we assume that, among the two contracted vertices constructed from a Type-I or Type-II packing set, at least one of them must be of even degree.

Lemma 4. $n\_odd_c \leq \frac{1}{4}w(Sol(I)_{SP}(G)) + \frac{1}{3}w(Sol(II)_{SP}(G)) + \frac{1}{3}w(Sol(III)_{SP}(G)) + \frac{3}{5}w(Sol(IV)_{SP}(G)))$, where n_{odd_c} is the number of odd degree contracted vertices in the modified tree $Tr(G)$.

By applying Lemma 3 and 4 and Eq. 1, we get

$$t_{ALG_2} = len(Tr(G)) + cost(MM_{Tr^*})$$
$$\leq n - w(Sol_{SP}(G)) + \frac{7 \cdot w(Sol(I)_{SP}(G))}{8} + \frac{5 \cdot w(Sol(II)_{SP}(G))}{6}$$
$$+ \frac{11 \cdot w(Sol(III)_{SP}(G))}{12} + \frac{9 \cdot w(Sol(IV)_{SP}(G))}{10} - 2 + \frac{h_1(G)}{2}$$
$$= n - \frac{w(Sol_{SP}(G))}{12} - 2 + \frac{h_1(G)}{2}$$

We have $w(Sol_{SP}(G)) \geq \alpha \cdot w(OPT_{SP}(G))$, where α is the approximation factor of the approximation algorithm Sol to the set packing problem max_6SPP. Furthermore, $w(OPT_{SP}(G)) \leq 2h_2(G) + 1$, as the maximum weight per configuration by the construction process is two. We also have $h_1(G) \leq 2h_2(G) + 1$, from Lemma 1 and $h_2(G) \geq (n - \frac{w(OPT_{SP}(G))}{2} - 1)$, from Lemma 2. Combining all these inequalities, we have the following.

$$t_{ALG_2} \leq n - \frac{\alpha \cdot w(OPT_{SP}(G))}{12} - 2 + h_2(G) - 1$$
$$\leq (n - \frac{w(OPT_{SP}(G))}{2} - 1) + (\frac{1}{2} - \frac{\alpha}{12})w(OPT_{SP}(G)) + h_2(G) - 2$$
$$\leq h_2(G) + (1 - \frac{\alpha}{6})h_2(G) + h_2(G) = (3 - \frac{\alpha}{6}) h_2(G)$$

Theorem 4. *There exists a $(3 - \frac{1}{21})$-approximation algorithm for 2-HWP. If the graph has no C_4, the approximation factor reduces to two.*

Proof. The best known approximation algorithm to max_6SPP is $\frac{2}{7}$ by Theiry and Hard [18]. Using their algorithm as Sol and setting $\alpha = \frac{2}{7}$, we have

$$t_{ALG_2} \leq (3 - \frac{1}{21})h_2(G)$$

If the graph has no C_4, the instance $\mathcal{I}_{SP}(G) = \emptyset$, implies that $w(OPT_{SP}(G)) = 0$. Additionally, all the transitions are being 1-transitions, $h_2(G) = h_2^r(G) \geq (n-2)$. Hence, from the inequality above, $t_{ALG_2} \leq (n-2) + (h_2(G) - 1) \leq 2h_2(G)$. □

4 k-HWP on Hypergraphs

Here, we formulate the problem k-HWP on hypergraphs and design an approximation algorithm to solve the problem. The formulation of the problem and the proposed solution will provide insight to obtain a solution for k-HWP on the graph. A hypergraph generalizes a graph by allowing each hyperedge to connect any number of vertices. In this paper, we consider the undirected k-uniform hypergraph without multiple edges, where each hyperedge connects exactly k vertices. We misuse $G = (V, E)$ to represent both the graph and the hypergraph. However, a hyperedge in an k-uniform hypergraph is a subset of V of size k. The line graph $L(G)$ of a hypergraph G is a graph where each vertex represents a hyperedge of G, and two vertices are adjacent if their corresponding hyperedges intersect. The hypergraph G is connected if $L(G)$ is connected.

Before defining the problem on the hypergraph, let us revisit the problem formulation on the simple graph with $k = 2$. In 2-HWP, we traverse the graph via the edges, with transitions classified as shifts or jumps. If the transition edge between (x_i, y_i) and (x_j, y_j) is a 1-transition edge, the pairs share a common vertex, and the move is called a "shift". Otherwise, it's a 2-transition edge, where one agent moves along (x_i, x_j) and the other along (y_i, y_j). After their movements, they reach (x_j, y_j) and the transition is called "jump". We introduce a similar notion for hypergraphs. Let all k agents initially lie on k distinct vertices $\{v_1^0, v_2^0, \cdots, v_k^0\}$ of G such that there is a hyperedge of G, say e_0, that connects all these vertices. In the next step, the movements are one of the following. (i) All agents move to a hyperedge $e_1 \in E$ such that e_0 and e_1 are adjacent, i.e., they share at least one vertex. This transition is named "shift". (ii) $\forall i : 1 \leq i \leq k$ the agent a_i moves from v_i^0 to v_i^1 such that there exists a hyperedge that contains $\{v_i^0, v_i^1\}$. Moreover, there exists a hyperedge that contains all the vertices $\{v_1^1, v_2^1, \cdots, v_k^1\}$. This transition is named "jump". Thus, we can assume each configuration to be one of the hyperedges, and the traversal is through those hyperedges. We formally define the problem below. The NP-hardness of the problem is directly derived from the NP-hardness of 2-HWP, since the 2-uniform hypergraph is equivalent to a simple graph.

Definition 5 (Problem: k-HWP on Hypergraph). *Consider an undirected connected k-uniform hypergraph G along with a collection of k agents. The task is to find a sequence of configurations $\{C_i\}$ with minimum length where each successive pair of configurations is adjacent, and every vertex in G is included at least once in one of these configurations.*

High-level Idea of the Approx. Algorithm for k-HWP on Hypergraph: We begin by computing the line graph $L(G)$ of the given hypergraph G. The graph $L(G)$ contains only the shift edges. We then modify $L(G)$ by introducing all possible jump edges and denote the resulting graph by $L^*(G)$. Next, we search for a minimum length walk of $L^*(G)$ that spans all the vertices of V. To achieve this, we create an instance $\mathcal{I}_{CSC}(G)$ of the *minimum connected set cover problem* (MCSC) [19] from the graph $L^*(G)$. In MCSC, we are given an universe of elements U, a family of subsets $\mathcal{F} = \{S\}$ where each $S \subseteq U$, and a connected graph where each vertex represents a unique $S \in \mathcal{F}$. The objective is to find a minimum size subfamily $\mathcal{F}' \subseteq \mathcal{F}$ such that each element of U is present in some of the members of $\mathcal{F}'$ and the vertices associated with $\mathcal{F}'$ induce a connected subgraph of the given graph. For $\mathcal{I}_{CSC}(G)$, we consider the vertex set V as the universe, the set of hyperedges E as the family of subsets, and $L^*(G)$ is the underlying connected subgraph. Using the best known approximation algorithm for MCSC by Zhang et al. [19], which is of factor $(1 + \ln k)$, we derive a connected subgraph of $L^*(G)$, say *Sol*, that covers all the vertices of V. Finally, we transform *Sol* into a walk by doubling all its edges, yielding a solution of k-HWP on the hypergraph G. The size of the solution is We omit a detailed description and analysis of the algorithm due to page constraints.

Theorem 5. *There exists a $2(1+\ln k)$-approximation algorithm for k-HWP on hypergraph.*

Theorem 6. *There exists a $2(1+\ln k)$-approximation algorithm for k-HWP on a simple graph, when $k = O(1)$.*

5 Conclusion

In this paper, we examine the Hamiltonian walk problem within the context of a connected group of mobile agents that minimally traverse the graph. The NP-hardness of the problem leads us to find some approximation algorithms. We propose an approximation algorithm for the problem with a set of two agents for any arbitrary graph. Then we define the problem on hypergraphs and provide an approximation algorithm. We also show some optimal results for the acyclic graph. Additionally, we define a restricted version of the problem in which each transition explores only one new vertex compared to the previous one. In the future, exploring tighter bounds for the problem and investigating the class of graphs in which a polynomial solution exists will be interesting.

References

1. Arkin, E.M., Hassin, R.: On local search for weighted k-set packing. Math. Oper. Res. **23**(3), 640–648 (1998)
2. Arora, S.: Polynomial time approximation schemes for Euclidean tsp and other geometric problems. In: Proceedings of 37th Conference on Foundations of Computer Science, pp. 2–11. IEEE (1996)
3. Chandra, B., Halldórsson, M.M.: Greedy local improvement and weighted set packing approximation. J. Algorithms **39**(2), 223–240 (2001)
4. Cheikhrouhou, O., Khoufi, I.: A comprehensive survey on the multiple traveling salesman problem: applications, approaches and taxonomy. Comput. Sci. Rev. **40**, 100369 (2021)
5. Christofides, N.: Worst-case analysis of a new heuristic for the travelling salesman problem. Oper. Res. Forum **3**(1), 1–4 (2022). https://doi.org/10.1007/s43069-021-00101-z
6. Demaine, E.D., Hajiaghayi, M., Mohar, B.: Approximation algorithms via contraction decomposition. Combinatorica **30**, 533–552 (2010)
7. Emek, Y., Halldórsson, M.M., Mansour, Y., Patt-Shamir, B., Radhakrishnan, J., Rawitz, D.: Online set packing. SIAM J. Comput. **41**(4), 728–746 (2012)
8. Goodman, S.E., Hedetniemi, S.T.: On Hamiltonian walks in graphs. SIAM J. Comput. **3**(3), 214–221 (1974)
9. Grigni, M., Koutsoupias, E., Papadimitriou, C.: An approximation scheme for planar graph tsp. In: Proceedings of IEEE 36th Annual Foundations of Computer Science, pp. 640–645. IEEE (1995)

10. Hoogeveen, J.: Analysis of christofides' heuristic: some paths are more difficult than cycles. Oper. Res. Lett. **10**(5), 291–295 (1991). https://doi.org/10.1016/0167-6377(91)90016-I
11. Jana, S., Italiano, G.F., Mandal, P.S.: Graph traversal via connected mobile agents (2025). https://arxiv.org/abs/2508.18683
12. Karlin, A.R., Klein, N., Gharan, S.O.: A (slightly) improved approximation algorithm for metric TSP. In: Proceedings of the 53rd Annual ACM SIGACT Symposium on Theory of Computing, pp. 32–45 (2021)
13. Karp, R.M.: Reducibility among combinatorial problems. In: 50 Years of Integer Programming 1958-2008: From the Early Years to the State-of-the-Art, pp. 219–241. Springer, Cham (2009)
14. Klein, P.N.: A linear-time approximation scheme for planar weighted tsp. In: 46th Annual IEEE Symposium on Foundations of Computer Science (FOCS 2005), pp. 647–656. IEEE (2005)
15. Mitchell, J.S.: Guillotine subdivisions approximate polygonal subdivisions: a simple polynomial-time approximation scheme for geometric TSP, k-MST, and related problems. SIAM J. Comput. **28**(4), 1298–1309 (1999)
16. Serdyukov, A.I.: O nekotorykh ekstremal'nykh obkhodakh v grafakh. Upravlyayemyye sistemy **17**, 76–79 (1978)
17. Sviridenko, M., Ward, J.: Large neighborhood local search for the maximum set packing problem. In: International Colloquium on Automata, Languages, and Programming. pp. 792–803. Springer, Cham (2013)
18. Thiery, T., Ward, J.: An improved approximation for maximum weighted k-set packing. In: Proceedings of the 2023 Annual ACM-SIAM Symposium on Discrete Algorithms (SODA), pp. 1138–1162. SIAM (2023)
19. Zhang, W., Wu, W., Lee, W., Du, D.Z.: Complexity and approximation of the connected set-cover problem. J. Global Optim. **53**(3), 563–572 (2012)

Time-Optimal Asynchronous Minimal Vertex Covering by Myopic Robots on Graph

Saswata Jana, Subhajit Pramanick, Adri Bhattacharya, and Partha Sarathi Mandal

Indian Institute of Technology Guwahati, Guwahati 781039, Assam, India
psm@iitg.ac.in

Abstract. In a connected graph with an autonomous robot swarm with limited visibility, it is natural to ask whether the robots can be deployed to certain vertices satisfying a given property using only local knowledge. This paper affirmatively answers the question with a set of *myopic* (finite visibility range) luminous robots with the aim of *filling a minimal vertex cover* (MVC) of a given graph $G = (V, E)$. The graph has special vertices, called *doors*, through which robots enter sequentially. Starting from the doors, the goal of the robots is to settle on a set of vertices that forms a minimal vertex cover of G under the asynchronous ($\mathcal{ASYNC}$) scheduler. We are also interested in achieving the *minimum vertex cover* (MinVC, which is NP-hard [14] for general graphs) for a specific graph class using the myopic robots. We establish lower bounds on the visibility range for the robots and on the time complexity (which is $\Omega(|E|)$). We present two algorithms for trees: one for single door, which is both time and memory-optimal, and the other for multiple doors, which is memory-optimal and achieves time-optimality when the number of doors is a constant. Interestingly, our technique achieves MinVC on trees with a single door. We then move to the general graph, where we present two algorithms, one for the single door and the other for the multiple doors with an extra memory of $O(\log \Delta)$ for the robots, where Δ is the maximum degree of G. All our algorithms run in $O(|E|)$ epochs.

Keywords: Graph algorithm · Filling problem · Vertex cover · Mobile robots

1 Introduction

Background and Motivation. Efficient sensor deployment is crucial in wireless sensor systems, especially in areas modeled as graphs, where coverage or

---

S. Jana—Supported by Prime Minister's Research Fellowship (PMRF) scheme of the Govt. of India (PMRF-ID: 1902165)
A. Bhattacharya—Supported by CSIR, Govt. of India, Grant Number: 09/731(0178)/2020-EMR-I.

placement must satisfy specific optimization goals. While static sensors rely on manual or random placement, which may not meet the coverage goals, mobile sensors, in contrast, can self-deploy without any central coordination. However, such autonomous behaviour requires complex, localized algorithm design, a central challenge in this line of research [7,10,11,16]. In this area, low-resource swarm robots [6] have been drawing the attention of researchers for many decades now. Under the classical *Look-Compute-Move* framework (which is formally defined later), many seminal problems have been studied in graphs, such as filling graph vertices [1,2,8,9], maximal independent set and dominating set [3–5,15], etc. In this context, a fundamental question emerges: *Can we achieve a specific graph property using autonomous mobile robots with local information?* In this paper, we affirmatively answer this question by exploring the vertex cover problem.

The *vertex cover* of a graph is a set of vertices such that every edge is incident to (or covered by) at least one vertex from the set. Since *minimum vertex cover* (MinVC) for general graph is NP-hard, we shift our attention to achieving a *minimal vertex cover* (MVC) of an arbitrary connected graph using a set of *autonomous* (no central control), *myopic* (having limited visibility range), *anonymous* (without identification) and *homogeneous* (the algorithm is same for all) mobile robots working under $\mathcal{ASYNC}$ scheduler. MVC is a computational problem with many theoretical and real-life applications, such as an area with multiple lanes, modelled as a graph needs to be minimally covered by guards.

In this paper, we study a constrained variant of the self-deployment problem, known as *filling MVC problem*, where robots, starting from specific *door* vertices, need to collaboratively fill a subset of vertices that forms an MVC of the graph. The *filling problem* using mobile robots, in which the robots are injected one at a time (using doors) into an unknown environment, has been introduced by Hsiang et al. [11]. A seminal result by Barrameda et al. [1] proved that the filling problem is impossible to solve deterministically using oblivious robots, even with unlimited visibility. To circumvent such impossibility, they considered persistent memory in the form of colors and proposed collision-free algorithms (two collocated robots make a *collision* that could damage the robots or the equipment) for robots with constant visibility range. We consider the bare-bone model in solving the filling MVC problem in the optimal time, considering $\mathcal{ASYNC}$ setting (the scheduler with the least assumptions), limited visibility with visibility range not depending on any graph parameter, no knowledge of the graph, luminous robots and no collision. Each robot has a persistent memory in the form of an externally visible persistent light that can flash a color from a predetermined color set. We judge algorithms on four metrics: (i) memory requirement, (ii) number of colors, (iii) visibility range, and (iv) time required to achieve the goal. Moreover, our interest lies in identifying some known graph classes where we can achieve the MinVC in optimal (or near-optimal) time.

Related Works. The filling problem is introduced by Hsiang et al. [11] in a setting where robots enter a region (modeled as a connected subset of an integer grid) through doors, aiming to occupy every cell. Barrameda et al. [1] showed that the problem is impossible with oblivious robots and thus considered persistent memory (in the form of colors) to solve the filling problem on a connected orthogonal space, partitioned into square cells (which they later model using graphs) with special door cells. They present two algorithms under $\mathcal{ASYNC}$: one for the single door, where sensors have 1 hop visibility and 2 bits of persistent memory, and the other for multiple doors, where sensors have 2 hops visibility and $O(1)$ persistent memory. Barrameda et al. [2] later extended the problem on orthogonal regions with holes using robots having 6 hops visibility. Under $\mathcal{ASYNC}$, Kamei and Tixeuil [13] solved the maximum independent set (Max_IS) filling problem on a finite grid with a door at a corner using 3 colors and 2 hop visibility with port-labelling and however it needs 7 colors and 3 hop visibility without it. Hideg and Lukovszki [8] studied the filling problem in orthogonal regions with doors. They propose two algorithms in $O(n)$ time under synchronous setting, one for single door and the other for multiple doors, where n is the number of cells. Later in [9], they presented the filling problem for an arbitrary connected graph under the asynchronous setting. The deployment of mobile robots on graph vertices with specific properties later gained popularity. Pramanick et al. [17] presented two algorithms for the maximal independent set (MIS) filling problem on arbitrary graphs: one for single door under $\mathcal{ASYNC}$ using 3 hop visibility and $O(\log \Delta)$ memory and another for multiple doors under semi-synchronous setting using 5 hop visibility and $O(\log(\Delta + k))$ memory, where Δ is the maximum degree and k is the number of doors. Pattanayak et al. [15] proposed algorithms for finding an MIS using mobile agents communicating face-to-face with each other. Chand et al. [4] investigated the problem of placing mobile agents on a dominating set of the given graph.

Contributions: Our contributions in this paper are the following:

- We show impossibility to solve the filling MVC problem with 1 hop visibility (Theorem 1) and a lower bound of $\Omega(|E|)$ on time complexity (Theorem 2).
- Algorithm: TREE_SINGLEDOOR, requires 2 hops of visibility and 4 colors. Interestingly, this algorithm achieves MinVC on trees in optimal time $O(|E|)$ and optimal $O(1)$ memory (Theorem 3).
- Algorithm: TREE_MULTIDOOR (H doors) requires 4 hops of visibility and $O(H)$ colors (which is also optimal) and runs in $O(|E|)$ epochs (Theorem 4).
- Later, we present two algorithms for a general graph: a time-optimal algorithm: GRAPH_SINGLEDOOR with 3 hops of visibility and 4 colors, and another GRAPH_MULTIDOOR algorithm (for H doors) with 4 hops of visibility and $O(H)$ colors. Both algorithms on general graphs use additional $O(\log \Delta)$ memory and run in $O(|E|)$ epochs (Theorem 5 and 6) without the knowledge of any graph parameter.

Due to page limitations, we deferred the detailed analysis and some components of the algorithms to the full version of this paper [12].

2 Model and Preliminaries

Graph Model: We consider an anonymous graph $G(V, E)$ with V as the set of vertices and E as the set of edges, where the vertices do not possess any unique ID. However, the ports corresponding to the incident edges of a vertex v are assigned a label from the set $\{1, 2, \cdots, \delta(v)\}$, where $\delta(v)$ is the degree of v. The edge between vertices u and v is denoted by $e(u, v)$ and Δ denotes the maximum degree of the graph. A vertex has neither memory nor computational ability. An edge between two vertices receives independent port numbering at either end. We use p_v to represent a port incident to the vertex v. When we say "port p of the edge $e(u, v)$", we refer to the port of the edge $e(u, v)$ incident to u. A vertex is called occupied if there is a robot positioned on it; otherwise unoccupied.

Door: The graph has some special vertices, referred to as *doors*, where a group of robots are initially collocated and no two adjacent vertices are doors. The robots on a door are serialized in a queue by a pre-processing algorithm (probably by any popular randomized leader election protocol, which is beyond our concern). When we say that the robot situated on a door executes the algorithm, we mean that the robot at the front of the queue executes the algorithm. When this robot leaves the door, the next robot in the queue comes to the front. The color of the robot on a door indicates the color of the robot at the front. A robot can identify whether it is at the door or not. We use H to denote the number of doors.

Robot Model: The robots are autonomous, myopic, anonymous and homogeneous. A robot at a vertex v with visibility range ϕ hops can see all the vertices and their associated port numbers along each path of length ϕ. Additionally, the robots are *luminous*, each having a light that determines a color from a predefined color set. A robot can see the color of all the robots in its visibility range, including itself. $r.color$ represents the color of the light for the robot r. At any given time, at most one robot can be located at a vertex, except for the door.

Activation Cycle: Each robot operates in the classical *Look-Compute-Move* (LCM) cycles. *Look:* The robot takes a snapshot of all visible vertices and the colors of the robots occupying them. *Compute:* It runs the algorithm using the snapshot to select a neighbouring vertex as its target or remains in place. It updates its color at the end of this phase if needed. *Move:* It moves to the target vertex, if any. A movement is not instantaneous.

Activation Scheduler: We consider the activation scheduler as asynchronous ($\mathcal{ASYNC}$), where the adversary is the strongest among all other schedulers. Under $\mathcal{ASYNC}$, any robot can be activated at any time and may be idle for an arbitrarily large number of LCM cycles. However, the robot must be activated infinitely often (fairness condition). The time is measured in terms of *epochs*, the smallest time interval in which each robot gets activated and executes a full LCM cycle at least once.

Problem (*Filling MVC*): We are given an anonymous port-labelled connected graph $G(V, E)$ with H door vertices, where luminous and myopic mobile robots operate. The objective is to settle the robots without collision on a set of vertices $V_1 \subset V$, such that V_1 forms a minimal vertex cover of G, all settled robots adopt a designated color to indicate termination so that no robot moves thereafter.

3 Impossibility, Lower Bound and Technical Overview

We first highlight the lower bounds on visibility range and the time complexity.

Theorem 1. *Under $\mathcal{ASYNC}$, the filling MVC problem cannot be solved without collisions using 1-hop visibility, even with robots having unbounded memory.*

Proof Sketch. Consider a simple path of 5 vertices, labeled v_1 through v_5, with a door at v_1. Vertex labels are provided for exposition only; the vertices themselves are anonymous. To cover the edge $e(v_4, v_5)$, a robot r_1 must eventually reach v_3 (by taking the edge $e(v_1, v_2)$ and then $e(v_2, v_3)$). If r_1 at v_3, moves back to v_2, the adversary can activate another robot r_2 in sync at the door, which moves to v_2, causing a collision. To avoid revisiting v_2, if r_1 uses memory to store port numbers in the direction of v_2, it moves to v_4 to cover $e(v_4, v_5)$ from v_3. After the movement, the adversary keeps r_1 idle at v_4 and activates r_2 at v_2. In this case, r_2 moves to v_3 from v_2 as it cannot move to the door at v_1 (since there is a robot on it). Next, with r_1 at v_4 and r_2 at v_3, the adversary again activates a third robot r_3 at the door. r_3 moves to v_2 as it cannot see any other robot with its 1 hop visibility from v_1. If r_1 settles at v_4, the minimality is violated. If instead r_1 moves and settles at v_5, the adversary can similarly direct r_2 to v_4 and r_3 to v_3, again violating minimality under $\mathcal{ASYNC}$ and 1 hop visibility. □

Theorem 2. *The time needed for an algorithm to solve the filling MVC problem on a graph G with a single door by myopic mobile robots is $\Omega(|E|)$.*

Proof. Let G be a path with a door at one of the endpoints. The first robot that leaves the door takes at least $|E| - 1$ epochs to reach the edge incident to the other endpoint and cover it. □

Remark 1. An argument similar to that in [1, Theorem 3] shows that $\Omega(H)$ colors are necessary for the robots when there are $H > 1$ doors.

Challenges and Our Technique. We begin by outlining the structure of our algorithms, which form the foundation for all subsequent sections. One can draw an analogy to depth-first search (DFS) graph traversal to have an intuitive understanding of our approach. The robots exploring the graph maintain a virtual chain-like structure (a similar idea is also used in [17], but failed to achieve time optimality because of the highly sequential movement of the robots), primarily helping them avoid collision. Our approach achieves both efficiency and time-optimality by enabling every alternate robot, starting from the head of the chain to the door, to move within a constant number of epochs, thereby introducing a parallelism in movement. For any two successive robots in the chain, referred to as the predecessor and the successor, we ensure that under $\mathcal{ASYNC}$, each of them remains (at least) 2 hops from its successor and (at most) 3 hops from its predecessor within constant epochs. This guarantees that such robots can move toward their predecessor in nearly constant epochs.

A robot primarily follows its predecessor until the predecessor can no longer proceed. Throughout the process, we ensure that the chain of robots never crosses itself and that chains originating from different doors remain disjoint. Additionally, to prevent collisions, a robot r that moves from a vertex v to a neighbouring vertex u is prohibited from returning to v. In the multiple-door case, to circumvent the impossibility shown in [1] (Theorem 3), we use distinct colors for the doors to establish a hierarchy among the robots entering through different doors, as two robots from two different doors having the same target vertex need to break the symmetry between them. In the case of a general graph, we use additional memory to maintain the predecessor-successor relationship between two consecutive robots and store their locations, as there can be multiple paths between two vertices. To give a structural overview of our algorithm, a brief execution example of the algorithm for the tree single-door case can be found in Sect. 4.1.

4 Algorithm for Filling MVC on Trees

Prior work on related problems, such as maximal independent set [17] and vertex filling [9], requires $O(\log \Delta)$ persistent memory. Similarly, our solution in Sect. 5 for MVC on general graph also uses $O(\log \Delta)$ memory. This raises a natural question: *Can we eliminate this memory requirement for specific graph classes, while preserving time optimality, at least for single-door?* Additionally, *how close can we get to the MinVC on such graphs?* We answer both questions affirmatively for trees. We begin with the following conventions.

Definition 1. *(k hops neighbour of v) A vertex with a shortest path of length k from the vertex v is called a k hops neighbour of v. We denote it by v_{nbr}^k.*

When we say that the vertex v' is a "k hop neighbour of v along the port p_v", we mean that there is a shortest path of length $(k-1)$ from v_{nbr}^1 to v', where v_{nbr}^1 is the neighbour of v along the port p_v. We also define the following predicates.
▶ $occupied(v_{nbr}^k, p_v, \texttt{COL})$: This means that there exists a k hops neighbour v_{nbr}^k of the vertex v along the port p_v, which is occupied by a robot with the color COL. When we write $\sim$ in place of COL, it indicates that the occupying robot can have any color from its color set. If we write $\neq$ COL instead of COL, it means that the occupying robot can have any color except COL.
▶ $\neg occupied(v_{nbr}^k, p_v, \sim)$: The vertex v_{nbr}^k exists along p_v, but unoccupied.
▶ $exists(p_v, k)$: There exists a k hops neighbour of v along the port p_v.
▶ $\neg exists(p_v, k)$: There does not exist a k hops neighbour of v along p_v.

For example, $\exists p_v \exists v_{nbr}^2 \; occupied(v_{nbr}^2, p_v, \neq \texttt{FINISH}))$ means that there is a port p_v (incident to v) along which there exists a 2 hops neighbour v_{nbr}^2 of v such that the vertex v_{nbr}^2 is occupied by a robot, say r' with $r'.color \neq \texttt{FINISH}$.

4.1 Algorithm (TREE_SINGLEDOOR) for Single Door

In this algorithm, robots use 2 hops of visibility and four colors: OFF-0, OFF-1, OFF-2 and FINISH. Initially, all the robots have the color OFF-0. A robot identifies its follower within its visibility range before executing a movement. A robot r with the color OFF-i ($i \in \{0,1,2\}$) considers the visible robot r' with $r'.color$ =OFF-j as its follower, where j =i+1 (mod 3). In each LCM cycle, this decision is made solely based on colors, without storing the follower's position. We now define an eligible port for a robot r situated at a vertex v.

Definition 2. *(Eligible Port from v) A port p_v incident with v is called an eligible port for r positioned at v if the following are satisfied. (i) An unoccupied v_{nbr}^2 exists along the port p_v. (ii) There is no robot r' with $r'.color \neq$ FINISH present at 2 hops away from v along the port p_v.*

Based on the position of r and its current color, we differentiate the following two cases. In all the cases, r does nothing when it sees a robot on the edges.
▶ **Case 1 (r is situated on the door):** We further identify two sub-cases.

- **Case 1.1** ($r.color$ = OFF-0): If $\exists p_v\ occupied(v_{nbr}^1, p_v, \text{OFF-i}) \vee \exists p_v \exists v_{nbr}^2$ $occupied(v_{nbr}^2, p_v, \text{OFF-i})$ for $i \in \{0,1,2\}$, r updates its color to OFF-j, where j = i+1 (mod3).
- **Case 1.2** ($r.color$ = OFF-1 or OFF-2): Since r is on the door and with the color OFF-1 or OFF-2, it must encounter a robot r' at 1 or 2 hops away from it in an earlier LCM cycle. Such a robot r is eligible to move either when r' changes its color to FINISH or moves further. Thus, r does nothing, if $\exists p_v\ (occupied(v_{nbr}^1, p_v, \neq \text{FINISH}) \vee \exists v_{nbr}^2\ occupied(v_{nbr}^2, p_v, \neq \text{FINISH}))$.

If neither of the predicates holds, then regardless of r having the color OFF-0, OFF-1 or OFF-2, it identifies the minimum eligible port (has the minimum label) p_v^{min} from the current vertex v. If p_v^{min} exists, r moves to v_{nbr}^1, the neighbour of v along the port p_v^{min}, with the current color. While r switches to FINISH, if p_v^{min} does not exist, and $\exists p_v \neg occupied(v_{nbr}^1, p_v, \sim)$.
▶ **Case 2 (r is not on the door & $r.color$ = OFF-i, $i \in \{0,1,2\}$):** r remains stationary till it does not see a robot r' with color OFF-j (the follower of r), where j = i+1 (mod 3). It also remains in place till it finds a robot r' with color OFF-j', where j' = i-1 (mod 3). Otherwise, r checks whether there is any eligible port incident to the current vertex v. If no such port exists, it changes its color to FINISH. If it exists, it selects v_{nbr}^1 along the minimum eligible port p_v^{min} as its target. Finally, r moves to v_{nbr}^1, maintaining the current color.
▶ **Termination Condition:** The algorithm terminates either when the door has a FINISH-colored robot or all the neighbours of the door are occupied with FINISH-colored robots.

Our analysis leads us to the following theorem.

Theorem 3. *Algorithm* TREE_SINGLEDOOR *fills a MinVC of a tree G with FINISH-colored robots having 2 hops visibility and 4 colors in $O(|E|)$ epochs under $\mathcal{ASYNC}$ and with no collision.*

Execution Example of the Algorithm TREE_SINGLEDOOR. The example provides a foundational understanding of the technique, which extends naturally to the multiple-door setting. Please refer to Fig. 1 and the following description.

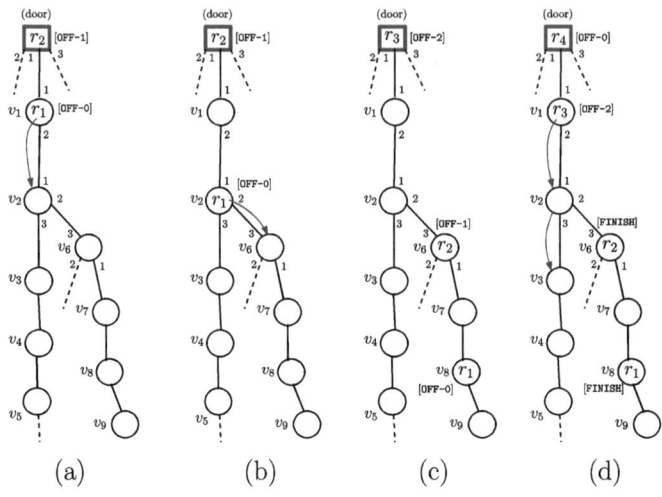

Fig. 1. An execution of the algorithm TREE_SINGLEDOOR

Initially, the robot r_1 appears at the door (which is indicated with a green square in Fig. 1) with the color OFF-0. After finding all the 1 and 2 hops neighbours unoccupied, it calculates $p_{door}^{min} = 1$ and moves to v_1 with OFF-0. Another robot r_2 is placed at the door after r_1 leaves. r_1 remains stationary till it finds an OFF-1-colored robot. r_2 switches its color to OFF-1, when it sees r_1 with color OFF-0 at one of its neighbour v_1. Now, r_1 discards the port 1 as the eligible port after seeing r_2 along the port 1 and computes $p_{v_1}^{min} = 2$. r_1 moves to v_2 with OFF-0, as shown in Fig. 1(a). Thereafter, r_1 moves to the neighbour v_6 of v_2 along the port $p_{v_2}^{min} = 2$ with OFF-0, while r_2 maintains status quo as it finds r_1 sitting at its 2 hops neighbour with color $\neq$ FINISH (refer to Fig. 1(b)). In the same way, r_1 and r_2 eventually move to v_8 and v_6 respectively (Fig. 1(c)). Meanwhile, another robot r_3 on the door sets its color OFF-2. Now, r_1 terminates at v_8 with color FINISH, as it finds r_2 at v_6 and no other 2 hops unoccupied neighbour. r_2 similarly changes its color to FINISH, when r_3 is at v_1, as depicted in Fig. 1(d). Next, r_3 moves to v_2 and then calculate $p_{v_2}^{min} = 3$ after disregarding the ports 1 and 2. Finally, r_3 moves to v_3 and continues the filling process.

4.2 Algorithm (TREE_MULTIDOOR) for Multiple Doors

We consider $H(> 1)$ doors, each assigned a unique color (can be thought of as ID) to establish a hierarchy, where the lower-ID doors dominate the higher-ID ones. Barrameda et al. [1] showed that $\Omega(H)$ colors are necessary to distinguish the robots entering from different doors. In this algorithm, robots use 4 hops visibility and use $O(H)$ colors. Initially, robots at the h-th lowest ID door are colored $\texttt{color}_h^0$, and two doors are not adjacent to each other. Due to space constraints, we could not include the detailed description of the algorithm, and hence, we present a high-level idea of it.

High-Level Idea: The strategy mirrors TREE_SINGLEDOOR, keeping a chain-like formation from each door, but with a distinct set of colors. Robots from h-th lowest ID door use the color set $\{\texttt{color}_h^0, \texttt{color}_h^1, \texttt{color}_h^2\}$, similar to $\{\texttt{OFF-0}, \texttt{OFF-1}, \texttt{OFF-2}\}$ in previous algorithm. The head of each chain explores the graph, while the other robots follow it. A head r at vertex v with the color $\texttt{color}_h^i$, moves to v_{nbr}^1 along the minimum eligible port to cover the edge $e(v_{nbr}^1, v_{nbr}^2)$, if v_{nbr}^2 is unoccupied. After moving, r remains stationary until it finds its follower with $\texttt{color}_h^{i+1}$ at a distance of 2 hops. If no eligible port is available, r terminates with FINISH, and the follower of r becomes the new head.

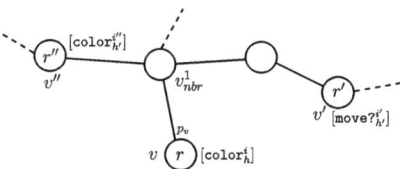

Fig. 2. r sees r' and r'' due to 3 hop visibility and do not move to v_{nbr}^1 to avoid possible collision

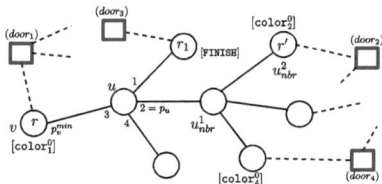

Fig. 3. r' moves to u_{nbr}^1 while r remains stationary in spite of r from higher ID door.

To ensure collision-free operation, robots perform additional checks beyond maintaining the chain. First, to prevent chain intersections, a robot r considers a port p_v *ineligible* if it detects two robots r' and r'' (from the same door but different from r) such that v_{nbr}^1 along p_v lies on the path between their positions v' and v'' (see Fig. 2). Second, if two head robots from different doors potentially target the same vertex, only the robot from the lower ID door proceeds.

We address a critical $\mathcal{ASYNC}$ scenario to avoid collision. Let r at v with $\texttt{color}_h^i$ finds both $v_{nbr}^1 (= u)$ and $v_{nbr}^2 (= u_{nbr}^1)$ unoccupied along its minimum eligible port. Meanwhile, another robot r' at u^2_{nbr} with $\texttt{color}^{i'}_{h'} (h' > h)$ sets u^1_{nbr} as its target but hasn't moved yet (see Fig. 3). r being a robot from a lower ID door than r', it might complete two LCM cycles: first moves to u and then to u^1_{nbr}, resulting in a collision with r'. To prevent this, r remains stationary at v, allowing the closer robot r' to proceed. However, if r' is initially outside the view of r (e.g., approaching u^2_{nbr} from $door_2$), r can target u without moving yet. Once r' reaches u^2_{nbr} and sees r at v, it may incorrectly assume itself as a robot closer to u^1_{nbr} than r and sets u^1_{nbr} as the target, leading to another collision. To resolve this, if r' first switches to $\texttt{move?}^{i'}_{h'}$ to signal its intent to move to u^1_{nbr} and waits for confirmation from r. In case r reaches u, r' in its next LCM cycle, after activating with $\texttt{move?}^{i'}_{h'}$, gives up its plan to move u^1_{nbr} and reverts to $\texttt{color}^{i'}_{h'}$. If instead, r is still at v, r' moves to u^1_{nbr} with $\texttt{color}^{i'}_{h'}$ safely.

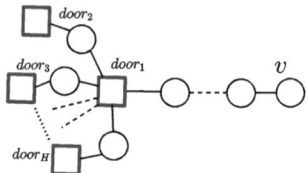

Fig. 4. Robots from $door_1$ fill the vertex cover of the path from $door_1$ to v

The termination condition remains the same as mentioned in the previous algorithm. Our analysis gives the following theorem.

Theorem 4. *Algorithm* TREE_MULTIDOOR *fills an MVC of a tree having H doors with FINISH-colored robots having 4 hop visibility and $O(H)$ colors in $O(|E|)$ epochs under $\mathcal{ASYNC}$ and without collision.*

Lower Bound on Time for Multidoor. Consider the graph as depicted in Fig. 4. The length of the path P from v to $door_1$ is $|E| - 2H$. All the edges on P must be covered by the robots entered through $door_1$. By Theorem 2, any algorithm needs $\Omega(|E| - H)$ epochs to cover P. This shows that our algorithm is time-optimal when there is a constant number of doors in the graph.

5 Algorithm for Filling MVC Vertices on General Graph

The algorithms designed for trees do not extend directly to general graphs, as multiple paths can exist between two vertices, making it difficult for a robot to accurately determine which robot it is following or which one is following it. Even if a robot has sufficient persistent memory, relying only on 2-hop visibility may lead to violating the minimality of the vertex cover. Robots maintain a *predecessor-successor* relationship during the execution of the algorithm In general graphs, we assume 3 hop visibility and $O(\log \Delta)$ additional memory in general graph to store the ports toward the predecessor and the successor.

5.1 Algorithm (GRAPH_SINGLEDOOR) for Single Door

Each robot initially has the color OFF and uses 4 colors in total. We define two variables $r.pred$ and $r.succ$ for a robot r situated at the vertex v.

Definition 3. *(Predecessor and Successor of r)* $r.pred$ *(resp. $r.succ$) is a tuple (p_1, p_2) (resp. (p'_1, p'_2)), implying that there is a 2-hop between the predecessor (resp. successor) robot of r situated at u and r situated at v such that p_1 (resp. p'_1) is the port of the edge $e(v, v^1_{nbr})$ and p_2 (resp. p'_2) is the port of the edge $e(v^1_{nbr}, u)$, where v^1_{nbr} is the neighbour of v along p_1 (resp. p'_1), see Fig. 5.*

We misuse the notation $r.pred$ and $r.succ$ to denote the predecessor and successor robot of r as well. The computation of $r.pred$ is possible when the predecessor is exactly at 2 hops away from v. Otherwise, r can only store the first component of the tuple $r.pred$. In that case, $r.pred = (p_1, \perp)$. r can also have $r.pred = (\perp, \perp)$, indicating that r does not have a predecessor, and we call such robot r as *head*. r also maintains a variable $r.avoid$, storing a port p incident to its current position, and all ports $p' < p$ are ignored when computing eligible port. Initially, r at the door has no predecessor or successor, i.e., $r.pred = r.succ = (\perp, \perp)$ and $r.avoid = 0$. We redefine the eligible port.

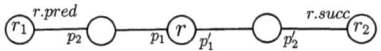

Fig. 5. Predecessor and successor of r

Definition 4. *(Eligible Port from v)* *A port p_v incident with v is called an eligible port for r positioned at v if the following conditions hold. (i) $p_v \neq p'_1$, where $r.succ = (p'_1, p'_2)$. (ii) There exists at least one unoccupied vertex 2 hops away from v along the port p_v. (iii) There is no robot r' with $r'.color \neq$ FINISH present at most 3 hops away from v along p_v.*

We distinguish the following cases based on the position and current color of r.

▶ **Case 1** ($r.color =$ OFF and r is situated on the door): If $\exists p_v occupied (v^1_{nbr}, p_v, \neq$ FINISH$)$, r does nothing. Elseif $\exists p_v \exists v^2_{nbr} occupied(v^2_{nbr}, p_v, \neq$ FINISH$)$ r stores $r.pred = (p_1, p_2)$, where $p_1 = p_v$ and p_2 is the port of $e(v^1_{nbr}, v^2_{nbr})$. r then changes its color to STORED and remains in place until the robot on v^2_{nbr} moves further or changes its color to FINISH. Otherwise, if $\exists p_v \exists v^2_{nbr} \neg occupied(v^2_{nbr}, p_v, \sim)$, r computes the minimum eligible port p^{min}_v. It now sets its target v^1_{nbr} along the port p^{min}_v and stores $r.succ = (p'_1, \perp)$, where p'_1 is the port of the edge $e(v^1_{nbr}, v)$. Then, it moves to v^1_{nbr} with the current color. If such p^{min}_v does not exist but $\exists p_v \neg occupied(v^1_{nbr}, p_v, \sim)$, r changes its color to FINISH.

▶ **Case 2** ($r.color =$ OFF or WAIT and r is not on the door): In this case, r may or may not be the head. So, we further divide this case into the following subcases. In case of r being the head, and situated more than 1 hop away from the door (Case 2.2), it might switch its color to WAIT.

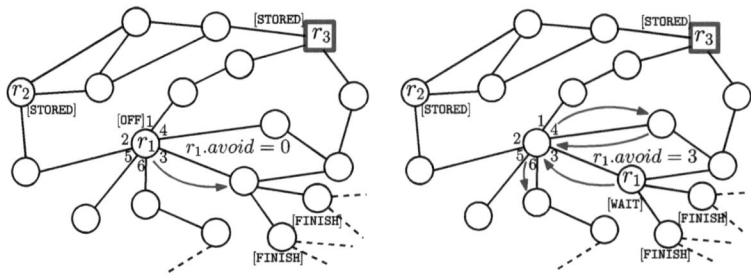

Fig. 6. r_1 is the head and $r_1.succ = r_2$ and $r_2.succ = r_3$. (left) r_1 moves along $p_v^{min} = 3$ (right) r_1 backtracks multiple times due to presence of r_3 at 3 hop neighbour

- **Case 2.1** ($r.pred = (\bot, \bot)$ and $r.succ = (p_1', \bot)$): It means that r is the head and 1 hop away from the door along p_1'. We slightly modify Definition 4 for such a robot, where the computation of the minimum eligible port p_v^{min} does not disregard a port p_v even when a 3 hop neighbour of v along p_v is occupied by (which is the door). If p_v^{min} exists, r updates $r.succ$ as (p_2'', p_1') and moves to the vertex v_{nbr}^1 along p_v^{min} with the current color, where p_2'' is the port of the edge $e(v_{nbr}^1, v)$. Otherwise, r sets its color FINISH without any movement.
- **Case 2.2** ($r.pred = (\bot, \bot)$ and $r.succ = (p_1', p_2')$): This indicates that the head r is situated at a vertex at least 2 hops away from the door. Let w be the neighbour of v along p_1'. Based on the values of the local variables, we segregate the following sub-cases.
  - $r.color = $ OFF: r waits until $occupied(w_{nbr}^1, p_2', $ STORED$)$ is satisfied. When the predicate becomes true, r computes p_v^{min}. If p_v^{min} exists, it moves to v_{nbr}^1 along p_v^{min} after updating $r.succ = (p_2'', p_1')$ and $r.color = $ WAIT, where p_2'' is the port of the edge $e(v_{nbr}^1, v)$ (refer to Fig. 6 (up)). If instead p_v^{min} does not exist, it terminates after changing its color to FINISH.
  - $r.color = $ WAIT and $r.avoid = 0$: In this case, r might have to backtrack in the direction of its successor. r calculates p_v^{min} and if it exists, r turns its color to OFF without any movement. If instead, p_v^{min} does not exist, and the predicate $\exists p(\neg occupied(v_{nbr}^1, p, \sim) \land \forall v_{nbr}^2 occupied(v_{nbr}^2, p, $ FINISH$))$ holds true, r switches its color to FINISH without any movement. Otherwise, if $\exists \ occupied(v_{nbr}^3, p_v, col\}$ is in $col \in \{$OFF, STORED$\}$, r moves to v_{nbr}^1 with the current colour and after updating $r.avoid = p^*$, where v_{nbr}^1 is the neighbour of v along the port p_1' and p^* is the port of the edge $e(v_{nbr}^1, v)$ (see Fig. 6 (down)). We call the movement toward $r.succ$ as backtracking.
  - $r.color = $ WAIT and $r.avoid = p^* > 0$: r first computes all the eligible ports $p > p^*$ and chooses the minimum among them as p_v^{min}. If no such port exists, it changes its color to FINISH without any movement. Else, it moves to v_{nbr}^1 along p_v^{min} after updating $r.succ = (p_2'', p_2')$, $r.avoid = 0$ and $r.color = $ WAIT, where p_2'' is the port of $e(v, v_{nbr}^1)$ incident to v_{nbr}^1.
- **Case 2.3** ($r.pred = (p_1, \bot)$): In this case, r has partial information about the position of its predecessor. So, it needs to find the exact position of the

predecessor. Let $u = v^1_{nbr}$, a 1 hop neighbour of v along the port p_1. A robot r' must exist with $r'.color \neq $ FINISH at a vertex 2 hops away from v along the port p_1. Let p_2 be the port of the edge $e(u, r')$, incident to u. r updates $r.pred = (p_1, p_2)$ and changes its color to STORED without any movement. We prove in our analysis that there can not be two such robots r' along p_1.

▶ **Case 3** ($r.color = $ STORED): Since the current color of r is STORED, there exists p_1, p_2 such that $r.pred = (p_1, p_2)$. The value of $r.succ$ depends on its distance from the door. If r is on the door, $r.succ = (\bot, \bot)$. If r is 1 hop away, $r.succ = (p'_1, \bot)$ and if at least 2 hops away, $r.succ = (p'_1, p'_2)$ for some ports p'_1 and p'_2. Let $w = v^1_{nbr}$ be the neighbour of v along p'_1. If $\exists w^1_{nbr}$ $occupied(w^1_{nbr}, p'_2, $ STORED$)$ does not hold, r remains stationary. Otherwise, regardless of the position of r, it considers the vertex u, a neighbour of v along the port p_1. If the predicate $occupied(u^1_{nbr}, p_2, \neq $ FINISH$) \vee occupied(u^2_{nbr}, p_2, $ WAIT$)$ holds, r maintains the status quo. If $occupied(u^1_{nbr}, p_2, $ FINISH$)$ holds, it updates $r.pred = (\bot, \bot)$ and $r.color = $ OFF, thus becoming the new head. However, if $\neg occupied(u^1_{nbr}, p_2, \sim)$ holds but $occupied(u^2_{nbr}, p_2, $ WAIT$)$ does not hold, r sets u as the target. Finally, r moves to u after updating $r.color = $ OFF, $r.pred = (p_2, \bot)$ and $r.succ = (p, \bot)$ or (p, p'_1), depending on whether it is on the door or not, where p is the port of the edge $e(u, v)$. The termination condition is the same as earlier.

The analysis of the above algorithm demonstrates the following theorem.

Theorem 5. *Algorithm* GRAPH_SINGLEDOOR *fills an MVC of an arbitrary graph G with FINISH-colored robots having 3 hops visibility, 4 colors and $O(\log \Delta)$ memory in $O(|E|)$ epochs under $\mathcal{ASYNC}$ and without collision.*

5.2 Algorithm (GRAPH_MULTIDOOR) for Multiple Doors

In this algorithm, the definitions of $r.pred$, $r.succ$, $r.avoid$ and $head$ remain same as in Sect. 5.1. The algorithm uses 4 hop visibility and $4H + 1$ colors: $\{$OFF$_h$, move?$_h$, STORED$_h$, WAIT$_h$ and FINISH$\}$, for $1 \leq h \leq H$. Initially, each robot r on the h-th lowest ID door ($door_h$) is with color OFF$_h$ and $r.pred = r.succ = (\bot, \bot), r.avoid = 0, 1 \leq h \leq H$. Here, we modify the definition of eligible port.

Definition 5. *(**Eligible Port from** v) A port p_v is called an eligible port for r, positioned at v with $r.color \in \{$OFF$_h$, move?$_h$, STORED$_h$, WAIT$_h\}$, if the following conditions hold. (i) $p_v \neq p'_1$, where $r.succ = (p'_1, p'_2)$. (ii) There exists at least one unoccupied vertex v^2_{nbr} along p_v. (iii) No 3-hop neighbour of v along port p_v is occupied by a robot r' with $r'.color \in \{$OFF$_h$, STORED$_h$, WAIT$_h\}$. (iv) r does not find two robots r' at v' and r'' at v'' such that v^1_{nbr} or v^2_{nbr} along the port p_v lies on the path between v' and v'', where $r'.color = $ col$_{h'}$ and $r''.color = $ col$'_{h'}$, for some col, col' $\in \{$OFF, move?, STORED$\}$, and $h' \neq h$.*

We distinguish the cases based on the position and current color of r. Several actions align with those in GRAPH_SINGLEDOOR, with minor adjustments to color transitions, specifically, each color col in Sect. 5.1 corresponds here to col_h, where h denotes the ID of the door through which the robot entered.

▶ **Case 1** ($r.color = \text{OFF}_h$ and r is on $door_h$): If $\exists p_v\ occupied(v^1_{nbr}, p_v, \ne \text{FINISH})$ $\vee\ \exists p_v \exists v^2_{nbr}\ occupied(v^2_{nbr}, p_v, \text{OFF}_h)$ holds, r follows the action as mentioned in Case 1, Sect. 5.1. Otherwise if $\exists p_v \exists v^2_{nbr}\ \neg occupied(v^2_{nbr}, p_v, \sim)$, r finds p^{min}_v and proceeds with the following steps sequentially. Let $u = v^1_{nbr}$ along p^{min}_v. Let p_u be the smallest port incident to u such that the 1-hop neighbour along it is unoccupied. Let p' be the port of the edge $e(u, v)$.

C1 IF $\exists u^3_{nbr}\ occupied(u^3_{nbr}, p_u, \text{col}^{i'}_{h'})$ with $h > h'$ holds, r remains in place.
C2 ELSEIF $\exists u^1_{nbr} occupied(u^1_{nbr}, p_u, \text{col}_{h'})$ for $h > h'$ and $\text{col} \in \{\text{OFF}, \text{move?},$ STORED, WAIT $\}$, r does nothing.
C3 ELSEIF $\neg exists(p_u, 2) \vee \forall u^2_{nbr}\ (\neg occupied(u^2_{nbr}, p_u, \sim) \vee occupied(u^2_{nbr}, p_u,$ FINISH)), r moves to u with the current color after updating $r.succ = (p', \bot)$.
C4 ELSEIF $\exists u^2_{nbr} \neg occupied(u^2_{nbr}, p_u, \sim) \wedge \exists u^2_{nbr} occupied\ (u^2_{nbr}, p_u, \text{col}_{h'})$ with $\text{col} \in \{\text{OFF}, \text{move?}, \text{WAIT}\}$ and h is smallest among all such h', r stays put.
C5 ELSEIF $\exists u^2_{nbr}\ \neg occupied(u^2_{nbr}, p_u, \sim) \wedge \exists u^2_{nbr}\ occupied\ (u^2_{nbr}, p_u, \text{OFF}_{h'})$ such that h is greater than the minimum among all such h', r switches to move?_h.
C6 ELSEIF $\forall v^2_{nbr}(\neg occupied(v^2_{nbr}, p^{min}_v, \sim) \vee (occupied\ (v^2_{nbr}, p^{min}_v, \text{OFF}_{h'}) \wedge (h < h')))$, r moves to u with its current color after updating $r.succ = (p', \bot)$.
C7 ELSEIF p^{min}_v does not exist and $\exists p_v \neg occupied(v^1_{nbr}, p_v, \sim)$, r turns to FINISH.

▶ **Case 2** ($r.color = \text{OFF}_h$ or WAIT_h and r is not on any door): We divide this case into the following sub-cases, based on whether r is a head robot or not.

- **Case 2.1** ($r.pred = (\bot, \bot)$): When $r.succ = (p'_1, \bot)$ for some port p'_1, i.e., r is one hop away from the door, it proceeds as described in Case 2.1, Sect. 5.1. When $r.succ = (p'_1, p'_2)$, some adjustments are made to prevent collisions with robots from the other door. If $r.color = \text{WAIT}_h$ and $r.avoid = 0$, it follows Case 2.2, Sect. 5.1. If $r.color = \text{OFF}_h$, r considers the vertex $w = v^1_{nbr}$ along p'_1 and waits until $occupied(w^1_{nbr}, p'_2, \text{STORED})$ is satisfied. Once true, it computes p^{min}_v. If $r.color = \text{WAIT}_h$ and $r.avoid = p^* > 0$, r considers all the ports $p > p^*$ and selects the minimum eligible port p^{min}_v among them. In the last two cases, if no p^{min}_v exists, r switches to FINISH; otherwise, r identifies u, p_u and p' as defined in Case 1. If $\exists u^1_{nbr} occupied(u^1_{nbr}, p_u, \text{move?}_{h'})$, r waits until u^1_{nbr} changes to $\text{OFF}_{h'}$. ELSEIF, r follows the steps C1, C2, C4 and C5 sequentially. ELSEIF $\forall v^2_{nbr}(\neg occupied(v^2_{nbr}, p^{min}_v, \sim) \vee (occupied\ (v^2_{nbr}, p^{min}_v, \text{OFF}_{h'}) \wedge (h < h')))$, r moves to u with WAIT_h after updating $r.avoid = 0$ and $r.succ = (p', p'_1)$ or (p', p'_2) depending on the current color of r is OFF_h or WAIT_h.

- **Case 2.2** ($r.pred = (p_1, \bot)$): Let $u = v^1_{nbr}$ along the port p_1. r first finds r', a 2-hops neighbour of v along p_1 and with $r'.color \in \{\text{OFF}_h, \text{STORED}_h, \text{move?}_h, \text{WAIT}_h\}$. Let p_2 be the port of the edge $e(u, r')$, incident to u. r updates $r.pred = (p_1, p_2)$ and changes its color to STORED_h without any movement.

▶ **Case 3** ($r.color =$ STORED$_h$): The action mirrors Case 3 of Subsect. 5.1, where r either moves toward its predecessor or becomes the new head.
▶ **Case 4** ($r.color =$ move?$_h$): Let $u = v_{nbr}^1$ along the port p_v^{min}. If all neighbours of u, except v, are unoccupied or occupied by robots with colors in {OFF$_{h'}$, move?$_{h'}$, STORED$_{h'}$, WAIT$_{h'}$, FINISH} for $h' > h$, it moves to u with the color WAIT$_h$. However, if r finds u_{nbr}^1 as occupied with OFF$_{h'}$-colored robot with $h' < h$, it switches to OFF$_h$ without movement. Otherwise, r does nothing.

The termination condition remains the same as earlier. Our detailed analysis establishes the following theorem.

Theorem 6. *Algorithm* GRAPH_MULTIDOOR *fills MVC of an arbitrary graph G having H doors with* FINISH*-colored robots having 4 hops visibility, $O(H)$ colors and $O(\log \Delta)$ memory in $O(|E|)$ epochs under $\mathcal{ASYNC}$ and without collision.*

6 Concluding Remarks

We are particularly interested in investigating a fundamental question in a barebone model: Can a group of mobile robots achieve a particular graph property with only local or limited knowledge? We affirmatively answered this question by considering the *filling MVC problem* on an arbitrary graph with robots operated under the $\mathcal{ASYNC}$ scheduler and with 4 hops visibility. The main highlight of this paper is to be able to achieve a deployment strategy that is time-optimal even under $\mathcal{ASYNC}$ scheduler. Interestingly, our strategy achieves MinVC for trees with the optimal time and memory. We believe a similar strategy can give time optimality in filling MIS problem [17]. Our method improves efficiency by allowing alternate robots on the chain to move in constant epochs, thereby significantly reducing the overall time complexity. As a future direction, one can also investigate other graph properties in the same model.

References

1. Barrameda, E.M., Das, S., Santoro, N.: Deployment of asynchronous robotic sensors in unknown orthogonal environments. In: Fekete, S.P. (ed.) ALGOSENSORS 2008. LNCS, vol. 5389, pp. 125–140. Springer, Heidelberg (2008). https://doi.org/10.1007/978-3-540-92862-1_11
2. Barrameda, E.M., Das, S., Santoro, N.: Uniform dispersal of asynchronous finite-state mobile robots in presence of holes. In: Flocchini, P., Gao, J., Kranakis, E., Meyer auf der Heide, F. (eds.) ALGOSENSORS 2013. LNCS, vol. 8243, pp. 228–243. Springer, Heidelberg (2014). https://doi.org/10.1007/978-3-642-45346-5_17
3. Barriere, L., Flocchini, P., Mesa-Barrameda, E., Santoro, N.: Uniform scattering of autonomous mobile robots in a grid. Int. J. Found. Comput. Sci. **22**(03), 679–697 (2011)
4. Chand, P.K., Molla, A.R., Sivasubramaniam, S.: Run for cover: dominating set via mobile agents. In: Georgiou, K., Kranakis, E. (eds.) Algorithmics of Wireless Networks, ALGOWIN 2023, pp. 133–150. Springer, Cham (2023)

5. Elor, Y., Bruckstein, A.M.: Uniform multi-agent deployment on a ring. Theoret. Comput. Sci. **412**(8), 783–795 (2011)
6. Flocchini, P., Prencipe, G., Santoro, N., Widmayer, P.: Hard tasks for weak robots: the role of common knowledge in pattern formation by autonomous mobile robots. In: ISAAC 1999. LNCS, vol. 1741, pp. 93–102. Springer, Heidelberg (1999). https://doi.org/10.1007/3-540-46632-0_10
7. Heo, N., Varshney, P.: A distributed self spreading algorithm for mobile wireless sensor networks. In: 2003 IEEE Wireless Communications and Networking, WCNC 2003, vol. 3, pp. 1597–1602 (2003)
8. Hideg, A., Lukovszki, T.: Uniform dispersal of robots with minimum visibility range. In: Fernández Anta, A., Jurdzinski, T., Mosteiro, M.A., Zhang, Y. (eds.) ALGOSENSORS 2017. LNCS, vol. 10718, pp. 155–167. Springer, Cham (2017). https://doi.org/10.1007/978-3-319-72751-6_12
9. Hideg, A., Lukovszki, T.: Asynchronous filling by myopic luminous robots. In: Pinotti, C.M., Navarra, A., Bagchi, A. (eds.) ALGOSENSORS 2020. LNCS, vol. 12503, pp. 108–123. Springer, Cham (2020). https://doi.org/10.1007/978-3-030-62401-9_8
10. Howard, A., Matarić, M.J., Sukhatme, G.S.: An incremental self-deployment algorithm for mobile sensor networks. Auton. Robots **13**(2), 113–126 (2002)
11. Hsiang, T.-R., Arkin, E.M., Bender, M.A., Fekete, S.P., Mitchell, J.S.B.: Algorithms for rapidly dispersing robot swarms in unknown environments. In: Boissonnat, J.-D., Burdick, J., Goldberg, K., Hutchinson, S. (eds.) Algorithmic Foundations of Robotics V. STAR, vol. 7, pp. 77–93. Springer, Heidelberg (2004). https://doi.org/10.1007/978-3-540-45058-0_6
12. Jana, S., Pramanick, S., Bhattacharya, A., Mandal, P.S.: Time-optimal asynchronous minimal vertex covering by myopic robots (2025). https://arxiv.org/abs/2508.14247
13. Kamei, S., Tixeuil, S.: An asynchronous maximum independent set algorithm by myopic luminous robots on grids. Comput. J. bxac158 (2022)
14. Karp, R.M.: Reducibility among combinatorial problems, pp. 85–103. Springer, Boston (1972). https://doi.org/10.1007/978-1-4684-2001-2_9
15. Pattanayak, D., Bhagat, S., Gan Chaudhuri, S., Molla, A.R.: Maximal independent set via mobile agents. In: Proceedings of the 25th International Conference on Distributed Computing and Networking, ICDCN 2024, pp. 74–83. Association for Computing Machinery, New York (2024)
16. Poduri, S., Sukhatme, G.: Constrained coverage for mobile sensor networks. In: IEEE International Conference on Robotics and Automation, Proceedings of ICRA 2004, vol. 1, pp. 165–171 (2004)
17. Pramanick, S., Samala, S.V., Pattanayak, D., Mandal, P.S.: Distributed algorithms for filling MIS vertices of an arbitrary graph by myopic luminous robots. Theoret. Comput. Sci. **978**, 114187 (2023). https://doi.org/10.1016/j.tcs.2023.114187

Linear Search for Capturing an Oblivious Mobile Target in the Sender/Receiver Model

Khaled Jawhar(✉) and Evangelos Kranakis

School of Computer Science, Carleton University, Ottawa, ON, Canada
khaledjawhar@cmail.carleton.ca

Abstract. We consider linear search for capturing an oblivious moving target by two autonomous robots with different communicating abilities. Both robots can communicate Face-to-Face (F2F) when co-located but in addition one robot is a Sender (can also send messages wirelessly) and the other also a Receiver (can also receive messages wirelessly). This is known as Sender/Receiver (S/R, for short) communication model. The robots can move with max speed 1. The moving target starts at distance d from the origin and can move either with speed $v < 1$ away from the origin in the "away" model or with speed $v \geq 0$ toward the origin in the "toward" model. We assume that the direction of motion of the target (i.e., whether it is the away or toward model) is known to the robots in advance. To capture the target, the two robots must be co-located with it.

We design new linear search algorithms and analyze the competitive ratio of the time required to capture the target. The approach takes into account various scenarios related to what the robots know about the search environment (e.g., starting distance or speed of the mobile, away or toward model, or a combination thereof). Our study contributes to understanding how asymmetric communication affects the competitive ratio of linear search.

Keywords: Autonomous robot · Capture · Competitive ratio · Sender/Receiver (S/R) · Knowledge · Oblivious target · Searcher · Speed

1 Introduction

Linear search and evacuation by one or more autonomous mobile robots (or agents) have been studied extensively and are applicable to many areas of theoretical computer science, including data mining, crawling, and surveillance, thus making them an area of significant interest. Linear search was first proposed for stochastic and game theoretic systems in [4,5], independently. Deterministic search by a single robot operating on the line was subsequently investigated

---

E. Kranakis—Research supported in part by NSERC Discovery grant.

© The Author(s), under exclusive license to Springer Nature Switzerland AG 2026
O. Michail and G. Prencipe (Eds.): ALGOWIN 2025, LNCS 16078, pp. 151–165, 2026.
https://doi.org/10.1007/978-3-032-09120-8_11

by several researchers including [2,3] and in other topologies, like star in [12]. Additional work on linear search can also be found in [1].

Linear search with multiple robots is also referred to as group search and is an important task arising from the need to design algorithms for multi-agent systems. More recently, group search has attracted the attention of researchers in distributed computing in order to understand the impact of communication faults [8,10] on linear search. In fact, one wants to know how the knowledge the robots have about the search environment affects the competitive ratio of linear search [15]. In particular, there is interest in designing algorithms and analyzing tradeoffs involving time, mobility, and communication model for finding a target. Proposed algorithms employ cooperating, communicating autonomous mobile agents in a distributed setting and operate over continuous domains (typically the infinite line). In such settings, designed algorithms should be fault-tolerant and their performance is measured by the competitive ratio.

The focus of the present paper is on linear search for capturing a mobile target; it involves two cooperating searchers communicating under the S/R model, whereby both robots can communicate in the F2F model but in addition there is communication asymmetry in that one robot is a Sender (can also send messages wirelessly) and the other also a Receiver (can also receive messages wirelessly). The S/R model was initiated in [9] in order to understand the impact of asymmetric communication. A key aspect of our analysis will involve comparing an algorithm designed for a specific knowledge model, where the robots have limited information about the input, to a full knowledge model, where the robots know everything about the input. Such information may include the half-line where the mobile started, its speed, direction of movement, or distance from the origin.

1.1 Model, Preliminaries, and Notation

The search domain is the bidirectional infinite line, in which the robots can move in either direction without affecting their speeds. The robots start at the origin and can travel with maximum speed 1. The target is oblivious, starts at distance d from the origin and can move either away from or toward the origin with a maximum speed v. We abbreviate mobile target either as mobile or target. If the target is moving away from the origin, we also assume that $v < 1$; if it is moving toward the origin, we allow $v \geq 0$ to be arbitrary. The robots and the mobile start at the same time. If $v = 0$ the target is static, so our approach generalizes linear search case for a static target. We consider three knowledge models, cf., [7], for the robots: in the NoDistance, v is known and d unknown, in the NoSpeed, v is unknown and d known, and in the NoKnowledge, neither v nor d is known.

A search algorithm for two robots is a complete description of their trajectories. For an algorithm A and an input instance I of the problem in the knowledge model, $T_A(I)$ is the time it takes algorithm A to solve instance I. If $T_{opt}(I)$ is the optimal time of an offline algorithm for the same instance I, then the competitive ratio for the capture time of an online algorithm A is defined by the ratio $CR_A := \sup_I T_A(I)/T_{opt}(I)$. If $\mathcal{A}$ is a class of algorithms solving an online version then its competitive ratio is defined by $CR_{\mathcal{A}} := \inf_{A \in \mathcal{A}} CR_A$; we omit the subscripts A and $\mathcal{A}$ when they are easily understood from context. When the target is not static it is customary to refer to capture as evacuation. Our goal is to design capture algorithms that achieve the best competitive ratio.

The robots can always communicate F2F (only when colocated). Additional communication is possible but is asymmetric in that one of the robots can also send communication wirelessly and is designated as the sender (denoted by S), while the other robot is designated as the receiver (denoted by R) and can also receive information wirelessly. Both robots are equipped with pedometers and computing capabilities, allowing them to deduce the location of the other robot from relevant communications exchanged. S and R can't switch roles.

1.2 Related Work

Linear search in a distributed setting with multiple robots subjected to possible crash faults was initiated in [11] and for Byzantine faults in [8]. One aspect of our current research is related to the communication model being used. The S/R communication model was introduced for an infinite line in [9]; for the case of two robots and an unknown static (non-mobile) target, it was shown that there exists an evacuation algorithm with competitive ratio $3 + 2\sqrt{2}$, which was also proven to be optimal among all possible linear search algorithms. Also related is the work of [13] which studies bike-assisted evacuation in the S/R model. The interested reader can find additional discussion and review of recent research on other search models in [15].

Another aspect of the present research is related to understanding how the mobility of the target affects the competitive ratio of linear search. McCabe [16] was first to investigate this problem in a stochastic setting whereby the mobile follows a Bernoulli random walk on the integers. In the deterministic (continuous) setting Alpern and Gal [1, p. 134, Eq. 8.25] were the first to compute the optimal competitive ratio of search as $1 + \frac{8(1+v)}{(1-v)^2}$ for a target moving with speed $0 \leq v < 1$. Extensions of this work, were investigated in [7] where also competitive ratio tradeoffs were analyzed depending on whether the target is moving toward or away from the origin of the inifinte line. For each of these two cases four subcases arise depending on which of the two parameters d and v are known to the searcher. Recent extensions of this work can be found in [6] where tight (in fact, optimal) bounds are obtained when the target is moving away from the origin.

The goal of our present paper is twofold. First we generalize the work of [9] from a static target to a mobile target, and second we extend the analysis of [7] from one to two robots in the asymmetric S/R model. We extend the work of [9] by generalizing their model to accommodate a moving target, where their setting becomes a special case of ours when the target speed is zero. With respect to [7], we introduce new algorithms under an asymmetric Sender/Receiver (S/R) communication model involving two robots. This allows us to achieve improved competitive ratios compared to the single-robot setting analyzed in [7], particularly in scenarios where the robots lack information about the target's distance, speed, or direction of motion. To this end we give new algorithms and study competitive ratio tradeoffs for linear search in several search models which take into account knowledge of aspects of the target's mobility by two autonomous robots. To the best of our knowledge this has not been investigated before.

1.3 Outline and Results of the Paper

The NoDistance model (v known, d unknown) is studied in Sect. 2. The main algorithm in the toward model consists of three subalgorithms with respective competitive ratios as follows: $\frac{\sqrt{v^2+2v+2}+1}{\sqrt{v^2+2v+2}-1}$ for Algorithm 1, $1+\frac{2(a^5+a^4)}{a^4+va^4+2av+v-1}$ for Algorithm 2, where a is the positive solution of Eq. (7), and $1+\frac{1}{v}$ for the waiting algorithm. In summary, Algorithm 1 performs best for $0 \leq v \leq \frac{1}{3}$, and the waiting algorithm outperforms the first one when $\frac{1}{3} \leq v \leq 1$. Figure 1 displays the range of v within which the algorithms are optimal. The main Algorithm 3 in the away model has competitive ratio $\frac{\sqrt{v^2-2v+2}+1}{\sqrt{v^2-2v+2}-1}$ (which for $v = 0$ is equal to $3+2\sqrt{2}$, thus generalizing the upper bound in [9] for arbitrary $v < 1$.)

The NoSpeed model (v unknown, d known) is studied in Sect. 3. For the toward model Algorithm 4 has competitive ratio 3, while for the away model Algorithm 5 has competitive ratio $1 + O(u^{\frac{10}{3}} \log u)$, where $u = \frac{1}{1-v}$. (The latter result is rather surprising given the communication asymmetry of the two searchers and should be compared to the single searcher case, where combining [7] with the more recent [6] the tight bounds $O(u^{4-(\log_2 \log_2 u)^{-2}})$, if $u > 4$ and $\Omega(u^{4-\epsilon})$, for any $\epsilon > 0$ were obtained.) We also prove in Theorem 7 that $1 + \frac{2}{1-v}$, is a lower bound for the competitive ratio of any algorithm in the NoSpeed away model.

Finally, the NoKnowledge model (both d, v are unknown) is studied in Sect. 4. In the toward model the optimal competitive ratio is $1+\frac{1}{v}$. In the away model we prove that $1+O(M^{\frac{16}{3}} \log(M) \log \log^{\frac{3}{2}} M)$ is an upper bound for the competitive ratio, where $M = \max\{d, \frac{1}{1-v}\}$. All omitted proofs are provided in the full version of this paper, available on arXiv [14].

2 The NoDistance Model

In this section, we consider the NoDistance model, in which d is unknown, but v is known to the robots. We distinguish the cases where the target is moving away from or toward the origin.

2.1 Target Moving Toward the Origin

The target moves toward the origin from either direction at any speed v. Agents S and R can move in any direction with a maximum speed of 1. Three algorithms are considered, two of which perform best over different ranges of the target's speed v.

2.1.1 Opposite Direction Algorithm

Assume that R moves in one direction with a maximum unit speed, and S moves in the other direction with speed u. Two cases are considered depending on which robot finds the target first. If S finds the target first, then it informs R, which proceeds to the target. Otherwise, if R finds the target first, it switches its direction to catch up to S, and then both robots move to the target with unit speed.

Algorithm 1. NoDistanceTowardOppositeDirection

1: S moves left with speed u and R moves right with speed 1;
2: **if** R finds the target first **then**
3:     It changes direction and catches up to S;
4:     The two robots change direction and move toward the target with unit speed;
5: **else**
6:     **if** S finds the target first **then**
7:         It informs R that the target has been found and moves with the target;
8:         R switches direction and moves with unit speed to the target;

Theorem 1. *The competitive ratio of Algorithm 1 is*

$$\frac{\sqrt{v^2 + 2v + 2} + 1}{\sqrt{v^2 + 2v + 2} - 1}. \tag{1}$$

Proof. (Theorem 1) Assume that S moves with speed u (in the course of the proof we will determine the optimal u) and R with unit speed. There are two cases to consider depending on which of S or R finds the target first. We fix the convention that movement to the right corresponds to the positive x-axis, and movement to the left corresponds to the negative x-axis.

- **S finds the target first.** For S to find the target, it needs time $\frac{d}{u+v}$. At that point, the receiver is at a distance of $\frac{d}{u+v} + \frac{du}{u+v}$ from the sender. The competitive ratio becomes:

$$CR = \frac{\frac{d}{u+v}}{\frac{d}{1+v}} + \frac{\frac{d}{u+v} + \frac{du}{u+v}}{\frac{d}{1+v}} = \frac{2 + v + u}{u+v} = 1 + \frac{2}{u+v}. \tag{2}$$

- **R finds the target first.** The time needed for R to reach the target is $\frac{d}{1+v}$. At this time, S would be away from the origin by a distance $\frac{du}{1+v}$. Thus, for R to capture S, it needs time:

$$\frac{\frac{d}{1+v} + \frac{du}{1+v}}{1-u} = \frac{d + du}{(1+v)(1-u)}. \tag{3}$$

Both robots would then be away from the target by:

$$\frac{d+du}{1+v} + \frac{du+du^2}{(1+v)(1-u)} - \frac{dv+duv}{(1+v)(1-u)} = \frac{du-dv-duv+d}{(1+v)(1-u)}.$$

Thus, for both robots to catch the target, they need time:

$$\frac{du-dv-duv+d}{(1+v)^2(1-u)}. \tag{4}$$

Combining Eqs. (3), and (4), the competitive ratio becomes:

$$CR = 1 + \frac{1+u}{1-u} + \frac{u-v-uv+1}{(1+v)(1-u)} = \frac{u-uv+3+v}{(1+v)(1-u)}. \tag{5}$$

As we will justify below, the optimal value of u is found by solving $\frac{u-uv+3+v}{(1+v)(1-u)} = \frac{2+v+u}{u+v}$.

We note that both competitive ratio functions derived for the two cases are monotonic in u. Specifically, in the first case where S finds the target first, the competitive ratio $\frac{2+v+u}{u+v}$ is decreasing in u for $u > 0$. In the second case where R finds the target first, the competitive ratio $\frac{u-uv+3+v}{(1+v)(1-u)}$ is increasing in u for $0 < u < 1$. Therefore, equating the two expressions gives the unique value of u that minimizes the maximum competitive ratio between the two cases. Solving this equation, we obtain $2u^2 + 4u + 4uv - 2 = 0$, whose solution is $u = \sqrt{v^2 + 2v + 2} - v - 1$. Substituting u into the competitive ratio formula, we get Eq. (1). This proves the theorem. □

2.1.2 ZigZag Till Meeting Algorithm

Both robots iterate a ZigZag strategy. They start at the origin. During the first iteration, robot S moves in one direction a distance of x_0, while robot R moves in the opposite direction a distance of x_1. If neither robot finds the target during this iteration, they reverse their directions and return to meet at some meeting point. If one robot finds the target, it stays with the target. If, upon reversing, one robot does not meet the other at the predetermined meeting point, the robot that arrives at the meeting point will proceed in the direction of the missing robot to catch up with the target. The algorithm is formalized as follows:

Algorithm 2. ZigZagTillMeeting

1: **for** $i \leftarrow 0$ to ∞ **until** the target is found **do**
   Sender's moves:
2:   S moves to the left a distance x_{2i} unless the target is found;
3:   **if** the target is not found **then**
4:     S reverses direction and moves back to meet R;
5:     **if** S does not meet R on the way **then**
6:       S continues in the same direction until it catches the target;
7:     **else**
8:       S reverses direction after meeting R and sets its next travel distance to x_{2i+2};
9:   **if** S reaches the target **then**
10:    S notifies R that it has reached the target;
11:    S stays with the target and moves with it;
   Receiver's moves:
12: R moves to the right a distance x_{2i+1} unless the target is found;
13: **if** the target is not found **then**
14:    R reverses direction and moves back to meet S;
15:    **if** R does not meet S on the way **then**
16:      R continues in the same direction until it catches the target;
17:    **else**
18:      R reverses direction after meeting S and sets its next travel distance to x_{2i+3};
19: **if** R reaches the target **then**
20:    R stays with the target and moves with it;
21: **if** R receives notification from S that it has reached the target **then**
22:    R reverses direction and proceeds to the target;

If neither robot finds the target during the first iteration, they proceed to the second iteration. In this iteration, robot S moves a distance of x_2, and robot R moves a distance of x_3. This pattern continues for subsequent iterations i, where, in each iteration i, robot S moves a distance of x_{2i}, and robot R moves a distance of x_{2i+1}. We define a sequence of distances x_i for $i \geq 0$ such that $x_i = a^{i+1}$, where a is a non-negative real number. During each iteration i, the robots meet at predetermined points y_i. We interpret y_i as the position on the line where both robots meet during iteration i. The origin is set at $y_0 = 0$. The sequence of points y_i is calculated based on the assumption that the robots meet at y_{i-1} during iteration $i-1$ and plan to meet at y_i during iteration i. This leads to the following recurrence relation: $x_{2i-1} - y_{i-1} + x_{2i-1} - y_i = y_{i-1} + 2x_{2i-2} + y_i$, which after simplification reduces to: $y_i = x_{2i-1} - x_{2i-2} - y_{i-1}$. The algorithm terminates when one of the robots finds the target. At that point, the other robot realizes the target has been found, as it does not encounter its counterpart at the expected intersection point. The second robot then proceeds directly toward the target. Although the sequence y_i is not used in the proof below, it is worth mentioning that it represents the points at which both robots meet during each iteration, and can be useful to understand the algorithm's behavior.

Theorem 2. *The competitive ratio of Algorithm 2 is upper bounded by*

$$1 + \frac{2(a^5 + a^4)}{a^4 + va^4 + 2av + v - 1}. \tag{6}$$

where a (as a function of v) is the positive root of the following equation

$$(1+v)a^5 + 8va^2 + (11v - 5)a + 4(v - 1) = 0. \tag{7}$$

2.1.3 Waiting Algorithm

The waiting algorithm is the strategy whereby both robots remain at the origin (indefinitely). This algorithm is easy to analyze and a proof can be found in [7].

Theorem 3. *When the target moves toward the origin, the competitive ratio for the waiting algorithm is $1 + \frac{1}{v}$.*

Figure 1 illustrates and compares the upper bounds of the three algorithms as a function of v.

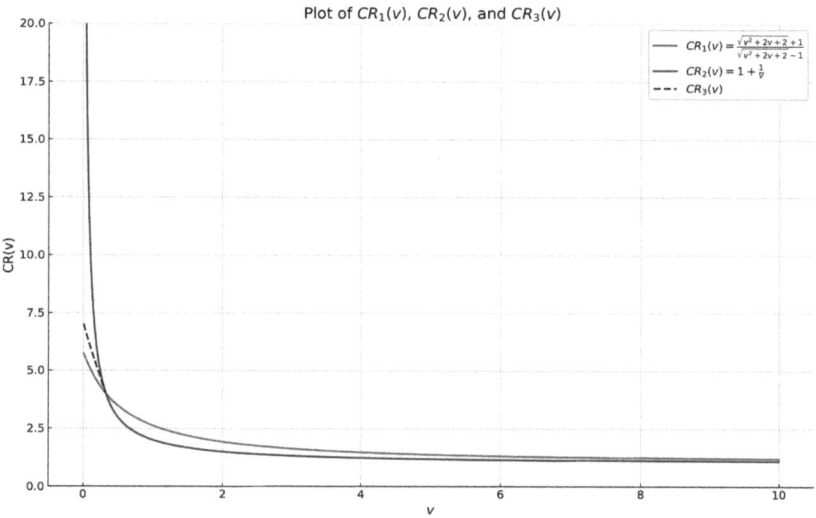

Fig. 1. Algorithm 1 achieves the best performance for $0 \leq v \leq \frac{1}{3}$, while Algorithm 2 outperforms the waiting algorithm within that same interval. For $v \geq \frac{1}{3}$, the waiting algorithm becomes the most competitive. Interestingly, all three algorithms share the same competitive ratio at $v = \frac{1}{3}$.

2.2 Target Moving Away from the Origin

The target moves away from the origin. We have no knowledge of the initial distance of the target from the origin. We have knowledge only of the speed of the moving target. Assume that R moves in one direction with maximum unit speed and S moves in the other direction with speed u. There are two cases to consider. Either S or R finds the target first. If S finds the target first, it informs R which proceeds to the target, otherwise if R does, it switches its direction to reach S, and then both robots move to the target with unit speed.

Algorithm 3. NoDistanceAway S/R

1: S moves to the left with speed u; R moves to the right with speed 1
2: **if** R finds the target first **then**
3:     it changes direction and catches up to S;
4:     The two robots change direction and move towards the target with unit speed;
5: **else**
6:     **if** S finds the target first **then**
7:         it informs R that the target has been found and moves with the target;
8:         R moves with unit speed to the target;

We prove the following result.

Theorem 4. *The competitive ratio of Algorithm 3 is*

$$\frac{\sqrt{v^2 - 2v + 2} + 1}{\sqrt{v^2 - 2v + 2} - 1}. \tag{8}$$

Proof. (Theorem 4) S moves with speed u and R with unit speed then we have two cases to consider depending on which of S or R finds the target first.

- **S finds the target first.** The competitive ratio is as follows:

$$CR = \frac{\frac{d}{u-v}}{\frac{d}{1-v}} + \frac{\frac{d}{u-v} + \frac{du}{u-v}}{\frac{d}{1-v}} = \frac{\frac{d}{u-v} + \frac{du+d}{(1-v)(u-v)}}{\frac{d}{1-v}} = \frac{2-v+u}{u-v}. \tag{9}$$

- **R finds the target first.** To reach the target, it needs time: $\frac{d}{1-v}$. At this time, S would be away from R by distance $\frac{d}{1-v} + \frac{du}{1-v}$, thus for R to capture S, it needs time:

$$\frac{\frac{d}{1-v} + \frac{du}{1-v}}{1-u} = \frac{d+du}{(1-v)(1-u)}. \tag{10}$$

Thus both robots would be away from the target by $\frac{d+du}{(1-v)(1-u)} + \frac{dv+dvu}{(1-v)(1-u)}$. It follows that for both robots to catch the target, they need time:

$$\frac{d + du + dv + dvu}{(1-v)^2(1-u)}. \tag{11}$$

Combining $\frac{d}{1-v}$ with equations (10), (11), the competitive ratio becomes:

$$\frac{\frac{d}{1-v} + \frac{d+du}{(1-v)(1-u)} + \frac{d+du+dv+dvu}{(1-v)^2(1-u)}}{\frac{d}{1-v}} = \frac{3 - v + u + vu}{(1-v)(1-u)}. \tag{12}$$

It is required to find the optimal value u. Setting the competitive ratios in Eqs. (9) and (12) to be equal, we get $\frac{3+u+uv-v}{(1-v)(1-u)} = \frac{2-v+u}{u-v}$. We conclude that $2u^2 + 4u - 4uv - 2 = 0$, thus $u = (v-1) + \sqrt{v^2 - 2v + 2}$. Substituting u above yields Eq. (8). This proves the theorem. □

3 The NoSpeed Model

In this section, we consider the NoSpeed model (d is known but v is not known to the robots) and distinguish the cases where the target is moving away from or toward the origin.

3.1 Target Moving Toward the Origin

Consider the following algorithm.

Algorithm 4. NoSpeedToward S/R

Input: Target Initial distance d

1: The two robots select the same direction and move together with unit speed, distance d
2: **if** Target is not found **then**
3:    Both robots change direction and move together until they encounter the target, at which point they stop.

Theorem 5. *The competitive ratio of Algorithm 4 is upper bounded by* 3 *and this is optimal.*

Proof. In the worst case scenario, if the target's speed is very small and one of the robots moves in the opposite direction to where the target is located, the robot will end up at a distance of approximately $2d$ from the target. At that point, the robot will be separated from the target by a distance $2d - dv$. Thus, the competitive ratio is $CR = \frac{d + \frac{2d-dv}{1+v}}{\frac{d}{1+v}} = 3$. This proves the upper bound. To prove the lower bound, we argue as follows. One of the two points $-d, d$ must be visited by either S or R, otherwise if the speed of the target is too small, then none of the robots would be able to capture the target. There are two cases to consider, either S or R reaches one of the two points $-d, d$. Let us consider the first case, Assuming that S reaches point d, the adversary can initially place the target at point $-d$. Thus for the robots to capture the target, considering that the speed of the target is v, the competitive ratio is at least: $\frac{d + \frac{2d-dv}{1+v}}{\frac{d}{1+v}} = 3$. For the second case, assuming that R reaches point d, then the adversary can initially place the target at point $-d$ and we end up having a similar competitive ratio 3. This proves the theorem. □

3.2 Target Moving Away from the Origin

The target moves away from the origin in any direction. Let us consider a monotone increasing sequence $\{f_i : i \geq 0\}$ of non-negative integers. The idea is to guess the speed of the target.

Algorithm 5. NoSpeedAway S/R

Input: Target's initial distance d
Given: Increasing integer sequence f_i with $f_0 = 1$, $f_i < f_{i+1}$; initial times $t_1 = t_2 = 0$
1: **for** $i \leftarrow 0$ to ∞ **until** the target is found **do**
    Sender's (S) moves:
2:     Set $v_{2i} = 1 - 2^{-f_{2i}}$, $x_{2i} = -\frac{d+t_1 v_{2i}}{1-v_{2i}}$
3:     S moves left by x_{2i} and returns to meet R
4:     **if** S does not meet R **then**
5:         S continues to pursue the target
6:     **else**
7:         S reverses and sets next guess v_{2i+2}
8:     **if** S finds the target **then**
9:         S stays with the target
    Receiver's (R) moves:
10:     Set $v_{2i+1} = 1 - 2^{-f_{2i+1}}$, $x_{2i+1} = \frac{d+t_2 v_{2i+1}}{1-v_{2i+1}}$
11:     R moves right by x_{2i+1} and returns to meet S
12:     **if** R misses S **then**
13:         R continues to pursue the target
14:     **else**
15:         R continues with S using v_{2i+1}
16:         **if** target not found **then**
17:             R reverses and updates to v_{2i+3}
18:     **if** R finds the target **then**
19:         R stays with the target
    Time Updates:
20:     $t_1 \leftarrow t_1 + 2|x_{2i}| + 2\times$(meeting time with R)
21:     $t_2 \leftarrow t_2 + 2|x_{2i+1}| + 2\times$(pursuit time with S and return)

The algorithm works through iterations. We will use the guess $v_i = 1 - 2^{-f_i}$. At the beginning, both robots S and R are situated at the origin. During each iteration i, robot S moves in one direction with a guess of v_{2i}, and R moves in the other direction with a guess of v_{2i+1}. If S finds the target first, it communicates with R to proceed to the target. Otherwise if R finds the target first, it moves with the target and waits for S to proceed to the target. If the target is not found by neither S nor R, then each robot returns back until they meet. At the meeting point, R would go back with S to confirm whether the target is caught with a guess of v_{2i+1} on the side where S was moving. If the target is not found by S and R, then R reverses its direction and proceeds with a guess of v_{2i+3}, while S continues in the same direction with a guess of v_{2i+2}. The competitive ratio is as follows.

Theorem 6. *The competitive ratio of Algorithm 5 is $1 + O(u^{\frac{10}{3}} \log u)$, where $u = \frac{1}{1-v}$.*

Theorem 7. *The competitive ratio of the NoSpeedAway S/R model is at least $1 + \Omega\left(\frac{1}{1-v}\right)$.*

Proof. Consider an algorithm A solving the capturing problem for two robots. Let d be the starting distance of the target from the origin and $v < 1$ its speed. For any $\epsilon > 0$ but arbitrarily small consider the first time one of the two robots reaches a distance $\frac{d}{1-v} - \epsilon$ away from the origin, following algorithm A, in either direction from the origin of the line. Let's call this the first robot. The adversary places the mobile in the opposite direction on the line. Regardless of where the second of the two robots is, the first robot will be distance $\frac{2d}{1-v} - 2\epsilon$ away from current position of the mobile. Therefore, the first robot needs time $\frac{d}{1-v} - \epsilon$ plus additional time

$$\frac{\frac{2d}{1-v} - 2\epsilon}{1-v} = \frac{2d}{(1-v)^2} - \frac{2\epsilon}{1-v}. \tag{13}$$

to move on the other side of the line where the mobile is. Consolidating the terms and simplifying Eq. (13) above we see that the total time for the first robot to reach the mobile (which is moving on the other side of the line) will be at least

$$\frac{d - 2\epsilon}{1-v} - \epsilon + \frac{2d}{(1-v)^2}. \tag{14}$$

As a consequence, the resulting competitive ratio of algorithm A must satisfy

$$CR \geq \frac{\frac{d-2\epsilon}{1-v} - \epsilon + \frac{2d}{(1-v)^2}}{\frac{d}{1-v}}. \tag{15}$$

Clearly, for d, v constants, the righthand side of Inequality (15) converges to $1 + \frac{2}{1-v}$, as $\epsilon \to 0$, which proves the lower bound. □

4 The NoKnowledge Model

In this section, we consider the NoKnowledge model (neither d nor v is known to the robots) and distinguish the cases where the target is moving away from or toward the origin.

4.1 Target Moving Toward the Origin

Theorem 8. *The optimal competitive ratio is $1 + \frac{1}{v}$ and is given by the waiting algorithm.*

Proof. The upper bound is well-known [7]. For the lower bound, consider an algorithm where the robot does not wait and instead moves a distance $x > 0$ in a certain direction, after waiting at the origin for time $t > 0$. Consider the scenario where the target with speed $v = \frac{d}{t+x}$ is at distance d away from the origin in the opposite direction. Thus, the target reaches the origin at the time the robot reaches x. The earliest meeting point is: $t + x + \frac{x}{1+v} = \frac{d}{v} + \frac{x}{1+v} \geq \frac{d}{v}$. It follows that the competitive ratio is at least $\frac{\frac{d}{v}}{\frac{d}{1+v}} = 1 + \frac{1}{v}$. This completes the proof of the theorem. □

4.2 Target Moving Away from the Origin

The target moves away from the origin in either direction. Let us consider two monotone increasing sequences of non-negative integers $\{f_i, g_i : i \geq 0\}$. The idea is to try to guess the speed and the initial distance of the target. The algorithm works through iterations. We will use the guesses $v_i = 1 - 2^{-f_i}$ and $d_i = 2^{g_i}$. At the beginning, both robots S and R are situated at the origin.

During each iteration i, robot S moves in one direction with a guess of v_{2i} for the speed and d_{2i} for the distance. R moves in the other direction with a guess of v_{2i+1} for the speed and d_{2i+1} for the distance. If S finds the target first, it communicates with R to proceed to the target. Otherwise, if R finds the target first, it moves with the target and waits for S to proceed to the target.

If the target is not found by either S or R, then each robot returns back until they meet. At the meeting point, R would go back with S to confirm whether the target is caught with a guess of v_{2i+1} for the speed and d_{2i+1} for the distance on the side where S was moving. If the target is not found by S and R, then R reverses its direction and proceeds with a guess of v_{2i+3} for the speed and d_{2i+3} for the distance, while S continues in the same direction with a guess of v_{2i+2} for the speed and d_{2i+2} for the distance.

Algorithm 6. NoKnowledgeAway S/R

1: **Given:** Increasing integer sequences f_i, g_i with $f_0 = 1$, $g_0 = 0$, $f_i < f_{i+1}$, $g_i < g_{i+1}$, and initial times $t_1 = t_2 = 0$
2: **for** $i \leftarrow 0$ to ∞ until target is found **do**
3:     S: Set $v_{2i} = 1 - 2^{-f_{2i}}$, $d_{2i} = 2^{g_{2i}}$, $x_{2i} = \frac{d_i + t_1 v_{2i}}{1 - v_{2i}}$
4:     Move left, then return to meet R
5:     **if** no meeting with R **then**
6:         Continue to pursue target
7:     **else**
8:         Reverse and update to v_{2i+2}, d_{2i+2}
9:     **if** target found **then**
10:         Move with target
11:     R: Set $v_{2i+1} = 1 - 2^{-f_{2i+1}}$, $d_{2i+1} = 2^{g_{2i+1}}$, $x_{2i+1} = \frac{d_i + t_2 v_{2i+1}}{1 - v_{2i+1}}$
12:     Move right, then return to meet S
13:     **if** no meeting with S **then**
14:         Continue to pursue target
15:     **else**
16:         Continue with S using v_{2i+1}, d_{2i+1}
17:         **if** target not found **then**
18:             Reverse and update to v_{2i+3}, d_{2i+3}
19:     **if** target found **then**
20:         Move with target
21:     $t_1 \leftarrow t_1 + 2|x_{2i}| + 2 \times$ (round-trip time with R)
22:     $t_2 \leftarrow t_2 + 2|x_{2i+1}| + 2 \times$ (time with S for guess coverage and return)

Theorem 9. *The competitive ratio of Algorithm 6 is upper bounded by* $1 + O\left(M^{\frac{16}{3}} \log(M) \log \log^{\frac{3}{2}} M\right)$ *where* $M = \max\{d, \frac{1}{1-v}\}$.

5 Conclusion

We considered the problem of capturing an oblivious moving target on an infinite line with two robots in the S/R model. Two cases were analyzed based on the target's movement: either moving towards or away from the origin. For each case, we took into account various constraints related to the knowledge the robots have about the target's speed and its initial distance from the origin. Establishing tight bounds for the scenario where the distance is unknown and the target is moving away from the origin remains an open problem. As a topic for future research it would be interesting to study competitive ratios in linear search for multi-robot systems and for capturing a mobile target with robots subjected to either crash or byzantine faults.

References

1. Alpern, S., Gal, S.: The Theory of Search Games and Rendezvous, vol. 55. Springer (2003)
2. Baeza-Yates, R., Culberson, J., Rawlins, G.: Searching in the plane. Inf. Comput. **106**(2), 234–252 (1993)
3. Baeza-Yates, R., Schott, R.: Parallel searching in the plane. Comput. Geom. **5**(3), 143–154 (1995)
4. Beck, A.: On the linear search problem. Israel J. Math. **2**(4), 221–228 (1964)
5. Bellman, R.: An optimal search. SIAM Rev. **5**(3), 274 (1963)
6. Coleman, J., Ivanov, D., Kranakis, E., Krizanc, D., Morales-Ponce, O.: Linear search for an escaping target with unknown speed. In: Rescigno, A.A., Vaccaro, U. (eds.) IWOCA 2024. LNCS, vol. 14764, pp. 396–407. Springer, Cham (2024). https://doi.org/10.1007/978-3-031-63021-7_30
7. Coleman, J.R., Kranakis, E., Krizanc, D., Morales-Ponce, O.: Line search for an oblivious moving target. In: Hillel, E., Palmieri, R., Rivière, E. (eds.) 26th International Conference on Principles of Distributed Systems, OPODIS 2022, 13–15 December 2022, Brussels, Belgium. LIPIcs, vol. 253, pp. 12:1–12:19. Schloss Dagstuhl - Leibniz-Zentrum für Informatik (2022)
8. Czyzowicz, J., et al.: Search on a line by byzantine robots. Int. J. Found. Comput. Sci. **32**(4), 369–387 (2021)
9. Czyzowicz, J., et al.: Group evacuation on a line by agents with different communication abilities. In: ISAAC 2021, pp. 57:1–57:24 (2021)
10. Czyzowicz, J., Kranakis, E., Krizanc, D., Narayanan, L., Opatrny, J.: Search on a line with faulty robots. Distrib. Comput. **32**(6), 493–504 (2019)
11. Czyzowicz, J., Kranakis, E., Krizanc, D., Narayanan, L., Opatrny, J.: Search on a line with faulty robots. Distributed Comput. **32**(6), 493–504 (2019)
12. Gal, S.: Minimax solutions for linear search problems. SIAM J. Appl. Math. **27**(1), 17–30 (1974)
13. Jawhar, K., Kranakis, E.: Bike assisted evacuation on a line of robots with communication faults. In: ALGOWIN 2024, Royal Holloway, University of London in Egham, United Kingdom, 5–6 September 2024, Proceedings. LNCS. Springer (2024)
14. Jawhar, K., Kranakis, E.: Linear search for capturing an oblivious mobile target in the sender/receiver model. arXiv:2508.04870 (2025)
15. Kranakis, E.: A survey of the impact of knowledge on the competitive ratio in linear search. In: Masuzawa, T., Katayama, Y., Kakugawa, H., Nakamura, J., Kim, Y. (eds.) SSS 2024. LNCS, vol. 14931, pp. 23–38. Springer, Cham (2024). https://doi.org/10.1007/978-3-031-74498-3_2
16. McCabe, B.J.: Searching for a one-dimensional random walker. J. Appl. Probab. 86–93 (1974)

A Logarithmic Approximation Algorithm for the Activation Edge-Multicover Problem

Zeev Nutov[1], Avner Huri[1], and Guy Kortsarz[2]

[1] The Open University of Israel, Ra'anana, Israel
nutov@openu.ac.il
[2] Rutgers University, Camden, USA
guyk@camden.rutgers.edu

Abstract. In the ACTIVATION EDGE-MULTICOVER problem we are given a multigraph $G = (V, E)$ with activation costs $\{c_e^u, c_e^v\}$ for every edge $e = uv \in E$, and degree requirements $r = \{r_v : v \in V\}$. The goal is to find an edge subset $J \subseteq E$ that minimizes the activation cost $\sum_{v \in V} \max\{c_{uv}^v : uv \in J\}$, such that every $v \in V$ has at least r_v neighbors in the graph (V, J). Let $k = \max_{v \in V} r_v$ be the maximum requirement and let $\theta = \max_{e=uv \in E} \frac{\max\{c_e^u, c_e^v\}}{\min\{c_e^u, c_e^v\}}$ be the maximum quotient between the two costs of an edge. The case $\theta = 1$ (when $c_e^u = c_e^v$ for all $e = uv \in E$) is the well studied MIN-POWER EDGE-MULTICOVER problem, that admits approximation ratio $O(\log k)$. On the other hand, for $k = 1$ the problem generalizes the FACILITY LOCATION problem, and admits a tight approximation ratio $O(\log n)$. This implies approximation ratio $O(k \log n)$ for general k and θ (c.f. [28]), and no better approximation ratio was known. Our main result is the first (poly-)logarithmic approximation ratio $O(\log k + \log \min\{\theta, n\})$, that bridges between two known approximation ratios – $O(\log k)$ for $\theta = 1$ and $O(\log n)$ for $k = 1$. This also implies approximation ratio $O(\log k + \log \min\{\theta, n\}) + \beta \cdot (\theta + 1)$ for the ACTIVATION k-CONNECTED SUBGRAPH problem, where β is the best known approximation ratio for the ordinary min-cost version of the problem. We also obtain the following improved approximation ratios for the MIN-POWER EDGE-MULTICOVER problem:
(i) $k + 0.2785$ for general costs, improving the ratio of [8] for $k \leq 22$.
(ii) $1 + \max_{x \geq 1} \frac{\ln x}{1 + x/\theta}$ for unit costs, improving the ratio 2.16 [8] for $k \leq 10$.

1 Introduction

In network design problems one seeks a cheap subgraph that satisfies a prescribed property. A traditional setting, motivated among others by wired networks, is when each edge has a cost, and we want to minimize the cost of the subgraph. A fundamental class of network design problems are "degree problems" when we want the subgaph to satisfy certain degree requirements. Given a set $R \subseteq V$

of terminals we say that an edge set J is an R-**edge-cover** if every $v \in R$ has some edge in J incident to it. In the MIN-COST EDGE-COVER problem we are given a graph with edge costs and a set R of terminals and seek a min-cost R-edge-cover. This problem can be solved in polynomial time [10]. More generally, given **degree requirements** $r = \{r_v : v \in V\}$ we say that an edge set J is an r-**edge-cover** if every $v \in V$ has at least r_v neighbors in the graph (V, J). In the MIN-COST EDGE-MULTICOVER problem the goal is to find a min-cost r-edge-cover. This problem can be solved in polynomial time by a reduction to to the MIN-COST EDGE-COVER problem, and it is one of the most fundamental problems in Combinatorial Optimization, cf. [33].

In wireless networks a communication between two nodes depends on our "investment" in both nodes – like transmission energy and equipment type. The node weighted setting captures just some of these scenarios. In 2011 Panigrahi [31] suggested a generalization, that captures many possible wireless networks scenarios. In Panigrahi's model, every edge uv has an activating function $f(x_u, x_v)$ to $\{0, 1\}$, such that an edge uv is activated if and only we invest x_u at node u and x_v at node v such that $f(x_u, x_v) = 1$. Here we use a simpler but less general setting suggested in [21], which is equivalent to that of Panigrahi for problems in which inclusion minimal feasible solutions have no parallel edges (but the input graph may have parallel edges), as in the problems we consider.

More formally, in **activation network design problems** we are given an undirected (multi-)graph $G = (V, E)$ where every edge $e = uv \in E$ has two (non-negative) **activation costs** $\{c_e^u, c_e^v\}$; here $e = uv \in E$ means that the edge e has ends u, v and belongs to E. An edge $e = uv \in E$ is **activated by a level assignment** $\{l_v : v \in V\}$ to the nodes if $l_u \geq c_e^u$ and $l_v \geq c_e^v$. The goal is to find a level assignment of minimum value $l(V) = \sum_{v \in V} l_v$, such that the activated edge set $J = \{e = uv \in E : c_e^u \leq l_u, c_e^v \leq l_v\}$ satisfies a prescribed property. Equivalently, the minimum value level assignment that activates an edge set $J \subseteq E$ is given by $\ell_J(v) = \max\{c_e^v : e \in \delta_J(v)\}$; here $\delta_J(v)$ denotes the set of edges in J incident to v, and a maximum taken over an empty set is assumed to be zero. We seek an edge set $J \subseteq E$ that satisfies the given property and minimizes $\ell_J(V) = \sum_{v \in V} \ell_J(v)$. Note that while we use l_v to denote a level assignment to a node v, we use a slightly different notation $\ell_J(v)$ for the function that evaluates the optimal assignment that activates an edge set J. We consider the following problem.

ACTIVATION EDGE-MULTICOVER (AEM)
Input: A multigraph $G = (V, E)$ with activation costs $\{c_e^u, c_e^v\}$ for every edge $e = uv \in E$, and degree requirements $r = \{r_v : v \in V\}$.
Output: An r-edge-cover J of minimal activation cost $\ell_J(V) = \sum_{v \in V} \max_{uv \in J} c_{uv}^v$.

Equivalently, AEM can be cast as a problem of assigning **levels** $\{l_v : v \in V\}$ to the nodes of minimum total value $l(V) = \sum_{v \in V} l_v$, such that the edge set $J = \{uv \in E : c_{uv}^u \leq l_u, c_{uv}^v \leq l_v\}$ activated by the assignment is an r-edge-cover. The **slope** θ of an instance of an activation network design problem is the maximum ratio between the two costs of an edge, namely

$$\theta = \max_{e=uv \in E} \frac{\max\{c_e^u, c_e^v\}}{\min\{c_e^u, c_e^v\}} \ .$$

Two main types of activation costs were extensively studied in the literature.

- **Node weights.** For all $v \in V$, c_e^v are identical for all edges e incident to v. This is equivalent to having node weights w_v for all $v \in V$ with the goal of finding a node subset $V' \subseteq V$ of minimum total weight $w(V') = \sum_{v \in V'} w_v$ such that the subgraph induced by V' satisfies the given property. Note that we may have $\theta = \infty$ in this case.
- **Power costs:** For all $e = uv \in E$, $c_e^u = c_e^v$. This is equivalent to having "power costs" $c_e = c_e^u = c_e^v$ for all $e = uv \in E$. The goal is to find an edge subset $J \subseteq E$ of minimum total power $\sum_{v \in V} \max\{c_e : e \in \delta_J(v)\}$ that satisfies the given property. Note that this is the case $\theta = 1$.

Node weighted problems include many fundamental problems such as SET COVER, SET MULTICOVER, NODE WEIGHTED STEINER TREE and many more c.f. [3,13,18,26,34]. Min-power problems were studied already in the 90's, c.f. [1, 17,32,35,37], followed by many more. They were also widely studied in directed graphs, usually under the assumption that to activate an edge one needs to assign power only to its tail, while heads are assigned power zero, c.f. [14,17,24,28]. The undirected case has an additional requirement - we want the network to be bidirected, to allow a bidirectional communication.

However these two particular cases don't capture many fundamental problems. Consider for example the (non-metric) FACILITY LOCATION problem (see Fig. 1(a,b,c)). Here we are given a bipartite graph with sides R (clients) and $V \setminus R$ (facilities), weights (opening costs) $\{w_v : v \in V \setminus R\}$, and distances (service/connection costs) $\{d_{uv} : u \in R, v \in V \setminus R\}$. We need to choose $S \subseteq V \setminus R$ such that $w(S) + \sum_{u \in R} d(u, S)$ is minimal, where $d(u, S) = \min_{v \in S} d_{uv}$ is the minimal distance from u to S. Equivalently, we need to chose a collection of stars with centers in $V \setminus R$ of minimal total value, where the value of a star is the weight of its center plus the costs of its edges. This is a particular case of the ACTIVATION EDGE-COVER problem, where for every $e = uv \in E$ with $u \in R$ and $v \in V \setminus R$ we have $c_e^u = d_{uv}$ and $c_e^v = w_v$. The ACTIVATION EDGE-COVER problem (and thus also the FACILITY LOCATION problem) admits a tight approximation ratio $O(\log n)$ and also approximation ratio roughly $\ln \theta - \ln \ln \theta$ [21]; note that the later ratio may be much better than $O(\log n)$ (for example, for $\theta = 10^6$ the approximation ratio in [21] is 11.5).

Now consider the FAULT TOLERANT FACILITY LOCATION problem introduced by Jain and Vazirani [15] (see Fig. 1(d,e,f)). Here the input is as in the FACILITY LOCATION problem, and in addition each client $u \in R$ has a degree requirement r_u and should connect to r_u facilities. The goal is to minimize the opening costs plus the sum of all connection costs. The metric version of the problem was studied in several papers, c.f. [4,15,36]. However, in the wireless scenario, each client represents a transmitter and the connection costs are determined by the transmission costs, that are usually not metric; each client pays

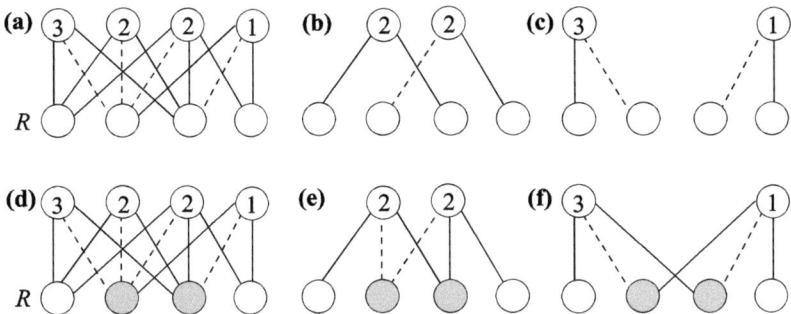

Fig. 1. (a) A FACILITY LOCATION instance: dashed edges have cost 1, solid edges have cost 2, and the numbers in the nodes in $V \setminus R$ are their weights. (b,c) Two feasible solutions, of value 11 and 10, respectively. (d) An instance of FAULT TOLERANT FACILITY LOCATION; in R, the requirement of a gray node is 2 and of a white node is 1. (e,f) Two feasible solutions, of value 14 both; in the wireless setting the solution values are 11 and 12, respectively.

only for the maximum transmission cost, as it allows to connect to all r_u facilities. Thus already very restricted instances of AEM capture the wireless version of the FAULT TOLERANT FACILITY LOCATION problem. And the general version captures more general fault-tolerant problems.

Kortsarz et al. [19] gave an $O(\log n)$-approximation algorithm for the min-power version (the case $\theta = 1$) of AEM, and Cohen & Nutov [8] improved the approximation ratio to $O(\log k)$, where $k = \max_{v \in V} r_v$. However, the node-weighted version is SET COVER hard even for $k = 1$, and thus has approximation threshold $\Omega(\log n)$. AEM admits an easy approximation ratio $O(\log n)$ for $k = 1$ (by a reduction to the SUBMODULAR COVER problem), and this implies ratio $O(k \log n)$ for any k, c.f. [28]. Note that this approximation ratio is not even polylogarithmic, if k is large. We obtain the first (poly-)logarithmic approximation ratio that generalizes and bridges between the known $O(\log k)$-approximation of [8, 19] for the case $\theta = 1$ and the $O(\log n)$-approximation for $k = 1$.

Theorem 1. AEM *admits approximation ratio* $O(\log k + \log \min\{\theta, n\})$.

The proof of Theorem 1 has two main ingredients.

- We will show that it is sufficient to prove approximation ratio $O(\log k + \log \theta)$, since it implies approximation ratio $O(\log n)$. In fact, we will give a generic reduction that applies on any activation network design problem: achieving approximation ratio ρ on instances with $\theta \leq n(\rho+1)/\epsilon$ implies approximation ratio $\rho + 2\epsilon$ for general instances.
- We will show that the problem admits approximation ratio $O(\log k + \log \theta)$. The algorithm extends the $O(\log k)$-approximation algorithm of [8, 19] for the case $\theta = 1$ to the case of arbitrary θ.

Our results and techniques show the advantages of studying the approximability of activation network design problem being parameterized by the slope, and suggest that some network design activation problems may be easier than they seem. We will illustrate this by two additional examples, as follows.

A graph is **k-outconnected from** s if it contains k internally disjoint sv paths for every node v. A graph is **k-connected** if it contains k internally-disjoint paths between every two nodes. In the k-CONNECTED SUBGRAPH problem we are given a graph G with edge costs and an integer k, and seek a minimum cost k-connected spanning subgraph H of G. In the activation version ACTIVATION k-CONNECTED SUBGRAPH problem, instead of ordinary edge costs we have activation costs and H should have minimum activation cost. The k-OUT-CONNECTED SUBGRAPH and ACTIVATION k-OUT-CONNECTED SUBGRAPH problems are defined similarly, where H should be k-out-connected. The min-power versions of these problems were studied in [14,22,25]. It is known that if $\deg_J(v) \geq k - 1$ for every node v, and if F is an inclusion minimal edge set such that $J \cup F$ is k-connected, or is k-out-connected from some node, then F is a forest; for k-connected graph this follows from Mader's Critical Cycle Theorem [23], while an analogous result was proved for k-out-connected graphs in [6]. It is known that if F is a forest then $\sum_{e \in E} \ell_e(V)/\ell_F(V) \leq \theta + 1$ [28, Lemma 15.1(ii) and Corollary 15.1(ii)]. This implies the following.

Corollary 1. *If* AEM *admits approximation ratio* α *and* k-CONNECTED SUBGRAPH *admits approximation ratio* β, *then* ACTIVATION k-CONNECTED SUBGRAPH *admits approximation ratio* $\alpha + \beta(\theta + 1)$. *Consequently,* ACTIVATION k-CONNECTED SUBGRAPH *admits ratio* $O(\log k + \log \min\{\theta, n\}) + \beta \cdot (\theta + 1)$. *A similar result holds for* ACTIVATION k-OUT-CONNECTED SUBGRAPH.

Let us briefly review the approximability status of these problems. The directed version of k-OUT-CONNECTED SUBGRAPH admits a polynomial time algorithm [12], and this implies approximation ratio 2 for the undirected version. The current approximability status of k-CONNECTED SUBGRAPH is more complicated; the following bounds on β are known (see a survey in [29]).

- $\beta = \lceil \frac{k+1}{2} \rceil$ for $2 \leq k \leq 7$ [2,9,16,20].
- $\beta \approx 4 + \frac{4 \lg k + 1}{\lg n - \lg k}$ [7,30]. In particular $\beta = 4 + \epsilon$ for any constant k and $\epsilon > 0$.
- $\beta = O\left(\log k \log \frac{n}{n-k}\right)$ for any k [11,27].

Thus from Corollary 1 we get the following.

Corollary 2. *For* $\theta = O(\log n)$, ACTIVATION k-OUT-CONNECTED SUBGRAPH *admits approximation ratio* $O(\log n)$, *and* ACTIVATION k-CONNECTED SUBGRAPH *admits approximation ratio* $O(\log n)$ *unless* $k = n - o(n)$.

The MIN-POWER EDGE-MULTICOVER (MPEM) problem is a particular extensively studied case of AEM when $\theta = 1$, namely, when $c_e^u = c_e^v$ for all $e = uv \in E$. This problem admits the following approximation ratios [8]:

(i) For general costs, $2\left[\lceil\log_{1/\alpha} k\rceil(1+\gamma)+2\right]$ for any $\gamma > 1$ and $\alpha = 1-(1-1/\gamma)(1-1/e)$; Using fundamental calculus and an approximate equation solver, one can show that the optimal value of γ is roughly $\gamma \approx 2.782105$.
(ii) For unit costs, a randomized expected approximation ratio 2.169.

Let $\omega(\theta) = \max_{x \geq 1} \frac{\ln x}{1+x/\theta}$; for large values of θ we have $\omega(\theta) \approx \ln\theta - \ln\ln\theta$. For MPEM we obtain the following improved approximation ratios.

Theorem 2. MPEM *admits the following approximation ratios:*

(i) $k + \omega(1) < k + 0.2785$ *for arbitrary costs.*
(ii) $1 + \omega(k) = 1 + \max_{x \geq 1} \frac{\ln x}{1+x/\theta}$ *for unit costs.*

Part (i) improves the approximation ratio of [8] for $k \leq 22$ (we used the WolframAlpha software to determined that this is so for $\gamma \approx 2.782105$), while part (ii) improves the approximation ratio 2.169 of [8] for $k \leq 10$ (specifically, $1 + \omega(10) < 2.157$ but $1 + \omega(11) > 2.2$).

2 A Logarithmic Approximation (Theorem 1)

In this section we prove Theorem 1. The following lemma shows that it is sufficient to prove just approximation ratio $O(\log k + \log \theta)$, since it implies approximation ratio $O(\log n)$.

Lemma 1. *If* AEM *admits approximation ratio* $O(\log(k\theta))$ *then it also admits approximation ratio* $O(\log n)$.

Proof. The idea of the proof is to construct a new AEM instance with "small" slope $\hat\theta = O(n \log n)$, such that solving the new instance will incur only a small factor in the approximation ratio. The method is somewhat similar to the "cost scaling" for the KNAPSACK problem, but the details are more involved. The construction is roughly as follows.

1. "Guess" the maximum edge cost M of some optimal solution.
2. Remove all edges that have cost $> M$; this does not affect the optimal solution value.
3. Divide all costs by $\frac{M}{n \log n}$ and round down, and then round zero costs to 1.

One can see that the new instance has slope $O(n \log n)$. Furthermore, the rounding incurs an additive factor of at most $\pm n$ in solution values, where $n = |V|$. We will show that this additive term incurs only a small additive term in the approximation ratio. Now we give a detailed formal proof.

Let $(G = (V,E), c, r)$ be an AEM instance. Fix some optimal solution J^*. Let $M^* = \max\{\max\{c_e^u, c_e^v\} : e = uv \in J^*\}$ be the maximum c-cost of an end of an edge in J^*. While M^* is not known, it is sufficient to have some estimate M for M^*, say $M^* \leq M \leq 2M^*$; for that, we apply the procedure below for every

$M \in \{2^i : i = 0, \ldots, \lceil \log C \rceil\}$, where $C = \max_{uv \in E} c_e^u$ is the maximum c-cost of an end of an edge in E, and return the best outcome. So in what follows we will assume that we know an estimate M for M^* such that $M^* \leq M \leq 2M^*$.

Let ρ be a parameter (eventually set to $\rho = O(\log n)$), let $\epsilon > 0$ be another parameter, and let

$$\alpha = \frac{\epsilon M}{n(\rho+1)}.$$

Remove from G all edges that have an end of cost greater than M. Note that J^* is a feasible solution of the obtained instance, since $M^* \leq M$. Define costs $\hat{c}$ by

$$\hat{c}_{uv}^u = \max\{\lfloor c_{uv}^u/\alpha \rfloor, 1\}.$$

Let us denote by $\hat{\ell}_J(v) = \max\{\hat{c}_e^v : e \in \delta_J(v)\}$ the optimal assignment w.r.t. costs $\hat{c}$ that activates a given edge set J. Let $J \subseteq E$ and let

$$V_0 = \{v \in V : \ell_J(v)/\alpha < 1\} \quad V_1 = \{v \in V : \ell_J(v)/\alpha \geq 1\}.$$

Note that $\hat{\ell}_J(V_0) = |V_0| \leq n$ and $\hat{\ell}_J(V_1) \leq \ell_J(V_1)/\alpha \leq \ell_J(V)/\alpha$. This implies

$$\hat{\ell}_J(V) = \hat{\ell}_J(V_0) + \hat{\ell}_J(V_1) \leq n + \ell_J(V)/\alpha.$$

Also note that $\ell_J(V_0)/\alpha \leq |V_0|$ and that $\ell_J(V_1)/\alpha \leq \hat{\ell}_J(V_1) + |V_1|$. This implies

$$\ell_J(V)/\alpha = \ell_J(V_0)/\alpha + \ell_J(V_1)/\alpha \leq |V_0| + \hat{\ell}_J(V_1) + |V_1| \leq n + \hat{\ell}_J(V).$$

Summarizing, we have $\ell_J(V)/\alpha - n \leq \hat{\ell}_J(V) \leq \ell_J(V)/\alpha + n$. From this we get that if J is a ρ-approximate solution w.r.t. costs $\hat{c}$ then

$$\ell_J(V) \leq \alpha(\hat{\ell}_J(V) + n) \leq \alpha(\rho \hat{\ell}_{J^*}(V) + n) \leq \alpha(\rho(\ell_{J^*}(V)/\alpha + n) + n) = \rho \ell_{J^*}(V) + \alpha n(\rho+1)$$

Note that $M \leq 2\ell_{J^*}(V)$ and thus $\alpha n(\rho+1) = \epsilon M \leq 2\epsilon \cdot \ell_{J^*}(V)$, by the definition of α. Consequently,

$$\ell_J(V) \leq \ell_{J^*}(V)(\rho + 2\epsilon).$$

Finally, note that the maximum $\hat{c}$-cost is bounded by $M/\alpha = n(\rho+1)/\epsilon$ while the minimum $\hat{c}$-cost is at least 1. Thus the slope $\hat{\theta}$ of the obtained instance is bounded by $\hat{\theta} \leq n(\rho+1)$. Summarizing, the obtained instance has slope at most $n(\rho+1)$ and approximation ratio ρ for the obtained instance implies approximation ratio $\rho + 2\epsilon$ for the original instance.

Now let $\rho = O(\log n)$ and suppose that the obtained instance admits approximation ratio $O(\log(k\theta))$. Then it also admits approximation ratio

$$O(\log(k\hat{\theta})) = O(\log(kn(\rho+1))) = O(\log(kn \log n)) = O(\log n).$$

This implies approximation ratio $O(\log n) + 2\epsilon = O(\log n)$ for the original instance, concluding the proof of the lemma. □

Remark. The reduction in Lemma 1 applies to any activation network design problem, showing that for any $\epsilon > 0$, if problem instances with $\theta \leq n(\rho+1)/\epsilon$ admit approximation ratio ρ, then general instances admit ratio $\rho + 2\epsilon$.

By Lemma 1, to finish the proof of Theorem 1 it is sufficient to prove approximation ratio $O(\log(k\theta))$. Naturally, the proof of the approximation ratio $O(\log(k\theta))$ extends the proof of [8,19] of the $O(\log k)$-approximation for the case $\theta = 1$. Our proof carefully follows the proof of [8,19] while adjusting the parameters to the case of arbitrary θ and investing more effort in showing appropriate bounds. As in [8,19], the proof eventually boils down to showing a constant approximation ratio for a certain coverage problem. In [8,19] this problem was shown to admit approximation ratio $(1 - 1/e)$. In our case we will show that the obtained coverage problem can be cast as maximizing a submodular function subject to one matroid constraint and one knapsack constraint, that in the value oracle admits a $(1 - 1/e - \epsilon)$-approximation scheme [5].

Following [8,19], we first reduce the problem with a loss of a factor of 2 in the approximation ratio to the following particular case.

BIPARTITE ACTIVATION EDGE-MULTICOVER (BIPARTITE AEM)

Input: A bipartite graph $G = (A \cup B, E)$ with activation costs $\{c_e^a, c_e^b\}$ for each edge $e = ab \in E$, and degree requirements $r = \{r_b : b \in B\}$ on B only.

Output: An r-edge-cover $J \subseteq E$ of minimum activation cost.

For that, add a copy V' of V and denote by v' the copy of $v \in V$. Then replace every edge uv by two edges $u'v$ and $v'u$ with activation costs as follows:

- $u'v$ has activation costs $\{c_{u'v}^{u'} = c_{uv}^{u}, c_{u'v}^{v} = c_{uv}^{v}\}$;
- $v'u$ has activation costs $\{c_{v'u}^{v'} = c_{uv}^{v}, c_{v'u}^{u} = c_{uv}^{u}\}$.

The degree requirements are $\{r_v : v \in V\}$, while nodes in V' have no requirements. It is not hard to see that ratio ρ for the obtained BIPARTITE AEM instance implies ratio 2ρ for the original instance, see [8,19].

So from now and on we will consider the BIPARTITE AEM problem. Whenever we consider an edge $e = ab$, it is assumed that $a \in A$ and $b \in B$. For $b \in B$, let w_b be the r_b-th least cost at b of an edge incident to b, where $w_b = 0$ if $r_b = 0$. The **residual requirement** of b w.r.t. an edge subset $J \subseteq E$ is defined by

$$r_b^J = \max\{r_b - \deg_J(b), 0\} \ .$$

Define the following potential function on edge subsets $J \subseteq E$

$$\Phi(J) = \sum_{b \in B} w_b r_b^J$$

Let opt denote the optimal solution value and let τ be an estimation for opt. The main step of the algorithm is given in the following lemma.

Lemma 2. *For any $\epsilon > 0$ there exists a polynomial time algorithm that given an edge set $J \subseteq E$, a parameter $\gamma > 1$, and an integer τ, returns an edge set $I \subseteq E \setminus J$ such that the following holds:*

(i) $\ell_I(B) \leq \gamma \tau$.
(ii) $\ell_I(A) \leq \tau$ if $\tau \geq$ opt.
(iii) $\Phi(J \cup I) \leq \alpha \cdot \Phi(J)$ if $\tau \geq$ opt, where $\alpha = 1 - \left(1 - \frac{1}{\gamma}\right)\left(1 - \frac{1}{e} - \epsilon\right)$.

Lemma 2 is proved in the full version. The next lemma bounds the activation cost of a feasible solution obtained by picking edges with least cost at B-nodes.

Lemma 3. *Let $J \subseteq E$ and let F be an edge set obtained by picking for every $b \in B$ a set of r_b^J edges incident to b in $E \setminus J$ of minimal cost at b. Then $J \cup F$ is an r-edge-cover and: (i) $\ell_F(B) \leq$ opt. (ii) $\ell_F(A) \leq \theta \cdot \Phi(J)$.*

Proof. Since F is an r^J-edge cover, $J \cup F$ is an r-edge-cover. By the definition of F, $\ell_F(b) \leq w_b$ for all $b \in B$. Any r-edge-cover has activation cost at least $\sum_{b \in B} w_b$. Thus we have

$$\ell_F(B) = \sum_{b \in B} \ell_F(b) \leq \sum_{b \in B} w_b \leq \text{opt} .$$

We prove (ii). Note that $c_{ab}^a \leq \theta c_{ab}^b$ for every $ab \in F$ and $\sum_{ab \in F} c_{ab}^b \leq w_b r_b^J$ for every $b \in B$. From this we get

$$\ell_F(A) = \sum_{a \in A} \ell_F(a) \leq \sum_{ab \in F} c_{ab}^a \leq \sum_{ab \in F} \theta c_{ab}^b = \theta \sum_{b \in B} \sum_{ab \in F} c_{ab}^b \leq \theta \sum_{b \in B} w_b r_b^J = \theta \cdot \Phi(J) ,$$

as required. □

Theorem 1 is deduced from Lemmas 2 and 3 as follows. We let γ to be a constant strictly greater than 1, say $\gamma = 2$, and we let $\epsilon = 1/2 - 2/e$. Then $\alpha = 3/4$. Using binary search, we find the least integer τ such that the following procedure computes an edge set J satisfying $\Phi(J) \leq \tau/\theta$.

Algorithm 1:

---
1 **initialization:** $J \leftarrow \emptyset$
2 **loop:** repeat $\lceil \log_{1/\alpha}(k\flat) \rceil$ times
   apply the algorithm from Lemma 2
   - If $\Phi(J \cup I) > \alpha \cdot \Phi(J)$ then return "ERROR" and stop
   - else do $J \leftarrow J \cup I$

After computing J, we compute an edge set F as in Lemma 3, so $J \cup F$ is a feasible solution.

Lemma 4. *If $\tau \geq$ opt then Algorithm 1 returns $J \subseteq E$ such that $\Phi(J) \leq \tau/\theta$.*

Proof. Note that $\Phi(\emptyset) = \sum_{b \in B} w_b r_b \leq k \sum_{b \in B} w_b \leq k \cdot$ opt. From this we get $\Phi(J) \leq \Phi(\emptyset) \cdot \alpha^{\lceil \log_{1/\alpha}(k\theta) \rceil} \leq \Phi(\emptyset) \cdot 1/k\theta \leq k \cdot$ opt$/k\theta =$ opt$/\theta \leq \tau/\theta$. □

By Lemma 4, the least integer τ for which the procedure does not return "ERROR" satisfies $\tau \leq$ opt. By Lemma 2(i) and since the number of iterations in Algorithm 1 is $\lceil \log_{1/\alpha}(k\theta) \rceil$, we have:

$$\ell_J(A \cup B) \leq \lceil \log_{1/\alpha}(k\theta) \rceil (1+\gamma)\tau = O(\log(k\theta)) \cdot \text{opt}.$$

Also, by Lemmas 3 and 4 we have:

$$\ell_F(A \cup B) = \ell_F(A) + \ell_F(B) \leq \theta \cdot \Phi(J) + \text{opt} \leq \theta \cdot \tau/\theta + \text{opt} \leq \tau + \text{opt} \leq 2 \cdot \text{opt}.$$

Consequently

$$\ell_{J \cup F}(A \cup B) \leq \ell_J(A \cup B) + \ell_F(A \cup B) = O(\log(k\theta)) \cdot \text{opt} + 2\text{opt} = O(\log(k\theta)) \cdot \text{opt}.$$

This concludes the proof of Theorem 1.

3 Improved Approximation for Power Costs (Theorem 2)

Here we prove Theorem 2, namely that MPEM admits approximation ratios: (i) $k + \omega(1)$ for arbitrary costs. (ii) $1 + \omega(k) = 1 + \max_{x \geq 1} \frac{\ln x}{1 + x/\theta}$ for unit costs.

In both algorithms we will use the RELATIVE GREEDY HEURISTIC. A set function f is decreasing if $f(A) \geq f(B)$ whenever $A \subseteq B$, and f is sub-additive if $f(A \cup B) \leq f(A) + f(B)$ for any A, B. Consider the following generic problem:

MIN-COVERING
Input: Non-negative set functions ν, τ on subsets of a ground-set U such that ν is decreasing, τ is sub-additive, and $\tau(\emptyset) = 0$.
Output: $S \subseteq U$ such that $\nu(S) + \tau(S)$ is minimal.

We call ν the **potential** and τ the **payment**. Let opt be the optimal solution value of a problem instance at hand. Fix an optimal solution A^*. Let $\nu^* = \nu(A^*)$, $\tau^* = \tau(A^*)$, so opt $= \tau^* + \nu^*$. The quantity $\frac{\tau(B)}{\nu(A) - \nu(A \cup B)}$ is called the **density** of B (w.r.t. A). The RELATIVE GREEDY HEURISTIC starts with $A = \emptyset$ and repeatedly adds to A a non-empty augmenting set $B \subseteq U$ of minimum density. The algorithm terminates when $\nu^* = 0$ or when the minimum density ≥ 1. It is known (c.f. [21, Theorem 2.1]) that the heuristic achieves approximation ratio

$$1 + \frac{\tau^*}{\text{opt}} \ln \frac{\nu(\emptyset) - \nu^*}{\tau^*} = 1 + \frac{\tau^*}{\text{opt}} \cdot \ln\left(1 + \frac{\nu(\emptyset) - \text{opt}}{\tau^*}\right). \tag{1}$$

3.1 Algorithm for General Costs

For the proof of part (i) of Theorem 2 we need to consider the following problem.

RESTRICTED MIN-POWER EDGE-COVER RESTRICTED MPEC
Input: A graph $G = (V, E)$ with edge costs, $R \subseteq V$, and bounds $\{b_u : u \in R\}$.
Output: An R-edge-cover J with $\ell_J^b(V) = \sum_{v \in V} \max\left\{\max_{e \in \delta_J(v)} c_e, b_v\right\}$ minimal.

Lemma 5 (Lemma 6 in [8]). *If* RESTRICTED MPEC *admits approximation ratio ρ then* MPEM *admits approximation ratio $(k - 1 + \rho)$.*

In [21] it is proved that MIN-POWER EDGE-COVER admits approximation ratio $1 + \omega(1)$. We will extend this to RESTRICTED MPEC.

Lemma 6. RESTRICTED MPEC *admits approximation ratio $1 + \omega(1)$.*

To prove Lemma 6 we formulate RESTRICTED MPEC as a MIN-COVERING problem with groundset U and functions ν and τ, such that the optimal values of the problems coincide. Let $\langle G, c, R, b \rangle$ be an instance of RESTRICTED MPEC. Define assignments w and q on V by $w_v = q_v = 0$ for $v \in V \setminus R$ and for $v \in R$:

- $w_v = \min_{e \in \delta(v)} c_e$; this is the minimum cost of an edge incident to v.
- $q_v = \max\{w_v, b_v\}$.

We let $Q = q(R)$. A **star** S is an edge set of a rooted tree (V_S, S) with at least one edge such that only its root may have degree ≥ 2. We say that a star S in G is a **proper star** if all the leaves of S are terminals. Given an instance $\langle G = (V, E), c, R, b \rangle$ of RESTRICTED MPEC define the corresponding MIN-COVERING instance $\langle U, \tau, \nu \rangle$ as follows. The groundset U is the set Λ_G of proper stars of G. For a star S let

$$\tau(S) = \ell_S^b(V_S) - q(V_S) .$$

For $\Lambda \subseteq \Lambda_G$ let R_Λ denote the set of terminals covered by the stars in Λ. Define

$$\tau(\Lambda) = \sum_{S \in \Lambda} \tau(S) \qquad \nu(\Lambda) = Q + w(R \setminus R_\Lambda)$$

It is easy to see that ν is decreasing, τ is additive, and $\tau(\emptyset) = 0$.

Note that any inclusion-minimal feasible RESTRICTED MPEC solution J is a union of a set $\Lambda \subseteq \Lambda_G$ of node disjoint stars that cover R. The next lemma shows that the obtained MIN-COVERING instance is equivalent to the original RESTRICTED MPEC instance. Let opt be the optimal solution value of a problem instance at hand. For the proof of the following lemma see Appendix B.

Lemma 7. *Let $\Lambda \subseteq \Lambda_G$ be a collection of node disjoint stars and let J be obtained by adding to the union of the stars in Λ the cheapest edge e_v incident to every $v \in R \setminus R_\Lambda$. Then $\ell_J^b(V) \leq \nu(\Lambda) + \tau(\Lambda)$, and if $R = R_\Lambda$ then $\ell_J^b(V) = \nu(\Lambda) + \tau(\Lambda) = Q + \tau(\Lambda)$. Consequently, both problems have the same optimal value, and MIN-COVERING has an optimal solution Λ^* such that $\nu(\Lambda^*) = Q$ and thus $\mathsf{opt} = \tau(\Lambda^*) + Q$.*

Proof. Since the stars in Λ are node disjoint and since $\ell_J^b(e_v) = q_v + w_v$ we have

$$\ell_J^b(V) \leq \sum_{S \in \Lambda} (\tau(S) + q(V_S)) + \sum_{v \in R \setminus R_\Lambda} (q_v + w_v)$$

$$= \sum_{S \in \Lambda} \tau(S) + \sum_{S \in \Lambda} q(V_S) + \sum_{v \in R \setminus R_\Lambda} q_v + \sum_{v \in R \setminus R_\Lambda} w_v$$

$$= \tau(\Lambda) + Q + w(R \setminus R_\Lambda) = \tau(\Lambda) + \nu(\Lambda) .$$

If $R = R_\Lambda$ then we have equality, hence $\ell^b_J(V) = \nu(\Lambda) + \tau(\Lambda) = Q + \tau(\Lambda)$. □

It is a routine to show that the RELATIVE GREEDY HEURISTIC can be implemented to run in polynomial time. Specifically, our function $\nu(\Lambda) = Q + w(R \setminus R_\Lambda)$ is supermodular and τ is additive. This implies that there exists a minimum density set that is a single star S (c.f. [21, Lemma 2.2]), and one can find such S in the same way as in [21, Lemma 3.3]. We show the approximation ratio $1 + \omega(1)$.

For the obtained MIN-COVERING instance, let us fix an optimal solution Λ^* as in Lemma 7, so $\tau^* = \tau(\Lambda^*)$, $\nu^* = Q$, and opt $= \tau^* + Q$. Let $\nu_0 = \nu(\emptyset) = Q + w(R)$.

Lemma 8. $\dfrac{\text{opt}}{\tau^*} \geq 2$ and $\dfrac{\nu_0}{\tau^*} \leq 2\left(\dfrac{\text{opt}}{\tau^*} - 1\right)$.

Proof. Note that $\tau^* + Q = \text{opt} \leq \nu_0 = Q + w(R) \leq 2Q$. In particular, $\tau^* \leq Q$, implying the first bound. The second bound is since $\nu_0 \leq 2Q = 2(\text{opt} - \tau^*)$. □

Let $x = \left(\dfrac{\text{opt}}{\tau^*} - 1\right)$ and $f(x) = \dfrac{\ln x}{1+x}$. By Lemma 8, $x \geq 1$. Substituting Lemma 8 second bound in (1) bounds the approximation ratio by

$$1 + \frac{\tau^*}{\text{opt}} \cdot \ln\left(1 + \frac{\nu_0}{\tau^*} - \frac{\text{opt}}{\tau^*}\right) \leq 1 + \frac{\ln x}{1+x} = 1 + f(x)$$

Consequently, the approximation ratio is bounded by $1 + \max\{f(x) : x \geq 1\} = 1 + \omega(1)$, concluding the proof of Lemma 6 and thus also of part (i) of Theorem 2.

3.2 Algorithm for Unit Costs

Given an instance of MPEM with unit costs let $D = \{v \in V : r(v) \geq 1\}$. Clearly, we may assume that $V \setminus D$ is an independent set. We can also assume that also D is an independent set; for that, we add all edges between nodes in D reducing the requirements accordingly, and then exclude from D the nodes whose requirement becomes zero.

For $\Lambda \subseteq \Lambda_G$ and $v \in D$ let $r^\Lambda(v)$ denote the residual requirement of v w.r.t. to the edges of the stars in Λ. The corresponding MIN-COVERING instance has groundset Λ_G and for $\Lambda \subseteq \Lambda_G$ we define

$$\tau(\Lambda) = |\Lambda| \qquad \nu(\Lambda) = |D| + r^\Lambda(D) \ .$$

Note that τ is additive and ν is decreasing.

Lemma 9. *The obtained* MIN-COVERING *instance is equivalent to the* MPEM *with unit costs instance (namely, both instances have the same optimal values), and the* MIN-COVERING *instance has an optimal solution Λ^* such that $\nu(\Lambda^*) = |D|$ and opt $= \tau(\Lambda^*) + |D|$.*

Proof. Let J be a feasible solution for MPEM with unit costs instance. Let $C = \{s \in V \setminus D : \deg_J(s) \geq 1\}$. For every $v \in C$ let S_v be a maximal star in the graph (V, J) that has center v and leaves in D and let $\Lambda = \{S_v : v \in C\}$. Note that $r^\Lambda(D) = 0$, hence $\tau(\Lambda) + \nu(\Lambda) = |\Lambda| + |D| + 0 = |C| + |D| = \ell_J(V)$.

Let $\Lambda \subseteq \Lambda_G$ be feasible solution for MIN-COVERING. Take all the edges of the stars in Λ into J and also for every $v \in D$ pick into J some additional $r^\Lambda(v)$ edges incident to v. Then $\ell_J(V) \leq |\Lambda| + |D| + |r^\Lambda(D)| = \tau(\Lambda) + \nu(\Lambda)$. □

It is again a routine to show that the RELATIVE GREEDY HEURISTIC can be implemented in polynomial time. We show the approximation ratio. Let opt be the optimal solution value of a problem instance at hand. Let Λ^* be an optimal solution as in Lemma 9, so $\tau^* = |\Lambda^*|$, $\nu^* = |D|$, and $\text{opt} = \nu^* + \tau^* = |D| + \tau^*$. We need the following bounds.

Lemma 10. $1 + \dfrac{\nu_0}{\tau^*} - \dfrac{\text{opt}}{\tau^*} \leq k\left(\dfrac{\text{opt}}{\tau^*} - 1\right)$ and $k\left(\dfrac{\text{opt}}{\tau^*} - 1\right) \geq 1$.

Proof. Note that $\nu_0 \leq (k+1)|D|$ and that $\text{opt} - \tau^* = |D|$. This gives

$$\tau^* + \nu_0 - \text{opt} \leq \tau^* + (k+1)|D| - \text{opt} = k|D| = k(\text{opt} - \tau^*) \ .$$

The first bound follows by dividing both sides by τ^*. The second bound follows from the observation that $k(\text{opt} - \tau^*) = k|D| \geq \tau^*$. □

Let $x = k\left(\dfrac{\text{opt}}{\tau^*} - 1\right)$. By Lemma 10 the approximation ratio is bounded by

$$1 + \dfrac{\tau^*}{\text{opt}} \ln\left(1 + \dfrac{\nu_0}{\tau^*} - \dfrac{\text{opt}}{\tau^*}\right) \leq 1 + \dfrac{\tau^*}{\text{opt}} \ln\left[k\left(\dfrac{\text{opt}}{\tau^*} - 1\right)\right] = 1 + \dfrac{\ln x}{1 + x/k}$$

By the second bound of Lemma 10, $x \geq 1$. Thus the approximation ratio is bounded by $1 + \max\limits_{x \geq 1} \dfrac{\ln x}{1 + x/k} = 1 + \omega(k)$, concluding the proof of part (ii).

4 Concluding Remarks

Our main result is the first polylogarithmic approximation for AEM. The approximation ratio is $O\left(\log k + \log \min\{\theta, n\}\right)$, bridging between the known approximation ratios $O(\log k)$ for $\theta = 1$ and $O(\log n)$ for $k = 1$. Our ratio is tight, since the problem is SET COVER hard. It is an open question whether for $\theta = 1$ (the min-power case) the approximation ratio $O(\log k)$ of [8] can be improved.

References

1. Althaus, E., Calinescu, G., Mandoiu, I., Prasad, S., Tchervenski, N., Zelikovsky, A.: Power efficient range assignment for symmetric connectivity in static ad-hoc wireless networks. Wirel. Netw. **12**(3), 287–299 (2006)
2. Auletta, V., Dinitz, Y., Nutov, Z., Parente, D.: A 2-approximation algorithm for finding an optimum 3-vertex-connected spanning subgraph. J. Algorithms **32**(1), 21–30 (1999)
3. Berman, P., DasGupta, B., Sontag, E.D.: Randomized approximation algorithms for set multicover problems with applications to reverse engineering of protein and gene networks. Discret. Appl. Math. **155**(6–7), 733–749 (2007)
4. Byrka, J., Srinivasan, A., Swamy, C.: Fault-tolerant facility location: a randomized dependent LP-rounding algorithm. In: IPCO, pp. 244–257, 2010

5. Chekuri, C., Vondrák, J., Zenklusen, R.: Dependent randomized rounding for matroid polytopes and applications. CoRR, abs/0909.4348, 2009
6. Cheriyan, J., Jordán, T., Nutov, Z.: On rooted node-connectivity problems. Algorithmica **30**(3), 353–375 (2001)
7. Cheriyan, J., Végh, L.A.: Approximating minimum-cost k-node connected subgraphs via independence-free graphs. SIAM J. Comput. **43**(4), 1342–1362 (2014)
8. Cohen, N., Nutov, Z.: Approximating minimum power edge-multi-covers. J. Comb. Optim. **30**(3), 563–578 (2015)
9. Dinitz, Y., Nutov, Z.: A 3-approximation algorithm for finding optimum 4, 5-vertex-connected spanning subgraphs. J. Algorithms **32**(1), 31–40 (1999)
10. Edmonds, J.: Paths, trees, and flowers. Can. J. Math. **17**, 449–467 (1965)
11. Fakcharoenphol, J., Laekhanukit, B.: An $O(\log^2 k)$-approximation algorithm for the k-vertex connected spanning subgraph problem. SIAM J. Comput. **41**(5), 1095–1109 (2012)
12. Frank, A., Tardos, É.: An application of submodular flows. Linear Algebra Appl. **114**(115), 329–348 (1989)
13. Guha, S., Khuller, S.: Approximation algorithms for connected dominating sets. Algorithmica **20**, 374–387 (1998)
14. Hajiaghayi, M., Kortsarz, G., Mirrokni, V., Nutov, Z.: Power optimization for connectivity problems. Math. Program. **110**(1), 195–208 (2007)
15. Jain, K., Vazirani, V.V.: An approximation algorithm for the fault tolerant metric facility location problem. Algorithmica **38**(3), 433–439 (2003)
16. Khuller, S., Raghavachari, B.: Improved approximation algorithms for uniform connectivity problems. J. Algorithms **21**(2), 434–450 (1996)
17. Kirousis, L.M., Kranakis, E., Krizanc, D., Pelc, A.: Power consumption in packet radio networks. Theor. Comput. Sci. **243**(1–2), 289–305 (2000)
18. Klein, P., Ravi, R.: A nearly best-possible approximation algorithm for node-weighted Steiner trees. J. Algorithms **19**(1), 104–115 (1995)
19. Kortsarz, G., Mirrokni, V.S., Nutov, Z., Tsanko, E.: Approximating minimum-power degree and connectivity problems. Algorithmica **60**(4), 735–742 (2011)
20. Kortsarz, G., Nutov, Z.: Approximating node-connectivity problems via set covers. Algorithmica **37**, 75–92 (2003)
21. Kortsarz, G., Nutov, Z., Shalom, E.: Approximating activation edge-cover and facility location problems. Theor. Comput. Sci. **930**, 218–228 (2022)
22. Lando, Y., Nutov, Z.: On minimum power connectivity problems. J. Discret. Algorithms **8**(2), 164–173 (2010)
23. Mader, W.: Ecken vom grad n in minimalen n-fach zusammenhängenden graphen. Archive der Mathematik **23**, 219–224 (1972)
24. Nutov, Z.: Approximating minimum power covers of intersecting families and directed edge-connectivity problems. Theor. Comput. Sci. **411**(26–28), 2502–2512 (2010)
25. Nutov, Z.: Approximating minimum-power k-connectivity. Ad Hoc Sens. Wirel. Netw. **9**(1–2), 129–137 (2010)
26. Nutov, Z.: Approximating steiner networks with node-weights. SIAM J. Comput. **39**(7), 3001–3022 (2010)
27. Nutov, Z.: Approximating minimum-cost edge-covers of crossing biset-families. Combinatorica **34**(1), 95–114 (2014). https://doi.org/10.1007/s00493-014-2773-4
28. Nutov, Z.: Activation network design problems. In: Gonzalez, T.F. (ed.), Handbook on Approximation Algorithms and Metaheuristics, Second Edition, volume 2, chapter 15. Chapman & Hall/CRC, 2018

29. Nutov, Z.: The k-connected subgraph problem. In: Gonzalez, T.F. (ed.), Handbook of Approximation Algorithms and Metaheuristics, Second Edition, volume 2, chapter 12. Chapman & Hall/CRC, 2018
30. Nutov, Z.: A $4+\epsilon$ approximation for k-connected subgraphs. J. Comput. Syst. Sci. **123**, 64–75 (2022)
31. Panigrahi, D.: Survivable network design problems in wireless networks. In: SODA, pp. 1014–1027, 2011
32. Rodoplu, V., Meng, T.H.: Minimum energy mobile wireless networks. In: IEEE International Conference on Communications (ICC), pp. 1633–1639, 1998
33. Schrijver, A.: Combinatorial Optimization. Polyhedra and Efficiency. Springer-Verlag, Berlin, Heidelberg, New York (2004)
34. Segev, A.: The node-weighted Steiner tree problem. Networks **17**, 1–17 (1987)
35. Singh, S., Raghavendra, C.S., Stepanek, J.: Power-aware broadcasting in mobile ad hoc networks. In: Proceedings of IEEE PIMRC, 1999
36. Swamy, C., Shmoys, D.B.: Fault-tolerant facility location. ACM Trans. Algorithms **4**(4), 51:1–51:27 (2008)
37. Wieselthier, J.E., Nguyen, G.D., Ephremides, A.: On the construction of energy-efficient broadcast and multicast trees in wireless networks. In: Proceedings of the IEEE INFOCOM, pp. 585–594, 2000

Capturing an Invisible Robber Using Separators

Igor Potapov, Tymofii Prokopenko, and John Sylvester(✉)

Department of Computer Science, University of Liverpool, Liverpool, UK
{potapov,t.prokopenko,john.sylvester}@liverpool.ac.uk

Abstract. We study the zero-visibility cops and robbers game, where the robber is invisible to the cops until they are caught. This differs from the classic game where full information about the robber's location is known at any time. A previously known solution for capturing a robber in the zero-visibility case is based on the pathwidth decomposition. We provide an alternative solution based on a separation hierarchy, improving capture time and space complexity without asymptotically increasing the zero-visibility cop number in most cases. In addition, we provide a better bound on the *approximate* zero-visibility cop number for various classes of graphs, where approximate refers to the restriction to polynomial time computable strategies.

Keywords: Pursuit-evasion game · zero-visibility cops and robbers · graph cleaning · separators · pathwidth · capture time · approximation

1 Introduction

Pursuit-evasion games model scenarios in which a group of pursuers attempts to capture an evader within a defined 'arena'. One of the most extensively studied pursuit-evasion games played on graphs is the *Cops and Robbers* game. This two-player game was introduced in [22] and [25], as a perfect-information game on a finite simple graph G. To begin, the k cops choose starting vertices; after seeing them, the robber chooses a vertex. Then in each round, any cop may stay or move to a neighbour and, then the robber moves likewise. Multiple cops may share a vertex, and all positions are visible to the players. The cops win if some cop ever occupies the robber's vertex; otherwise the robber evades forever.

The original formulation actually considered a single cop ($k = 1$) chasing a single robber and leads to a characterisation of graphs where the cop can always guarantee a capture, known as cop-win graphs. Since then, the game has been the subject of significant research, including generalizations involving multiple cops, robbers, and variations in rules. For a comprehensive overview of the topic, we refer the reader to the book by Bonato & Nowakowski [5]. There are many variants of the Cops and Robbers game, distinguished by the restrictions placed on the cops and the robber. It is natural to restrict the speed or edges that can be used by the cops or robber [12,14]. Another important variant restricts the cops' information about the robber's position during the game, leading to the concept of ℓ-*visibility Cops and Robbers* [7], where the cops can detect the robber only within a limited distance.

In this paper, we focus on the **zero-visibility Cops and Robbers** variant, in which the cops have no information about the robber's position at any point during the game. This version was first introduced in [27] and later investigated further in [8,10]. It can be viewed as a special case of the ℓ-*visibility Cops and Robbers* with parameter ℓ equal to 0. A characterisation for the ℓ-*visibility cop number* of a tree based on its structure was given in [7] and shows that the difference between the ℓ-visibility cop number and the cop number can be arbitrarily large. Moreover, both variants of the game are closely related to the *limited visibility graph search problem*, in which the cops move at speed one and the robber has infinite speed. This problem was recently introduced in [18], providing an algorithm for capturing the robber under these conditions.

The problem of estimating the *zero-visibility cop number*, i.e. the minimum number of cops to win the zero-visibility Cops and Robbers game, was initiated in [28]. Tang [26] gives lower bounds for connected graphs, showing that the zero-visibility cop number exceeds half of the minimum vertex degree of the graph, also establishing the connection to the pathwidth, and characterisation of zero-visibility cop-win graphs. Moreover, [26] constructs a graph with an arbitrarily large *zero-visibility cop number* and capture the robber using an optimal path decomposition. Later, a class of graphs on which two cops are sufficient in the *zero-visibility Cops and Robbers* game was provided in [16].

In [10], the authors studied monotonic strategies to capture the robber, making a connection between the *zero-visibility cop number*, its monotone variant, and the pathwidth of a graph. They proposed an algorithm for trees, and exhibited graphs of zero-visibility cop number two with arbitrarily large pathwidth. The same authors, later in [9], addressed the computational complexity of the *zero-visibility Cops and Robbers* game, presenting a linear-time algorithm to compute the *zero-visibility cop number* of a tree. They also showed that the corresponding decision problem is NP-complete on a non-trivial class of graphs.

In [30], the authors developed a partition method to establish lower bounds on the *zero-visibility cop number* in graph products. Subsequently, they analysed the *zero-visibility Cops and Robbers* on graph joins, lexicographic products, complete multipartite and split graphs. In these studies, they refined the lower bounds on the *zero-visibility cop number* for these classes of graphs compared to [26] and established a connection to the graph matching number. In [31] the authors provide an algorithm for computing optimal cop-win strategies on a tree in the *one-visibility Cops and Robber* game and show the relationship between the *one-visibility cop number* and *zero-visibility cop number* of trees.

For arbitrary graphs, the best-known strategy for bounding the *zero-visibility cop number* is based on the initial idea of pathwidth decomposition [26]. However, the weaknesses of the pathwidth solution in respect to capture time, computational complexity and quality of the approximation has not been addressed in the literature and motivated our study for alternative solutions, for example based on separators that have been used in full visibility case, see [17,21].

In this paper, we design an alternative algorithm based on a separation hierarchy that improves the capture time for a robber without an increase to the zero-visibility cop number in most cases. More specifically, our algorithm provides $O\big(D \cdot \frac{n}{f(n)}\big)$ capture time compared to $O(D \cdot n)$ of the PW algorithm in any hereditary f-separable class of graphs with diameter D. Also, since the optimal pathwidth decomposition is NP-complete, with the alternative separation hierarchy approach we can improve the approximate zero-visibility cop number required to win in several classes of graphs. Our approach provides a wider applicability and improvement facilitated by the existence of better approximation algorithms for computing the separation sets of graphs. Moreover, the approach allows us to cover classes of graphs where an optimal pathwidth decomposition, or a good approximation, has not been established yet.

As an example, we also demonstrate the applicability of the algorithm to the hyperbolic random graph. Finally, the space complexity of pathwidth decomposition has only a trivial $O(n^2)$ upper bound, and with the alternative approach we show that $O(n)$ space is enough.

2 Preliminaries

Graphs

We consider finite undirected graphs $G = (V, E)$, without loops or multiple edges, and let $V(G)$, or just V if clear from context, be the vertex set of G, and $E(G)$ or E be the edge set. The *diameter* D_G of a graph $G = (V, E)$ is the maximum distance between any pair of vertices, where, the distance between two vertices is the minimum number of edges on any u-v path. Given a graph G and a vertex subset $S \subseteq V$, we let $G[S]$ be the graph induced by S, i.e. the graph with vertex set S and edge set $\{uv \in E : u, v \in S\}$. A class of graphs is *hereditary* if it is closed under taking induced subgraphs, i.e. for any hereditary class $\mathcal{C}$ of graphs, if $G \in \mathcal{C}$ then $H \in \mathcal{C}$ for all induced subgraphs H of G.

A *path decomposition* of a graph $G = (V, E)$ is a sequence $B = (B_1, \ldots, B_r)$ of subsets of V (or 'bags') if the following conditions are satisfied: 1) $\bigcup_{i=1}^{r} B_i = V$ 2) for every edge $vw \in E$ there exists $i \in 1, \ldots, r$ with $\{v, w\} \subseteq B_i$ 3) For $1 \leqslant i \leqslant j \leqslant k \leqslant r, B_i \cap B_k \subseteq B_j$. In other words, in the path decomposition, every vertex appears in at least one bag; for every edge, both endpoints appear together in some bag and for any vertex, the bags containing it appear consecutively along the path. The *width* $\mathsf{pw}(B)$ of B is defined as $\max_{i \in [r]} |B_i| - 1$. The *pathwidth* $\mathsf{pw}(G)$ of G is the minimum width of any path decomposition of G.

Let $\frac{1}{2} \leq \alpha < 1$ be a real number, $s \geq 0$ an integer, and $G = (V, E)$ a graph. A subset $S \subset V$ is said to be an (s, α)-*separator* of G, if there exist subsets $A, B \subset V$ such that 1) $V = A \cup B \cup S$ and A, B, S are pairwise disjoint; 2) $|S| \leq s$, $|A|, |B| \leq \alpha|V|$; and 3)$|\{ab \in E : a \in A, b \in B\}| = 0$. We will refer to A, B as *separated sets* and S as the *separator*. The *separation number* $\mathsf{s}(G)$ of G is the smallest s such that all subgraphs G' of G have an $(s, 2/3)$-separator. For a function $f : \mathbb{N} \to \mathbb{N}$, we say that a class $\mathcal{C}$ is f-*separable* if any n-vertex graph $G \in \mathcal{C}$ satisfies $\mathsf{s}(G) \leq f(n)$.

By a *separation algorithm*, we refer to an algorithm $\mathcal{S}$ that takes a graph $G = (V, E)$ as input and returns subsets A, B, and S of V, such that S is an (s, α)-separator of G. We say that an f-*separable* class $\mathcal{C}$ has an $(f, T(n))$ - *separation algorithm* if there exists a separation algorithm $\mathcal{S}$ such that for any n-vertex graph $G \in \mathcal{C}$, the algorithm returns an $(f(n), 2/3)$-separator of G in time at most $T(n)$, where $f(n)$ and $T(n)$ are functions from $\mathbb{N} \to \mathbb{N}$. As an example, in our notation, the celebrated result of Lipton-Tarjan [20] gives an $(O(\sqrt{n}), O(n))$-*separation algorithm* for planar graphs.

Let G be an n-vertex graph and $g(n) \geq 0$ be a function that defines a threshold based on n. The *binary separation tree* $\mathcal{T}_{\mathsf{sep}}$ of a graph G, with respect to a separation algorithm $\mathcal{S}$ and a threshold function $g(n)$, is defined as follows: the nodes of $\mathcal{T}_{\mathsf{sep}}$ are subsets of $V(G)$, derived by starting with the root node ε corresponding to the subset $V(G)$. For each node $\omega \in \mathcal{T}_{\mathsf{sep}}$, if $|\omega| > g(n)$, we apply $\mathcal{S}$ to $G[\omega]$ to obtain subsets $\omega \cdot \text{``1''}$, $\omega \cdot \text{``0''}$, and $\text{Sep}(\omega)$. The subsets $\omega \cdot \text{``1''}$ and $\omega \cdot \text{``0''}$ are added as nodes in $\mathcal{T}_{\mathsf{sep}}$ if they are not already present. The children of $\omega \in \mathcal{T}_{\mathsf{sep}}$ are defined as follows: ω has children $\omega \cdot \text{``1''}$ and $\omega \cdot \text{``0''}$ if $|\omega| > g(n)$ and the two are obtained by applying $\mathcal{S}$ to $G[\omega]$. A node ω is a leaf in $\mathcal{T}_{\mathsf{sep}}$ if and only if $|\omega| \leq g(n)$, indicating that $G[\omega]$ cannot be separated further by $\mathcal{S}$. This is similar to the notion of *separator hierarchy*, when the iterative separation is continued until the separated sets are of size one, see [2].

Cops and Robbers. The original cops and robber game [1] is played on an undirected n-vertex graph $G = (V, E)$ with two players: one controls a set of $k \geq 1$ cops, indexed by the integers $0, \ldots, k-1$, and the other controls a single robber. We will generally refer to the moves of the cops and robbers rather than to the players themselves. In round 1, the cops choose their initial positions on the graph, occupying a set of vertices $c_0(0), \ldots, c_{k-1}(0)$. The robber then selects an unoccupied vertex $r(0)$ to begin. In each subsequent round $t = 2, 3, \ldots$, the cops move first, with each cop moving from their current vertex $c_i(t-1)$ to a vertex $c_i(t) \in N^+(c_i(t-1))$, where $N^+(v) := N(v) \cup \{v\}$ is the closed neighbourhood of vertex v and $N(v) := \{u \in V \mid (v, u) \in E\}$ is the open neighbourhood of vertex v. The robber then moves in a similar way, choosing a new position $r(t) \in N^+(r(t-1))$. If a cop or the robber chooses to remain on their current vertex, this is referred to as a pass. We will refer to this variant of the game as the *classic Cops and Robbers* game. In the version where cops are allowed to move to any vertex $c_i(t) \in V$ of the graph G, the game is called *node search* (or *teleporting Cops and Robbers* game) [23,29] i.e. the cops are not restricted to moving only to neighbouring vertices, while the robber continues to move along the edges of the given graph as before.

The original game is played with perfect information: both the cops and the robber know each other's positions at all times. The cops win if, in some round, one of them moves to the vertex occupied by the robber, thereby capturing the robber. In contrast, the robber wins if they can avoid capture indefinitely. Both the cops and the robber are assumed to play optimally: the cops aim to minimise the number of rounds until capture, while the robber seeks to maximise it. The cop number of a graph G, denoted by $\mathsf{cop}(G)$, is the minimum number of cops required to guarantee the capture of the robber in G.

A graph G is said to be a k cop-win graph if it admits a cop strategy that guarantees capture using at most k cops. The *capture time of a strategy* is defined as the maximum number of rounds until capture is achieved [6]. The *capture time of a graph G*, $\mathsf{capt}(G, k)$, is then defined as the minimum capture time of any cop strategy on G with k cops. The *capture time of a graph* was first considered by Bonato, Golovach, Hahn & Kratochvíl [4], who mostly considered the *capture time of cop-win graphs*. The *capture time of planar graphs* using three cops was shown to be at most $2n$ in [24]. One can show that if the *capture time* by k cops is finite, then it is at most $O(n^{k+1})$; surprisingly, this bound is tight [6]. We study a variant of the classic Cops and Robber game on a graph $G = (V, E)$, known as the *zero-visibility Cops and Robbers* game, first introduced in [27] and further explored in [8, 10, 26] where the bounds on the zero-visibility cop number, denoted by $\mathsf{cop}_0(G)$, in terms of path width were established, and an algorithm was developed for capturing a robber. In this version, the robber is invisible to the cops, who can only detect and capture the robber by occupying the same vertex. The cops move without knowing the location of the robber, while the robber, who sees the cops, moves optimally to evade capture. Similarly, we let $\mathsf{capt}_0(G, k)$ be the capture time by k cops in the zero-visibility setting.

A Cops and Robbers Path Width (PW) *Algorithm* In [26], a strategy to capture the robber using an optimal path decomposition has been proposed, which we refer to further as the PW algorithm. The minor modification of the algorithm was used in [10] to study the monotonic strategies and investigate the connection between the monotone zero-visibility cop number, the zero-visibility cop number, and the pathwidth of a graph.

The PW algorithm is based on finding a path decomposition $B = \{B_1, \ldots, B_r\}$ of a connected graph G such that $\mathsf{pw}(B) = \mathsf{pw}(G)$, with the additional condition that $\forall i \in \{1, \ldots, r-1\}$, the sets $B_i \setminus B_{i+1}$, $B_{i+1} \setminus B_i$, and $B_i \cap B_{i+1}$ are not empty. In the algorithm, $k = \mathsf{pw}(G)$ cops are used, which move from the bag B_i to B_{i+1} for each $i \in \{1, \ldots, r-1\}$ in such a way that the robber's territory R_i monotonically decreases after each round i. Initially, the k cops are placed on the vertices of B_1. If $k > |B_1|$, then multiple cops can be placed on the same vertex of B_1. The algorithm then proceeds by sequentially moving the cops from B_i to B_{i+1}, so that they are moved from $B_i \cap B_{i+1}$ to $B_{i+1} \setminus B_i$, ensuring that the robber cannot enter B_i for any $i \in \{1, \ldots, r\}$. The movement in each step can be described as follows: for each $i \in \{1, \ldots, r-1\}$, the cops are moved from $B_i \cap B_{i+1}$ to $B_{i+1} \setminus B_i$, while the robber cannot move into B_i. The algorithm halts when the robber is caught in any round i. Since the robber's territory R_i monotonically decreases with each round i, in the worst case, the algorithm will need to pass through all r bags of the decomposition.

Neither [10] nor [26] consider using this algorithm to bound the capture time, however a simple analysis of the algorithm gives the following result.

Proposition 1. *The capture time of the* PW *algorithm with* pw(G) *cops for a graph G with n vertices and diameter D_G, is bounded above by $O(D_G \cdot n)$ and the space complexity by $O(n^2)$.*

Proof. Following the PW algorithm in [10,26] we move the cop team from one bag B_i to the next bag B_{i+1} following a path decomposition $B = (B_1, \ldots, B_r)$ for all $i \in 1, \ldots, r-1$. The number of bags in the path decomposition is bounded above by $O(n)$, and to move a cop from B_i to B_{i+1}, we need D_G moves. Since the size of each bag can be as large as $O(n)$, and the total number of bags is bounded above by n, we need to store all bags to follow the PW algorithm. So, the PW algorithm requires $O(n^2)$ memory. □

3 Capturing Invisible Robber Using Separation Hierarchy

We present an algorithm for capturing a robber based on the traversal of the separation tree which is an alternative to the existing algorithm based on a pathwidth decomposition [10]. During the design of the overall strategy, we first reason with respect to the node search (or teleporting Cops and Robbers) game [29]. In the node search model, cops are allowed to be placed on or removed from any vertex (i.e. not restricted to adjacent moves), while the robber still moves along edges. Then, when we analyse the capture time and other aspects, we add back in the travel times of the cops (restricted to travel over edges).

The core idea of the algorithm is to iteratively apply a separation algorithm $\mathcal{S}$ that partitions the graph G into three parts: a separator of size at most $f(n)$, and two subgraphs with no edges between them. The separator is guarded by $f(n)$ cops, and two separate sets can be cleaned independently and recursively. Our "Separation Tree Traversal" (STT) algorithm operates on a separation hierarchy of the graph, but it does not require building the full separation tree in advance. Instead, the algorithm incrementally traverses this implicit hierarchy, which can be represented by tree structure, cleaning one subgraph at a time. At each step, it uses separators to isolate "uncleaned" regions, placing cops as static guards on the separator vertices to prevent the robber from moving into the already cleaned parts of the graph. If at any point an isolated uncleaned subgraph G' of size at most $f(n)$ remains, it can be cleaned directly by deploying $f(n)$ cops to cover all its vertices simultaneously. This process is monotonic, so once a region of the graph is cleaned, it remains secure, and the robber cannot re-enter it. By maintaining this invariant controlling the cops' movements and use of separators, the algorithm ensures that the entire graph is eventually cleaned and the robber is captured. We demonstrate the correctness of the algorithm and evaluate the capture time for a robber on a graph as well its time/space complexity by analysing a recursive function that estimates the number of vertices in the binary separation tree of the graph.

3.1 Separation Tree Traversal (STT) Algorithm

The Separation Tree Traversal Algorithm (STT) takes as input an n-vertex graph $G \in \mathcal{C}$, where $\mathcal{C}$ is an f-separable hereditary class, and defined with respect to a

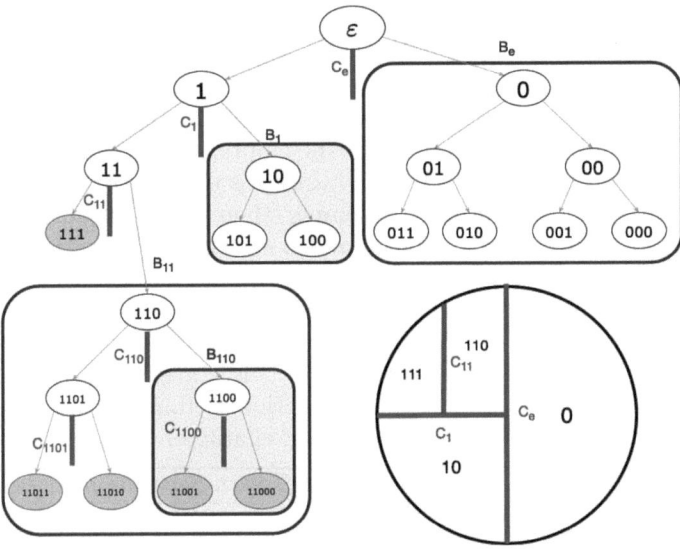

Fig. 1. The STT algorithm: Separation Tree, Stack Updates, and Graph Partitioning.

separation algorithm $\mathcal{S}$ and had a related separation tree $\mathcal{T}_{\text{sep}}$. In G, an unknown vertex u contains a robber. It gives a sequence of cop moves, moving $O(f(n))$ cops during an iteration, which guarantee the capture of an invisible robber.

The STT algorithm consists of three functions: Scheduler, Separate, and Clear. The main component of the STT algorithm is the Scheduler, which calls the Separate and Clear methods during its execution. Scheduler uses two stacks: STACK-B which stores separated sets; and STACK-C containing separators. The algorithm terminates after monotonically after clearing all vertices (Fig. 1).

The Clear(H) function simply moves a cop to each vertex of the input graph H for a round then removes them, catching any robber that is confined to H.

The input to Separate is an induced subgraph $H \subseteq G$, the index $V(H)$, and an integer n (the size of the original graph G). If $|V(H)| \leq f(n)$, then Clear is called to catch any potential robber in H. Otherwise $\mathcal{S}(H)$ is called, that is, the separation algorithm partitions $V(H)$ into three parts A, B, C. The separated subsets A, B, with indices extending that of $V(H)$ by a 0 or 1, are placed on STACK-B, and the separator C, with the index of $V(H)$, is placed on STACK-C.

The Scheduler uses two stacks, STACK-B and STACK-C where it stores separated sets and separators obtained by the separation algorithm $\mathcal{S}$, respectively. Each of these sets is indexed by its place in the separation tree, stored is a binary string. STACK-B stores sets of separated vertices, and their indices, which have yet to be cleared. The subsets of vertices contained in STACK-B are disjoint. Similarly, the disjoint separators, corresponding to sets in STACK-B, are stored together with their indices in STACK-C. The idea is that cops are temporarily placed on vertices of sets in C to restrict movement of the robber between the two corresponding separated sets (from STACK-B) so that these two separated sets can be cleaned independently. The role of the scheduler is to keep track (via the indices and stacks) of which sets are cleaned and assign cops accordingly.

The Scheduler starts by initially setting STACK-C to be empty, and STACK-B to contain the set $V(G)$ with index ε (the empty string). The outermost while loop of the Scheduler runs until the STACK-B is empty, i.e. when there are no 'uncleared' vertices. If STACK-B is not empty, then the top element U is popped. Its next step is to check if cops can be pulled off some of the separators. It does this by seeing if the separator at the top of STACK-C separates the U from its sibling in the separation tree, as if not then both of its corresponding separated sets must already be clear - so the separator can be popped and its cops removed. The Scheduler then calls Separate on $G[U]$ and starts the loop again.

Given a string $w = w_1 w_2 \cdots w_n$ the function DelLast(w) returns the string $w_1 w_2 \cdots w_{n-1}$, i.e. it simply removes the last character from w.

Algorithm 1 *Separation Tree Traversal of G with Separation Algorithm $\mathcal{S}$*

Function Scheduler(G):
　STACK-B.push($(V(G), \varepsilon)$)　　　　　　　　　%Place $(V(G), \varepsilon)$ in STACK-B
　while STACK-B is not empty **do**
　　$(U, index_U) \leftarrow$ STACK-B.pop()　　%Get $(U, index_U)$ from top of STACK-B
　　$pre \leftarrow$ DelLast($index_U$)　　　%Remove last character from $index_U$
　　if STACK-C is not empty **then**
　　　while $pre \neq$ to the index of STACK-C.peek() **do**
　　　　$(S, index_S) \leftarrow$ STACK-C.pop()　　　　　%Pop from STACK-C
　　　　Remove cops from all vertices in S
　　　end while
　　end if
　　Separate(G[U], $index_U$, $|V(G)|$)
　end while

Function Separate(H, index, n):
　if $|V(H)| \leqslant f(n)$ **then**
　　Clear(H)　　　　　　　　　　　　　　　　　　　　　%Clear H
　else
　　$(A, B, C) \leftarrow \mathcal{S}(H)$　　　　　　%Call Separation algorithm on H
　　Place cops in C
　　STACK-C.push((C, w))　　　　　　　%Push (C, w) onto STACK-C
　　STACK-B.push($(B, w \cdot 0)$)　　　%Push $(B, w \cdot 0)$ onto STACK-B
　　STACK-B.push($(A, w \cdot 1)$)　　　%Push $(A, w \cdot 1)$ onto STACK-B
　end if

Function Clear(H):
　Place cops in all vertices of H
　Remove cops from all vertices of H

3.2 Correctness of the STT Algorithm

Let us consider a node w of a binary separation tree $\mathcal{T}_{\text{sep}}$ with respect to the separation algorithm $\mathcal{S}$ applied to a graph G that corresponds to the subset of

$V(G)$. Clearly, the node can be denoted by a binary string. Upon applying $\mathcal{S}$ to $G[w]$, three sets are obtained: A_w, B_w, and C_w. In our notation, the set A_w is denoted as a sting $w \cdot$ "1", the set B_w as a sting $w \cdot$ "0", and the set C_w as $\text{Sep}(w)$, respectively. The following lemma is key to the analysis of the STT algorithm. Note that we take x_1 to be the empty string ε.

Lemma 1. *Let a robber be on some vertex of a graph G and $x_1 \cdots x_n \in \{0,1\}^*$, where $n \geq 1$ and $\{0,1\}^*$ is the family of all binary strings. If there is a cop at each vertex of $\cup_{i=1}^{n} \text{Sep}(x_1 \cdots x_i)$, then the robber in $x_1 \cdots x_n \cdot$ "1" or $x_1 \cdots x_n \cdot$ "0" cannot leave their respective set without being caught.*

Proof. We prove the lemma by induction on n. For the base case $n = 1$, we apply the separation algorithm $\mathcal{S}$ to G and obtain three sets $(1, 0, \text{Sep}(\varepsilon))$. Now place one cop on each vertex of the set $\text{Sep}(\varepsilon)$. Since $\text{Sep}(\varepsilon)$ separates set 0 from 1, a robber in either of set 0 or 1 cannot move to the other set without being caught.

Assume the statement holds for $n = k$. Thus, w.l.o.g. the robber is at a vertex in $G[x_1 \cdots x_{k+1}]$ and cannot leave this subgraph without being caught by a cop in the set $\cup_{i=1}^{k} \text{Sep}(x_1 \cdots x_i)$. Applying $\mathcal{S}$ to $G[x_1 \cdots x_{k+1}]$ gives three sets: $x_1 \cdots x_{k+1} \cdot$ "1", $x_1 \cdots x_{k+1} \cdot$ "0", and $\text{Sep}(x_1 \cdots x_{k+1})$, where we place cops in the latter. Since the robber cannot leave $G[x_1 \cdots x_{k+1}]$, if it was not caught by the placement of cops in $\text{Sep}(x_1 \cdots x_{k+1})$, then it must be in one of the two sets $x_1 \cdots x_{k+1} \cdot$ "1", $x_1 \cdots x_{k+1} \cdot$ "0". However, by virtue of $\mathcal{S}$, it cannot reach the other set without passing though $\text{Sep}(x_1 \cdots x_{k+1})$, where it will be caught. □

Let the robber's territory in round $i \geq 0$ of the game be the set of vertices in the graph G where a robber, which has not yet been caught, can possibly be located at the end of the round with respect to the cops' strategy. For example, in round $i = 0$, the robber's territory is given by $V(G) \setminus \{c_0(0), c_1(0), \ldots, c_{k-1}(0)\}$.

Theorem 1. *Let R_i be the territory of the robber after the i-th iteration of the outer while loop of* Scheduler(G). *Then, $\forall k \in \mathbb{N}$ such that $|R_k| > 0$, we have $R_{k+1} \subsetneq R_k$. Furthermore, the STT algorithm terminates in a finite number of steps with the robber being caught.*

Proof. Let W denote the set of vertices contained in some set on STACK-B. We will prove the following invariant (I) of the while loop holds by induction: (I) At then end of the ith loop, $R_i = W$.

For the base case, $R_0 = V(G)$, this holds as before the while loop begins $(V(G), \varepsilon)$ is pushed to the stack and no cops have been placed yet.

Suppose that invariant (I) holds at the end of the ith iteration, and that $R_i \neq \emptyset$. Thus, by induction, STACK-B is non-empty and the first element $(U, index_U)$ is popped from STACK-B. The next step of the outer while loop, is a check to see if STACK-C is empty, followed by an (inner) while loop. This inner while loop pops elements from STACK-C until the top one is a separator S corresponding to an output (U, U', S) from $\mathcal{S}$, that is, S separates U from its sibling U' in the separation tree. Note that a separator is only popped from STACK-C if the two sets it separates have already been cleared. By Lemma 1, and since all separators above S in the separation tree are still on STACK-C, we have that this step does not change R_i. The final step in the loop is to call Separate$(U, index_U, n)$. During this call, either the whole set U is cleared with cops (thus $R_{i+1} = R_i \setminus U$) and thus (I) holds since U was the only set of vertices removed from STACK-B. Or $f(n)$ cops are placed on a separator of $G[U]$, and the two corresponding separated sets are added to STACK-B. Thus also in this case, since the robber cannot be in the separator, invariant (I) holds.

Observe that the (potentially empty) union of the sets added during one iteration is a strict subset of the set U popped at the start of the iteration, i.e. a positive number of vertices is removed in each iteration. Since the graph is finite it follows that the while loop terminates in a finite number of iterations.

Since invariant (I) holds, at the end of the final iteration the set $R_i = \emptyset$, and so the robber must be caught. Additionally, if $|R_i| > 0$, then there will another iteration of the loop and so, by the above paragraph, we have $R_{i+1} \subsetneq R_i$.

Finally, although the STT algorithm is defined for teleporting cops, using cops which travel over edges (waiting for them to arrive) does not affect correctness - as the robber can't escape its current territory in the meantime. □

Theorem 1 shows that for teleporting cops the STT algorithm gives a monotonic strategy in the sense of [10]. However, for cops moving over edges the robber's territory may not be monotonically decreasing, as this depends on the paths taken by the individual cops when travelling between separator sets.

3.3 Capture Time, Cop Number and Computational Complexity

In this subsection, we define a recursive function that provides an estimate of the number of vertices in the binary separation tree. The estimate will be used in the next subsection to derive upper bounds on the STT algorithm's computation time and memory usage, upper bounds on the cop number, and capture time associated with the STT algorithm.

For any $f : \mathbb{N} \to \mathbb{N}$ and $n \in \mathbb{N}_+$, let $\varphi(x) := \varphi_{f(\cdot),n}(x)$ denote the maximum number of nodes in the binary separation tree corresponding to subgraphs of size x, assuming we place $f(x)$ cops on each separator, and stop the recursion when we reach a graph of size $f(n)$. This mirrors what happens in Algorithm 1. For simplicity, we assume each separation of a subgraph on x vertices uses exactly $f(x)$ cops, even if the actual separator is smaller. This removes $f(x)$ vertices, leaving $x - f(x)$ vertices in two disconnected parts, each with at most $\frac{2x}{3}$ vertices. Thus, the following recurrence holds:

$$\varphi(x) = \begin{cases} 0 & \text{for all } x < 1; \\ 1 & \text{for all } 1 \leq x \leq f(n); \\ \max_{\lceil x/3 \rceil \leq y \leq \lfloor 2x/3 \rfloor} \{\varphi(y) + \varphi(x - f(x) - y)\} + 1 & \text{otherwise.} \end{cases} \quad (1)$$

The recurrence reflects two cases: when $x \leq f(n)$, the region can be cleaned directly with one full group of cops, so $\varphi_k(x) \leq 1$. For $x > f(n)$, we place $f(x)$

cops on a separator and split the remaining $x - f(n)$ vertices into two parts. The recurrence adds 1 for the current separator node, and recursively counts the nodes in the two resulting subtrees. The maximisation over y ensures all $(f(x), 2/3)$-separators are considered.

Proposition 2. *For any $f : \mathbb{N}_+ \to \mathbb{N}_+$ and $n \in \mathbb{N}_+$, let $\varphi_{f(\cdot),n}(x)$ given by (1). Then, for all $x \geq f(n)$,*

$$\varphi_{f(\cdot),n}(x) \leq \frac{6x}{f(n)} - 1.$$

Corollary 1. *Let $\mathcal{C}$ be any f-separable hereditary class, and $G \in \mathcal{C}$ have n vertices. Then, the number of nodes in the binary separation tree $\mathcal{T}_{\mathsf{sep}}$ is $O\left(\frac{n}{f(n)}\right)$.*

We can then use this to bound the time and memory complexity of STT.

Proposition 3. *The STT algorithm runs in time $O\left(\frac{n}{f(n)} \cdot T(n)\right)$, where $T(n)$ is the running time of a separation algorithm.*

Proof. The computational time of the STT algorithm is dominated by the number of calls within the `while` loop that repeatedly invokes the separation algorithm $\mathcal{S}$, which takes as input a set of vertices from a subgraph of graph G.

Observe that $\mathcal{S}$ is executed once for each internal node of the binary separation tree $\mathcal{T}_{\mathsf{sep}}$. Consequently, the runtime is dominated by $T(n)$, the max running time of a call to $\mathcal{S}$, multiplied by the number of internal vertices of the tree $\mathcal{T}_{\mathsf{sep}}$, which is $O\left(\frac{n}{f(n)}\right)$ by Corollary 1. Thus, the time complexity is $O\left(\frac{n}{f(n)} \cdot T(n)\right)$. □

Let us introduce a function $\ell : \mathbb{N} \to \mathbb{N}$ that will be used to evaluate the cop number and space complexity. The function $\ell : \mathbb{N} \to \mathbb{N}$ is given by

$$\ell(n) := \left\lceil \log_{3/2} n \right\rceil + 1. \tag{2}$$

Note that $\ell(n) \approx 2.466 \cdot \ln n$, for large n. For $f : \mathbb{N}_+ \to \mathbb{N}_+$ define

$$C_f(n) = f(n) + \sum_{i=0}^{\ell(n)} f\left(\left\lfloor \left(\frac{2}{3}\right)^i \cdot n \right\rfloor\right). \tag{3}$$

Thus $C_f(n) = O(f(n) \log n)$, but the $\log n$ factor may vanish if $f(n)$ grows fast.

Proposition 4. *The STT algorithm uses $O(n)$ memory in the RAM model for any connected graph G as input to the algorithm.*

Proof. In the STT algorithm, memory is used only to push subgraphs and their indices in STACK-B and STACK-C. Since STACK-B and STACK-C contain the same number of sets, we need to only estimate the number and size of sets stored in STACK-B. Additionally, we assume that the indices are negligible compared to the corresponding sets. The maximum height h of the binary separation tree is given by $\ell(n) = \lceil \log_{3/2} n + 1 \rceil$.

Since the algorithm stores in STACK-B all sets B along the path from the root of the tree to its leaf, and the size of each set at level i is at most $\left(\frac{2}{3}\right)^i n$, we will need $M = \sum_{i=0}^{\lceil \log_{3/2} n \rceil + 1} \left(\frac{2}{3}\right)^i n = O(n)$ memory. □

So far, we have shown the correctness of the STT algorithm in Theorem 1, and we have obtained the results on the time and space complexity in Propositions 3 and 4. Now, we will analyse the number of cops used by the STT algorithm in order to bound the zero-visibility cop number of a graph G and derive an upper bound on the capture time with respect to the algorithm.

Theorem 2. *Let $\mathcal{C}$ be any f-separable hereditary class, and $C_f(\cdot)$ be given by (3). Then, for any n-vertex $G \in \mathcal{C}$, the STT algorithm uses $C_f(n)$ cops, and thus $\mathsf{cop}_0(G) \leq C_f(n)$.*

Proof. The number of 'teams' of cops deployed by the STT algorithm on the separation sets, where the size of the i-th team is $f(\lfloor (2/3)^i n \rfloor)$, is at most the height h of the binary partition tree $\mathcal{T}_{\mathsf{sep}}$. To bound h, observe that the output sizes of A and B by the separation algorithm $\mathcal{S}$ used in the STT algorithm are at most $2/3$ times the size of the input. Also, once sets have size at most $f(n)$ then they are just cleared using at most $f(n)$ cops. Since $f(n) \geq 1$, it follows that $(2/3)^{h-1} n \geq 1$, and so rearranging gives $h \leq \ell(n)$, where $\ell(n)$ is given by (2). Summing the cops in all these teams, and not forgetting the last team of size $f(n)$ used to clear the sets at the leaves, gives $C_f(n)$ cops. □

A function $f : D \to \mathbb{R}$ is multiplicative if $f(xy) = O(f(x)f(y))$ for all $x, y \in D$.

Proposition 5. *Let $f(x) \leq x$ be a non-decreasing multiplicative function, and $\mathcal{C}$ be an f-separable hereditary class. Then, for any n-vertex $G \in \mathcal{C}$, the STT algorithm uses $O(f(n))$ cops, and thus $\mathsf{cop}_0(G) = O(f(n))$.*

We also show a novel bound on the zero-visibility capture time.

Theorem 3. *Let $\mathcal{C}$ be any hereditary class that is f-separable, $G \in \mathcal{C}$ and D_G be diameter of G. Then, the capture time of G with respect to the STT algorithm is bounded above by $O\left(D_G \cdot \frac{n}{f(n)}\right)$.*

Proof. The cop team must visit every vertex of the binary separation tree $\mathcal{T}_{sep}$ of G to capture the robber. Let u, v be two vertices of the tree $\mathcal{T}_{sep}$. In the worst case, to go from u to v, steps of D_G are required. By *Proposition* 2, the number of nodes in $\mathcal{T}_{\mathsf{sep}}$ is bounded above by $\frac{n}{f(n)}$, where $f(n)$ is the size of the separator. Since the team of cops must traverse each of the vertices of $\mathcal{T}_{sep}$, we will get the desired estimate $O(D_G \cdot \frac{n}{f(n)})$. □

We get the following from the Lipton-Tarjan separation algorithm [20].

Corollary 2. *Let G be a planar graph with diameter D_G, and $k = C_{\sqrt{\cdot}}(n) = O(\sqrt{n})$ be given by (3). Then, the SST algorithm gives $\mathsf{capt}_k(G) = O\left(D_G \cdot \sqrt{n}\right)$.*

3.4 Applications of STT Algorithm

In order to demonstrate our bounds on the zero-visibility cop number and capture time, we apply these result to the hyperbolic random graph. In addition, we demonstrate the advantages of the STT algorithm in the context finding the approximate zero-visibility cop number $\mathsf{apxcop}_0(G)$ which is the restriction of $\mathsf{cop}_0(G)$ to stratgies that can be computed in polynomial time.

The hyperbolic random graph exhibits many properties of large real-world networks, such as a power-law degree distribution, a constant clustering coefficient, polylogarithmic diameter, and other relevant structural features [2,3,19] - which make it a popular model. Moreover, to the best of our knowledge, there are currently no known exact results on the pathwidth of hyperbolic random graphs, so application of the PW algorithm remains undesirable at this stage.

The hyperbolic random graph has three parameters: the number of vertices n; the parameter $\alpha \geq \frac{1}{2}$, which controls the power-law exponent; and the parameter C, which controls the average degree. For our purposes, as often in the literature, we just assume that C is some suitably large constant. The hyperbolic random graph $G \sim \mathcal{G}_{\mathrm{hyp}}(n, \alpha)$ can be obtained by sampling n points in the disk D_R of radius $R = 2\log n + C$, using radial coordinates (r, θ) with the center of D_R as the origin. The angle θ is drawn uniformly from $[0, 2\pi]$, while the radius r is chosen according to the density $d(r) = \frac{\alpha \sinh(\alpha r)}{\cosh(\alpha R)-1}$.

Proposition 6. *Let G be any largest component of $\mathcal{G}_{\mathrm{hyp}}(n, \alpha)$ given with its geometric representation, where $\alpha \geq \frac{1}{2}$. Then, w.h.p. the run time of the STT algorithm is $O(n^{1+\min\{\alpha,1\}})$, and gives $\mathsf{cop}_0(G) \leq k$ where*

$$k = \begin{cases} O(n^{1-\alpha}) & \text{for } \alpha < 1, \\ O(\log^3 n) & \text{for } \alpha = 1, \\ O(\log^2 n) & \text{for } \alpha > 1. \end{cases} \quad \& \quad \mathsf{capt}_k(G) = \begin{cases} O(n^\alpha \log n) & \text{for } \alpha < 1, \\ O(\frac{n}{\log^2 n}) & \text{for } \alpha = 1, \\ n^{1+\frac{1}{2\alpha}} \log^{O(1)} n & \text{for } \alpha > 1. \end{cases}$$

Since finding an optimal pathwidth decomposition or optimal separation set is NP-complete, we show an improved approximate zero-visibility cop number using the alternative approach based on separation hierarchy. Applying the available approximation algorithms in the literature for finding separators and path decompositions [13], we provide a comparison of the approximate zero-visibility cop numbers obtained by the STT and PW algorithms on various classes.

Proposition 7. *Let $\mathcal{C}$ be any f-separable hereditary class, $G \in \mathcal{C}$ have n vertices, and $C_f(n) = O(f(n) \log n)$ be given by (3). Then, the STT algorithm gives*

$$\mathsf{apxcop}_0(G) = \begin{cases} O\big(C_f(n) \cdot \sqrt{\log f(n)}\big) & \text{if } G \in \mathcal{C}, \\ O\big(C_f(n) \cdot |V(H)|^2\big) & \text{if } G \text{ is } H\text{-minor-free, ,} \\ O\big(C_f(n) \cdot g\big) & \text{if } G \text{ has genus at most } g. \end{cases}$$

Similarly, we can apply the best known approximation for Pathwidth [13].

Proposition 8. *Let $\mathcal{C}$ be any f-separable hereditary class, $G \in \mathcal{C}$ have n vertices. Then, the PW algorithm gives*

$$\mathsf{apxcop}_0(G) = \begin{cases} O\big(\mathsf{pw}(G) \cdot \sqrt{\log(\mathsf{pw}(G))} \cdot \log n\big) & \text{if } G \in \mathcal{C}, \\ O\big(\mathsf{pw}(G) \cdot |V(H)|^2 \cdot \log n\big) & \text{if } G \text{ is } H\text{-minor-free}. \end{cases}$$

Generally speaking, $\mathsf{pw}(G)$ is harder to approximate than $\mathsf{s}(G)$, and the best known approximations [13] all carry an additional $\log n$ factor over those for $\mathsf{s}(G)$. As a concrete examples of where the STT algorithm outperforms the PW algorithm in its bound of $\mathsf{apxcop}_0(G)$ we can consider planar graphs. Since the separator number is $O(\sqrt{n})$ and planar graphs are K_6-minor-free, we can apply Propositions 8 and 5 to give $\mathsf{apxcop}_0(G) = O(\sqrt{n})$ via the STT algorithm, however the corresponding bound from PW is only $\mathsf{apxcop}_0(G) = O(\sqrt{n} \log n)$. In particular a constant factor approximation to $\mathsf{pw}(G)$ is only known for outerplanar graphs [15]. A similar gap holds for K_t-minor-free graphs, where $t \geq 6$.

Conclusion. As the future direction the reduction of space complexity of the STT algorithm could be analysed further, e.g. by storing only the order of separations and potentially using the LOGSPACE algorithm for recursively computing separation sets on the way, following [11], with careful application and analysis.

Acknowledgements. Tymofii Prokopenko was supported by the Centre for Doctoral Training in Distributed Algorithms.

References

1. Aigner, M., Fromme, M.: A game of cops and robbers. Discret. Appl. Math. **8**(1), 1–12 (1984)
2. Bläsius, T., Friedrich, T., Krohmer, A.: Hyperbolic random graphs: Separators and treewidth. In: 24th Annual European Symposium on Algorithms, ESA 2016, volume 57 of LIPIcs, pp. 15:1–15:16, 2016
3. Boguná, M., Papadopoulos, F., Krioukov, D.: Sustaining the internet with hyperbolic mapping. Nat. Commun. **1**(1), 62 (2010)
4. Bonato, A., Golovach, P.A., Hahn, G., Kratochvíl, J.: The capture time of a graph. Discret. Math. **309**(18), 5588–5595 (2009)
5. Bonato, A., Nowakowski, R.J.: The game of cops and robbers on graphs. Student Mathematical Library, vol. 61. AMS, Providence, RI (2011)
6. Brandt, S., Emek, Y., Uitto, J., Wattenhofer, R.: A tight lower bound for the capture time of the cops and robbers game. In: 44th International Colloquium on Automata, Languages, and Programming, ICALP 2017, volume 80 of LIPIcs, pp. 82:1–82:13, 2017
7. Clarke, N.E., Cox, D., Duffy, C., Dyer, D., Fitzpatrick, S.L., Messinger, M.E.: Limited visibility cops and robber. Discret. Appl. Math. **282**, 53–64 (2020)
8. Dereniowski, D., Dyer, D., Tifenbach, R.M., Yang, B.: Zero-visibility cops and robber game on a graph. In: Fellows, M., Tan, X., Zhu, B. (eds.) AAIM/FAW - 2013. LNCS, vol. 7924, pp. 175–186. Springer, Heidelberg (2013). https://doi.org/10.1007/978-3-642-38756-2_19
9. Dereniowski, D., Dyer, D., Tifenbach, R.M., Yang, B.: The complexity of zero-visibility cops and robber. Theor. Comput. Sci. **607**, 135–148 (2015)
10. Dereniowski, D., Dyer, D., Tifenbach, R.M., Yang, B.: Zero-visibility cops and robber and the pathwidth of a graph. J. Comb. Optim. **29**, 541–564 (2015)
11. Elberfeld, M., Jakoby, A., Tantau, T.: Logspace versions of the theorems of bodlaender and courcelle. In: 51th Annual IEEE Symposium on Foundations of Computer Science, FOCS 2010, pp. 143–152, 2010

12. Enright, J., Meeks, K., Pettersson, W., Sylvester, J.: Cops and robbers on multi-layer graphs. In: Paulusma, D., Ries, B. (eds.) Graph-Theoretic Concepts in Computer Science. WG 2023. LNCS, vol. 14093, pp. 319–333. Springer, Cham (2023). https://doi.org/10.1007/978-3-031-43380-1_23
13. Feige, U., Hajiaghayi, M.T., Lee, J.R.: Improved approximation algorithms for minimum weight vertex separators. SIAM J. Comput. **38**(2), 629–657 (2008)
14. Frieze, A., Krivelevich, M., Loh, P.-S.: Variations on cops and robbers. J. Graph Theory **69**(4), 383–402 (2012)
15. Govindan, R., Langston, M.A., Yan, X.: Approximating the pathwidth of outerplanar graphs. Inf. Process. Lett. **68**(1), 17–23 (1998)
16. Jeliazkova, D.: Aspects of the cops and robber game played with incomplete information. PhD thesis, Acadia University, 2006
17. Joret, G., Kamiński, M., Theis, D.O.: The cops and robber game on graphs with forbidden (induced) subgraphs. Contrib. Discret. Math. **5**(2) (2010)
18. Kehagias, A., Papazoglou, A.C.: An algorithm for limited visibility graph searching. *arXiv preprint*arXiv:2105.06150, 2021
19. Krioukov, D., Papadopoulos, F., Kitsak, M., Vahdat, A., Boguná, M.: Hyperbolic geometry of complex networks. Phys. Rev. E-Stat. Nonlinear Soft Matter Phys. **82**(3), 036106 (2010)
20. Lipton, R.J., Tarjan, R.E.: Applications of a planar separator theorem. SIAM J. Comput. **9**(3), 615–627 (1980)
21. Loh, P.-S., Siyoung, O.: Cops and robbers on planar-directed graphs. J. Graph Theory **86**(3), 329–340 (2017)
22. Nowakowski, R., Winkler, P.: Vertex-to-vertex pursuit in a graph. Discret. Math. **43**(2), 235–239 (1983)
23. Peng, S.L., Ho, C.W., Hsu, T.S., Ko, M.T., Tang, C.Y.: Edge and node searching problems on trees. Theor. Comput. Sci. **240**(2), 429–446 (2000)
24. Pisantechakool, P., Tan, X.: On the capture time of cops and robbers game on a planar graph. In: Chan, T.-H.H., Li, M., Wang, L. (eds.) COCOA 2016. LNCS, vol. 10043, pp. 3–17. Springer, Cham (2016). https://doi.org/10.1007/978-3-319-48749-6_1
25. Quilliot, A.: Jeux et pointes fixes sur les graphes. PhD thesis, Ph. D. Dissertation, Université de Paris VI, 1978
26. Tang, A.: Cops and robber with bounded visibility. National Library of Canada Bibliothque nationale du Canada, Ottawa (2005)
27. Tosic, R.: Vertex-to-vertex search in a graph. In: Graph Theory (Dubrovnik 1985), pp. 233–237, 1985
28. Tošić, R.: Vertex-to-vertex search in a graph. In: Proceedings of the Sixth Yugoslav Seminar on Graph Theory, pp. 233–237. University of Novi Sad, 1985
29. Zsolt Adam Wagner: Cops and robbers on diameter two graphs. Discret. Math. **338**(3), 107–109 (2015)
30. Xue, Y., Yang, B., Zhong, F., Zilles, S.: A partition approach to lower bounds for zero-visibility cops and robber. In: Colbourn, C.J., Grossi, R., Pisanti, N. (eds.) IWOCA 2019. LNCS, vol. 11638, pp. 442–454. Springer, Cham (2019). https://doi.org/10.1007/978-3-030-25005-8_36
31. Yang, B.: One-visibility cops and robber on trees: optimal cop-win strategies. Theor. Comput. Sci. **928**, 27–47 (2022)

Author Index

A
Adamson, Duncan   1
Agdur, Vilhelm   17
Alafin, Oluwatobi   32
Araújo, Júlio   104

B
Betti Sorbelli, Francesco   46
Bhattacharya, Adri   135
Bilò, Davide   61

C
Corsini, Timothée   76

D
Davot, Tom   89
de Andrade, Davi   104

E
Enright, Jessica   17, 76, 89

G
Ghobadi, Sajjad   46
Gualà, Luciano   61

H
Huri, Avner   166

I
Ibiapina, Allen   104
Italiano, Giuseppe F.   119

J
Jana, Saswata   119, 135
Jawhar, Khaled   151

K
Kortsarz, Guy   166
Kranakis, Evangelos   151

L
Larios-Jones, Laura   17, 76, 89
Leucci, Stefano   61

M
Mandal, Partha Sarathi   119, 135
Marino, Andrea   104
Meeks, Kitty   17, 76
Mertzios, George B.   32

N
Nutov, Zeev   166

P
Palazzetti, Lorenzo   46
Pinotti, Cristina M.   46
Potapov, Igor   181
Pramanick, Subhajit   135
Proietti, Guido   61
Prokopenko, Tymofii   181

R
Rosenbaum, Will   1

S
Schoeters, Jason   104
Silva, Ana   104
Skerman, Fiona   17
Spirakis, Paul G.   1, 32
Straziota, Alessandro   61
Sylvester, John   181

Y
Yates, Ella   17

© The Editor(s) (if applicable) and The Author(s), under exclusive license to Springer Nature Switzerland AG 2026
O. Michail and G. Prencipe (Eds.): ALGOWIN 2025, LNCS 16078, p. 197, 2026.
https://doi.org/10.1007/978-3-032-09120-8

If you have any concerns about our products,
you can contact us on
ProductSafety@springernature.com

In case Publisher is established outside the EU,
the EU authorized representative is:
**Springer Nature Customer Service Center GmbH
Europaplatz 3, 69115 Heidelberg, Germany**

Printed by Libri Plureos GmbH
in Hamburg, Germany